RENEWALS 4

DATE

D0721880

MAX WEBER'S 'OBJECTIVITY' RECONSIDERED

GERMAN AND EUROPEAN STUDIES

General Editor: James Retallack

EDITED BY LAURENCE McFALLS

Max Weber's 'Objectivity' Reconsidered

WITHDRAWN
UTSA Libraries

UNIVERSITY OF TORONTO PRESS
Toronto Buffalo London

© University of Toronto Press Incorporated 2007
Toronto Buffalo London
Printed in Canada

ISBN 978-0-8020-9224-3

Printed on acid-free paper

Library and Archives Canada Cataloguing in Publication

Max Weber's 'objectivity' reconsidered / edited by Laurence McFalls.

(German and European studies)
Includes bibliographic references and index.
ISBN 978-0-8020-9224-3

1. Weber, Max, 1864–1920.   2. Objectivity.   3. Social sciences – Philosophy.
I. McFalls, Laurence H.   II. Series.

H61.M38 2007   300'.1   C2006-905057-0

Library
University of Texas
at San Antonio

University of Toronto Press acknowledges the financial assistance to
its publishing program of the Canada Council for the Arts and the
Ontario Arts Council.

University of Toronto Press acknowledges the financial support for
its publishing activities of the Government of Canada through the
Book Publishing Industry Development Program (BPIDP).

Contents

Part Three: Weber and Contemporary Social Science:
An Opportunity Missed?

Acknowledgments

The editor and authors of this volume wish to thank the Social Sciences and Humanities Research Council of Canada, the German Academic Exchange Service (DAAD), and the Centre canadien d'études allemandes et européennes at Université de Montréal for the financial and logistical support that made the publication of this book possible.

MAX WEBER'S 'OBJECTIVITY' RECONSIDERED

Introduction: Towards a Comparative Reception-History of Max Weber's Oeuvre

LAURENCE McFALLS WITH AUGUSTIN SIMARD AND
BARBARA THÉRIAULT

In 1904, Max Weber published two of his most seminal works, his essay 'The "Objectivity" of Knowledge in Social Science and Social Policy'[1] and the first of two instalments of *The Protestant Ethic and the 'Spirit' of Capitalism*. The former is no doubt his most widely read methodological piece, the latter his most celebrated empirical study. Despite their different topics and genres, these works share more than their date and their place of publication (the *Archiv für Sozialwissenschaft und Sozialpolitik*, of which Weber assumed the co-editorship that year). As contemporaneous works, the 'Objectivity' essay and *The Protestant Ethic* can and, in light of the personal context of their production, must be read as expressions of one another. After almost five years of mental illness following an acute Oedipal conflict with his father[2] and perhaps expressing an elective affinity, if not causal connection, with his alleged philosophical nihilism,[3] Weber had made his return to professional intellectual life only the previous year with the publication of his tortuous methodological critiques of *Roscher and Knies*.[4] Intended for broader audiences, Weber's essays of 1904 marked the comeback at the age of only forty of a public scholar who, before his illness, had already been the fastest rising intellectual star of Wilhelmine Germany, as Weber weighed in on the most important intellectual and social debates of his day: the *Methodenstreit* and the 'Social Question.' While in the 'Objectivity' essay Weber proffered nothing less than his solution to the dispute opposing the interpretive approach of the German 'historical school' of economics and social science and the nomothetic approach extolled by the marginal utility theorists, the *Protestant Ethic* represented his original incursion into the scientific and political debate that Karl Marx had initiated on the origins and dynamics of capitalist development. What is more, as the qualifying quotation marks around the terms 'objectivity' and 'spirit' signalled, Weber was also taking on major philosophical questions of the day, respectively the epistemological debates of the neo-Kantian school,[5] and the ghost of Hegel's philosophy of history that still haunted historical and social thought.[6]

Weber's 1904 works launched 'a tidal wave of productivity and creativity'[7] and defined his intellectual agenda for the sixteen years up to his untimely death, from sequelae of the Spanish flu, in 1920. *The Protestant Ethic* initiated his encyclopedic sociology of the world's religions and established the scientific discipline of comparative historical sociology, whereas the 'Objectivity' essay began to lay the conceptual groundwork for the theoretical treatise of *Economy and Society*, part 1. It is hardly surprising that Weber wrote his path-breaking methodological and substantive works simultaneously. Even before explicitly stating as much in the 'Objectivity' essay, Weber never saw method or even theory as an end in itself, but only as tools for his *Wirklichkeitswissenschaft*,[8] his empirical science of historical and social reality (as opposed to the logico-deductive 'dogmatic' sciences such as jurisprudence, esthetics, or marginal utility theory). In this sense, the 'Objectivity' essay could be read, and often has been, as a mere companion piece to the *Protestant Ethic*, for in the methodological essay Weber articulates for the first time the analytic utility of the ideal-type. Explicitly following this method, the *Protestant Ethic* first defines the ideal-types of Protestant worldly asceticism and of the rationality of modern capitalism and then establishes the empirical plausibility of a causal link between the former and the latter – a link understood, of course, as only partially explanatory, merely one 'finite segment of the vast chaotic stream of events, which flows away through time.'[9] At the same time, however, as the closing dramatic passages of the 'Objectivity' essay (from which the preceding quote is taken) suggest, it is possible to interpret the 'Objectivity' essay as a recasting of Weber into the role of the ascetic hero whose ethical commitment to the rational pursuit of truth more or less unintentionally[10] slammed the modern world into the 'iron cage' of soulless scientific specialization.[11] Indeed, anticipating his lecture 'Science as a Vocation'[12] to come thirteen years later, Weber's 'Objectivity' essay concludes that modern scientific inquiry, like modern capitalism, has roots in an ethical calling that proved effective only within a particular cultural and historical constellation, namely that of early modern Western Europe.[13]

With a century of hindsight, we might argue that Weber's works of

1904 were of 'world-historical' significance in that they established the conditions of possibility for a scientific understanding of the cultural processes characteristic of our age, including the most significant of those processes – modern capitalism and its iron-cage-like consequences for our social existence – as well as our reflexive scientific analyses situated within those processes. In that sense, Weber's 1904 essays marked the birth of truly modern self-reflexive social science – or even *post*modern social science in that the epistemological relativism of the 'Objectivity' essay, along with the *Protestant Ethic*'s exposure of the radical contingency of social development, stripped modern social thought of its crypto-Hegelian faith in progress and ultimate, teleological meaning. At the time, of course, the significance of Weber's essays went largely unnoticed, at least outside of Germany. In the Wilhelmine Reich, Weber's scientific interlocutors and targets of criticism engaged him in ongoing – at times parochial – debates, with Gustav Schmoller, for example, defending the ethical orientation of the historical school,[14] and with Weber himself publishing in 1910 an *Anti-Kritik* of what proved to be only the first round of debate elicited by the so-called Protestant-ethic thesis.[15] In 1904 coincidentally, Weber, at the height of his intellectual powers, visited the United States. While personally enriching for him,[16] his visit went unnoticed by American scholars, with the significant exception of the marginalized African-American sociologist W.E.B. Du Bois.[17] Indeed, Weber's oeuvre remained unknown in the international social-scientific community until well after his death, and even in Germany, where he was a public celebrity by the time of his death, the originality, rigour, and integrity of Weber's scientific thought were rapidly forgotten. Of his three most brilliant students, only Karl Jaspers heeded the lesson, first spelled out in the 'Objectivity' essay, that scientific neutrality is a precondition for ethical and political integrity (as well as vice versa).[18] By contrast, Georg Lukacs on the left and Carl Schmitt on the right proved willing to sacrifice their intellect on the altar of faith in the Party or the Führer. Similarly, if less perniciously, the founders of the Frankfurt School of social philosophy also rejected Weber's rigorous distinction between facts and values, as Horkheimer's invention of the engaged concept of 'critical theory' made abundantly clear.[19] Ironically, it was only after Weber was discovered by postwar social science abroad that he was re-imported, in earnest only in the 1970s, into the social-scientific thought of the nation Weber had so vehemently defended.[20]

The vagaries of this international reception and retransmission of

Weber's oeuvre over the past century constitute the central concern of this volume. The essays collected here do not and cannot provide a reception-history (*Rezeptionsgeschichte*) of Weber's thought; such an enterprise would surpass the confines of a single volume, as the full book length of Alan Sica's recent *un*-annotated bibliography of Weberian literature in English alone proves.[21] Although histories of Weber's reception in different national contexts do exist,[22] no theoretically systematic and comparative study of Weber's reception across disciplines and cultural contexts exists. This book represents the first step of such a study. It presents essays by sociologists, political scientists, anthropologists, and philosophers from four continents to illustrate, in the first instance, how Weber's thought has been taken up in different cultural and disciplinary contexts. Written with the methodological prescriptions of the 'Objectivity' essay in mind, the fourteen essays range from the celebratory to the highly critical, from the exegetic to the applied. Together they demonstrate that just as the *Protestant Ethic*'s Puritan heroes' desire to lead a life of ascetic vocation gave rise to a broad variety of practical orientations within the cosmos of rationalized capitalism, so too has Weber's thought engendered a multiplicity of social-scientific practices and self-understandings. Indeed, Weber's oeuvre has given rise – and in recent years at a seemingly exponential rate – to numerous, often contradictory, interpretations and practical applications, so that today everyone from neo-liberals to Trotskyites,[23] from rational choice theorists to neo-Marxists, historical institutionalists, and post-structuralists[24] can claim to defend Weber's intellectual heritage.

In this introductory chapter, before briefly presenting the fourteen essays, the logic of their order, the criteria for their selection, and the insights they offer into modes of Weber-reception, we propose an initial theoretical reflection on Weber as an author and continuing scientific authority as a way of providing an overview of how Weber has been read and used to different ends over the past century. Weber would have recognized the diverse and often contradictory uses of his oeuvre in actual scientific practice as so many unintended consequences of the effectiveness of ideas in history, in this case his own. The ambition of this volume is to contribute to a history of the reception and practical effects – or what the Germans call a *Rezeptions- und Wirkungsgeschichte* – of Weber's oeuvre as Weber himself might have conducted such an inquiry. We do not pretend, of course, even to begin to match Weber's encyclopedic intellect, or to have privileged insight into his work's 'true' meaning. Instead, we contend that Weber's sociology offers a heretofore under-exploited key for interpreting and explaining the divergent practices (or what Weber calls *Lebensführungen*) that his oeuvre has inspired in contemporary social sciences and humanities.

Although the diffusion of Weber's thought is an interesting historical and sociological question in itself, understanding this phenomenon involves a more fundamental issue: the truth status of social-scientific knowledge. In the 'Objectivity' essay, Weber sets out to identify the conditions of possibility for such scientific, or 'objective,' knowledge of the cultural phenomenon of human social existence.[25] Within the context of the late nineteenth-century *Methodenstreit* in German academics, Weber stakes out a position for his *Sozialwissenschaft* that is *not* the *juste milieu* between the individualizing, interpretive, hermeneutic science of the *Geisteswissenschaften* and the generalizing, objectifying, positivist method of the *Naturwissenschaften* (and their social-scientific imitators in the tradition of Auguste Comte), for as he makes unmistakably clear in the essay, the truth does not lie 'somewhere in the middle' of opposing positions. Instead, Weber draws a very fine line at the intersection of the two epistemic forms where valid knowledge of social and historical phenomena might tenuously and tentatively be possible. Giving comfort to his readers who wish to claim him for the interpretive approach, Weber explains that 'objective' knowledge can exist only relative to subjective value orientations (hence the qualifying quotation marks around 'objectivity'), since science can elucidate only those parts of an infinitely complex reality that the scientist evaluates as interesting. What is more, the conceptual tools for analysing reality, ideal-types, are interpretive constructs. At the same time, however, Weber seems to side with the positivists in arguing that it is possible to establish causal relations between ideal-typically conceived phenomena according to the same empirical and logical rules as apply to the natural sciences, hence his claim that a social-scientific 'truth' must be demonstrable to someone as subjectively foreign as 'a Chinese.'[26] Contrary to the positivists, though, the existence of empirically and logically 'adequate' socio-cultural knowledge does not allow for the construction of a systematic, general theory of social reality, because that reality constantly shifts, as do the value orientations of those who seek scientific truth.[27] Indeed, scientific truth is valid anyway only for those who *want* or *will* the truth, as Weber writes in one of his more Nietzschean moments.[28] Weber's manic productivity, like that of the Puritan worldly ascetic in search of the *certitudo salutis*, testified to his will for scientific knowledge, but do those who have followed Weber (temporally and scientifically) share his will for scientific truth?

Leaving aside the question of the metaphysical validity of Weber's relativist epistemological position,[29] we can nonetheless see that his readers have rarely succeeded in embracing it. Some have latched onto his positivist elements, others onto his defence of interpretive *Verstehen*, but more importantly no clear or coherent Weberian school of social science has ever formed. To be sure, many social scientists claim a Weberian filiation. That is, independently of whether they emphasize his (post)positivist or interpretive tendencies, they either work with, and often reify, one or another of his conceptual tools without much regard for its epistemological premises, or else they adopt a relativist epistemological attitude inspired by Weber's with an eye more towards scientific criticism and meta-theory than empirical research. To a certain extent, the emergence of a Weberian school would seem impossible since, as Weber writes, the questions and concepts of social-scientific inquiry, inasmuch as it is even culturally valued and actually practised, change across time and space. And yet Weber's ideal-typical method provides a *form*, if not the substance (that is, the value-rooted concepts) for acquiring valid social-scientific knowledge. Weber establishes the formal rationality of science while remaining agnostic about its substantive ends. This formalism raises the question of whether Weber's methodological thought articulates a method for valid social-scientific research or a philosophy of science, the inescapable cognitive horizon of any scientific practice, or perhaps both, a scientific praxis that unites a valid practical method with theoretical recognition of its own contingency. In other words, what is at stake in the reception of Weber's social-scientific methodology, as first articulated in the 'Objectivity' essay and most famously applied empirically in *The Protestant Ethic*, is whether his readers and followers have seized upon the fragile possibility for scientific truthfulness that his oeuvre instantiates or whether they have missed the opportunity to make social science into something other than glorified ideology.[30]

The question of Weber's success in founding a methodologically grounded, 'objective' science of social reality recalls a problem that Michel Foucault raised in his well-known lecture of 1969, 'Qu'est-ce qu'un auteur?'[31] Foucault's reflections merit brief recapitulation, for his distinction between founders of a scientific discipline and what he calls founders of discursiveness (*discursivité*) can help us articulate Weber's status as a founder of the science of *verstehende Soziologie*. Foucault makes this distinction at the end of his narrative – a metonymy for his genealogy of the modern subject[32] – of the 'birth' and (imminent or already achieved) 'death,' along with modernity, of the author, or rather of the 'author-function,' in order to distinguish the epistemic concept from the physical being who actually inscribes words. Although the author-function lends voice, it also restricts the proliferation of meaning, binding discourse to more or less arbitrary criteria, such as coherence and authenticity, that define an oeuvre, just as the arbitrary construction of mental health, criminality, or sexuality (to name some of Foucault's genealogical themes) both enable(d) and confine(d) the modern subject. In Weber's language, the author-function is but another 'iron cage,' a form of rationality where the means of written expression become an end in themselves. Text or discourse becomes a closed system, whose precise meaning may be subject to dispute, but only on the premise that it has a coherent meaning. We might say, though Foucault does not use the term borrowed from Kuhn,[33] that an author's oeuvre becomes paradigmatic when it becomes the norm for other texts. Such is the case for the founders of a scientific discipline. Their work establishes a discourse that subsumes its founding oeuvre so that even different interpretations of the founder's work compete and are at least potentially reconcilable within the normative framework of the established paradigm.

Foucault, however, admits that certain authors escape the iron cage of the author-function. These are what he calls the 'founders of discursiveness,' of whom the (paradigmatic?) examples are Marx and Freud. Their works, according to Foucault, generate a proliferation of possible meanings whose normative references are found not in a scientific paradigm but in the founding author's oeuvre. In other words, their oeuvres subsume competing proto-paradigms and are not themselves subject to paradigmatic verification. Foucault explains this most clearly with the example of the discovery of a new text by a founding author, such as the posthumous publication of Freud's *Entwurf einer Psychologie* of 1895,[34] though a better example might have been Marx's *Economic and Philosophic Manuscripts* of 1844. These discoveries throw the entire oeuvre into a wholly new light and thereby prevent paradigmatic consolidation. In a conflation of Kuhn and Trotsky, we might say that the founder of a discipline has carried out a successful scientific revolution, while a founder of discursiveness has launched permanent revolution. Although debates among Weberians have not been as fratricidal as those among Marxists and Freudians (perhaps because the partisan and professional stakes are lower), students of Weber have fundamental differences, which typically express themselves in references to different parts of Weber's oeuvre. These differences are due in part, no doubt, to the availability and quality of translations, to the canonization of certain texts and passages by established disciplines that have laid claim to parts of Weber's work, and to readers' personal idiosyncrasies and patience with Weber's dense prose. But more importantly, do they point to unbridgeable tensions, or even incoherencies, in Weber's thought? Or to the failure, so far, of an overarching scientific synthesis to occur? Is a 'definitive,' paradigmatic interpretation of Weber, an interpretation to end all interpretations, possible? If it were possible to derive from Weber's work an overarching Weberian paradigm that subsumes competing interpretations as well as the work itself, then we could attribute to Weber status of a founder of a scientific discipline, however inchoate it may still be; if not, then he too may be a founder of discursiveness, a rare thinker whose intellectual legacy escapes 'disciplining.'

While Foucault's normative preference clearly lies with the founders of discursiveness who spur a proliferation of meanings, his distinction of them from founders of a science (and implicitly from derivative authors whose work falls within an established disciplinary paradigm) suggests an interesting avenue for studying an author's reception, regardless of how one might evaluate each status. Thus, while the reception of derivative thinkers occurs generally through the assimilation of their thought to the contours of an existing paradigm, the founder of a science or discipline articulates the terms in reference to which readers and interpreters at least implicitly formulate their understanding of the founder. If it proves impossible, however, to identify within a non-derivative author's oeuvre the terms of reference of its subsequent reception, then we may have found a scientific 'permanent revolutionary.'[35] In the case of Max Weber's reception, it is difficult, if not impossible,[36] to claim that we are dealing with a derivative thinker. To be sure, Weber's oeuvre had its intellectual antecedents – he himself acknowledged his debt to Marx and to Nietzsche[37] as well as to the German historical school and to numerous contemporary colleagues[38] – but the diversity of his influences as well as his disciplinary competence in history, philosophy, economics, law, and even music theory meant that his oeuvre could hardly be anything less than an original synthesis. But does his oeuvre propose coherent[39] terms that define the universe of its possible subsequent interpretations?

One possible ideal-typical schema for interpreting the different usages of Weber's work could be Weber's sociology of domination.[40] After all, scholars who turn to Weber for some practical reason enter into a relation similar to that of legitimate domination: as an author, Weber exercises authority over those who read him, authority that we can consider legitimate inasmuch as readers act, insofar as they continue to read him, as if they believe that Weber has something worthwhile to teach them (even if only negatively). The form of this submission to Weber's putatively authoritative texts can vary in, among others, the following respects (implicit in Foucault's distinction between what we can call 'paradigmatic' and 'revolutionary' authors): (1) according to whether the reader/user considers a text's individual propositions as inextricably linked expressions of one and the same 'author' (here Weber) or autonomous, decontextualizable premises subject to individual verification, that is, whether they are personal (bound to the author as an ethical actor) or impersonal (abstract rational propositions independent of the personal authority of the actor who articulates them); (2) according to whether the use of the text is 'ordinary' (that is, embedded in a practical scientific regime of continuity) or 'extraordinary' (in a revolutionary context of rupture with existing scientific practice).

These two axes describing the reader/user's relation to Weber's texts correspond, of course, to those that define Weber's three ideal-types of legitimate domination: traditional (personal, ordinary), charismatic (personal, extraordinary), and legal-rational (impersonal, ordinary). Interestingly, Weber does not propose a fourth form of impersonal, extraordinary legitimate domination, probably because, in keeping with the premises of ideal-typical concept construction, he developed this typology on the basis of known historical forms of domination[41] and not in an abstract a priori deductive manner. Thus, just as it is hard to imagine a political revolution without exemplary personal leadership,[42] it is hard – though, as we shall suggest in the Conclusion, not impossible – to conceive of a practical reception of a scientific author that is revolutionary without appealing to the personal, integrative authority of an author and the allegedly overarching paradigmatic character of his or her oeuvre. Leaving this problem aside for now, we can adapt Weber's tripartite typology of legitimate domination in proposing three ideal-typical practical receptions of Weber, and more precisely of his methodological thought as formulated in his 'Objectivity' essay of 1904. Rather than offering a systematic review of the relatively large literature that Weber's methodological writings have prompted, we propose briefly to examine a handful of well-known readings of Weber that approximate the traditional, the legal-rational, and the charismatic ideal-types.

The most common reading of Weber, the traditional one, casts him typically as a 'founding father.' As with other customary or habitual social action, such paying of respect to Weber's scientific authority verges on the unthinking or the irrational: Weber is an important thinker because everyone and all the textbooks say so and have done so for a long time. Indeed, for most social scientists, Weber's name slides off the tongue automatically alongside those of the other two members of the holy trinity of modern sociology, Durkheim and Marx. The incantation is not entirely ritual, however. Traditional authorities serve not only as mythological progenitors. Like gods, they can intervene in daily affairs. The claim to be their successors imbues pretenders with power. Hence, one of the incentives for the continued exegesis of a 'classic'[43] author such as Weber resides in the traditional authority conferred on those who propose the doctrinally most correct interpretation. An additional strategy for the appropriation and perpetuation of such authority is the surpassing but *not* supplanting of the master, so that in a regime of continuity it is possible to claim to 'stand on the shoulders of giants' who came before. Thus, the traditional mode of reception of Weber's oeuvre is consistent with a 'building block' model of cumulative scientific progress, Weber and the other 'fathers' having laid the foundation stones for the allegedly prodigious edifice of modern social science.

This traditional reading of Weber has naive and more subtle, sophisticated forms. Perhaps most exemplary of the latter is that of Talcott Parsons, who more than anyone else shaped the conventional understanding of Weber's oeuvre in the English-speaking world.[44] We cannot expose the complexities of Parsons's social theory and of its relation to Weber's thought here,[45] but offer as an illustration of his ideal-typically 'traditional' reception of Weber a brief analysis of Parsons's speech before the German Sociological Congress on the centennial of Weber's birth in 1964, a time when Parsons was at the height of his own scientific power and prestige.[46] Such occasions lend themselves to ritual encomium, and Parsons does not fail to laud Weber for his innovative response to the scientific, political, and ideological crises of the early twentieth century. His speech, however, remains largely descriptive of Weber's methodological rapprochement of the cultural and natural sciences, of his articulation of philosophical alternatives to historicist idealism, individualist utilitarianism, and Marxist socialism, of his attaining a post-ideological position in politics, and of the theoretical centrality of Weber's sociology of law in relation to his sociology of religion. Between the lines, though, there emerges an assimilation of

Weber's positions to Parsons's scientific program: the forging of a general theory of social action,[47] of the social system,[48] and ultimately of the entire human condition.[49] Thus, in his centennial speech, Parsons argues that Weber's methodological innovations laid the groundwork for a general theoretical sociology, which only his particular empirical interests and foreshortened life prevented him from realizing himself. Substantively, according to Parsons, Weber's preoccupation with the sociology of law and its formal autonomy demonstrated the integrative social function of the normative order, while the allegedly universalist, evolutionary nature of his comparative sociological thought allowed him to transcend the partial conservative, liberal, and socialist ideological and theoretical positions that characterized pre-scientific social thought. It hardly matters, of course, whether Parsons was speaking about Weber's or his own accomplishments; the point of his address, probably with no cynical intention, was to inscribe Weber's and his own thought into a regime of scientific continuity and progress, in the process enhancing his own authority by donning the mantle of Weber's time-honoured intellectual prowess.

When an interpreter such as Parsons allows himself to criticize shortcomings in the work of a traditional authority, he moves towards what we can call a legal-rational mode of reception. In this type of relationship between an author and readers, legitimate authority does not inhere to the author's person but to the autonomously verifiable rational propositions of his or her work. Whether the author be derivative or paradigmatic, the validity of his or her work depends on the norms of the scientific discourse to which it belongs. Just as under legal-rational political authority 'no one is above the law,' author and interpreter stand as equals before the rules of their shared paradigm. In other words, under this mode of reception, readers engage with an author such as Weber as they would with any colleague according to the ordinary rules of debate of an established discipline, even if Weber is credited as a founder. Among Weberian scholars, this type of reception has occurred most frequently with regard to the so-called *Protestant Ethic* thesis. It ranges from more or less informed attempts empirically to prove or to disprove the applicability to one or another region of the world of what is taken for Weber's thesis, on the one hand, to serious, if not pedantic, scholarly disagreement with details of historical interpretation, on the other.[50] Numerous attempts to link contemporary economic performance to the vitality of Protestantism characterize the former,[51] while among the latter we might cite Tatsuro Hanyu's philological critique of Weber's anachronistic attribution of the term *Beruf* to Luther.[52]

With regard to Weber's methodological writings, Guy Oakes's work represents an ideal-typical example of their legal-rational reception. As translator and commentator of Weber's most difficult early methodological essays,[53] Oakes had to immerse himself in the turn-of-the-century neo-Kantian philosophical context of the twilight of the *Methodenstreit* and to acquire expertise in the legal, economic, social, and philosophical thought of Weber's interlocutors (Stammler, Jellinek, Roscher, Knies, Simmel, Tönnies, Windelband, Rickert, Dilthey, etc.). Thus, when Oakes engages in highly erudite methodological critiques of Weber's alleged reliance on Windelband's epistemology and, in particular, on Rickert's assumption of the objectivity of value-relevance,[54] he recasts himself in a sense into the role of a co-equal, rational interlocutor of Weber within the discursive context of Weber's writing. To be sure, by questioning the methodological tenability of a 'classic' author, Oakes might also be simultaneously perpetuating and arrogating Weber's traditional authority, but unlike Parsons's use of Weber in which the past legitimates present scientific practice, Oakes's relation to Weber collapses past and present into the timeless rationality of a particular scientific discourse.[55]

The third ideal-typical form of reception of a 'classic' oeuvre, the charismatic, is no doubt the most complex, and not only because it treats the oeuvre of an author from the past as presently still prophetic of the future. Although the concept is, along with the 'Protestant (work) ethic,' one of the two that Weber developed that have entered the popular consciousness, charisma is among the least easy to understand,[56] and describing the varieties of Weber's oeuvre's charismatic reception would require volumes, in part because it has been primarily the mode of interpretation among philosophers.[57] Borrowed from the historian of canon law Rudolf Sohm,[58] who used it to describe the communal relation among early Christians inspired by the example of Christ's rapport with his disciples,[59] Weber's concept above all expresses the negation of formal rules and time-honoured practices. Thus, he writes, 'From a substantive point of view, every charismatic authority would have to subscribe to the proposition [or Biblical formulation of prophecy], 'It is written ... but I say unto you ... '[60] In light of this ideal-typical formulation, the charismatic reception of an author's oeuvre would be all but impossible. Only a living being free from all constraints of human convention (rational or traditional) can exercise such authority, and yet the charismatic reception of Weber's writings began immediately following his death. In a eulogy of Weber for students at Heidelberg on 17 July 1920, Karl Jaspers praised Weber as the greatest philosopher of our time, who, precisely because he rejected philosophical speculation, lived a philosophy that contested existing philosophical and scientific discourses and their boundaries.[61] In such a reading, Weber's works become sacred relics of an exemplary life practice. To be sure, Weber's works are not themselves invested with magical powers, the exposure to which suffices to confer ethical benefit. According to the charismatic interpretation, however, they are traces of Weber's exemplary scientific *Lebensführung* whose 'correct' reading permits uplifting – or disenchanting – emulation of the prophetic master.

Perhaps the most influential charismatic interpreter of Weber in the contemporary Anglo-American context, political theorist Sheldon Wolin, identifies Weber's methodological texts, the 'Objectivity' essay in particular, as most revealing of his prophetic example. Claiming that 'methodology is mind engaged in the legitimation of its own political activity,'[62] Wolin argues that Weber's methodological texts are acts of political as well as scientific foundational violence. Not only do they destroy existing scientific practices and their theoretical truth claims, but by establishing the autonomy of the sphere of rational science, they contribute to the subjugation of modern social life to the '*Herrschaft* of facticity,'[63] or the tyranny of order over right, as Weber's scientific method becomes an ersatz political philosophy, implicitly critical of the very order in whose establishment it participates. Thus, like the Puritan founders of bourgeois rational capitalism, Weber is a tragic hero who has the courage to face the disenchantment of the world that his own action achieves. Finally, underscoring the paradox of the religious character of Weber's purely scientific revolution, Wolin expresses his own ambivalence about Weber's legacy when he describes how Weber, in his 1920 preface to *The Protestant Ethic*, performs his own 'secular crucifixion,' acknowledging the scientific imperfection and mortality of his own work, thereby admitting the anachronism as well as the 'powerlessness of the prophet in a "prophetless and godless" world' and exposing the 'the meaning of meaninglessness to be power without right.'[64] Ultimately, Weber's prophetic example – an 'objective' scientific practice that revealed science's incapacity to lend meaning to the world, 'a worldly asceticism at the service of a will to unconditioned truthfulness'[65] – made him the anti-hero as well as the hero of modern social science.

Coming back to Foucault's typology of authors, we can see that the extraordinary and personal charismatic mode of reception corresponds to the effects produced by founders of discursiveness, whose works escape the conventions of ordinary scientific discourse, standing outside of it and challenging even their own legitimacy and truth claims. By contrast, the other two modes characterize ordinary scientific discourse, with the traditional mode tending to apply more to the paradigmatic founding fathers of disciplines, and the impersonal legal-rational mode applying to derivative authors and to founders subjected to the norms of their own paradigm. The fact that some of the greatest thinkers of the twentieth century have read Weber as a charismatic authority, however, does not prove that he was a founder of discursiveness in Foucault's sense. Indeed, it would be possible to argue that Weber's elaboration of the concept of charisma (as well as his self-conscious articulation of his revolutionary methodological relativism) anticipated his charismatic reception and thus subsumed it to his emergent scientific paradigm. Such a facile argument, though, would result from a superficial, tautological reading of Weber, for his ideal-typical forms of legitimate domination are not intended to explain actual social relations, be they between political leaders and followers or between authors and readers. Instead, the ideal-types set the asymptotic logical limits within which social reality must vary; they are purely descriptive parameters.[66] Thus, the ideal-types of reception cannot correspond to actual scientific practice. Scholars who draw on Weber mix the forms, addressing him simultaneously, but to varying degrees, as founding father, prophet, and rational interlocutor. Nonetheless, the ideal-types proffer an analytical tool for comparing different readings and uses of Weber's thought such as those presented in the essays of this volume. Some of the essays do tend more towards one of the ideal-types (for example, anthropologist James Boon offers a performative celebration, complete with sexual innuendo, of Weber's charismatic scientific leadership; sociologist Anthony Oberschall inscribes Weber into a tradition of cumulative social-scientific progress; political theorist Peter Breiner engages rationally with an apparent antinomy in Weber's concept of the ideal-type), but the relationship of each essay's author to Weber (just like that of Parsons, Oakes, or Wolin) is in fact constantly shifting.

In short, the value of Weber's 'pure forms' is analytically descriptive; they do not propose a static categorization of reality, but in shifting combinations allow for a dynamic description of the history of social relations. The challenge for any *Wirklichkeitswissenschaft*, as exemplified by Weber's huge empirical oeuvre, is to establish the causal connections between ideal-typically described configurations of social relations (including their ideal representations). Thus, for a reception-history of Weber's oeuvre, the ideal-typical description of the different combined modes of reception constitutes only a first step. The simple typological schema that we have proposed here, following the vocabulary of Weber's *Herrschaftssoziologie*, allows us to distinguish between different kinds of reception. Explanation, however, can proceed only empirically; that is, we cannot dogmatically and idealistically deduce Weber's reception from the contents of the oeuvre itself, though as we shall argue in the Conclusion to this volume, Weber's empirical practice instantiates a method for causal social analysis that applies to his own scientific reception. For now, though, let us turn to the volume's empirical contents.

The texts presented here are not the work of scholars who have made a career or reputation primarily through the theoretical exegesis of Weber.[67] Instead, we have collected essays from scholars working in different disciplinary, institutional, and cultural contexts and who have encountered or turned to Weber in their practical scientific research on problems ranging from the history of ideas to social movements and electoral behaviour. Their readings of Weber are necessarily selective and pragmatically oriented. Unlike theologians, legal theorists, or professional 'Weberologists,' they do not pursue the dogmatically correct interpretation of a doctrine (in this case Weber's oeuvre) but translate his work into their practical scientific *Lebensführung*.

In selecting our authors, we excluded German scholars working in a Weberian perspective for two reasons: one theoretical, the other more pragmatic, if not political. On the one hand, we are interested in the diffusion and interaction effects of Weber's reception (including unavoidable but at times creative cultural and linguistic mistranslations) within different national as well as disciplinary milieus, the phenomenon of intellectual diffusion being moreover particularly interesting from a Weberian perspective, since it allows for an assessment of the causal autonomy of ideas within different ideational and interest contexts. On the other hand, partly because German scholars do have privileged access to Weber's language and intellectual referents as well as a more personal stake in his legacy for German social and political thought, the German reception of Weber adds certain complexities that we choose not to address here.[68] As we already noted, Weber was 're-imported' into German academics after the Second World War, but Weber's 'ghost' had always been there. Much of the social thought of the Weimar period, from Carl Schmitt to Karl Mannheim and the early Frankfurt School was a response to his work. After 1933, German émigré scholars continued their debate on Weber, notably his fact–values distinction, in the United States,[69] whence 'Weber' returned to Germany, Americanized and 'Parsonized,' in the work, among others, of Jürgen Habermas, for example. An additional complication of Weber's postwar reception in Germany arises from the fact that, like other thinkers of the Wilhelmine and Weimar periods, Weber is read through the lens of the catastrophe of 1933–45. While the founders of the Federal Republic had recuperated Weber as a liberal, even transatlanticist forefather,[70] the young historian Wolfgang Mommsen, in his 1959 thesis *Max Weber und die deutsche Politik, 1890–1920*, accused Weber of 'mak[ing] the German people inwardly willing to acclaim Adolf Hitler's leadership position.'[71] While this kind of political evaluation has lost its acuity in Germany today, and Weber-scholarship has experienced a renaissance thanks to the continuing publication project of a critical edition of his entire oeuvre, Weber is still mobilized within the context of German academic politics, with a recent book calling for the authentic Weberian 'Heidelberg School' (under the leadership of Wolfgang Schluchter) to assume at last its rightful place alongside if not above the dominant paradigms of Luhmann's systems theory, Habermas's theory of communicative action, and rational-choice theory.[72] Weber has also been held hostage to debates between historians and social scientists, with Wilhelm Hennis notably contesting the misappropriation of Weber as a founder of sociology.[73] The editors of this volume have chosen to avoid these Germano-German debates.

The non-German reception of Weber is of course no simpler, nor without its politico-academic pitfalls. Other scholars, for example, might be considered better qualified in, or more representative of, Weberian scholarship within their disciplinary or national contexts than some of those presented in this volume. Our purpose here, however, is to illustrate the variety of understandings and uses of Weber, with an eye to explaining this variation. A more significant problem with the essays selected here arises from the fact that the essays were written for a volume marking the centennial of Weber's methodological manifesto of 1904: we invited the authors to be self-reflexive in considering the role that Weber has played in their own work and within their respective disciplines at large. The essays thus pose an interpretive challenge in that, in most of them, the authors explicitly articulate their own ideal-typical intellectual representations of Weber at the same time as they implicitly reveal the interests, competing ideas, and cultural as well as disciplinary biases that co-determine their understandings and uses of Weber. We shall return to this problem of levels of self-representation and mediation in the Conclusion.

In taking up our invitation to reflect on Weber's methodology, the authors tended to adopt one of three practical approaches, which of course shade into one another: (1) a close (re-)reading of Weber's methodological texts and/or practice as exemplified in his empirical texts, (2) an assessment of the reception and interpretation of Weber's methodology within their own scientific communities, or (3) an evaluation of actual scientific practice inspired by Weber within their disciplines. Different, shifting combinations of the three ideal-typical modes of reception are implicitly evident within each type of approach. We have not attempted to organize the chapters' presentation by reception types but rather more obviously by the authors' practical approaches. Thus, the first four essays (respectively by sociologist John Drysdale, political theorists John Gunnell and Peter Breiner, and the philosopher of science Mario Bunge) directly and critically take up the epistemological issues raised in the 'Objectivity' essay, such as the role of value orientations in concept formation, the truth value of ideal-types, and the relationship of scholarship to partisanship. The second group of six essays (by philosopher Catherine Colliot-Thélène, sociologist Guy Rocher, anthropologist Roberto Motta, philosopher Naoshi Yamawaki, anthropologist Jack Goody, and sociologist Anthony Oberschall) addresses the reception of Weber outside of his historical and national context as well as the relevance of his thought to the non-Western world. The final four essays (by sociologist Robert Fishman, political scientists Jeffrey Kopstein and Stephen Hanson, and anthropologist James Boon) consider the place of Weber's thought in contemporary empirical social science and question its apparent marginalization despite its fecundity and relevance.

The volume's three sections thus respectively treat Weber's thought as doctrinal text, examine its diffusion, and assess it as practical conduct. This sequence corresponds, in fact, to the levels of analysis the Weber employs in his comparative historical sociology of religion, in which he establishes how doctrines (such as Calvinist predestination), with their inherent logics, translate into life practices (worldly asceticism) and social institutions (capitalism) by way of particular social carriers with other material and ideal interests as well as technical means. In the volume's conclusion, we shall return to Weber's comparative historical sociological method as a model for a reception-history of his oeuvre that might allow us both to understand and to explain Weber's varied legacy within contemporary international social science. In doing so, we may also be able, at last, to discern Weber's status as a founding author.

NOTES

1 The 'standard' English translation of this essay, complete with mistranslations and typographical errors (notably the frequent substitution of *casual* for *causal*), appeared in Max Weber, *The Methodology of the Social Sciences*, trans. and ed. Edward Shils and Henry Finch (Glencoe, IL: Free Press, 1949). A new translation by Keith Tribe is now available in *The Essential Weber*, ed. Sam Whimster (London: Routledge, 2004). Testifying to the explosion of interest in Weber, this translation, like Stephen Kalberg's new translation of the *Protestant Ethic* (Los Angeles: Roxbury, 2003), does not appear in Alan Sica's *Max Weber: A Comprehensive Bibliography* (New Brunswick, NJ: Transaction, 2004), which, with 4,888 entries, attempts to offer an exhaustive inventory of publications by and about Weber in the English language only.

2 See Alan Sica, *Max Weber and the New Century* (New Brunswick, NJ: Transaction, 2004), 10–11.

3 See the section entitled 'From Philistinism to Insanity' in Nasser Behnegar, *Leo Strauss, Max Weber, and the Scientific Study of Politics* (Chicago: University of Chicago Press, 2003), 83–7, for a close reading of Strauss's assimilation of Weber to Nietzsche's philosophy and insanity.

4 Max Weber, *Roscher and Knies: The Logical Problems of Historical Economics*, trans. and ed. Guy Oakes (New York: Free Press, 1975).

5 See Guy Oakes, 'Max Weber and the Southwest German School: The Genesis of the Concept of the Historical Individual,' *Politics, Culture, and Society* 1, no. 1 (Fall 1987): 115–31.

6 See Catherine Colliot-Thélène, *Le désenchantement de l'État: de Hegel à Max Weber* (Paris: Les éditions de Minuit, 1992).

7 Sica, *Max Weber*, 12.

8 Max Weber, 'Die "Objektivität" sozialwissenschaftlicher und sozialpolitischer Erkenntnis,' *Gesammelte Aufsätze zur Wissenschaftslehre* (Tübingen: Mohr, 1988), 170 [Shils and Finch, *Methodology of the Social Sciences*, 72].

9 Ibid., 213–14 [111].

10 Unlike the Puritans, who were unaware of the economic consequences of their religiously motivated action, Weber assumed responsibility for the iron cage of science when in the final paragraph of the 'Objectivity' essay he wrote, '[Research in an age of specialization] will lose its awareness of its ultimate rootedness in the value ideas in general. And it is well that should be so.' He immediately added, however, 'But there comes a moment when the atmosphere changes. The significance of the unreflectively utilized viewpoints becomes uncertain and the road is lost in the twilight.' Ibid., 214 [111].

11 The best-known version of this interpretation, as we shall explore further below, is that of Sheldon Wolin, 'Max Weber: Legitimation, Method, and the Politics of Theory,' *Political Theory* 9, no. 3 (August 1981): 401–24. Also see Tracy Strong, 'Max Weber and the Bourgeoisie,' in *The Barbarism of Reason: Max Weber and the Twilight of Enlightenment*, ed. Asher Horowitz and Terry Maley, 113–38 (Toronto: University of Toronto Press, 1994).

12 Hans Gerth and C. Wright Mills, trans. and eds., *From Max Weber: Essays in Sociology* (1946: repr. New York: Oxford University Press, 1958), 129–58.

13 See Weber's preface to his *Religionssoziologie*, 3 vols. (Tübingen: Mohr, 1988), which Talcott Parsons in his translation presents as the 'Author's Introduction' to the *Protestant Ethic* (London: Allen and Unwin, 1930 [reprinted in paperback by Scribner's, New York, 1958]). Thus presented, religious, scientific, and economic rationalization appear to be facets of a universal rationalizations process initiated in the West. For more on Parson's creative misinterpretation of Weber, see below, as well as Guy Rocher's contribution to this volume.

14 See Naoshi Yamawaki's contribution to this volume.

15 David Chalcraft and Austin Harrington, eds., *The Protestant Ethic Debate: Max Weber's Replies to His Critics, 1907–1910* (Liverpool: Liverpool University Press, 2001).

16 See James Boon's contribution to this volume.

17 Thanks to his encounter with Du Bois in St Louis and their subsequent correspondence, Weber, whose disparaging remarks about Polish workers in his 1895 Inaugural Lecture earned him accusations of racism, actually sketched the first social-constructivist theory of race during his famous debate with the racial hygienist Alfred Ploetz at the first German Sociological Congress of 1910. See Elke Winter, *Max Weber et les relations ethniques* (Quebec: Presses de l'Université Laval, 2004).

18 For more on this lesson, see John Gunnell's and Peter Breiner's contributions to this volume.

19 See Raymond Morrow, 'Mannheim and the Early Frankfurt School: The Weber Reception of Rival Traditions of Critical Sociology,' in Horowitz and Maley, *Barbarism of Reason*, 169–94.

20 The not-yet-complete project of a critical edition of Weber's oeuvre, under the editorial supervision of prominent professors, did not begin until 1976. Before then the institutional 'carriers' of Weber's legacy had been the legal scholar and retired banker Johannes Winckelmann and Weber's widow, Marianne. See Dirk Käsler, *Max Weber: An Introduction to His Life and Work* (Chicago: University of Chicago Press, 1988).

21 Sica, *Max Weber*.

22 For example, Guenther Roth and Reinhard Bendix, 'Max Webers Einfluss auf die amerikanische Soziologie,' *Kölner Zeitschrift für Soziologie* 11, no. 1 (1959): 38–53; Agnes Erdelyi, *Max Weber in Amerika: Wirkungsgeschichte und Rezpetionsgeschichte Webers in der anglo-amerikanischen Philosophie und Sozialwissenschaften* (Vienna: Passagen Verlag, 1992); Michaël Pollack, 'Max Weber en France: l'itinéraire d'une oeuvre,' *Cahiers de l'IHTP* 3 (July 1986); Käsler, *Max Weber*; Peter Kivisto and William H. Swatos Jr, 'Weber and Interpretive Sociology in America,' *Sociological Quarterly* 31, no. 1 (1990): 149–63; Irving Horowitz, 'Max Weber and the Spirit of American Sociology,' *Sociological Quarterly* 5, no. 4 (Autumn 1964): 344–54.

23 On the political instrumentalization of Weber by these ideological currents in France, see Michael Pollack, 'La place de Max Weber dans le champ intellectuel français,' *Droit et société* 9 (1988): 195–209. Guenther Roth, 'Interpreting and Translating Weber,' *International Sociology* 7, no. 4 (December 1992): 457, notes that while American neo-conservatives attack Weber as a dangerous cultural relativist, their German counterparts have elevated Weber to the status of 'moral preceptor of the nation.'

24 See Richard Swedberg, 'The Changing Picture of Max Weber's Sociology,' *Annual Review of Sociology* 29 (2003): 283–306.

25 For a more thorough and systematic analysis of the content and structure of the 'Objectivity' essay, see John Drysdale's and John Gunnell's contributions to this volume.

26 Weber, '"Objektivität"' 155 [58 in Finch and Shil's translation].

27 Such a general theory has, of course, proven impossible in the natural sciences as well. As with Heisenberg's electron, whose position and charge can never both be known, it may be possible to retrace some of the path taken by a historical subject (as in history) or partially describe its position (as in social statistics), but even with a combination of both types of information, it is impossible to predict where it is headed.

28 'Denn wissenschaftliche Wahrheit ist nur, was für alle gelten *will*, die Wahrheit *wollen* [literally: For scientific knowledge is only that which *wants* to be valid for those who *want* the truth].' Weber, '"Objektivität,"' 184. Shils and Finch in their translation (84) slightly water down the relativism of this famous sentence: 'For scientific truth is precisely what is valid for those who *seek* the truth' (all emphases in the original text and translation).

29 Leo Strauss and Eric Voegelin did precisely this in their philosophical critiques of Weber, yet also held him up as the quintessential social scientist of the twentieth century. See John G. Gunnell, 'Reading Max Weber: Leo Strauss and Eric Voegelin,' *European Journal of Political Theory* 3 (April 2004): 151–66. Also, see Guy Oakes, 'Methodological Ambivalence: The Case of Max Weber,' *Social Research* 49, no. 3 (Autumn 1982): 584–615, for a critique of Weber's 'methodologically untenable' reliance on Rickert's and Windelband's neo-Kantian epistemology; and John Drysdale, 'How Are Social Scientific Concepts Formed? A Reconstruction of Max Weber's Theory of Concept Formation,' *Sociological Theory* 14, no. 1 (March 1996): 71–89, for a refutation of Oakes's critique.

30 This question was, of course, central to the sociology of knowledge of Karl Mannheim; see Peter Breiner's contribution to this volume.

31 Michel Foucault, *Dits et écrits I, 1954–1975* (Paris: Gallimard, 2001), 817–49; first published in the *Bulletin de la Société française de philosophie*, 63, no. 1 (July–September 1969): 73–104, and in English translation in *The Foucault Reader*, ed. Paul Rabinow (New York: Pantheon Books, 1984).

32 Foucault was introduced at the beginning of the lecture as the 'real live' author of *Les mots et les choses* (Paris: Gallimard, 1966), which ends with the famous image of the erasure of the modern subject like a face drawn in the sand at the edge of the sea.

33 Thomas Kuhn, *The Structure of Scientific Revolutions* (Chicago: University of Chicago Press, 1962).

34 Foucault, *Dits et écrits I*, 837.

35 Foucault's distinction may not be exhaustive, as we suggest in the Conclusion to this volume.

36 For example, Alan Bloom, *Dwarfs and Giants* (New York: Simon and Schuster, 1990), 238, claims that his mentor, Leo Strauss, 'recognized the seriousness and nobility of Max Weber's mind, but he showed that he was a derivative thinker, standing somewhere between modern science and Nietzsche, unable to resolve their tension.' Cited in Sica, *Max Weber*, 176.

37 Notably, following a debate with Oswald Spengler, as reported by Eduard

Baumgarten, *Max Weber: Werk und Person* (Tübingen: Mohr, 1964), 354, Weber told one of his students that these two thinkers defined the contemporary intellectual field, and to deny so would be intellectually dishonest.

38 Much of the 'Weberological' work since the 1980s, notably by Thomas Burger, Guy Oakes, Guenther Roth, Lawrence Scaff, and Stephen Turner (see Sica's exhaustive bibliography, *Max Weber*) has been devoted to the intellectual origins and context of Weber's work.

39 Again, coherency is a historically contingent feature of the author function and therefore does not apply to the 'post-authorial' founders of discursiveness.

40 Max Weber, *Economy and Society*, ed. Guenther Roth and Claus Wittich (Berkeley: University of California Press, 1978 [1968]), pt 1, chap. 3, 212–301.

41 As presented in *Economy and Society*, pt 2, chaps. 11–16, concrete historical analyses that temporally preceded the elaboration of the formal typologies of part 1.

42 A possible exception may be the peaceful revolutions of 1989 that brought down communism with little or no personal leadership or abstract revolutionary doctrine. See Laurence McFalls, *Communism's Collapse, Democracy's Demise?* (New York: New York University Press, 1995).

43 For a discussion of the concept of the 'classic' author, see Jeffrey Kopstein's contribution to this volume.

44 Swedberg, 'Max Weber's Sociology,' labels Parsons's interpretation, with its emphasis on the causal importance of norms and values, the 'traditional' view of Weber, though in a typology that opposes it to the newer views offered by 'analytical' or rational-choice Weberians and by 'structural' interest theorists. In the French-speaking world, Raymond Aron, *La sociologie allemande contemporaine* (Paris: Presses Universitaires de France, 1935), had a similar influence on the reception of Weber.

45 See Guy Rocher's contribution to this volume. Parsons's interpretation of Weber, along with his own theory, came under polemical attack in the 1970s, notably by Jere Cohen, Lawrence E. Hazelrigg, and Whitney Pope, 'De-Parsonizing Weber: A Critique of Parson's Interpretation of Weber's Sociology,' *American Sociological Review* 40 (April 1975): 229–41.

46 Talcott Parsons, 'Evaluation and Objectivity in Social Science: An Interpretation of Max Weber's Contribution,' *International Social Science Journal* 17, no. 1 (1965): 46–63.

47 Talcott Parsons, *The Structure of Social Action* (New York: Free Press, 1968 and 1949 [1937]).

48 Talcott Parsons, *The Social System* (New York: Free Press, 1951).

49 Talcott Parsons, *Action Theory and the Human Condition* (New York: Free Press, 1978).

50 See Hartmut Lehmann and Guenther Roth, eds., *Weber's* Protestant Ethic: *Origins, Evidence, Context* (Cambridge: Cambridge University Press, 1993); Philippe Besnard, *Protestantisme et capitalisme: La controverse post-wébérienne* (Paris: Armand Colin, 1970); or for an overview, Alistair Hamilton, 'Max Weber's *Protestant Ethic*,' in *The Cambridge Companion to Weber*, ed. Stephen Turner, 151–71 (Cambridge: Cambridge University Press, 2000).

51 For example, Niall Ferguson, 'Why America Outpaces Europe (Clue: The God Factor),' *New York Times*, 8 June 2003, cited in Sica, *Max Weber*, 75; or Peter Berger's foreword to David Martin, *Tongues of Fire: The Explosion of Protestantism in Latin America* (Oxford: Blackwell, 1990), xiii–ix: 'Max Weber and Elie Halévy have analyzed the manner in which the previous Protestant explosion transformed the world ... The same ethos also continues to evince its time-honoured affinities with the "spirit of capitalism," with individualism, with a hunger for education and (last but not least) with a favorable disposition toward democratic politics.'

52 Tatsuro Hanyu, 'Max Webers Quellenbehandlung in der Protestantischen Ethik: Der Berufs-begriff,' *Archives Européennes de Sociologie* 35, no. 1 (1994): 72–103. See also Roberto Motta's contribution to this volume.

53 Max Weber, *Critique of Stammler*, trans. Guy Oakes (New York: Free Press, 1977); Weber, *Roscher and Knies*.

54 Guy Oakes, *Weber and Rickert: Concept Formation in the Cultural Sciences* (Cambridge, MA: MIT Press, 1988); also see note 29.

55 For an interesting discussion of the temporality of different modes of legitimate authority, see Stephen Hanson's contribution to this volume. Also see Terry Maley, 'The Politics of Time: Subjectivity and Modernity in Max Weber' in Horowitz and Maley, *Barbarism of Reason*.

56 In *Economy and Society*, pt 1, Weber purposely presents it third, in order to contrast it with the forms historically more familiar to his readers.

57 Notably Karl Jaspers, *On Max Weber* (New York: Paragon House, 1988); Karl Löwith, *Max Weber and Karl Marx* (London: Routledge, 1992); Maurice Merleau-Ponty, 'The Crisis of Understanding,' *Adventures of the Dialectic*, chap. 1 (Evanston, IL: Northwestern University Press, 1973); Leo Strauss, 'Natural Right and the Distinction between Facts and Values,' *Natural Right and History*, chap. 2 (Chicago: University of Chicago Press); Eric Voegelin, 'Introduction, Part Three: The Traditional Position of Max Weber,' in *The New Science of Politics: An Introduction* (Chicago: University of Chicago Press, 1952); Wolin, 'Max Weber.' Among these philosophers, Strauss and Voegelin might be said to have a 'negative charismatic' read-

ing of Weber in that each holds him up as an example of a hero *not* to be emulated.

58 Weber, *Economy and Society*, 216.
59 See Peter Haley, 'Rudolf Sohm on Charisma,' *Journal of Religion* 60, no. 2 (1980): 185–97. By describing the charismatic organization of the original Christian community, Sohm was of course engaging in a critique of the traditional and legal-rational institution of the Catholic Church.
60 Weber, *Economy and Society*, 243.
61 Karl Jaspers, *Max Weber: Eine Gedenkrede* (Tübingen: Mohr, 1926). Elsewhere, Jaspers put Weber on an equal footing with not only Plato and Saint Augustine but Jesus Christ and Confucius.
62 Wolin, *Max Weber*, 406.
63 Ibid., 420.
64 Ibid., 421–2.
65 Philippe Despoix, *Éthiques du désenchantement* (Paris: L'Harmattan, 1998), 58: 'une ascèse intramondaine au service d'une volonté de véracité indéterminée.' Despoix is in fact paraphrasing Karl Löwith's attribution to Weber of a 'Willen zur unbedingten Wahrhaftigkeit' in his centennial essay 'Die Entzauberung der Welt durch Wissenschaft, *Merkur* 6 (1964): 515.
66 Weber's typology would in fact be *logically* exhaustive of all possible forms of domination/reception if he had defined the impersonal-extraordinary quadrant. We shall return to this issue in the Conclusion.
67 One exception is Catherine Colliot-Thélène, probably the leading 'Weberologist' in France today, who has most comparatively reflected on Weber's reception in France. However, she came to Weber from the perspective of philosophy and not social theory. Her works include *Max Weber et l'histoire* (Paris: Presses Universitaires de France, 1990); *Le désenchantement de l'État*; and *Études wébériennes* (Paris: Presses Universitaires de France, 2001).
68 On the German reception of Weber, see Walter M. Sprondel, Constans Seyfarth, et al., '"Soziologie soll heissen ... "' *Kölner Zeitschrift für Soziologie und Sozialpsychologie* 32, no. 1 (1980): 1–11.
69 See John G. Gunnell, *The Descent of Political Theory: The Genealogy of an American Vocation* (Chicago: University of Chicago Press, 1993), on what he calls the 'Weimar conversation.' For the first important introduction to American scholars, notably a series of articles in *Social Research* by Albert Salomon, see Bryan S. Turner, ed., *Max Weber: Critical Responses*, vol. 2, *Methods and Theory* (London: Routledge, 1999).

70 See the rehabilitation of Weber's politics by the German editor of *Economy and Society*: Johannes Winckelmann, *Legalität und Legitimität in Max Webers Herrschaftssoziologie* (Tübingen: Mohr-Siebeck, 1952).

71 Cited in Sven Eliaeson, 'Constitutional Caesarism: Weber's Politics in Their German Context,' in Turner, *Cambridge Companion to Weber*, 144. Although Mommsen subsequently toned down the accusation, the damage was done.

72 Wolfgang Schluchter, 'Handlung, Ordnung und Kultur: Grundzüge eines weberianischen Forschungsprogramms,' in *Das Weber-Paradigma: Studien zur Weiterentwicklung von Max Webers Forschungsprogramm*, ed. Gert Albert, Agathe Bienfait, Steffen Sigmund, and Claus Wendt, 42–76 (Tübingen: Mohr-Siebeck, 2003).

73 Wilhelm Hennis, *Max Webers Fragestellung* (Tübingen: Mohr-Siebeck, 1987) and *Max Webers Wissenschaft vom Menschen: Neue Studie zur Biographie des Werks* (Tübingen: Mohr-Siebeck, 1996). See Peter Baehr, review of these works, 'Heart, Character, and a Science of Man,' *Political Theory* 31, no. 1 (February 2003): 116–24.

PART ONE

The Partisan and the Scholar: Weber's 'Objectivity' between Theory and Practice

1 Weber on Objectivity: Advocate or Critic?

JOHN DRYSDALE

Introduction: Weber and the Language of 'Objectivity'

Weber's reputation with respect to objectivity has been pulled in contradictory directions. On the one hand Weber can be portrayed as the classic modernist spokesman for objectivity, understood as the cool, detached attitude of the scientific specialist. In this view, objectivity is associated with the production of value-free, rational knowledge on the model of the natural sciences. On the basis of this image, Weber can be associated with the positivist and rationalist traditions of social science. Proponents of this image tend to applaud Weber for at least 'preaching,' if not always practising, a notion of objectivity understood as an ideal standard of value-freedom.[1] On the other hand, Weber can also be viewed as the champion of *Verstehen* in the socio-cultural studies, the 'warm' hermeneutic method of empathetic understanding (after all, he defined sociology as an *interpretive* science of social action, and action was to be 'interpretively understood' before it could be explained in causal terms). Empathy implies a kind of emotional intimacy with people and their actions, the very opposite of the impersonal objectivity usually associated with science. According to this model, knowledge of the social world is viewed as essentially intuitive, non-rational, and anti-positivistic.[2]

These polarized images of Weber – 'cool' objectivist versus 'warm' hermeneuticist, proponent of value-free, rational, causal explanation versus intuitive, empathetic understanding – of course, are not easily reconciled. Proponents of the objectivist, rationalist Weber have to either ignore or else reject Weber's *verstehende* approach as a gratuitous lapse from rational models of scientific explanation. Champions of the *verstehende* or hermeneutic Weber need to ignore, if not reject, the doctrine of value-freedom along with the value-fact dichotomy, and indeed Weber's emphasis on causal explanation. From this second perspective, Weber's apparent advocacy of objectivity and value-freedom are treated as unfortunate slips.

The very persistence of these contradictory, if distorted, images requires that we read more closely the essay that is the *locus classicus* of Weber's ideas concerning objectivity. The single point of agreement between these two opposing interpretations of Weber's legacy appears to be an acceptance that he indeed advocated objectivity in social science, a fact applauded by the one side, grudgingly conceded by the other. Our aim in the following remarks is to explore in some detail the question of Weber's own understanding of, and orientation toward, objectivity. Thus, the main purpose of this essay is explication and interpretation rather than critique. For that reason, reference to the immense secondary literature is confined to a minimum.

Although '"Objectivity" in Social Science and Social Policy' was published in 1904 as a statement of editorial policy by the new editors (Max Weber, Werner Sombart, and Edgar Jaffé) of *Archiv für Sozialwissenschaft und Sozialpolitik*, it served a larger purpose for its primary author. Addressed in part to potential contributors interested in ascertaining the editorial 'line' or policy-orientation of the journal, the essay includes several indications of editorial intent toward openness to diverse points of view and value commitments with respect to social policy. Beyond the content normally expected of the editorial genre, however, Weber took the opportunity to lay out in considerable detail his views concerning core methodological and even epistemological issues facing the social and cultural sciences, including, but not limited to, economics.

On more than one occasion Weber suggests that extended reflection on methodological norms and presuppositions is justified only under certain conditions. Under ordinary conditions (similar to what Thomas Kuhn has called 'normal science') when there is consensus on the most basic questions of method, the ordinary social scientist can pursue research without constantly having to reflect on the methodological and theoretical presuppositions of one's research. In Weber's assessment, his own time was not ordinary; it was a period in which the emerging social sciences still suffered deep confusion over a wide range of issues that had plagued economics and related fields for a generation. Under such conditions of confusion and controversy, the scholar in general and journal editors in particular have extraordinary obligations with respect to scientific communication and accountability. The 'progress' of science (understood broadly as scholarship) depended on the clear accounting for the premises and presuppositions of one's own work. This accountability applied to communication 'horizontally' with colleagues in specialized fields or contexts, but also 'vertically,' so to speak, with philosophers (logicians) and methodologists. Thus, historians need to be able to express the theoretical-philosophical underpinnings of their specialized historiographical practices. The same is true for political economists and specialists in all the social sciences.

The major division within the framework of the earlier, and still to be resolved, methodological controversies was the split between the two major schools of economics, the so-called historical and theoretical schools. Weber himself had been trained as a member of the historical school and continued to identify himself, with certain reservations, as a member of that school. From 1903 to 1906 Weber undertook an extensive critical analysis of the ideas of the founders of the historical school, Wilhelm Roscher and Karl Knies. Much of the content of the objectivity essay is to be understood as a contribution to Weber's ongoing critical appropriation of the methodological ideas of the historical school. On this occasion Weber places the key issues in the context of the claims of the two schools and their respective methodologies based on historical concreteness in the one case and theoretical abstraction in the other. Although the issues are manifold, Weber settles on the theme of 'objectivity' as the criterion for sorting out the controversies. He appears to aim at nothing less than a resolution of the *Methodenstreit*.

By placing the word *objectivity* prominently in the title of his essay, Weber announced his main theme to prospective readers. By further highlighting the word in quotation marks he implied that the reader should expect the concept of objectivity to bear close attention and critical scrutiny. Those who have read widely in Weber's writings know that he often used this particular rhetorical device of placing terms in quotes, though not always with obvious intent. Although it is far from self-evident why or with what meaning Weber placed *objectivity* in quotes in this essay, his doing so at least alerted the reader to a term whose meaning should not be taken at face value.

In an essay of almost seventy pages and bearing the term *objectivity* in its title, the reader might expect that the term would be both carefully defined and frequently used. Yet neither seems to be the case. Weber used the terminology of objectivity strikingly few times. In a recent rereading of this essay, I tracked the number of Weber's explicit uses of the terms related to *objectivity*. According to this word count, Weber used the terms only a few times, especially as terms specifically related to the cognitive processes associated with scientific knowledge. In an essay of more than 21,000 words Weber used the noun *Objektivität* (objectivity) only six times in the body of the essay. On each occasion he flagged the special status of the term, either by placing the term in quotes (five times) or by asking explicitly, 'What is the meaning here of objectivity?' Yet he never attempted to define *objectivity*. He never, we are tempted to say, made it explicitly into a concept (in the way he made 'ideal-types' a concept in the same essay). Although much of the essay can be construed as somehow related to issues of objectivity in one or more of its senses, often the discussion bears only an oblique relation to the question most on the reader's mind: 'What, then, is objectivity?'

The situation is essentially the same with respect to Weber's use of the adjective. Of eighteen cases where he used the adjective *objektiv* (objective), three instances refer to the status of values rather than knowledge, and two other cases refer to the idea of 'objective possibility,' which Weber used in a special sense that does not refer to the main issues at stake in this essay. So Weber used the terminology of objectivity, either the noun or the adjective, fewer than twenty times to refer to the processes of knowledge. Even making allowances for the fact that much discussion of the issues of objectivity can be framed in terms that elucidate the issues without relying on repetitive literal uses of the same terms, many readers have had their expectations for a direct and explicit focus on objectivity as a concept somewhat frustrated.

In the foreword to the essay Weber attempted to delineate authorial responsibility for the essay in terms of its two main parts. In taking complete responsibility for the long second part (Shils/Finch translation 63–112, designated in the following page citations as ET, for English translation), Weber clearly implied that the first section (ET 51–63) had the full endorsement of his two co-editors, Werner Sombart and Edgar Jaffé. He identified three major points of agreement among the editors: (1) the positive value of theoretical knowledge from 'one-sided' points of view, (2) the construction of precisely defined concepts, and (3) the rigorous distinction between empirical knowledge and value judgments (*Werturteile*) (146 [in Winkelmann's German edition], ET 49). There is reason to believe that Weber wrote a draft version of the first section and then secured the agreement of the co-editors. The exact extent of contributions of Sombart and Jaffé to the emphases and content in this part is not clear. In any case, the essay as a whole was published under Weber's name. With respect to the three points of agreement, the focus of discussion in the first part is disproportionately weighted on the distinction between empirical knowledge and value judgments – a topic that also reappears in Weber's other writings. Insofar as the terminology of *objectivity* comes into play in this opening section it is only in the sense of making a distinction in principle between the putative objectivity of empirical knowledge and the realm of values and value judgments associated with practice. Exploration of objectivity was postponed to the second and major section of the essay.

In the closing paragraph of the first section Weber established the context in terms of which he wished to launch and to justify the extended discussion of issues of objectivity in the second part. Having so far only deployed the distinction in principle between value judgments and empirical knowledge, the task at hand in the second part would be, instead of merely presupposing the existence of 'an unconditionally valid type of knowledge in the social sciences,' to explore 'the meaning of objectively "valid" truth in the social sciences' (160, ET 63). He identified the contentious issues at play in contemporary social-scientific discourse: the conflicts over methods, over 'fundamental concepts' and presuppositions, and over the 'incessant shift of "viewpoints," and the continuous redefinition of "concepts."' Anyone who was aware of these issues and 'who sees that the theoretical and historical modes of analysis are still separated by an apparently unbridgeable gap (*eine scheinbar unüberbrückbare Kluft*)' (161, ET 63) would recognize the seriousness of the divisions in the social sciences and especially in economics.[3] Weber cites sympathetically the lament of a Viennese examinee that as a result of these methodological differences there are *two* sciences of economics (161, ET 63). At this point Weber connects the meaning of *objectivity* with the methodological rift between the two schools, each wedded to its own exclusive 'method': in the one case 'historical,' and in the other, 'theoretical.' In view of the rift between the two schools/methods, what is the meaning in such a situation of 'objectivity' (*'Was heißt hier Objektivität?'*) (161, ET 63)?

In recounting these issues Weber acknowledged that the methodological controversies and the consequent gap opened a generation earlier between the historical school of economics, led by Gustav Schmoller, and the theoretical (Austrian) school, headed by Carl Menger, remained unresolved. This far-flung struggle (as Weber calls it, a *Kampf um Methode*) incorporated issues concerning the goals and methods of economics, as well as the relation of economics to other social sciences, and the question of the status of its concepts as instruments of social-scientific knowledge. By referencing this divisive and ongoing set of controversies, Weber derives a mandate to address a broad range of issues concerning the status of economic, and more broadly, social-scientific, knowledge. He placed the question of 'objectivity' at the centre of these issues.

If we were to pose Weber's central question in a Kantian form it would read, How is social-scientific knowledge possible? That is, assuming that such knowledge is possible, how, or by what means, can the knower (Kant's knowing subject) gain access to the object (Kant's phenomenal object)? Weber is more interested in the methodological than in the strictly epistemological dimensions of the question. Having dealt in the first part of the essay with values and value judgments as potential dangers to the subject (or subjectivity), Weber, pursuing his interest in objectivity, focused in the long second part on those features of the subject–object relation that allow or facilitate access to the object of knowledge. This focus on objectivity, then, requires attention to two questions: How can an object of social-scientific knowledge be constituted? By what path or means can the social-scientist gain access to the object, thereby gaining objective knowledge?

It is my contention that in Weber's hands objectivity is not a univocal concept. A great deal of Weber's attention was given to what could be called false or misleading concepts of objectivity. Weber was a firm critic of a number of misguided paths to objective social-scientific knowledge. At the same time, of course, he attempted to establish a methodological framework for a limited, but credible, path to objective knowledge. The framework he advocated retained elements of both the historical and the theoretical modes of inquiry. His apparent intention was nothing less than a resolution of the generation-long 'struggle over methods.'

In what follows I have selected three conceptions of objectivity that drew Weber's critical attention. I propose to sketch the outline of his position on each of these misconceptions of objectivity before turning to three conceptions of objectivity and objective knowledge promulgated by Weber in this essay. This approach requires that we view Weber as both advocate and critic of objectivity in the social sciences. This does not mean that he was ambivalent towards objectivity; rather, it means that objectivity, for Weber, had many faces, some benign, others malign.

Weber as Critic of Objectivity and Objectivism

Here we can only sketch each of three notions of objectivity targeted by Weber as misconceptions. The first view of objectivity to be considered by Weber is one that conflates scientific objectivity with political non-partisanship. The second view Weber criticizes is an overly descriptive view of knowledge as concerned with the cognitive reproduction of the object or event as it exists or happened – a view of knowledge Weber associates with the historical school of economics. Finally, theoretical economics is associated with the third view of objectivity. This view is criticized by Weber as the attempt to 'reduce' objective social-economic reality to a set of general laws, after the model of the exact natural sciences.

1. *Objectivity as the Middle Ground between Opposing Positions*

Here, as in other essays, Weber attacks the confusion between objectivity and the pursuit of the middle ground between conflicting ideas, values, opinions, or sectarian interests. Whereas in politics it may be desirable in particular cases to mediate between antagonistic points of view, in science, on the other hand, truth is not to be identified with compromise between two opposing claims. Mediation between antagonistic points of view, insists Weber, 'has nothing whatsoever to do with scientific "objectivity." *Scientifically the "middle course" is not truer even by a hair's breadth*, than the most extreme party ideals of the right or the left' (154, ET 57; emphasis in original). Along with the other co-editors, Weber committed the journal to 'struggle relentlessly against the severe self-deception which asserts that through the synthesis of several party points of view, or by following a line between them, practical norms of *scientific validity* can be arrived at' (155, ET 58; emphasis in original).

Whereas mediation and compromise may be entirely appropriate in a field of conflicting values or competing interests, disputes over rival truth claims are never to be settled by mediation or compromise. Objective knowledge is achieved by following norms for establishing scientific validity rather than norms of conflict resolution, reduction, or avoidance.

If political non-partisanship is a false path to objectivity, so is moral indifference or detachment. Weber's position on this question is unequivocal: 'An attitude of moral indifference has no connection with scientific "objectivity"' (157, ET 60). Like everyone else, particular social scientists may be, to use a Weberian term from another context, 'carriers' of strong partisan interests, value positions, and moral commitments. However, when they enter the circle of scientific discussion, social scientists are obliged to play by the rules of validation of truth claims. The scholar who brings strong value commitments to the threshold of science is nevertheless bound by 'the elementary duty of scientific self-control' (200, ET 98). The social scientist who either is, tries to be, or claims to be politically non-partisan or morally indifferent has no advantage on the playing fields of scientific validation of competing truth claims.

2. Objectivity as the Reproduction of the Object

One of Weber's chief targets was the notion of objective knowledge as the reproduction of the object. According to the 'copy theory' of knowledge, a version of correspondence theory, concepts are supposed to reproduce or duplicate the objects they represent as completely and accurately as possible. This view was especially prevalent, according to Weber, among researchers associated with the historical school of economics. Although Weber attributes this copy theory of knowledge specifically to the historical school of economics (followers of Schmoller), this view of historical knowledge could have been traced further back to Leopold von Ranke, who had famously called on historians to produce purely descriptive accounts of the past *'wie es eigentlich gewesen ist'* ('as it actually was'). The historians and followers of the historical school assumed – mistakenly, according to Weber – the function of concepts 'to be the reproduction of "objective" reality in the analyst's imagination' (208, ET 106). Under this view, objective knowledge consists of, or at least begins with, the duplication of the object of inquiry in a mental image or concept. Concepts were supposed to reflect or reproduce events, individuals, and other phenomena, as in the analogy of a photographic image. The task of a concept was to capture and represent – if not all, then the essential – aspects of an object. Concepts then, according to this mistaken view, were assumed to bear an unproblematic relation to reality.

Weber counters this view by warning repeatedly that the relation between concept and reality is always problematic. He clearly rejects the view that historical knowledge 'can or should be a "presuppositionless" copy of "objective" facts' (192, ET 92). No concept can ever be assumed to exhaust the richness or even the 'essence' of a potential object of knowledge. Rather it must be accepted that a concept, properly understood as a conceptual construct, 'is neither historical reality nor even the "true" reality' (194, ET 93). It is in the nature of constructed concepts that they 'diverge from reality' (195, ET 94). 'Nothing is more dangerous,' Weber claims, than 'the confusion of theory and history stemming from naturalistic prejudices. This confusion expresses itself in the belief that the "true" content and the essence of historical reality is portrayed in such theoretical constructs' (195, ET 94). By *theory* and *theoretical constructs* Weber is referring to the function of concepts. Later in the essay Weber warns against 'the danger that the ideal type [concept] and reality [the object] will be confused with one another' (203, ET 101).

'Naturalism' (or 'naturalistic prejudices') in this context appears to Weber to entail a naive form of conceptual realism, whereby it is mistakenly presumed that there is a one-to-one correspondence between a concept and the object it tries to represent, that the concept is a copy of the real object. For Weber the relation between concept and reality is always problematic in that it is unavoidably partial and selective. The naïveté of naturalism in this context consists of the failure to realize the necessary role of the theoretical contribution of the knower in the process of conceptual construction.

3. Objectivity as the Nomological Representation of Historical Reality

'Naturalism' is involved in a second sense in the view that historical reality (that is, economy, society, culture) can be represented adequately as the operation of a set of general laws. Weber considered the culprit in this misguided view to be 'the naturalistic prejudice that the goal of the social sciences must be the reduction of reality to "laws"' (203, ET 101). Weber's frequent references to 'laws' relate to the pursuit of what he calls 'nomological' knowledge and are to be understood against the background of, first, epistemological distinctions derived from neo-Kantian philosophy, and second, aspects of the methodological differences between the two major current schools of economics, the historical and the theoretical schools.

WEBER AND NEO-KANTIAN IDEAS ABOUT METHOD
Weber's treatment of nomological knowledge presupposes familiarity with some of the ideas of the neo-Kantian philosophers Wilhelm

Windelband and Heinrich Rickert. Weber uses the term *nomological* to refer to knowledge of general and recurrent patterns, leading to the formulation of a set of general 'laws' as in the analogy of Newtonian laws, which are then applied in the explanation of events or other phenomena. Windelband had earlier made a strong distinction between two fields of science (*Wissenschaft*, understood broadly to include scholarly fields such as the humanities): natural science and history or historical science. The distinction between the two realms of science/scholarship is based on the type of method characteristic of each. The natural sciences use the *nomothetic* method, understood as a focus on the general, common, and recurrent features of phenomena, with a view to establishing a set of general laws by which to explain the occurrence of classes of phenomena. As Rickert pointed out, such a procedure necessarily abstracts from the concrete level of our perception of phenomena, so that in their most general formulations laws are devoid of all content. Historical science, on the other hand, is rooted in our cognitive interest in concrete, individual, and particular characteristics of phenomena, especially as viewed from the standpoint of values. This focus on the concrete aspects of phenomena, thought to be valuable in their individuality, exemplifies what Windelband called the *idiographic* method.

Weber regarded the social and cultural sciences fundamentally, but not exclusively, as historical sciences. As such, these fields are defined by their interest in social and cultural phenomena from the standpoint of concrete and individual specificity and cultural significance (for example, the rise of modern, Western capitalism). On account of the interest in historical specificity and concreteness along with cultural significance, the historical sciences, including economics, necessarily rely essentially on the use of historical methods, such as the search for genetic cause-and-effect relationships (Weber avoids the term *idiographic* apparently on the grounds that he regarded it as overly restrictive; the historically oriented social sciences use a broader range of methods).

Weber's term, *nomological*, is similar but not identical to Windelband's and Rickert's term, *nomothetic*. If there is a semantic difference, it is that for Weber *nomological* refers to knowledge of the general, whereas for his neo-Kantian colleagues the *nomothetic* refers to a *method* of attaining knowledge. One could say, then, that the application of the generalizing nomothetic method leads to the production of nomological knowledge (that is, knowledge of the general and the recurrent). Weber acknowledged that 'laws are important and valuable in the exact natural sciences' (179, ET 80), in that those sciences are concerned with factors that are general, indeed universal, in application. In the social sciences, on the other hand, generality of concept and method becomes the chief issue. The more general a concept (or law, for general laws require general concepts), Weber explains, 'the more it leads us away from the richness of reality since in order to include the common elements of the largest possible number of phenomena, it must necessarily be as abstract as possible and hence *devoid* of content' (180, ET 80). However appropriate such a nomological approach might be for the natural sciences, it was clearly of limited use in the social or cultural sciences, where knowledge of some degree of historical concreteness is valuable. In the cultural sciences, as opposed to the natural sciences, Weber claims, 'knowledge of the universal or the general is never valuable in itself' (180, ET 80). That Weber saw the naturalistic nomological approach as inimical to social-scientific objectivity is shown in the conclusion that he draws from these considerations: 'An "objective" analysis of cultural events, which proceeds according to the thesis that the ideal of science is the reduction of empirical reality to "laws," is meaningless' (180, ET 80).

It must be said that, from Weber's perspective, there is nothing wrong in principle with nomological knowledge or even with its limited use in the cultural sciences. For instance, the attribution of causality in practice always requires consistency with previously accumulated nomological knowledge in the social sciences. In this respect, nomological knowledge, according to Weber, plays a positive role in the social sciences: 'A valid imputation of any individual effect without the application of "nomological" knowledge ... would in general be impossible' (179, ET 79). (See also Weber's discussion of the notions of *causal adequacy* and *objective possibility* in this essay as well as elsewhere in his methodological writings.) The proper use of nomological knowledge in the social sciences is, however, always limited to that of a means, never as the goal or the aim of social-scientific research.

While Weber's position vis-à-vis nomological knowledge can be usefully compared to the neo-Kantian distinctions between idiographic and nomothetic methods, his ideas, here as elsewhere in his methodology, depart from neo-Kantianism. In the first place, Weber, writing as a practising social scientist, acknowledged the usefulness of both nomological and particularistic knowledge in the social sciences. Unlike the philosopher, the social scientist cannot afford the luxury, as it were, of adopting only one approach, the idiographic or the nomothetic, in its

purity. In any case, secondly, Weber's objection was not to the properly
restricted use of the nomothetic method or of nomological knowledge
in the social sciences. His objection was, rather, against what he called
the 'reductionism' entailed by the view that it was the goal of the social
sciences to generate or discover general laws. Not *nomology* (to coin a
term) per se, but nomological reductionism, is the target of his critique.
In this context, *reductionism* refers to the above-cited view 'that the ideal
of science is the reduction of empirical reality to "laws"' (180, ET 80). By
the reduction of empirical reality to laws he refers to 'the deducibility of
reality from "laws"' (187, ET 87) as the one and only legitimate methodological approach in the social sciences, the view Weber attributes to the
founder of the theoretical school of economics (Carl Menger).

WEBER AND THE CONTROVERSY OVER HISTORICAL VERSUS THEORETICAL METHOD IN ECONOMICS

Although he avoids explicit reference by name to the Austrian theoretical school of economics and its main representative, Carl Menger, it
is clear that Menger's '"abstract"-theoretic method' (Weber's term) is
the target of some of Weber's most serious critique on account of its
presuppositions concerning the role of the social sciences and the relation of scientific knowledge to reality. Menger and the proponents of
this method believe, mistakenly, that 'the construction of a system of
abstract and therefore purely formal propositions analogous to those
of the exact natural sciences is the *only* means of analyzing and intellectually mastering the complexity of social life' (187, ET 87, emphasis
mine). Menger, Weber believes, wrongly 'claims empirical validity in
the sense of the deducibility of reality from "laws" for the propositions
of abstract theory' (187–8, ET 87). This is a case of 'naturalistic monism' in economics, tied to the view that 'there was in general no
conceivable meaning of scientific work other than the discovery of the
laws of events' (186, ET 86). Again, with Menger in mind, Weber chas-
tises him for the 'fantastic claim' that economic theories can be applied
in the explanation of reality 'by ostensibly following the analogy of
physical science propositions' (188, ET 88). Finally, Menger's abstract-
theoretic method entails, according to Weber, 'the naturalistic prejudice that every concept in the cultural sciences should be similar to
those in the exact natural sciences,' which leads to a fundamental
misunderstanding of the relation of 'theoretical construction' to reality
(188, ET 88).

Weber's critique of Menger's presuppositions about the 'abstract-theoretic' method can be applied by extension to the positivism of Auguste Comte and Herbert Spencer in sociology, insofar as their views of science envisioned the determination of a set of general laws representing the operational principles of society and the supposed 'laws' of evolution.[4]

In his critique of the theoretical method in economics Weber gives voice to the standpoint of the historical school. The single most problematic element of the methodology of the theoretical school is its (naturalistic) reductionism. It operates on the premise that the most essential aspects of reality can be represented in a set of general laws, which are then used to explain deductively all historically concrete events. From Weber's perspective, this is a meaningless and impossible enterprise. Social science must always recognize that historical specificity and concreteness can never be represented in a set of general laws, no matter how large. What disappointed Weber was that even some followers of the historical school shared the view of the theoretical school that 'the ideal which all the sciences, including the cultural sciences, serve and towards which they should strive even in the remote future is a system of propositions from which reality can be "deduced"' (171–2, ET 73). This view of the future development and purpose of science is, in Weber's view, patently absurd.

4. Weber's Critique of Objectivism

When we look back over the targets of Weber's critiques, we can see that Weber was mounting an attack on an extreme view of knowledge that might be called 'objectivism.' This is the view that, with respect to the relation of the knower (subject) to reality (object), privileges the object. Whereas Weber's view of objectivity allows for a balance or reciprocity between subject and object (more on this below), objectivism rests on the claim that the object exists, as Kant would say, *an sich*, independent of the subject and the processes of knowledge. The allegedly autonomous object is simply there to be discovered and known. Knowledge occurs by the adaptation of the subject to the object. The subject's only role is to reflect or reproduce an image that seeks to duplicate the real object. This appears to be a largely passive process; the object impresses itself on the subject.

But what reason do we have to suppose that the object is fully and accurately disclosed or represented in the resulting image received by the subject? How can we ever know that we have received a complete representation of an object? Failing that, how can we even know what are the *essential* aspects of an object? In Weber's view, the answer to all these questions is that we cannot know the complete object or even its objectively essential traits. In his view, the chase after full and accurate representation of any object, or even of its essential aspects, is a fool's errand. According to Weber, as with Kant, the object in-itself is unknowable. It is the epitome of hubris to seek, much less to claim, full, complete, total, and accurate knowledge of an object, or even of its 'essential' aspects. For Weber as for his neo-Kantian contemporaries, any object is inexhaustibly rich in aspects of potential knowledge. Knowledge is always, therefore, partial with respect to its object. The object is intensively infinite; therefore it always outreaches the capacity of any given (finite) knower or act of knowledge.

There is a certain even-handedness in Weber's treatment of the historical and theoretical modes of inquiry and schools of economics. In effect, if not explicitly, each stands accused by Weber of objectivism, albeit in different forms. The historical school erred in supposing that it could grasp objective reality mainly by description of historical particulars and by focusing single-mindedly on the 'historical individual.' It committed the fallacy of objectivism in presuming that it could discover and represent actual objects of economic-historical inquiry and place them within causal chains in order to explain the course of events. The theoretical school went astray in presuming that it could grasp objective reality by representing it in terms of the operation of a set of general 'laws' equivalent to those of the natural sciences. In Weber's view, this reliance on general laws amounted to 'reductionism' in the face of the infinitude of any and all potential objects of knowledge. Yet both schools – the historical and the theoretical – were guilty of an arrogant objectivism in presuming that their mode of inquiry led to a full, accurate, and adequate representation of an objective reality. From Weber's standpoint, the knower as subject never can claim to do full justice, as it were, to the object of knowledge.

Weber as Advocate of Objectivity

While it is clear that Weber distanced himself from the specific notions of objectivity discussed above – the moderation of extreme views, the copy theory of knowledge, and nomological reductionism – it is equally clear that, properly understood, objectivity is both possible and desirable. It is now our task to sketch three notions of objectivity supported by Weber in this essay.[5]

1. Objectivity and Value Neutrality

Weber speaks often in this essay of problems stemming from confusion about the role of science with respect to values. Some of the confusion has to do with the question of whether science has a role to play in the validation of values and value judgments. Further problems have arisen from the confusion of reality with values, and the possible intrusion of value judgments into the context of scientific work. Here, as in his later writings, Weber attempts to make a strong distinction in principle between the realm of empirical fact ('is') and the domain of values, valuations, and value judgments or commitments ('should be'). One ramification of this distinction is Weber's warning against the delusion that empirical (including historical) phenomena contain within them principles of development toward the realization of our own (or any) values. This is the very first issue Weber takes up.

It is a delusion, Weber asserts, to believe that what is 'normatively' right' is identical with either 'the immutably existent' or 'the inevitably emergent' (148, ET 51–2). From the context it is clear that the target of his critique is, first, the natural law tradition, which identified the 'normatively right' with the 'immutably existent,' and, secondly, various evolutionary views in the nineteenth century, including those associated with Roscher and Marx, which identified the normatively right with the 'inevitably emergent.' Both the natural law tradition and the evolutionists deluded themselves with the view that (their) values were immanent within reality, either as being or becoming.

Science has a role to play with·respect to values, but it is not in a position to validate values or value judgments. What science can offer especially is knowledge of the consequences of the pursuit of values (ends) through chosen means in the context of action. Scientific knowledge can illuminate the possible consequences beyond the attainment of the desired ends of proposed action: 'We can answer the question: what will the attainment of a desired end "cost" in terms of the predictable loss of other values?' (150, ET 53). While the contribution of science to action is direct in the case of evaluating means, it is indirect with respect to ends (values) where science can only show whether the pursuit of a valued end is feasible or meaningful in practical terms. Weber has more to say about this subject in later writings, especially in his famous lecture 'Science as a Vocation.'

In the context of scientific work we can speak, with caution, of *value-neutrality* (not Weber's term) if we understand this term to refer to both (1) the attempt to neutralize the effects of value judgments or commitments of the scholar, and (2) the avoidance of the intrusion of *unconsciously held* value judgments on the processes of inquiry. Value neutrality in this context refers to a normative ideal or standard, establishing a clear obligation on the part of the scholar to become aware of one's own value commitments and to attempt to neutralize their impact on the conduct of research.

Given the terms of Weber's discussion in this essay, there is no justification for equating value-neutrality with objectivity. While Weber speaks often of value judgments, and the need to recognize the gulf between facts and values, he never speaks directly of value-neutrality or value-freedom (*Wertfreiheit*) as such in this essay. He was to develop his views on value-freedom many years later in the 1917/1918 *Logos* essay 'The Meaning of "Ethical Neutrality" [*Wertfreiheit*] in Sociology and Economics.' In any case, the role of value-neutrality is not constitutive of objectivity or objective scientific knowledge. At most it is a negative (the negating or nullifying or neutralizing of value judgments), even if necessary, condition for the pursuit of knowledge. That is, if we imagine that a scholar is successful in becoming conscious of one's value judgments and in deliberately holding them aside from infiltrating the process of empirical or historical inquiry, this preliminary step in no way guarantees success in gaining objective scientific knowledge.

Weber is careful not to condemn scholars for holding value commitments. It is worth noting that values are not for Weber what the 'idols' were for Francis Bacon. While unconscious or uninformed value commitments may be deleterious in some circumstances to either rational action or scientific inquiry, values are not in general culprits to be barred from the fields of politics or science. From Weber's perspective, it is not values per se that are pernicious; it is ignorance of the effects of value commitments that is the source of a range of problems. In Bacon's view, the subject needed to be purified of idols as contaminants nestled within the knower-subject. To cleanse the subject of values for Weber would be nonsensical and undesirable, even if it were possible.

2. Objectivity and Perspective

'All knowledge of cultural reality,' Weber tells us, 'is always knowledge from particular points of view' (181, ET 81). He has in mind in this context particularly the viewpoint of the scholar in relation to specific values (*Wertbeziehungen*), but it seems clear that Weber also has in mind the fact that the scholar is also necessarily situated in a particular social and cultural location from which to view social and cultural phenomena. Elsewhere in the essay Weber makes the emphatic point that 'there is no absolutely "objective" scientific analysis ... of "social phenomena" independent of special and "one-sided" viewpoints according to which ... they are selected, analyzed and organized for expository purposes' (170, ET 72).

Weber's notions of the necessity of perspective (standpoint, viewpoint) can be explicated usefully by drawing on Edmund Husserl's contemporaneous treatment of the phenomenon of perceptual perspective. The following references to Husserl are intended only to provide an analogy for understanding Weber's ideas of standpoint or perspective. No implication of kinship with Husserl's phenomenology is intended.[6]

During his tenure at the University of Göttingen, beginning around 1901, Husserl is said to have enjoyed the view of an apple tree that stood in his garden. This tree, or Husserl's perception of this tree, served several illustrative purposes in his philosophical writings during this period. In the *Ideen*, published in 1913, he uses the perception of the tree to make several points about the relation of the subject to the object in the everyday act of perception. I would like to recount the basic outline of some of his points and extend them by analogy in order to illuminate Weber's approach to conceptual knowledge.

Imagine yourself looking at the tree, an object of some size and complexity. As you look at the tree, certain points become obvious. First, assuming for the moment that what you see is a 'real' phenomenal object, you see only a *part* of this three-dimensional object. You see its 'front' side. Second, you develop expectations such as the following. You assume or expect that the tree has a 'back' side that lies beyond your *horizon* of vision. The horizon represents the limits of your perception from your current viewing position. If you were to move around the tree, you anticipate that you would see this back side (which would then become the front side). Of course, Husserl goes into great technical detail about various issues and distinctions that exceed our present interests. For instance, there are issues of time (for example, memory, expectation) and questions about the status of the object, etc. For our purposes, however, we can summarize the main points about the relation of the subject (as knower) to the perceived object (the tree):

1 Our perception of the tree (the object) is always *partial*. We can never see the whole object at any given moment. Even if we move around the tree, we can see only a limited aspect at any given moment.

2 Our perception of the tree is necessarily made from a given stand-

point, position, or *perspective*. This has to do with the fact that the knowing, perceiving subject is tied to a particular location or position just as much as the object is similarly positioned or situated at any given moment.

3 Finally, it is worth noting, with Husserl, that even though we cannot perceive the entire tree, our experience of perception gives us no reason to doubt the existence of the tree as a whole object. As we continue to look at the tree, perhaps moving around the tree, we develop expectations that lead us to have confidence in our belief in the existence or reality of the tree.

Now these points, although they apply to the situation of a perceiving subject in relation to a physical object, when applied by extension to *conception* instead of *perception*, help us to understand Weber's methodological ideas related to perspective.

Both the perspectival and partial nature of knowledge are among Weber's main points.

The knowing subject faces an object, a historical individual, that is an infinite manifold. The object is intensively infinite. The number of possible perspectives from which the object can be approached is likewise, in principle, infinite. The fact that knowledge of a socio-cultural phenomenon (object of knowledge) is always necessarily from a particular perspective or viewpoint (Weber's preferred term, *Gesichtspunkt*, interestingly refers both to *aspects of the object* and to the *standpoint of the knower* in relation to the object) means that the resulting knowledge is also partial in relation to the potentially knowable aspects of the object. Not only 'large' objects such as 'capitalism' but apparently 'small' objects such as Bismarck are, from a logical point of view, infinite in the range of knowable aspects and the corresponding perspectives that can be taken toward them.

In the end we can see that, for Weber, objective knowledge is tied inextricably to perspectival knowledge. Objects of potential knowledge are chosen from particular 'locations,' which provide distinctive 'angles of vision.' At the same time, these objects of potential knowledge are chosen with respect to their cultural significance and relevance to values. Both the subject (as knower) and the object of knowledge are situated in certain locations within both a field of logical possibility and a landscape of cultural signification. These parameters of knowledge are not regarded by Weber as handicaps to be lamented. It is simply not given to the empirical (also historical) scholar-scientist to have total knowledge of reality, or of any possible object as a whole, or even of its particular constituent parts. Without perspective there is no possibility of knowledge.[7]

3. Objectivity and Conceptually Mediated Knowledge

If it has been sufficiently established that, in Weber's view, objective scientific knowledge is always perspectival, it remains to be shown that, for Weber, objective scientific knowledge of cultural objects is necessarily always mediated by concepts.

In this essay, as in his companion essays from the same period on the historical economists Wilhelm Roscher and Karl Knies, Weber makes a firm distinction between discursive knowledge and knowledge based on immediate intuition. Theories of knowledge based on intuition characteristically claim or presuppose that the knower has immediate, which is to say unmediated (Weber says *unmittelbar*), mental access to phenomena or experience. That is, the mental experience of the knower is such that no deliberate cognitive operations are required in order to apprehend the object of knowledge; there is no reflection or manipulation (for example, framing) of the object by the mind. It is a view of direct access to the object, as presupposed, for instance, in the Rankean formula to describe the past 'as it really happened,' as well as in theories of 'empathy' or 'empathetic intuition' and notions of 're-living' of experience in memory. Intuition in this context short-circuits all forms of conscious mental processes operating on the contents of the mind. Weber deals harshly with all exponents (such as Croce, Gottl, and to some extent, Simmel and Dilthey) of such views, more so in the Roscher and Knies essays than in the present essay.

In Weber's view, immediate or unmediated knowledge of the object is simply not possible. All scientific knowledge is *discursive*, according to Weber, who explains that 'the discursive nature of our knowledge' means that 'we comprehend reality only through a chain of intellectual modifications' (195, ET 94). Chief among these 'intellectual modifications' (*Vorstellungsveränderungen*) are processes associated with the formation of concepts of the objects of scientific inquiry. The only way open to us to gain cognitive access to any socio-cultural object is through the concepts we adopt or construct as an attempt to 'represent' (*darstellen*, *vorstellen*) a potential object of investigation, albeit partially and from a given perspective.

This brings us to Weber's well-known discussion of 'ideal-type' concepts, a subject that occupies much of his attention in this essay. With the ideal-type (*Idealtypus*) Weber believed himself to be discovering the nature of conceptualization as already often practised rather than inventing a new kind of concept. When they are not strictly classificatory in purpose or use, social-scientific concepts are constructed as ideal-types.[8] Often but not always representing historical individuals (the 'medieval city,' 'Western capitalism'), ideal-type concepts are deliberately formed to accentuate certain significant features of a putative object of inquiry, abstracted from concrete reality and synthesized into a unified construct. The constructed ideal-type is not to be confused with the illusory ideal that a concept 'can or should be a "presuppositionless" copy of "objective" facts' (192, ET 92), the impossibility of which was discussed above. Weber is emphatic that the ideal-type 'is not a *description* [Darstellung] of reality' (190, ET 90). Compared to any putative object of inquiry, the ideal-type concept is a very selective and partial representation. Moreover, ideal-type concepts are formed from the standpoint of the cultural significance and value-relevance of their objects. Considerations of cultural significance serve to define the standpoint or perspective of the knower and at the same time limit the parameters of the object to the few that are relevant for the heuristic purposes of an inquiry.

Weber also cautions that, as a concept, the ideal-type differs from a hypothesis: 'It *is* no "hypothesis" but it offers guidance to the construction of hypotheses' (190, ET 90). Whereas hypotheses have the logical status of judgments that may be true or false, ideal-type concepts are methodological constructions that can be judged only as more or less useful or adequate in identifying culturally significant objects. For instance, 'capitalism' can be conceptualized (that is, formed into an ideal-type) in an indefinitely large number of ways. To ask whether a given way of conceiving capitalism is true or false is to make a category mistake. A given concept of capitalism can be judged only as more or less adequate in representing culturally significant features of actual phenomena and as being more or less useful for the specific heuristic purposes at hand. Weber refers to ideal-types as a 'heuristic means' (*heuristisches Mittel*) (102, ET 203). By designating specific objects, ideal-type concepts are intended to be used as elements within hypothetical claims about causal relationships among empirical-historical phenomena. It is the hypotheses, not the concepts, that are ultimately judged as true or false.[9]

Concept formation is a process that illuminates reality by focusing attention on a few facets of an object whose features are infinite and hence unknowable in their totality. Without concepts, objects are unknowable; phenomena cannot even be identified as objects or discriminated from the formless background or infinite chaos of reality. In this respect, the formation of concepts is akin to the shining of a focused light, which brings into relief particular elements or facets of an otherwise indiscriminate background. Weber's prescription for the constructed concepts of the social sciences can be read as a testament against the myth of 'total enlightenment.' As social scientists and cultural beings, it is simply not possible to have direct, full, immediate, and 'presuppositionless' access to reality. Objective knowledge of socio-cultural phenomena requires the use of ideal-type concepts. Freed from the illusions and 'naturalistic prejudices' associated with the naive identification of concept and reality, it is the use of ideal-type concepts in social-scientific investigations that makes objective knowledge possible.

Conclusion: Objectivity without Objectivism

One of the many possible interpretations of the quotation marks that embrace the word *objectivity* in Weber's essay is that they flag the very elusiveness of the idea of objectivity. Weber has much more to say about what objectivity is not than about what it is. On virtually every one of the six occasions when he uses the term, he deploys it to reject a wrong or misguided interpretation: scientific objectivity is ... not mediation between opposing positions ... not a presuppositionless copy of reality ... not a set of general laws. Granted, but then, as Weber himself asks tantalizingly at the end of the first section of the essay, what is objectivity?

One of the results of our analysis has been to see that Weber wanted above all else to construct an ideal of objectivity free of what we have called objectivism. By this term we intend to include all the problematic views Weber called variously 'naturalism,' 'naturalistic prejudices,' and all forms of reductionism. The fatal flaw of objectivism in all its forms is hubris, an unjustifiable pride in the illusion that the knower can apprehend reality directly, accurately, and comprehensively. If objectivity is to have a positive function for social science, it must be understood as beginning with a critical self-awareness of the presuppositions that underlie our research practices as social scientists. Through critical reflection we gain at least the possibility of escaping the compulsions that would otherwise be blind prejudices and self-deceptions.

Weber points to possible paths to objective scientific knowledge: critical self-consciousness and constraint with respect to our value commitments, and the construction of conceptualizations of those objects in the world that are significant to our time and place within the stream of history. These are paths that lead to limited, partial knowledge from situated perspectives. Only certain facets of reality can be illuminated by our theoretical constructions before the knowing subjects and the known objects change their shapes and move on. The intellectual humility of Weber's epistemology is the counterpart of hubristic objectivism. We must reconcile ourselves to knowledge of the (possible) object that is partial, culture-bound, and historically specific.

Weber could be criticized for, among other things, failing to provide a comprehensive and systematic theory of objectivity, a theory that would more thoroughly illuminate the subject–object relation in the process of acquiring knowledge. Such a theory would ideally help us to understand better the subject's access to the object in terms of a set of epistemological as well as methodological principles. However, to place 'objectivity' within the bounds of a theoretical system would not be in keeping with Weber's intellectual modus operandi. His approach is rather to develop specific ideas as 'types' (in this case, of 'objectivity') to serve as reference points to move toward an object of inquiry, and then in a further step, to implement them in practice.

Written in the same year as the objectivity essay, Weber's *Protestant Ethic and the 'Spirit' of Capitalism* is, I submit, an implementation par excellence of his ideas of objectivity. Several of Weber's themes and concerns in the essay on objectivity are reflected in his now-classic study of the rise of the modern capitalistic 'spirit.' First, at the conceptual level, Weber constructs a carefully nuanced and historically specific notion of 'modern rational capitalism' whose 'spirit' or ethos is related genetically and through 'elective affinities' to specific forms of Protestant asceticism. All the relevant concepts (for example, vocation, spirit of capitalism, sect, and inner-worldly asceticism, among others) are framed for use in the 'genetic' explanation of the rise and development of the spirit of this particular form of capitalism in its historical context of origin. Speaking of his constructed ideal-type of the 'spirit of capitalism,' Weber says that it represents a *historical individual*: 'Such a singular entity is nothing more than a complex of relationships in historical reality. We join them together, from the vantage point of their *cultural significance*, into a conceptual unity' (Weber, 1920, 39, ET [Kalberg] 13).

Second, the very framing of the question that animates the entire study, the question of how to understand and explain the rise of a specific modern Western form of capitalism with its distinctive ethos and associated patterns of life provides a model for historically oriented inquiry stemming from cognitive interests shaped by assessments of cultural significance. Weber suggests that we embark on such an inquiry because of our interest in understanding the historical genesis of aspects of modern Western culture. The 'spirit' of such an inquiry is far removed from 'abstract-theoretic,' deductive-nomological models of explanation. The *Protestant Ethic* is not a general theory of moderniza-tion, in part because it is not a general theory of anything. On the other hand, it displays an interest in both historical causation and cultural interpretation. By the same token, the *PE* offers both more and less than historical description: more because it attempts to go beyond historical particulars to connect patterns in social, economic, religious, and cultural phenomena; less because it does not pretend to offer a perspective-free 'copy' of historical reality 'as it really hap-pened.' The *PE* represents the case par excellence of conceptually medi-ated knowledge from the standpoint of self-consciously chosen perspectives of cultural significance. It is clearly a study in the tradition of the historical school, now reconstituted in Weber's hands, with a single concession to the theoretical school of economics, that is, the notion of conceptualization as a self-conscious act of 'theorization,' but one that is free from the universalistic ambitions of abstract theory.[10]

In both the objectivity essay and the *PE* Weber renounces the totaliz-ing and reductionistic tendencies associated with, on the one hand, the earlier historical school (the copy theory of knowledge) and, on the other hand, the theoretical school of economics (nomological deduc-tionism). In their place he upholds the ideal of objective social-scientific knowledge, understood as conceptually mediated knowledge of his-torically specific phenomena from culturally significant perspectives. Originally framed as a charter of editorial policy for a leading social science journal, Weber's vision of objective social-scientific knowledge remains, a century later, a central and compelling facet of his legacy.

NOTES

Note: Except where otherwise indicated, page references in parentheses, for example (180, ET 81), in the text of this paper refer first to pages in the Ger-man edition and second to pages in the Shils/Finch English translation (ET) of Weber's essay on objectivity.

1 For instance, the positivistic philosopher of science Ernest Nagel, in his influential *Structure of Science*, applauded Weber's strong distinction in principle between factual judgments and value judgments and praised Weber as a 'vigorous proponent of a "value-free" social science' who main-

tained that although 'social scientists must appreciate (or "understand") the values involved in the actions or institutions they are discussing ... it is not their business as objective scientists to approve or disapprove either those values or those actions and institutions,' 485. Other key statements in the positivist reception of Weber's methodology, often selectively critical, include Carl G. Hempel, *Aspects of Scientific Explanation*; J.W.N. Watkins, 'Historical Explanation in the Social Sciences'; and W.G. Runciman, *A Critique of Max Weber's Philosophy of Social Science*. Objectivity was tied to the notion of value-freedom by Talcott Parsons in 'Value-Freedom and Objectivity.' See also the response to Parsons by Jürgen Habermas, 'Discussion.'

2 On the reception and uses of *Verstehen* see William Outhwaite, *Understanding Social Life*. For various perspectives on *Verstehen* see Rob Shields, 'Meeting or Mis-meeting?' and the exchange between Theodore Abel and Murray Wax in *Sociology and Social Research* 51 (1967): 323–33. Fred Dallmayr's edited collection, *Understanding and Social Inquiry*, provides a range of perspectives on the subject. For a positivistic critique of *Verstehen* see Theodore Abel's 'The Operation Called *Verstehen*.'

3 Later in the essay Weber refers again to the 'unmediated and ostensibly irreconcilable cleavage' (*unvermittelter und anscheinend unüberbrückbarer Schroffheit*) [187, ET 87] between the 'abstract-theoretic' method and historical research in economics.

4 By the same token it seems clear that Weber's critique would apply equally to mid-twentieth-century neo-positivistic philosophies of science, including especially Hempel's 'deductive-nomological' methodology as well as Hempel's treatment of 'covering laws,' a term attributed by him to William Dray. See Hempel, *Aspects of Scientific Explanation*, 335–47. Likewise Weber's critique would seem to apply to Nagel's philosophy of science, anchored as it was in notions of deductive explanation on the basis of laws. Other versions current at the same time were the 'hypothetic-deductive' methods advocated by Karl Popper and his followers. In keeping with their positivistic views, each of these three philosophers staunchly defended methodological monism in science, that is, the view that all the sciences, natural and social, are obliged to follow the same deductive-nomological methodology, the same view critiqued by Weber as 'monistic' and reductionistic.

5 Guy Oakes has argued (*Weber and Rickert*) that Weber's claim for the objectivity of knowledge in the cultural sciences depends on the objectivity of values. Oakes believes that because Weber's notion of objectivity depends on the logically defective arguments of Rickert for the objective status of values, Weber's claim for the objective status of knowledge in the

cultural sciences cannot be sustained. In a subsequent article I have taken issue with Oakes on the ground that Weber's idea of value is historical and contingent rather than objective, making Rickert's argument irrelevant to Weber. See John Drysdale, 'How Are Social-Scientific Concepts Formed?' Neither set of arguments can be pursued here.

6 In his essay on Knies, Weber commented on specific distinctions found in Husserl's *Logical Investigations*. While his references to Husserl are not critical, they cannot be taken as evidence for broader agreement with Husserl's phenomenological project.

7 For a recent account of the issue of perspective in relation to objectivity, see Lorraine Daston, 'Objectivity and the Escape from Perspective.'

8 Weber says that 'every concept which is not purely classificatory diverges from reality' (195, ET 94). The classical logic of classification proceeds according to the principles of *genus proximum* (nearest kind) and *differentia specifica* (specific differences). In Weber's thinking, concept formation for use in taxonomic classifications, derived from Aristotelian logic, is represented in modern natural-scientific knowledge most extensively in biology, as for example in the work of Linnaeus. Here entities are organized logically together on the basis of as little as a single shared trait, such as feathers. Such an approach is deficient in the historically oriented cultural sciences because the differentiation of species within genera is likely to miss the aspects of cultural significance and value-relevance. Furthermore, classificatory concepts are the logical ally or tool of deductive-nomological explanation, which, for all its power in the natural sciences, is deficient in the cultural sciences for the reasons mentioned above. Ideal-type concepts, on the other hand, are most often *genetic*, that is, they are tools within *genetic* explanations of cause-and-effect relations in historically specific contexts. Weber also distinguishes *genetic* (ideal-types) from *generic* (classificatory) concepts.

9 Weber's views concerning the heuristic function of ideal-types further separate his position from the copy theory of knowledge, specifically from the view that concepts are copies or images of reality. This has been an issue of dispute in the secondary literature. In an earlier essay I have tried to draw out further implications of Weber's position in relation to the *interpretive* function of concepts as distinguished from the *explanatory* function of hypotheses. See Drysdale, 'How Are Social Scientific Concepts Formed,' especially 78–87.

10 For further exploration of the implications of ideal-types as conceptually mediated knowledge, see ibid. For a discussion of the largely unrealized theoretical relevance of Weber's *PE* in American social science, see Kalberg, 'On the Neglect of Weber's *Protestant Ethic*.'

REFERENCES

Abel, Theodore. 'A Reply to Professor Wax,' *Sociology and Social Research* 51 (1967): 334–6.
-   'The Operation Called *Verstehen*.' *American Journal of Sociology* 54 (1948): 211–18.
Dallmayr, Fred R., and Thomas A. McCarthy, eds. *Understanding and Social Inquiry*. Notre Dame: University of Notre Dame Press, 1977.
Daston, Lorraine. 'Can Scientific Objectivity Have a History?' *Mitteilungen der Alexander-von-Humboldt-Stiftung* 75 (2000): 31–40.
-   'Objectivity and the Escape from Perspective.' In *The Science Studies Reader*, edited by Mario Biagioli, 110–23. New York: Routledge, 1999.
Dray, William. *Laws and Explanation in History*. Oxford: Oxford University Press, 1957.
Drysdale, John. 'How Are Social-Scientific Concepts Formed? A Reconstruction of Max Weber's Theory of Concept Formation.' *Sociological Theory* 14 (1996): 71–88.
Habermas, Jürgen. 'Discussion.' In *Max Weber and Sociology Today*, edited by Otto Stammer, 59–66. New York: Harper and Row, 1971.
Hempel, Carl G. *Aspects of Scientific Explanation and Other Essays in the Philosophy of Science*. New York: Free Press, 1965.
Husserl, Edmund. *Ideas: General Introduction to Pure Phenomenology*. Translated by W.R. Boyce Gibson. London: Allen & Unwin; New York: Macmillan, 1931. Published as 'Ideen zu einer reinen Phänomenologie und phänomenologischen Philosophie.' In *Jahrbuch für Philosophie und phänomenologische Forschung*, 1–323. Halle a.d.S., 1913.
-   *Logical Investigations*. Translated by J.N. Findlay. New York: Humanities Press, 1970. Published as *Logische Untersuchungen*. Parts 1 and 2. Halle: Max Niemeyer, 1900, 1901.
Kalberg, Stephen. 'On the Neglect of Weber's *Protestant Ethic* as a Theoretical Treatise: Demarcating the Parameters of Postwar American Sociological Theory.' *Sociological Theory* 14 (1996): 49–70.
Nagel, Ernest. *The Structure of Science: Problems in the Logic of Scientific Explanation*. New York: Harcourt, Brace & World, 1961.
Oakes, Guy. *Weber and Rickert: Concept Formation in the Cultural Sciences*. Cambridge, MA: MIT Press, 1988.
Outhwaite, William. *Understanding Social Life: The Method Called Verstehen*. London: Allen & Unwin, 1975.
Parsons, Talcott. 'Value-Freedom and Objectivity.' In *Max Weber and Sociology Today*, edited by Otto Stammer, 27–50. New York: Harper and Row, 1971.

Popper, Karl R. *The Logic of Scientific Discovery.* London: Hutchinson, 1959.

Rickert, Heinrich. *The Limits of Concept Formation in Natural Science: A Logical Introduction to the Historical Sciences.* Translated and edited by Guy Oakes. Abridged ed. New York: Cambridge University Press, 1986. Published as *Die Grenzen der naturwissenschaftlichen Begriffsbildung.* 5th ed. Tübingen: J.C.B. Mohr, 1921.

Runciman, W.G. *A Critique of Max Weber's Philosophy of Social Science.* Cambridge: Cambridge University Press, 1972.

Shields, Rob. 'Meeting or Mis-meeting? The Dialogical Challenge to Verstehen.' *British Journal of Sociology* 47 (1996): 275–94.

Watkins, J.W.N. 'Historical Explanation in the Social Sciences.' *British Journal for the Philosophy of Science* 8 (1957): 104–17.

Wax, Murray. 'On Misunderstanding Verstehen: A Response to Professor Abel.' *Sociology and Social Research* 51 (1967): 323–33.

Weber, Max. 'The Meaning of "Ethical Neutrality" in Sociology and Economics.' In *The Methodology of the Social Sciences.* Translated and edited by Edward A. Shils and Henry A. Finch. New York: Free Press, 1949. Published as 'Der Sinn der "Wertfreiheit" der soziologischen und ökonomischen Wissenschaften.' In *Gesammelte Aufsätze zur Wissenschaftslehre.* Edited by Johannes Winckelmann, 489–540. 4th ed. Tübingen: J.C.B. Mohr, 1973.

– '"Objectivity" in Social Science and Social Policy.' In *The Methodology of the Social Sciences.* Translated and edited by Edward A. Shils and Henry A. Finch, 49–112. New York: Free Press, 1949. Published as 'Die "Objektivität" sozialwissenschaftlicher und sozialpolitischer Erkenntnis,' in *Gesammelte Aufsätze zur Wissenschaftslehre.* Edited by Johannes Winckelmann, 146–214. 4th ed. Tübingen: J.C.B. Mohr, 1973.

– *The Protestant Ethic and the 'Spirit' of Capitalism.* Translated and introduced by Stephen Kalberg. 3rd Roxbury ed. Los Angeles: Roxbury, 2002. Published as 'Die protestantische Ethik und der "Geist" des Kapitalismus.' In Weber, *Gesammelte Aufsätze zur Religionssoziologie,* 17–206. Rev. ed. Tübingen: J.C.B. Mohr, 1920.

– *Roscher and Knies: The Logical Problems of Historical Economics.* Translated and edited by Guy Oakes. New York: Free Press, 1975. Published as 'Roscher und Knies und die logischen Probleme der historischen Nationalökonomie.' In *Gesammelte Aufsätze zur Wissenschaftslehre,* edited by Johannes Winckelmann, 1–145. 4th ed. Tübingen: J.C.B. Mohr, 1973.

2 The Paradoxes of Social Science: Weber, Winch, and Wittgenstein

JOHN G. GUNNELL

Despite the vast secondary literature that now surrounds, and maybe smothers, Max Weber's 'The "Objectivity" of Knowledge in Social Science and Social Policy,' there has been little detailed interpretation of the work.[1] During the past three decades, there have been many enlightening and stimulating characterizations, descriptions, and assessments of Weber's methodological arguments, but there has been little attempt to reconstruct in depth and detail the internal structure and substance of the 1904 essay.

One tendency has been to decontextualize the piece and view it, often anachronistically, as if it were an intervention in contemporary discussions in the philosophy of social science. Weber has been characterized, quite contradictorily, either as a representative of positivist social science or the harbinger of post-positivism,[2] and, more recently, as a neo-rationalist and as a constructivist.[3] Another approach, however, has been to over-contextualize the essay and assume that its meaning could be extrapolated from its philosophical ambience. His arguments have sometimes been contextualized to such a degree that they appear as an impossibly complex and unreconciled amalgam of the ideas of thinkers such as Heinrich Rickert, Wilhelm Dilthey, George Simmel, Wilhelm Roscher, Georg Lukacs, Karl Marx, John Stuart Mill, Karl Menger, Eduard Meyer, Friedrich Nietzsche, Gustav Schmoller, Rudolf Stammler, Wihelm Windelband, etc. The essay has on occasion been carefully scrutinized in terms of its relationship to Weber's other methodological writings, but while this is an important exploration, it is probably a mistake to view this corpus as simply a collection of occasional pieces or as elements of a consistent, or evolving, and carefully formulated methodological position.

In order to free the essay from the patina of secondary literature that now encrusts it, I begin with a close internal, but contextually sensitive, reading. My particular distribution of emphasis is on the essay's location within what I refer to as the *orders of discourse*: the first-order realm of social and political life; the meta-practical second-order claims of activities such as social science; and the third-order reflections of the philosophy of social science.[4] An essential dimension of my discussion involves clarifying how Weber conceived of these realms and particularly the *cognitive* and *practical* relationships between them. More specifically, I argue that the essay was an element of a *rhetoric of inquiry* that functioned at two levels. While it was involved in negotiating the character and role of the social sciences within their own domain and within the academy as a whole, with respect to such issues as concept formation and the extent to which these fields were logically symmetrical with the natural sciences, it was also involved in justifying social science to the world from which, as Weber pointedly recognized, these fields had in part sprung and to which they were now intended to speak. Although this rhetoric was embedded in the practice of social science, Weber, in this instance, was, strictly speaking, writing neither as a social scientist nor as a philosopher of social science, even though he was intersecting both forms of discourse. In large part, the essay addressed what I refer to as the cognitive and practical paradoxes of social science. The cognitive paradox arose from the fact that, although social phenomena are conventionally and discursively constituted, their *interpretation* by social science entails the application of an external or supervenient language. The closely related practical paradox was that social science could gain political purchase only by seeking an epistemic authority distinct from politics.

Weber was not primarily a philosopher of social science, and he was not engaging in detail many of the philosophical issues that his claims represented and intimated. Although there may be some distortion in classifying Weber as a social scientist by criteria that are appropriate to contemporary disciplinary practices, this is nevertheless the basic lineage of the essay. The language of social science, however, was not one-dimensional. In Weber's context, substantive claims were entwined with a language of validation, and part of his purpose in the essay was to explicate the character of emerging social-scientific discourse and its relationship to the practices of philosophy and politics. It is now widely recognized that Weber was quite explicit about the fact that he became involved in epistemological and methodological issues by necessity rather than choice and that many of his arguments, about such matters as factual and evaluative statements, were part of a rhetorical strategy designed to clarify and defend his research.[5] My analysis of Weber's essay is intended to stand on its own, but it is followed by an examination of the position of Peter Winch, a philosopher who, more than a half-century later, enlisted the image of Weber in formulating his 'idea of a social science' and who engaged many of the same issues that Weber had confronted. And I conclude with a brief promissory consideration of certain dimensions of the work of Ludwig Wittgenstein on whom Winch most directly relied in presenting his claims about the nature of social-scientific knowledge but whose work also points toward some insights into Weber's essay and particularly Weber's account of the ideal-type.

The essay on objectivity was written shortly after Weber, along with Edgar Jaffe and Werner Sombart, assumed the editorship of the *Archiv für Sozialwissenschaft und Sozialpolitik*. This was during the last days of his long, debilitating, and probably neurotic illness, and the same year as the publication of the *Protestant Ethic and the 'Spirit' of Capitalism* and his visit to the United States. Although he took on the editorship somewhat reluctantly, it was the beginning of his return to *both* academic and political life and among his earliest involvements in discussions of methodology. Methodological discourse had become the arena in which diverse persuasions in social science regarding both the nature of these disciplines and the relationship between social science and politics confronted one another, and these methodological disputes drew the conversations of social science into the orbit of philosophy.

In introducing his essay, Weber claimed that the plural composition of both the editorial board and the contributors to the *Archiv* would ensure that no 'one particular school of thought' on 'methodological' matters could dominate. This diversity of '"one-sided" view points' was part of his answer to the problem of objectivity, and Karl Mannheim would later elaborate this idea as a more general prescription for escaping 'ideology and utopia.' But Weber argued that this pluralism of perspectives must be supplemented by a simultaneous commitment by all social scientists to the 'value of *theoretical* knowledge,' 'the *formation of clear concepts*,' and 'the strict *distinction between empirical knowledge and value-judgment*' (emphasis in original). What he meant, and, maybe more importantly, did *not* mean, by 'objectivity' and 'objectively valid truths' was closely related to what he would later refer to as the tenets of 'ethical neutrality' and the distinction between the 'vocations' of

science and politics, but 'objectivity' also had to do with the nature of
what might be called the objects of knowledge or, in this case, social
reality. And the two senses of 'objective' were closely linked in his
discussion. His rendering of the term 'objectivity' in quotes indicated
both that it was a contested notion and that he was referring to the word
and thereby suggesting the numerous concepts to which it might refer.

Weber abjured an intention to make any major contribution to philosophy or epistemological and logical analysis in favour of emphasizing what he presented as selected 'results,' arising from the work of
individuals such as Windelband, Simmel, and Rickert, and ensuring
that 'their significance' was 'made plain to the lay-person.' What is
often neglected is who Weber indicated as the principal audience of his
essay. This audience, as he explicitly noted, was neither other social
scientists nor philosophers but rather those 'detached from practical
scientific activity' who required some enlightenment with respect to
'"self-evident" matters' regarding '"social-scientific" work.' Although
the essay was directed in part toward social scientists and presented as
an intervention in controversies about method and the relation between
social science and politics, it was also designed to vouchsafe, before a
wider tribunal, the cognitive – and consequently practical – authority of
social science in terms of its relationship to public life. The audience
was both internal and external. Although he stressed that the commitment of the journal was to the scientific pursuit of 'the *facts* of social
life,' it was concerned with 'social policy' and 'the training of *judgment*
in respect of *practical problems* arising from these social circumstances.'
This raised an issue about the compatibility of 'aim' and 'means' or,
more specifically, about how the empirical claims of social science were
related to, and could be reconciled with, 'value judgments' and a 'critique of socio-political work,' which were, at least de facto, the province
of political actors and legislators (359–60).[6]

Weber was not embracing either pole of what would become, a
generation later, the philosophical and social-scientific debate about
value judgments revolving around the issue of whether or not it was
possible to employ a language that was free of value connotation. He
was not caught up in what the philosopher J.L. Austin would refer to as
the 'value/fact fetish,' which failed to see that there were more than
two things that one can do with words. We cannot equate Weber's
argument about separating empirical and normative claims with the
verificationist theory of linguistic meaning, and his argument about the
manner in which values-informed research was not a claim that a

purely empirical language was impossible to achieve. Although Weber tended to subsume a number of quite different things under the categories of fact and value (interests, perspectives, and ethical positions, as opposed to specifications and descriptions of events), he was talking less about forms of speech and judgment than about the existential problem of the relationship between the practices of social science and politics, as well as the commitments that should, in his view, define and distinguish them.

At the very beginning of section 1, which focused primarily on the difference and relationship between social science and its subject matter, Weber pointed out that the social sciences 'arose historically from *practical* perspectives' and, more specifically, for the purpose of making value judgments about public policy. Although he did not elaborate this point, it was a historically accurate claim. In nearly every country during the nineteenth century, the institutionalization of the social sciences was the confluence of two discursive tributaries: elements of academic philosophy devoted to practical purposes, and ideologically informed social reform movements invoking the authority of science. As these tributaries intellectually coalesced and were institutionalized in the context of the modern university during the later part of the nineteenth century, in countries such as Germany, England, Hungary, and the United States, and evolved as academic or 'scientific' disciplines, they had failed, Weber noted, to take full account of their new situation and to formulate adequately a 'principled distinction' between 'existential knowledge' of what 'is' and 'normative' claims about what 'should be.' He argued that although a mistaken image of the unity of empirical and ethical claims had persisted 'among practical men of affairs' as well as among some social scientists, it was necessary to realize that 'the task of an experimental science can never be the determination of binding norms and ideals, from which in turn guidelines for practical application might be derived' (360–1). This was less a philosophical imperative that he was announcing than the need to recognize a practical difference, and often a difference denied or unrecognized by his contemporaries, but he was also suggesting that the renunciation of value judgments by social science was, paradoxically, the key to its playing a practical role in value decisions.

It was not that it was logically incorrect or impossible for science to engage in making value judgments but rather that it was not its proper or practicable role. Even if it wished to do so, it was, in an increasingly ideologically and culturally pluralized society, in no position to perform this function, since social science was no longer an integral part of the structures of political power. Furthermore, if it attempted to take on this function, it would undermine its epistemic authority, which, with the imminent passing of the German 'mandarins,' was the only kind of authority that it, in effect, now possessed and was the only actual source of potential practical authority. Only by separating social science and politics could the former have an impact on the latter.

Renouncing the task of making value judgments, or at least making a clear distinction between the two forms of discourse, did not mean, Weber insisted, that values were not to be matters of critical discussion or that social science had nothing to contribute to the formulation and assessment of such judgments. His distinction between empirical and evaluative claims, and later between the 'vocations' of science and politics, was again in large part to show how each might impinge, favourably or unfavourably, upon the other. Without demonstrating that, in both principle and practice, they were different endeavours, it was impossible to discuss these relationships cogently.[7] Unless both social scientists and political actors recognized the difference, the matter of connections could not be articulated or confronted. What was important was to determine the appropriate '*meaning* and *purpose* of the scientific criticism of ideals and value-judgments.' This distinction could include such things as understanding, analysing, and clarifying the 'ideas' and 'values' in 'meaningful human action' that defined various normative ends, and demonstrating the likelihood of attaining a certain end by a certain means (361). There were many ways in which empirical and normative claims were, and might be, connected, but these were contingent and ultimately depended on the actual relationship between the practices of social science and politics. There was no way formally to extrapolate, either logically or practically, normative conclusions from empirical premises.

Weber argued that acting on the basis of empirical knowledge was not, and could not be, either philosophically or sociologically, the 'business' and goal of science. It was the 'desiring person' in the political world who bore the burden and responsibility for the act of choice. By doing such things as telling social actors what they could do, and maybe even clarifying what they actually wished to do, and by assessing the real and hypothetical consequences, science might, if it carried authority, significantly constrain and guide practical decisions, but in the end it could not conclude what these decisions should or would be, that is, it could not replace practical, that is, political, judgment. In the case of values and ultimate meaning, *'validity'* was a practical matter. It was individually, historically, and culturally relative – no matter what transcendental or extra-political standards one might call upon as justification. The province of science, he claimed, was the search for universally valid empirical knowledge or truths, and this claim was essential to the rhetorical force of his essay. If this was not the manner in which the role and capacity of social science was perceived externally, these disciplines would have little influence, and if this was not the actual commitment of social science, it would soon be exposed as disguised ideology. The question was how social science achieved or was to pursue this goal, and Weber's answer was that it was to be accomplished by *'conceptually ordering* empirical reality' and producing results that, as he famously said, would be 'recognized as correct even by a Chinaman.' The problem, then, was to determine what 'objectivity' in this context meant and entailed, that is, what this activity of 'conceptual ordering' involved (362–5).

In section 2, then, the much longer portion of the essay, Weber turned directly to the cognitive problem of concept formation in the social sciences. Here he began by pointedly and expansively claiming that what constituted social facticity was not a function of inherent properties attaching to the objects of knowledge. These facts, the facts represented in the language of social science, were, he maintained, analytical constructions reflecting criteria of significance and interest that, in the end, were indigenous to the practice of social science. Such specifications of fact were conceptually extracted from a prior cultural whole, but this whole, that is, 'society,' was itself not an intelligible object any more than the 'world' investigated by natural science was such an object. 'Scientific domains are constituted not by the *"objective"* relation of *"things,"* but by the relationship of *problems in thought*: a new "science" emerges wherever new methods are applied to a new problem and, in this way, truths discovered which disclose significant and new perspectives' (371).

For Weber, this conception of social science entailed liberation from such things as the one-dimensional materialist account of history and economics and its universalistic pretensions. Such *'one-sided'* analysis of cultural reality from specific 'perspectives' was, however, acceptable, if there was a plurality of such analyses, since a plurality of relatively arbitrary perspectives would not only facilitate a more comprehensive and neutral overall representation but provide wider access to the infinite dimensions of social phenomena, while achieving the kind of delimitation that would allow claims about causal explanation. The 'unreality' of dominant economic constructs, whatever their particular deficiencies, reflected a basic principle that was generally 'valid for the whole of scientific knowledge of cultural reality.' The implication of this principle was that there was '*no* absolutely "objective" scientific analysis of cultural life,' that is, of 'social phenomena *independent* of special and "one-sided" perspectives' (373–4). But by 'absolutely objective,' Weber was, quite pointedly, referring to a conception for which there were no criteria. He was stressing that objectivity was a value that required being cashed out in the currency of some scientific practice. The reason that it was impossible to achieve 'absolute' objectivity was not so much that the goal was out of reach as that there was not, and could not be, any such definable goal. There simply were no trans-contextual criteria of objectivity, because there was no transcendental form of scientific practice. Objectivity could be conceived in terms of the concerns and standards of a variety of practices, but there was no objectivity as such in which all the practices participated. Consequently, it was vain to seek criteria of objectivity either by postulating the cognitive independence of social phenomena or by creating a single privileged domain of social-scientific constructions.

What Weber was, and was not, getting at here is surely one of the most difficult dimensions of his work. He defined his image of social science as a '*science of reality*,' but, once again, his point was that this reality could not in itself be an object of inquiry. It consisted of infinite '*uniqueness*' and multiplicity, and as a whole it was an object that lacked scientific identity and significance. This might seem, on its face, to be an outright appropriation of Rickert's neo-Kantian position about concept formation in the natural sciences, but Weber did not endorse emulating the natural sciences, and Rickert's claim had limited application to social science. Although hypothetical laws might be employed as a heuristic or means in the process of social inquiry, social phenomena did not, he argued, lend themselves to the deductive law-governed images of what he dubbed the '"*astronomical*" knowledge' sought by many economists. What bothered Weber about the constructions typical of natural science, and of those who professed to emulate it, was that they obliterated historical and cultural uniqueness and the meaning indigenous to such particularity. Social science was more like natural history, which assumed a theoretical account of the natural world but involved a focus on the individual and historical. A social phenomenon was 'historical' or significant in its individuality as well as '*qualitative*' and part of a situated cultural '*constellation*,' which must be interpreted in order to be causally explained.

Despite all this, Weber went on to insist that the study of cultural values was, however, distinguished less by any prior fixed character and location than by the intellectual orientation and interest of the investigator, which was, in the end, what transformed any instance of empirical reality into a social fact (375–7). What constituted a social fact could not, in the end, be concluded outside the language of science and its conception of social reality. 'The stream of infinite events flows constantly toward eternity.' It was only through the presuppositions of an investigator that a phenomenon and its cause could be factored out of the spatial and temporal infinitude of social life. Otherwise, there would be a 'chaos of "existential judgments" with respect to innumerable individual judgments' (378). There were no facts that spoke for themselves, and to believe that they did was merely to be unaware of the cognitive orientation that one brought to selection and conceptualization. Significance was ultimately a function of the concerns of the social scientist, 'for scientific truth is only valid for those who *seek* the truth' (383).

At this point in the essay, however, as well as in other well-known portions of his work,[8] Weber shifted his emphasis away from how the language of social science created social facts to an examination of how social phenomena are pre-constituted and already meaningful when encountered by scientific investigators. Despite his insistence on the *constructive* role of social-scientific concept formation, there was another sense in which the objects of social inquiry *did* possess a kind of independent objectivity and quality of facticity. While the language and concepts of natural science were constitutive of the facts that comprised the category of natural phenomena, social objects were, in the first instance, conventionally meaningful in terms of the understanding of social actors and thus part of a realm discursively independent of the language of social science. This brings us to what might appear as a fundamental paradox, and what might even seem to be an outright contradiction, in Weber's argument. Social phenomena were particular and historical yet intelligible only in the language of social science. It would, however, be a mistake to seek to extricate his claims from this paradox. He viewed this cognitive paradox as endemic to social inquiry, just as much as the practical paradox of the difference and relationship between social science and its subject matter.

Although he claimed, in what might at first seem an extreme neo-

Kantian sense, that the social world becomes intelligible only in terms of the categories through which the social scientist orders it, he was also saying that social phenomena are ontologically and epistemologically 'given' in a way that natural phenomena are not. The issue, however, is more complex than these stark alternatives allow. We might say that while social science creates facts as classes or kinds of things in terms of its theories and attending categories, it does not conceptually construct facts as particularities. In the case of all second-order analysis, there are two discursive universes. There is, however, no such distinction in the case of natural science. If we are persuaded by an argument such as that of Thomas Kuhn,[9] we would say that the facts of the natural 'world' are rendered and accessible only in the language and theories of natural science (or religion, common sense, or some other first-order discourse). We cannot compare the 'world' with science's construction of the world. Metaphysical realism, or the notion that somehow the unrepresented 'real' world both sustains and limits scientific claims, is an option of faith, but that world still remains epistemologically unintelligible and something that we cannot call upon to resolve either conflicts between claims in science or conflicts between science and other first-order discourses. While the 'world' at large toward which social science directs its attention is also something that in itself cannot be articulated or even said, in terms of any theoretically neutral criteria, to exist, the particular elements from which that vacuous image is adduced are not like the facts of natural science. The reason that the natural 'world' is itself not an intelligible object is not exactly the same as the reason that the social 'world' is not as a whole intelligible. The problem with the social world is its pre-constituted historical and conventional diversity and complexity, and although we might metaphorically say the same about the natural world, the real problem is that the natural world is always, and only, represented in, for example, the language of natural science. It is a *constructed* rather than *reconstructed* world. Social facts, or at least a large domain of social facts, involve something quite different.

As conventional objects they, logically and temporally, precede the theory, language, and concepts of social science. The social-scientific account of facts can be juxtaposed and compared to how social actors have constructed elements of the social universe, and thus the products of social science are, as Weber distinctly referred to them, *reconstructions* and, in some sense, rivals of the perceptions and *constructions* of social actors. If this were not basically how Weber construed the situation, his whole scheme, including not only his account of meaningful action but also his concern about producing political clarity and showing actors the consequence of their beliefs and motives, would not make sense. So, then, in what respect was the social world an infinite chaotic universe of unintelligibility that required external conceptual ordering, and in what respect was it already historically and meaningfully constituted? The answer lies in the concept of interpretation, which entails both a prior and intelligible object and a language of interpretation and reconstruction. Interpretation presupposes a text, but an interpretation is another text, which is both cognitively and practically distinct. And this cognitive difference entails a practical difference.

Both the historical particularity and meaningful character of social phenomena implied that they, in contrast to the facts generated by the abstractions of natural science, were culturally infused with meaning and possessed a cultural identity, yet they nevertheless required conceptual reconstruction and interpretation in the language of social science. Since cultural significance was not self-evident and was, in the end, a consequence of the perspective from which the investigator approached social practices, explanation was primarily, as Weber pointedly stressed, a matter of '*interpretation*' and not the subsumption of data under laws that not only concealed their particularity or historicity but obliterated the conventional nature of social phenomena by treating them as natural data. It was as much a 'mistake' as treating physical phenomena as if they were a text authored by God. The search for universal laws was less relevant in social science, not simply because conventional objects were often not governed by laws, but because viewing them from this perspective would not produce adequate knowledge about the internal conceptual grounds of, and relationship between, such phenomena.

Weber emphasized, however, that neither the manner in which the presuppositions of the investigator determined the selection and identity of facts nor the individuality and historicity of social phenomena negated the search for generality, causal knowledge, and universally valid scientific truth. It would be a distinct mistake to construe Weber's use of *cause* in a narrow sense, such as referring to the deduction and prediction of particulars from nomothetic premises. What he often meant by *causes* were the concepts that informed action and the contexts that, in turn, provided a repertoire of concepts as well as the manner in which a concatenation of events produced other events. And although the orientation of the investigator governed the '*construction of the conceptual scheme*,' the results were another matter and something about which, in principle, anyone committed to the scientific enterprise would be able to agree. The issue of how and why investigators were able to agree might seem to have been left hanging, since Weber had already ruled out the common answers – that is, determinacy of either the object or its apprehension. Part of the solution was simply that there was no *general* answer to the question of how scientific agreement was achieved and that it was a mistake to seek such an answer, but part of the solution was tied to the objective character of social phenomena. They were there to be seen by anyone who would look, apart from the cultural perspective from which one might view them. If this were not the case, translation and communication across cultures would be impossible. But what, then, Weber asked, did all this entail *'methodologically'* with respect to objectivity, concept formation, and theory (383)?

Weber argued that the 'naturalistic prejudice' that every concept in the cultural sciences should be similar to those in the exact natural sciences and involve deduction from laws had led to a number of mistakes in seeking to account for the 'psychological' grounds of social action and institutions as well as to an 'apparently unbridgeable gulf in our discipline between "abstract"-theoretical method and empirical-historical research.' What was required was not deduction from general premises about human beings and their psychology, including those advocated by either Dilthey or Menger, but knowledge of 'social institutions' and individual cultural elements and their 'interpretative susceptibility for our empathetic understanding.' There should be no need at this point in the scholarship on Weber to emphasize that by such 'understanding' or *Verstehen* he did not mean some form of intuitive apprehension but rather sensitivity to social contexts and practices. There had, he argued, been a failure to grasp the basic character of 'conceptual formation characteristic of the sciences of human culture.' This kind of formation was exemplified in the 'ideal-type' (385–7).

Although, in Weber's view, marginal utility economics was wrong in its search for universal laws, it did provide him with an example of the application of these 'synthetic constructs.' They were like a *'utopia'* produced by an 'accentuation of particular elements of reality' and the bringing together of 'certain relationships and events of historical life into an internally coherent *conceptual* cosmos.' Such constructs were a means or heuristic, rather than logically exclusive hypotheses or descriptions, that could be judged true or false. They were used to interpret social phenomena and make them and their cultural significance understandable and thus provide a basis for making hypotheses. The ideal-type was neither an 'ethical' ideal nor a *'representation* of the real' but a vehicle of interpretation. Such constructs were 'formed by the one-sided *accentuation* of one or *several* perspectives, and through the synthesis of a variety of diffuse, discrete, *individual* phenomena, present sometimes more, sometimes less, sometimes not at all, subsumed by such one-sided, empathetic viewpoints, so that they form a uniform construction *in thought.* In its conceptual purity this construction can never be found in reality,' but 'historical research' could determine how closely it approximated an individual instance of what was specified (387–8).

It was only through such constructs that the social scientist engaged reality, since there was no '"disinterested" representation of "objective facts."' The cognitive paradox was that the language of social science was a necessary medium for reaching a prior realm of conventionally constituted social facts. Ideal-types were not simply tools of classification but a kind of generalized conventionality. He referred to a certain class as 'genetic concepts,' because they referred to 'cultural meanings,' and such *'limiting'* constructs were to be judged by the extent of their 'success in developing knowledge of concrete cultural phenomena and their context, their causal determination, and their *significance.'* These 'categorical' concepts or 'thought constructs' allowed the particulars of social life to be generalized and made it possible to go beyond 'the mere registration of material relationships.' Whether the social scientist was aware of it or not, they were demanded, since the 'discursive nature of our knowledge – the circumstance that we grasp reality only through a chain of modifications in our apprehension of it – presumes such a conceptual shorthand.' It was necessary, however, to guard against assuming that these constructs were isomorphic representations, attempting to force all historical phenomena into such a 'Procrustean bed,' and allowing their 'hypostatization' or reification into 'ideas' or 'forces' behind history. Finally, since social science was concerned with 'practical *significance,'* there was always a danger of moving beyond their logical and cognitive significance. The danger was that they sometimes represented, or came to represent, what the investigator believed was 'essential' and *'valuable'* and were transformed into ethical ideals. The subject matter of the investigator was value-informed behaviour, but since the constructs employed might involve 'value-judgments,' it was necessary to exert *'scientific self-control,'* which demanded 'a sharp distinction between the logically *comparative* relation of reality to ideal *types* in their logical sense, and the evaluative *judgment* of reality directly in terms of *ideals'* (389–4). What separates Weber's ideal-types from some of the conceptual frameworks of later social science, or even the economics of his time, was the fact that they were presented as multiple and changing and they exemplified a never-ending attempt to encompass and keep pace with historical social phenomena.

There was no getting away from the fact that since social science was a matter of interpretation, there must be a *language* of interpretation. And an interpretation is an argument about, or an account of, what is interpreted, which is predicated on the assumption of difference. In a strange way, the positivists were right, in the case of social science, about the heterogeneity of theory and fact but wrong in the case of natural science. In the case of social science, there could not be an identity between the interpretation and the object of interpretation, and it would be a mistake to read Weber as an exponent of what is today often referred to as the claim that 'interpretation goes all the way down.' Interpretation, in fact, came up abruptly – cognitively and practically – against the immanent understanding *within* the discursive universe of the subject matter of social science, which was a universe of meaning quite independent of the renderings of social science. The *'concept of the state'* was, Weber suggested, a prime example.

Weber noted that what corresponded to the everyday use of the term *state* was 'an infinity of diffuse and discrete active and passive human actions' and ideas. From this, social science might abstract an ideal-typical 'synthesis,' which would constitute the theoretical heuristic of the 'scientific conception of the state.' Here the 'practical' idea of the state, embraced by political actors, and the ideal-typification, created by the social scientist, might 'approach each other very closely and constantly tend to merge with each other,' but they were, in the end, elements of two different languages and practices. And ideal-types also applied in instances where there was a considerable cultural gap between the interpreter and the datum of interpretation as well as in the cases of historical research and of phenomena involving various levels of abstraction including *'developments.'* Although these last constructs were not 'history,' as Marxism had assumed, they could be used in causal explanations of historical events (394–6). For Weber, then, virtually the entire vocabulary of social science was composed of kinds and levels of ideal-types. The ideal-type represented the essential difference between the language of social science and the language of society but also the necessity to take account of both.

Even the description and classification of particular phenomena re-quired the imposition of a language of social science. The use of the ideal-type was simply emblematic of the discursive distinction between meta-practical languages and their objects of analysis. 'Theory and history' were two different things, and it was necessary to be vigilant in distinguishing them. While what he called the 'genetic' ideal-types referred to specific origins and causes such as beliefs, he distinguished the more 'generic' kind as referring to more general cross-cultural simi-larities. Weber argued that the past and progress of the social sciences amounted to a continuing and open-ended quest to impose conceptual order on the complex and ever-changing world of social reality. In that respect, these disciplines were 'destined to eternal youthfulness,' since there was an inevitable 'transience of *all* ideal-typical constructions' and the need of 'constantly forming *new* constructions.' There was no 'exhausting reality's infinite wealth' or end to the process of trying to 'bring order into the prevailing chaos of facts' through 'cognitive *recon-struction*,' since both the particulars of social reality and the interest of the investigator were undergoing constant change. This realization 'that there is no *direct* representation ... of "objective" reality' and that the concepts of science are only the 'cognitive means for the purpose of intellectually mastering the empirically given,' was, Weber suggested, the discovery of Kant, and it entailed the limited validity of such con-cepts and the need to *continually* construct them in order to achieve clarity. The neglect of such concepts by those engaged in 'policy' discus-sion and activity was something that Weber claimed was 'especially dangerous,' since the '*collective* concepts taken from everyday life have had an especially unhappy impact' and often created a kind of verbal confusion,' which could be remedied only by the introduction of a careful and systematic analysis of the possible standpoints through ideal-typical concept construction (397–402). Such clarity was not sim-ply for the satisfaction of social science but for the edification of society.

Weber was emphasizing the therapeutic function of social science, and there can be no doubt that notwithstanding his remarks about the simultaneous 'meaningfulness' and 'chaos of facts,' what he was saying was that, despite the pre-constituted character of social phenomena, social science was necessarily involved in reconstructing the object of its interpretation and that in doing so it had a potential practical effect on social and political action. What has bothered many commentators, as philosophically and ideologically diverse as Leo Strauss and Jürgen Habermas, was Weber's failure to postulate some transcendental critical standard for social-scientific judgment, but the essence of Weber's message was the impossibility of philosophically resolving the cognitive and practical paradoxes involved in what is often called the difference between theory and practice.

Weber concluded his essay by stressing that there was, in the end, only a 'fine line that separates science and belief' and that the 'objective validity of experimental knowledge rests, solely rests, upon the fact that given reality is ordered by categories which are in a specific sense *subjective*: they represent the *presupposition* of our knowledge and are based on the presupposition of the *value* of those truths which experimental knowledge alone is able to give us.' Even the value of scientific truth itself was culturally relative, along with all the other diverse and specific value orientations that informed science. Social science was predicated on values, and it investigated values, but it could not, as a matter of either logic or practice, yield definitive judgments about the validity of values. Yet a practical belief in ultimate values, Weber argued, was not incompatible with social science and its constantly changing viewpoints about the significance of empirical phenomena. Science and politics were simply two different ways of coming to terms with the 'ever-changing finite part of the monstrously chaotic stream of events that flows through time' (403–4). It is little wonder that Weber ended with a quotation from *Faust*.

What, then, exactly, did Weber mean by objectivity in social science? One might reasonably conclude that his goal was less to say what it was in some definitive sense than to indicate what it was not. What comes across most clearly is the rejection of what was, and still is, often assumed to be the basis of objectivity, that is, either the image of phenomena as accessible through some form of immediate experience or the neutrality of their conceptualization. In one sense, he suggested, as already noted, that the solution was to be found in the problem: the inevitability of multiple viewpoints had the virtue of inhibiting the dominance of any one viewpoint, which he believed would be the most dangerous threat to the creation and progress of knowledge. Another dimension of objectivity was the construction and application of concepts that were distinctly the product of social science rather than extractions from the amorphous discourses of society itself. Finally, and what is most often neglected, was his emphasis on the objective, or discursively independent, character of social phenomena. It might seem that Weber was also arguing for something like what philosophers of science Carl Hempel and Karl Popper would later refer to as the difference between the context of discovery and the context of justification and the assumption that objectivity and validity are matters pertaining to the latter. But then what did he mean by *validity* as empirical truth? What was he getting at when he claimed that a scientific proof in the social sciences must be acknowledged as correct, even by someone from a radically different culture such as that of China? This statement is particularly problematical in view of his subsequent reference to the 'Chinese ossification of intellectual life.'

Clearly Weber did not mean that scientific claims were self-evident, since he noted that the kind of validity he was speaking of was something that we must '*strive* to attain' and that 'faulty data,' the failure of some cultures to accept scientific values, and other problems could inhibit knowledge. In the end, his answer tended to be a negative one. Maybe more than anything else he was dissolving the myth that *objectivity* was a word that, despite its universal force or connotation, had some trans-contextual criteria of application. It was a term that referred to different concepts that were relative to different forms of practice. Objectivity in social science was obviously not the same as in natural science. It is important, however, not to be overly quick to read into Weber what would often seem to be the import of some of Nietzsche's aphorisms about the unreality of truth or certain less-than-careful assertions of self-ascribed postmodernists. Truth was not an object but rather the name applied to certain claims for which a practice such as science possessed communally agreed upon criteria. It was not that terms like *truth, objectivity*, and *validity* had no meaning or referred to mythical entities, but rather that they designated multiple concepts and possessed an excess of meaning that required restricting them to a relevant context.

Weber's basic, positive answer to the problem of objectivity was given in his claim that the '*objective* validity of all empirical knowledge rests exclusively upon the ordering of the given reality according to categories.' The criteria of validity and objectivity were, at any time and place, internal to the discourse of science and its vocation of providing a systematic account of the world. And, one might ask, where else could they possibly reside? Such criteria were certainly not to be found in the world of politics, and they were not located in the abstract pronouncements of philosophy. What Weber was in part seeking was the autonomy and identity of the social sciences and their freedom from both politics and philosophy. This did not mean, however, that he wished to sever relations with either, since he believed that philosophy had something to say to and about social science and that despite its necessary distance from politics, both the past and future of social science were rooted in its relationship to public life. What Weber was in effect saying, much like Kuhn many years later, was that the criteria of scientific truth are located within the practice of science. Although a certain culture may be resistant to the values of science, there was nothing about, for example, the Chinese mind that inhibited its participation in a scientific community, and in the case of social phenomena, they, like language itself, could be understood cross-culturally. Scientific validity is a matter of scientific agreement, and it was the very possibility of that kind of agreement, which was so remote in both politics and philosophy, that might secure the cognitive, and therefore practical, authority of social science.

My principal purpose in discussing Winch's 'idea' of a social science is to examine how many of the issues that Weber confronted appear when approached from within another order of discourse – in this case the third-order realm of the philosophy of social science.[10] Like Weber's essay, Winch's work was also a kind of rhetoric of inquiry, even a polemic, but one external to the practice of social science. Although his work would have an impact on the theory and activity of social science, Winch was no more a social scientist than Weber was a philosopher, and he spoke only in a derivative manner about and to social scientists, and really not at all to social actors. But although he made little reference to the actual practice of social science, it was to Weber that Winch turned in seeking to clarify and exemplify his claims about the explanation of what he referred to as 'meaningful behaviour' expressing 'reasons' and 'motives' and about what objectivity in such explanation would involve. He argued that such behaviour was what Weber had designated as actions that are 'subjectively intended,' or with which 'the agent or agents associate a subjective *sense*.' Although individual actions were the 'paradigm' case, Winch argued that Weber included more in the concept of meaningful behaviour than that for which an actor possessed specific and consciously held and articulated intentions and purposes. The normative force of 'tradition,' for example, went beyond a reference to mere habit and physical acts and carried a 'sense' that made it 'symbolic' and allowed it to be viewed in terms of actions that, by commitment to the rule implied, had some bearing on future patterns of conduct (45–50).

Winch found in Weber's work a basis for defending the idea of an interpretive social science based on 'understanding' rather than a posi-

tivist image of causal explanation in terms of natural laws. This idea of
a social science had come under severe attack, by philosophical empiricism and similarly inclined social scientists, for its putative lack of
objectivity. Although it was Wittgenstein's conception of the public
character of intentionality manifest in language that Winch most fully
and directly drew upon, and although he concluded that Weber did not
provide 'a clear account of the *logical* character of interpretive understanding' (*Verstehen*), he insisted that Weber was not, in the end, talking
about something such as 'intuition' and had maintained that claims
about social-scientific understanding 'must be tested by careful observation' (112). Where Winch deviated from Weber was in what Winch
believed was Weber's assimilation of causal explanations to those based
on 'events of consciousness' and his 'wrong account of the process of
checking the validity' of such interpretations by reference to statistical
laws (113–15). This, however, was a relatively minor issue and more a
matter of terminological use than substantive disagreement. What was
important was that Winch credited Weber with emphasizing the fact
that 'all meaningful behaviour must be social,' since it is 'governed by
rules, and rules presuppose a social setting' or cultural context. Thus,
Winch claimed, one of the most persistent criticisms of Weber could be
met, that is, the notion that he was defending explanations based on
grasping some 'inner sense,' since any such sense was the internaliza-
tion of '*socially* established' concepts (117–20). Winch began his book by
challenging what he took to be the 'platitude amongst writers of textbooks' that the social sciences were in their 'infancy' and would evolve,
as had the natural sciences, beyond their philosophical origins by embracing the 'methods of the natural sciences' (1). Winch's work became
relevant to social scientists primarily because many had adopted the
positivist philosophical *idea* of science that he was calling into question.
His immediate acquaintance with both the social and natural sciences
was, however, limited, and he was, as he pointedly noted, writing as a
philosopher about an issue in the philosophy of social science, rather
than engaging in 'what is commonly understood by the term methodology' or debates about how social scientists should go about their business (136). This in part explains the fact that what he characterized as
the logic and epistemology of natural science was itself less a description of any practice than a philosophical image that had come to dominate the discourse of philosophical practice. Within a few years, this
image would be called into question as an account of both natural and
social science.

The most basic task that Winch defined for himself, however, was broader and more formidable than conjuring up an anti-positivist or post-positivist idea of social-scientific explanation. His goal was 'to attack' what had become, in both philosophy and social science, the received 'conception of the relation between the social studies, philosophy and the natural sciences.' Like Weber, he focused on distinguishing these orders of discourse and sorting out the relationships between them. Even more particularly, he wished to critically engage a certain account of the relationship between 'philosophy and the social studies,' or what in general amounted to the relationship between second-order analysis and its subject matter. Winch made it very clear that he was not advancing an 'anti-scientific' position but rather seeking to clarify the true nature of social science by demonstrating how a certain concept of such inquiry was demanded by the nature of social phenomena. Yet despite the cultural approbation enjoyed by the institution of science, he wanted to warn against the 'extra-scientific *pretensions* of science,' which included any suggestion that it could replace philosophy (1–2). Much of the failure to understand Winch's argument has been a consequence of his infelicitous, or rhetorically motivated, lack of distinction between philosophy (especially metaphysics and epistemology) as an intellectual or academic practice and as a functional category referring to theoretical conceptions of reality and the entailed criteria for the acquisition of knowledge.

At the root of his work was an issue in the field of philosophy about which many social scientists had little cognizance but was structurally parallel to the issue of the relationship between social science and its subject matter as well as, in principle, the relationship between any second-order analysis, such as the philosophy of natural science, and its object of inquiry. This was what Winch parsed as the difference between the images of the philosopher as a 'master-scientist' and as an 'underlabourer.' This was not unlike Weber's attempt to find a middle ground between the pretensions of earlier social thinkers and certain images of an antiseptic social science. Winch considered his own conception of philosophy, what might be called his third way, as 'essential' to the book but as 'heretical as my conception of social science itself' (2). Thus the 'opening chapter' and the statement of his 'philosophical bearings,' and of the bearing of philosophy on social science, were presented as crucial.

Here he announced his thesis that 'to be clear about the nature of philosophy and to be clear about the nature of the social studies amount to the same thing' (3). While much of the philosophical response to Wittgenstein had been to move the practice of philosophy in the 'underlabourer' direction of a technical 'ordinary language' analysis, Winch maintained that this trend had gone too far. As a consequence, the practice of philosophy had begun to relinquish the belief that it could 'contribute to any positive understanding of the world' – a world that included both nature and human activity. Philosophy was often conceived as 'parasitic' and assigned the largely 'negative role' of 're-moving impediments' associated with problems of language and logic that attended 'non-philosophical investigations' such as natural science, religion, and social science (4). Although Winch rejected something such as what he took to be Hegel's 'a priori' and 'pseudo-scientific speculations,' he did not want to surrender the traditional core territory of philosophy to either the empirical sciences or special branches of philosophical investigation. The critique of the 'master-scientist' image of philosophy had, he argued, been mistakenly extended to 'a priori philosophizing of a sort which is quite legitimate.' He claimed that while 'the scientist investigates the nature, causes and effects of particular real things and processes, the philosopher is concerned with the nature of reality as such and in general,' with the very concept of 'externality' and with our cognitive connection to that external reality. This was not a matter to be settled by 'pure science' and its experimental methods, since it constituted a 'conceptual' rather than an 'empirical' question and raised the problem of 'the nature of thought' and its relation to 'the nature of language' and how language is connected to reality (7–11).

In discussing language philosophically we are in fact discussing *what counts as belonging to the world*. Our idea of what belongs to the realm of reality is given for us in the language that we use. The concepts we have settle for us the form of the experience we have of the world [since] when we speak of the world we are speaking of what we in fact mean by the expression 'the world': there is no way of getting outside the concepts in terms of which we think of the world ... The world *is* for us what is presented through these concepts. That is not to say that our concepts may not change; but when they do, that means that our concept of the world has changed too. (15; emphasis in original)

Winch claimed that this point was important for the 'philosophy of the social sciences,' because 'many of the more important theoretical issues which have been raised in those studies belong to philosophy rather than to science and are, therefore, to be settled by *a priori* conceptual analysis rather than by empirical research.' This included the question of 'what constitutes social behaviour,' which was really a 'demand for an elucidation of the *concept* of social behaviour' rather than a matter that could be determined by 'empirical research' (17). Since these statements of Winch have been the object of the most contentious interpretations of his work,[11] it is important to be clear about exactly what he was saying.

First of all, what Winch meant by the term *a priori* was not what was analytically or deductively true or beyond argument but rather what might be more accurately referred to as theoretical. When he claimed that the theoretical issues of social science belonged to philosophy, he meant philosophy in a functional sense, in that the issues were conceptual and preceded particular statements of fact that were the result of empirical research conducted within a theoretical paradigm. Both the social sciences and what he designated as the 'peripheral philosophical disciplines,' which studied special subjects such as science or religion, presupposed an account of reality and the manner of its intelligibility (18). Philosophers would properly be seeking to illuminate the kind of reality and intelligibility sought by communities such as science, religion, and social science, and the comparative product should, he claimed, shed some general light on the very concepts of reality and intelligibility and on the fundamental 'conditions' required for there to be 'criteria' for applying these concepts. Thus there was, or should be, a dialectical relationship between the general and specialized endeavours, and, in the same manner, philosophy was relevant to social science – and, in a functional manner, embedded in the theoretical dimension of social science (20–1).

In this generic sense, metaphysics and epistemology were part of *both* social science and its subject matter. The very idea of a social science entailed a theory of social phenomena and assumptions about the criteria of knowing such phenomena, and social actors were also, in effect, metaphysicians and epistemologists, since social life was based on fundamental visions of social reality and knowledge. The latter was, in Winch's view, the basis of the core difference between natural science and social science. A social-scientific interpretation of society required a grasp of the particularities of understanding that were indigenous to various human societies. Since 'social relations are expressions of ideas about reality,' to understand a society is to understand the view of reality shared by the members of society (25).

It was here, at the end of his presentation of his 'philosophical bear-ings,' that Winch turned to an extended discussion of Wittgenstein's analysis of rules and rule-following and the public or social character of such behaviour and its relationship to language, but he commenced his exploration of 'the nature of meaningful behaviour' with a more direct consideration of the relationship between 'philosophy and sociology.' Various branches of philosophy sought, Winch claimed, to illuminate what Wittgenstein had referred to as the 'forms of life,' and the modes of understanding and concepts of reality peculiar to them, but the larger task was to 'try to elucidate what is involved in a form of life as such.' This, Winch argued, was the contribution that Wittgenstein had made. It was not, however, simply a task for the field of philosophy, since social science, in its 'theoretical part,' also required 'a discussion of the nature of social phenomena in general' (41). Since this discussion was the province of the epistemologist, there was, at the theoretical level, a fundamental sort of identity between social science and episte-mology, and thus Winch concluded that 'the central part of sociology, that of giving an account of the nature of social phenomena in general, itself belongs to philosophy,' and 'this part of sociology is really misbe-gotten epistemology' rather than a strictly 'scientific problem' (43).

While one might suggest that Winch was arguing that social science was really an outpost, or even the bastard offspring, of philosophy, an argument that carried a certain degree of historical truth, the more important point was that both philosophy and social science were forms of second-order discourse and thus functionally the same and mutually relevant, whatever the specific tasks they might set for themselves. The most fundamental issues were those involving the nature of second-order activities as well as the nature of their subject matter – and particularly the relationship between them. Both were conventional human activities, constituted in part by an image of the realities in which they were embedded and their own vision of truth and right. His reference to social phenomena as 'rule-governed' certainly invited an unduly narrow construal and the charge that this implied a reflective stance on the part of the social actor. On the whole, however, it is evident that he used the concept of a rule as equivalent to conventional phenomena in general and that his emphasis was on the fact that most conventional activity is habitual or tacit. What he was drawing from Wittgenstein was precisely the essentially public character of conven-tional phenomena, which was most evident in language, but included both action and thought and provided an answer to the persistent social-scientific problem of accessing other minds. His point about reflection was only that all this involved the *possibility* of self-reflection just as social action was open to external observers. The fundamental difference between natural and social science was that in the physical sciences the objects that constitute reality are connected by the scientist's theory, but in social science the connections are also pre-constituted. This was the very paradox with which Weber had grappled.

After half a century, Winch's discussion of rules and meaningful behaviour, and his comparison of the interpretation or understanding of such phenomena with the causal and law-like explanations of natural science, might seem somewhat dated – often because of his equation of natural science with the obsolescent positivist reconstruction. What has remained more important is the manner in which he, like Weber, confronted the problem of the relationship between the language of social science and the language of social life. Winch stressed the similarity, but, nevertheless, the irreducible difference, between the two. They were both conventional realms, but each constituted a different order of concepts and rules as well as different criteria for the application of the concept of sameness. Winch, much like both Rickert and Weber, argued that in the case of the natural scientist 'we have to deal with only one set of rules, namely those governing the scientist's investigation itself,' which determines both the practice of science and the theoretical constitution of the subject matter. He claimed that to adequately understand social phenomena, social scientists must perforce utilize their own language and concepts, but, like Weber, he claimed that in the case of social science it was necessary to apprehend and describe phenomena in a manner that recognized and illuminated the social actor's vision of the world. Thus, Winch concluded, the relation between the social scientist and a social practice 'cannot be just that of observer to observed' but in part like the participation of scientists in their own community, or at least like an 'apprentice' seeking to learn the rules of the practice (87–8).

Although some critics have fastened on Winch's remarks that 'a historian or sociologist of religion must himself have some religious feeling if he is to make sense of the religious movement,' or that a 'historian of art must have some aesthetic sense if he is to understand the problems confronting artists of his period,' this was not, any more than in the case of Weber, a reversion to claims about intuitive understanding but rather, quite the opposite, an affirmation of the conventional, and therefore, in principle, cognitively accessible character of meaningful action. Winch stressed that although second-order understanding was not really like the apprentice's more unreflective mode of learning, a 'reflective understanding' by the social scientist must 'presuppose ... the participant's unreflective understanding.' Although reflective students of society, or of a particular mode of social life, may find it necessary to use concepts that are not taken from the forms of activity that they are investigating, but are taken from the context of their own investigation, still these technical concepts of theirs will imply a previous understanding of those other concepts that belong to the activities of investigation (89). And this point led Winch to once again claim that the activities of the philosopher and the social scientist were 'closely connected' (91). Here, however, he was fastening on a different theme, which had to do more specifically with the issue of objectivity.

While theorists such as Durkheim and Pareto had stressed that objectivity resided in the application of scientific criteria and a mode of explanation that disregarded the understanding and consciousness of actors within the social forms being investigated, Winch argued that this led to evaluative judgments about the logic and rationality of these forms, which distorted or neglected their internal meaning. According to Winch, what made philosophy a model and analogy for social science was not only the fact that they were both second-order endeavours, that is, activities that studied other activities, but 'the peculiar sense in which philosophy is *uncommitted* enquiry' in that it reflected on 'its own account of things' and its 'own being,' which tends to 'deflate the pretensions of any form of enquiry to enshrine the essence of intelligibility as such, to possess the key to reality. For connected with the realization that intelligibility takes many and varied forms is the realization that reality has no key' (102) – not even that of science. While

> non-philosophical unself-consciousness is for the most part right and proper in the investigation of nature [except at critical and revolutionary junctures], it is disastrous in the investigation of a human society, whose very nature is to consist in different and competing ways, each offering a different account of the intelligibility of things. To take an uncommitted view of such competing conceptions is peculiarly the task of philosophy ... It is not its business to advocate any *Weltanschauung* ... In Wittgenstein's words, 'Philosophy leaves everything as it was.' (103)

Winch noted R.G. Collingwood's remark that the work of 'scientific' anthropologists often masks 'a half-conscious conspiracy to bring into ridicule and contempt civilizations different from their own' (103). He also noted Wittgenstein's remark that when we encounter 'philosophical difficulties over the use of some of the concepts of our language, we are like savages confronted with something from an alien culture,' and he suggested the 'corollary' that 'sociologists who misinterpret an alien culture are like philosophers getting into difficulty over the use of their own concepts' (114). He suggested that the analogy was 'plain,' but although he was obviously drawing a parallel between conceptual clarification in philosophy and social-scientific interpretation, the parallel required further elaboration. These somewhat unexplicated remarks, however, led quite directly to Winch's controversial confrontation with the issue of 'understanding a primitive society'[12] and his claims about how to understand without judging. In addition to hypothetically putting into practice his *idea* of a social science, Winch, in this essay, more specifically addressed a matter left somewhat in abeyance in the book. He made it quite clear that his conception of philosophy was one that assumed that philosophy had something practical to contribute, that clarity both about the reality of its subject matter and about itself was a goal and value for social science; and that if there was a fundamental identity shared by philosophy and social science, it implied some practical possibilities for social science. Winch, like Weber, has often been taken to task by those on the left and right for his relativism or, despite his rejection of an 'underlabourer' image of philosophy, his failure to provide philosophy and social science with grounds of critical judgment. Although Winch did not claim some substantive transcendental authority for social science and philosophy any more than Weber did, Winch made it clear that social science had potential practical effects and consequences, that there was a practical as well as cognitive relationship between social science and its subject matter.

Since Winch did not fully draw out the connection that he implicitly perceived between the claims of Weber, as a social scientist, and Wittgenstein, as a philosopher, it is worthwhile making them more explicit or, maybe more accurately, extending the conjunction.[13] There would not seem to be any clear evidence that Wittgenstein read Weber, but they shared important dimensions of the same philosophical context. But while Weber was writing his essay on objectivity, Wittgenstein was in Linz, Austria, attending the same school as Adolf Hitler, and while Weber was delivering his lectures on the 'vocations,' Wittgenstein was a prisoner of war in Italy and completing the statement of his early philosophy in the *Tractatus*. In a recent symposium on the work of Winch, Peter Lassman stated that, even after all these years, 'Winch's work is the best indication that we have of what an approach to political philosophy inspired by Wittgensteinian ideas might look like.'[14] I strongly endorse that proposition and would extend it to include social-scientific inquiry in general.

First and foremost, Wittgenstein emphasized the irreducible conventionality and pre-constituted character of social phenomena as the object of not only philosophy but of all second-order analysis, as opposed to the manner in which natural science 'constructs' its object of inquiry. As Wittgenstein famously put it,[15] 'What has to be accepted, the given, is – so one could say – *forms of life*' (226; emphasis in original). Second, the language and perspectives of second-order analysis could not be collapsed into the discursive universe of its subject matter, and this disjuncture between orders of discourse entailed confronting the cognitive and practical relationship between the two realms. All meta-practical analysis required a language of description and typification – a language of interpretation and reconstruction. Although Winch explicitly recognized this point and stressed the need to gain access to the understanding of actors, he said very little about the specific problems of seeking such understanding through the medium of the interpreter's language, or about the manner in which Wittgenstein's work might be brought to bear on this issue as well as on the problem of the practical relationship between the two realms. It is here that one might suggest a Wittgensteinian corrective or addition to Winch, which at the same time would speak to Weber's dilemma. Third, Wittgenstein stressed the manner in which words such as *objectivity* and *truth* gained full meaning only in the context of practices, which supplied criteria of application. Despite a certain sameness or kinship between the uses of these terms, they did not partake of some common essence.

Wittgenstein might be construed as identifying something approximating Weber's image of ideal-types when he spoke of the manner in which philosophy, or any meta-practice, might approach its conventionally constituted subject matter. Wittgenstein suggested that what was required in giving an account of a *Lebensform* and *Weltbild*, that is, what might be called cultural objects, was a 'perspicuous representation' or 'sketches of a landscape' that 'produces just that understanding which consists in "seeing connections."' He asked if this was a *Weltanschauung*, but he did not directly answer the question. He might have concluded, like Weber, that it was not, but that it was nevertheless rooted in a philosophy or world view. The kind of representation that he sought would be accomplished by 'inventing *intermediate cases*' that determined 'the way we look at things.' The subject matter consisted of 'language games' embedded in various social practices and forms of life, but he recommended, and saw the necessity of creating, second-order language games that would be 'set up as *objects of comparison*' and were 'meant to throw light on the facts ... by way not only of similarities, but also dissimilarities.' Here one might generalize in the sense of seeking 'family resemblances' but not succumb to the kind of 'craving for generality' that characterized so much of philosophy and modern thought in general. Such a model would, again, be 'an object of comparison ... a measuring rod; not as a preconceived idea to which reality *must* correspond (§67, 122, 130, 131).

It would be difficult to imagine a better account of the kind of thing that Weber talked about as an ideal-type. Such typifications involved what Wittgenstein spoke of as 'noticing an aspect' that was central to the activity of interpretation. Interpretation involved seeing something but, in addition, seeing it in a certain way and thus the necessity to first '*see*' something and then '*interpret* it' (193), and consequently interpretation was different from the kind of understanding that took place within a practice or what Kuhn referred to as a paradigm. When Weber talked about the need to impose social-scientific concepts on phenomena during the course of inquiry, he was not, in the end, suggesting that this was like the manner in which natural facts gained their identity in terms of the concepts that composed a scientific theory. That was one kind of 'seeing,' but there is another kind, which is characteristic of interpretation. Both Weber and Wittgenstein were talking about what it was 'to see an object according to an *interpretation*,' which mode of seeing presupposed a prior identity of the phenomenon and involved seeing it aspectively. In natural science, or any first-order discourse, we just *see* a fact, but in social science we interpret and thus characterize a fact *as* a 'this' or a 'that' identified in the language and description of social science.

Wittgenstein suggested that 'it is easy to recognize cases in which we are *interpreting*. When we interpret we form hypotheses, which may prove false' (212). Theories in natural science are not refuted by The Facts but by *the facts of another theory*. In social science, we often find, as Wittgenstein indicated, that our interpretation is inadequate and that what we need, as Winch stressed, is another interpretation. And adequacy is most often judged by the extent to which a description and interpretation are viewed as producing a satisfactory reconstruction. Wittgenstein also made the same point when he stressed the difference between, on the one hand, following a rule, and in that sense understanding it in the course of performing it in the context of a practice, and, on the other hand, interpreting it. The latter required a supervenient language and descriptions that could, in principle, be quite infinite in number. There were many things that we might wish to call descriptions, but 'there is not *one genuine* proper case of such description' (200).

Another dimension of Weber's work that can be illuminated by reference to Wittgenstein, and although not ruled out by Winch even if not emphasized, was the practical therapeutic possibilities of social science. Wittgenstein's criticisms were primarily internal to the practice of philosophy, and although he may not have been optimistic about the impact of philosophy on the practices that it might make its object of analysis, clarity was the general goal of philosophy. Truth for Wittgenstein, as for Weber, was something to be defined in the practices that possessed criteria for the application of the concept, yet there was the possibility of immanent critique. Philosophy, like social science, in one sense, as he said, 'leaves everything as it is' (§124, 126), in that the world that was its object did not automatically change as a consequence of philosophy's reconstructions, but such reconstructions inevitably challenged the social construction of reality. Wittgenstein repeatedly noted the manner in which conceptual analysis potentially involved a *de*-struction of social reality and combated the bewitchments of language, thereby freeing people from the pictures that held them captive and the dilemmas that lack of clarity had induced. Neither Weber nor Winch claimed some transcendental status for the claims of social science, but each recognized the critical dimension of these discourses as well as the practical problems involved in their relationship to their subject matter.

In a recent television interview regarding his role as Sir John Falstaff in Shakespeare's *Henry IV*, Kevin Kline noted that he systematically avoided reading reviews of his performance – but not because he was impervious to, or contemptuous of, criticism. It was because he believed that he could not read an interpretation of his work without having it affect his portrayal. We might analogize Kline's stance to the reluctance of a political actor to heed the descriptions and judgments of political science, but we might also view it as the prudential hesitancy of a social scientist to listen to the siren call of philosophy.

NOTES

1 See, for example, W.G. Runciman, *A Critique of Max Weber's Philosophy of Social Science* (Cambridge: Cambridge University Press, 1972); Thomas Burger, *Max Weber's Theory of Concept Formation* (Durham, NC: Duke University Press, 1976); Toby E. Huff, *Max Weber and the Methodology of the Social Sciences* (New Brunswick, NJ: Transaction Publishers, 1984); Stephen P. Turner, *Max Weber and the Dispute over Reason and Value* (London: Routledge and Kegan Paul, 1984); Fritz Ringer, *Max Weber's Methodology* (Cambridge: Harvard University Press, 1997); Jay A. Ciaffa, *Max Weber and the Problems of Value-Free Social Science* (Lewisburg, PA: Bucknell University Press, 1998); Ola Agevall, *A Science of Unique Events: Max Weber's Methodology of the Social Sciences* (Uppsala: Uppsalla University Press, 1999); George E. McCarthy, *Objectivity and the Silence of Reason: Weber, Habermas, and the Methodological Dispute in German Sociology* (New Brunswick, NJ: Transaction Publishers, 2001); Sven Eliaeson, *Max Weber's Methodologies* (Cambridge: Polity, 2002).

2 For a discussion of the former, see John G. Gunnell, 'Reading Max Weber: Leo Strauss and Eric Voegelin,' *European Journal of Political Theory* 3 (April 2004): 151–66.

3 One of the more egregious of these interpretations is the equation in Ringer, *Max Weber's Methodology*, of Weber's position with contemporary scientific realism and claims about universal rationality, such as those represented in Martin Hollis and Steven Lukes, eds., *Rationality and Relativism* (Cambridge, MA: MIT Press, 1982).

4 For a fuller discussion of this schema, see John G. Gunnell, *The Orders of Discourse: Philosophy, Social Science, and Politics* (Lanham, MD: Rowman and Littlefield, 1998). My discussion also presupposes in some respects my account of Weber's place in what I have called the 'Weimar Conversation' (*The Descent of Political Theory* [Chicago: University of Chicago Press, 1993]).

5 See Guy Oakes, ed., *Max Weber, Roscher and Knies: The Logical Problems of Historical Economics* (New York: Free Press, 1975), for a discussion of Weber's attitude toward epistemology. ·

6 All quotations from Weber are from the translation by Keith Tribe in Sam Whimster, ed., *The Essential Weber* (London: Routledge, 2004), 359–413, but the translation from Max Weber, *The Methodology of the Social Sciences*, ed. Edward A. Shils and Henry A. Finch (Glencoe, IL: Free Press, 1949), was initially utilized in interpreting the essay and employed comparatively in the present revision.

7 For a fuller discussion of Weber's argument about these matters in the context of the subsequent Weimar conversation about theory and practice, see John G. Gunnell, *The Descent of Political Theory*.

8 See 'Basic Sociological Concepts,' in Whimster, *The Essential Weber*.

9 Thomas S. Kuhn, *The Structure of Scientific Revolutions* (Chicago: University of Chicago Press, 1962).

10 Peter Winch, *The Idea of a Social Science and Its Relation to Philosophy* (London: Routledge and Kegan Paul, 1958).

11 Among these critics, see Richard Rudner, *Philosophy of Social Science* (Englewood Cliffs, NJ: Prentice-Hall, 1966); Ernest Gellner, 'The New Idealism: Cause and Meaning in the Social Sciences,' in *Problems in the Philosophy of Science*, ed. Imre Lakatos and Alan Musgrave (Amsterdam: North Holland, 1973), 377–406, 426–32.

12 Peter Winch, 'Understanding a Primitive Society,' *American Philosophical Quarterly* 1 (1964): 307–24.

13 For a more detailed discussion of the implications of Wittgenstein's work for social science and political theory, see John G. Gunnell, 'Desperately Seeking Wittgenstein,' *European Journal of Political Theory* 3 (2004): 77–98.

14 Peter Lassman, 'Politics and "the Fragility of the Ethico-Cultural,"' *History of the Human Sciences* 13 (2000): 125.

15 Ludwig Wittgenstein, *Philosophical Investigations*, trans. G.E.M. Annscombe (New York: Macmillan, 1958).

3 Ideal-Types as 'Utopias' and Impartial Political Clarification: Weber and Mannheim on Sociological Prudence

PETER BREINER

Naturally in individual cases the practical politician can subjectively find himself duty-bound to mediate between antagonistic opinions, or alternatively take sides with one of them. But this has nothing at all to do with *scientific* 'objectivity' [Weber's emphasis].

Max Weber

Where ... the realm of politics begins, in which everything is in the process of becoming, where the collective knowing subject shapes this process of becoming in us, where thought is *not the contemplation of the spectator* [*Betrachtung*], but rather the active participation, the reshaping of the process, a new type of knowledge appears to emerge, namely that in which *decision and viewpoint* are inseparably bound up together.

Karl Mannheim

In this paper, I would like to address a paradox at the heart of Weber's essay on 'Objectivity' that few commentators have noticed. On the one hand, the essay seeks to account for the conditions under which social science in general and historical economics in particular might achieve a degree of impartiality in its modes of inquiry. In doing so, Weber famously appeals to the possibility of attaining a unique kind of objectivity through the use of the ideal-type. However, the ideal-type for Weber is partial and perspectival in all its aspects. It is dependent on cultural values in the selection of its object and on practical values in its construction, and it is a subjectively constructed distillation of relevant facts about a social tendency, belief, or activity and therefore cannot be a representation of historical or social reality. It is, as Weber says, a utopia – though in a logical not normative sense. Yet Weber's ideal-typical driven account of social inquiry is the basis for his claim that social science can provide an impartial clarification for (political) partisans of various positions about the logic and the conditions for putting their ultimate aims into practice. Indeed, it is precisely in part 1 of the 'Objectivity' essay that Weber first makes a claim that will be repeated many times without revision throughout his work: historical sociology based on the ideal-type can provide an impartial method for testing the meaning and feasibility of political-ethical projects. How can a social science whose concepts are subjectively constructed distillations of the facts of social reality claim to provide a resolutely impartial basis for clarifying partisan political action in that reality, indeed claim a unique authority to do so? It is Weber's answer to this paradox that I propose to examine here.

As it will turn out, Weber never successfully squares this circle – indeed, he demonstrates the problem to be irresolvable. In doing so, he sets an agenda for a new kind of sociologically informed political judgment that to this day has been addressed by only a few political theorists (see Brecht 1959; Freeden 1996; Gramsci 1971; Mannheim 1936; Schmitt 1996). At the close, I will examine the way one such theorist, Karl Mannheim, sought to solve this problem. Mannheim, we shall see, was intensely conscious of the inadequacies of Weber's solution. Rejecting Weber's claim to impartiality based on concept construction, he proposes a dynamic overview of changing political fields through a synthetic construct of the particular ideological notions of competing actors constituting that field. While Mannheim's solution is often criticized for also trying to gain an impartial standpoint toward political situations through an artificial notion of 'synthesis,' I shall want to argue that he merely makes explicit the irresolvable tension between the claims of social science and the viewpoints of political actors – a tension that constantly has to be calibrated anew as we seek to understand the relation between conflicting political wills and the dynamic forces impinging on the opportunities to achieve political goals.

The Tension between Political Clarification and the Methodology of Social Inquiry in the 'Objectivity' Essay

Interpreters usually view Weber's '"Objectivity" of Knowledge in Social Science and Social Policy [*Sozialpolitik*]'[1] as his first systematic attempt to set out the proper method for engaging in social inquiry, as well as to examine the degree – or better yet, the kinds – of 'objectivity' any human science can attain. However, there is another part to this work that interpreters have chosen either to ignore or to treat as containing a distinctly separate set of arguments with only a peripheral relation to the arguments about social inquiry. I refer here to the preface and part 1 of this essay in which Weber explicitly addresses the practical-political uses of social science. In this opening to the essay, Weber lays out the fundamental tension that informs the whole rest of the piece: on the one hand, the journal of which this is to be a programmatic essay was and continues to be concerned with 'the training of *judgment* about *practical problems* [*die Schulung des* Urteils *über* praktische Probleme]' arising from social contexts, and this mission immediately forces us to confront the role of value judgments in social inquiry; on the other hand, the journal will be concerned with the sense in which there could be 'objectively valid truths' in the human and cultural sciences (GAW, 147; Weber 1949, 51; Weber's emphases). Weber then goes on in part 1 to lay out systematically what a social science can do to clarify practical political positions without necessarily taking a stand on the values at stake – his famous notion of the 'scientific' clarification of convictions, means, ends, and consequences. He then makes his even more famous argument on the existential fact that every value and world view is always forged and criticized from within a struggle of values and world views, and hence has no 'objective' grounding. Having driven a wedge between value judgments and social-scientific inquiry, Weber then prepares the way for the second prong of his inquiry to which the rest of the essay is devoted: the conditions for claiming the truths of social sciences to be objective. But before he opens this second line of inquiry, he vigorously claims that practical value problems [*praktische* 'Fragen'] provide the stimulus for social-scientific inquiry (GAW, 158; Weber 1948, 61; Weber's emphasis). Thus, before Weber even starts the discussion for which the essay has become so famous, there is an intimation that the two problems already alluded two in the title – social politics and objectivity of social knowledge – are intimately tied to one another. Indeed, given the essayistic rather than systematic nature of this piece, one would suspect that the preface and first section on the limits and possibilities of social science as practical advice and the latter sections on conceptualization in social science inform each other. Curiously, most commentators do not give much attention to the relation between these two parts of the essay.[2] It is precisely how these two parts of the essay fit together – or more properly, the tension between them – that I intend to pursue here.

The 'Utopian' Nature of Ideal-Types and the
Claim to Objectivity

Weber's strongest methodological recommendations in the 'Objectivity' essay do not initially rotate around political clarification at all. Rather, they rotate around the defence of genetic concepts and a demonstration of the inadequacies of generic concepts in political economy. Writing this article at virtually the same time as his famous *Protestant Ethic and the Spirit of Capitalism*, Weber uses it to demonstrate precisely the force of his ideal-typical approach to social inquiry in general and his defence of genetic historical concepts in particular.[3]

At the centre of his famous defence of the ideal-type is his criticism of the use of general concepts, especially in deductive theories of economics as practised by marginal utility theory.[4] Without going into a full discussion of this knotty question in Weber, I want merely to point to his strategy of argument for the reason that deductive theories of economics fail if they claim to provide generic concepts and general laws applicable to all economies.[5] Weber does not directly challenge the goal of deducing economic behaviour from a simple psychological motive such as human acquisitiveness or a general maxim of conduct such as the principle of marginal or final utility. Rather, he claims that such constructs are not what they claim to be. They are, in fact, ideal-types: concepts in which the distinctive features of some aspects of historical and cultural life are forged into an internally consistent construct. In producing such concepts, as Weber so famously put it, we engage in a 'one-sided accentuation' of what we take to be the unique features of a social relationship or culture so as to produce a 'utopia' of that form in the true sense of the word (GAW, 191; Weber 1949, 90): this concept does not exist in reality (GAW, 188–91; Weber 1949, 87–91).[6] But of course it allows us to clarify and understand this reality in its uniqueness relative to other concepts from which we can draw similarities and contrasts. But what we find to be distinctive is itself related to the interests governing our inquiry, and different interests will generate different complexes of ideal-types (GAW, 192; Weber 1949, 91; Weber 2002, 8–9). So, for example, Weber finds marginal utility theory to be not a general theory of economic conduct, though it incorporates generic concepts like exchange, but in fact a genetic concept describing a perspective on the unique features of 'capitalist culture' and the behaviour it seeks to cultivate (GAW, 201, 192; Weber 1949, 100, 91; Weber 2002, 9). And this is true of all theories of political economy, despite their generic claims.

Of course, we may want something more solid, susceptible to histori-cal or empirical confirmation, when we engage in social inquiry. Weber responds with four powerful arguments for our inevitable reliance on the ideal-type. First, he claims that as soon as we try to characterize any social phenomenon, make any stream of social action intelligible, we are compelled to use ideal-typical concepts. That is, whenever we seek to characterize historical or social phenomena by their common but distinctive traits, such as imperialism, capitalism, or mercantilism, we inevitably invoke ideal-types. They are the means by which we make analytical distinctions within descriptions insofar as we want to focus attention on the distinctive differences between classes of phenomena (GAW, 192; Weber 1949, 92). In brief, whether we want to acknowledge it or not, we inescapably make use of such 'distorted' concepts, when-ever we draw social-scientific generalizations.

The second claim, which seems a bit more controversial, is just as unavoidable as the previous one: since the ideal-type cannot be 'ob-served' in empirical reality (Weber 1949, 91), it can provide us with only a set of motivations and outcomes that are *possible*, given already con-ceptually constructed antecedent conditions. Ideal-types are in ef-fect imagined constructs of *what could have happened* to produce a certain outcome given 'these conditions': 'It is a matter of constructing relation-ships which our imagination accepts as plausibly motivated and hence as "objectively possible" and which appear as *adequate* from a nomo-logical standpoint' (GAW, 192; Weber 1949, 92). We should note the very careful vocabulary Weber is using here: 'imagination,' 'plausibly motivated,' 'objectively possible,' and 'adequate' with regard to law-like statements. Both the ideal-typical understanding of the self-under-standing of agents or the social relations that they constitute and the explanation of their conduct are couched in a language of tentativeness. The notions of 'objectivity' and 'law-like generalizations' are connected to possibility in the sense that this is what we could plausibly expect, given the internal relations between these beliefs or these social rela-tions and these outcomes.[7]

The reason that ideal-types must inevitably consist of imaginative constructs of possible outcomes has to do with a third claim: the reality that these constructs capture is so intertwined that we can capture only some small portion of this causal nexus by disentangling a part of it through concepts and relating these concepts to one another. There is no capturing social or historical reality in its full multiplicity (Weber 1949, 81, 84). Thus the contrasting types of agent, beliefs, and social action that can be constructed using the ideal-type allow us to capture possible streams of conduct within a causally intertwined reality, rather than a representation of that reality itself: 'We present the religious ideas in a logically consistent form, compiled as an "ideal type," which rarely existed in historical reality. For precisely *because of* the impossibility of drawing clear boundaries in historical reality, we can only hope to arrive at the specific effects of these ideas by examining their *most logically consistent* form' (Weber 2002, 69, Weber's emphasis; see GAW, 191–2; Weber 1949, 90).

This point leads us finally to a fourth claim, which has proven perhaps to be the most controversial. Since ideal-types are utopias that synthesize distinctive features of a social phenomenon, they are not susceptible to confirmation or disconfirmation by reference to brute empirical data. They already contain the relevant data, albeit it in a simplified – one should say explicitly distorted – and one-sided form. Therefore, if they fail to register some crucial feature of the historical activity being analysed, the proper response is to point to a new set of features and relations that the previous set failed to account for and forge them into a set of ideal-types from a new perspective (Weber 1949, 95).[8] Thus Weber's ideal-types provide streams of cultural, social, economic, or political action and their effects, but they do not, as it were, represent a particular set of empirical facts 'out there.' They provide possible histories or possible streams of action whose plausibility depends on the typologies and narratives in which they are placed.

Curiously, it is this hypothetical reality constituted by these 'heuristic' ideal-typical constructs of distinctive beliefs, social practices, tendential developments, and social constellations that forms the backdrop for Weber's claim that the social sciences have a distinctive authority to inform agents about their highest political and social commitments. In what sense can these 'utopias,' which 'in their conceptual purity are not to be found anywhere in empirical reality' (GAW, 191; Weber 1949, 90), give us a greater self-consciousness of the practical contexts in which we pursue our most deeply held partisan values and principles?

Science, Partisanship, and Political Advice

To understand Weber's contribution to providing a dynamic sociological backdrop to political advice – and its limits – one first must turn to a distinction from his later work: his most famous and much belaboured distinction between partisanship and science. In 'Science as a Vocation' he invokes this distinction not initially for analytic purposes but to distinguish the practical commitments of the scholar from those of the partisan political actor: 'Party politics ... does not belong in the lecture-room as far as the lecturer is concerned and it belongs least of all when he is scientifically concerned with politics. For opinions on practical political issues and the scientific analysis of political structures and party positions are two different things' (Lassman, Velody, and Martins 1989, 20; Weber 1982, 60).[9] They are 'two different things' for Weber in the sense that the duty of the scholar is not to avoid addressing practical political issues but to provide an analysis that will enable the members of his or her captive audience to evaluate their individual political commitments from an impartial vantage point. The scholar's job is to provide, as it were, a political sociology and a generic account of political responsibility that all members of the audience would find plausible apart from their substantive political goals. To press one's own political position on the audience is to exploit it.

Thus, in 'scientific analysis of political structures and party positions,' one deploys concepts in such a way that even individuals of such divergent positions as a Catholic and a Free Mason would agree to the same analysis. Instead of seeking to win over the listener, one turns the democratic forum itself into an object of analysis. One considers, for example, the various forms of democracy, analyses the way in which they function, establishes the consequences that the adoption of each form has for the living conditions of those who must live under it, and compares these conditions with those of non-democratic forms. 'The goal of the analysis is to put the listener in the position to find the point when he can take a stand on it from his ultimate standpoint' (GAW, 601; SV, 21). The goal is most definitely not to convince listeners of one's personal standpoint as part of a struggle against opposing standpoints. Respect for the listeners and presumably their capacity to evaluate and choose in accordance with their ultimate value axioms is paramount.

By contrast, practical political positions are characterized by 'partisanship,' 'rhetorical persuasion,' and above all 'struggle' (*Kampf*): 'When one speaks in a popular assembly about democracy one does not hide one's personal standpoint; indeed to take a clearly recognizable partisan position there is one's damned duty and responsibility. The words that one uses are not means of scientific analysis but means of winning over another to one's own position. They are not plowshares to loosen the soil of contemplative thinking but rather swords to be used against enemies: they are weapons (*Kampfmittel*)' (GAW, 601; SV, 20). In political action, analysis is used merely as a means of prevailing over others in struggle. It is not neutral or objective and does not seek to understand perspicaciously the position of the opponent. On the contrary, political analysis is a direct means of persuasion, convincing the as-of-yet unconverted to one's partisan stance and, above all, preparing one's audience for a struggle against opposing positions. In playing one's role as a partisan political actor, one is in effect morally bound by one's role to advance one's cause, using whatever political arguments one has at one's disposal. Unlike the scholar, one is not duty bound by one's role to provide a political sociological analysis in which all partisans can find a location.

The basic assumption here is that as a political actor, one is immediately implicated in partisan struggle; hence, all political analysis is used to promote one's own position. In the sociological clarification of political action, on the other hand, one allows the members of the audience to choose, once their ultimate viewpoints are analysed for logical coherence, for the necessary means to their realization, and for the consequences that follow, once these means are applied. Agreement is attained not on values but on the objectivity of the ideal-typical analysis of action, an objectivity, however, that inheres in the process of concept construction itself, not in any correspondence between ideal-type and reality. A kind of individual moral autonomy, not partisan agreement, is enhanced by this process of analysis.

Interpreters of Weber's defence of the distinctiveness of (social) scientific analysis of politics have tended to see it as essentially a claim about the epistemological status of social science, as opposed to ordinary understanding of politics and society, much akin to Weber's distinction between factual and value claims.[10] However, as John Gunnell has quite rightly pointed out, Weber draws this distinction not in order to separate social science from politics, but rather to support the notion that social science, properly understood, may claim a unique authority in informing political choice of the most significant kind: one's choice of ultimate political commitments in light of the historical and sociological possibilities of realizing them (Gunnell 1993, 148–52). That is, for Weber, sociology in general and political sociology in particular has the ability to give an impartial account of political structures and alternative possibilities for acting within them, and therefore it can claim to educate potential political actors to a comprehensive understanding of politics that ordinary political discussion cannot provide.[11]

In what ways can social science clarify political action that mere partisan understanding cannot? Weber addresses this problem, and in much the same way in virtually all of his methodological essays (see Brunn 1972, 235), but he gives his most succinct answer in 'Science as a Vocation': in addition to logically testing whether one's political commitments and the subsidiary goals that follow from them are consistent with one's highest value assumptions, it can provide an instrumental clarification of political action:

> We can make clear to you the following: to the problem of values [Wertproblem] that is at stake – for simplicity's sake please think of social phenomena as examples – you can in practice take this or that particular stand. If you take such and such a stand, then according to scientific experience you have to apply such and such a means in order to carry it out practically. These means may be in themselves such that you believe you must reject them. Then one must simply choose between the end and the unavoidable means. Does the end [Zweck] 'justify' ['heiligt'] the means or not? *The teacher can demonstrate to you the necessity of the choice, more he cannot do* ... Of course he can go further and tell you if you want such and such an end, then you must accept such-and-such secondary results, which experience shows to occur. (GAW, 607; SV, 25–6; my emphasis)

Although Weber invokes here the traditional vocabulary of political prudence – *examples, experience*, ends and means – he clearly believes that 'science [Wissenschaft],' broadly conceived, can provide a more reliable form of political knowledge than mere 'experience.' At this point, we must turn to his account in the 'Objectivity' essay and his late essay 'Value-Freedom,' as they both lay out precisely the force and the limits of the ideal-type in providing both clarification and prognostication for partisan actors. First, Weber famously argues, quite apart from any instrumental understanding that it may provide, social-scientific clarification relying on ideal-type constructs may assess an agent's ultimate values for consistency between his or her ultimate ends and the subsidiary goals that follow from it – what Weber calls axiomatic reasoning. Furthermore, given any number of ultimate ends among the conflicting ones that we might pursue in politics, it can give an account of the necessary means to achieve them, if such means are available. Even more significantly it can determine 'the factual consequences' of using a particular means to a proposed end. Certain means will produce certain foreseeable consequences that are directly compatible with the end being pursued, and these consequences will in turn be accompanied by subsidiary consequences that are frequently both unforeseen and unwanted. This determination of consequences, both intended and unintended, enables the agent to weigh different possible means against each other according to whether the consequences of deploying them achieve or undermine the end (GAW, 150; Weber 1949, 53; GAW, 510; Weber 1949, 20; GAW, 539; Weber 1949, 35). Such weighing may be decisive in deciding whether a particularly intrinsically bad means is still compatible with the end aimed for.

But the clarification of consequences may have even a more profound effect on practical decisions, for the result of determining both the desirable and undesirable consequences of applying certain means to a given end, as well as the necessary means to do so, may very well compel individual agents to revise their ultimate value axioms in the most fundamental of ways. The political agents may discover that there are no means available to achieve the political end – even if the end is consistent with the agents' highest values. Or the means may simply conflict with values held equally dear. Or even if the consequences of pursuing the end using political means – for example, power backed by force – are consistent with one's ultimate end, the subsidiary consequences may undermine its achievement or simply be too costly to other values held to be equally significant (GAW, 149–50; Weber 1949, 53; GAW, 607, 608). Considerations of this kind, Weber argues, impose on potential political agents a kind of dialectical form of deliberation (GAW, 151; Weber 1949, 54). By pursuing their ultimate ends through politics, agents may discover logical or factual consequences resulting from the use of political means that are inconsistent with the political commitments that they originally derived from their highest values. The agents may be then be compelled to revise their subsidiary goals or reformulate their ultimate goals, or abandon them entirely for new ones. But having revised their original position in any number of these ways, the agents must then subject their new political commitments to similar social-scientific clarification until they finds a satisfactory stopping point (GAW, 510–11; Weber 1949, 12).

Where this stopping point is to be found rests entirely with the agent (GAW, 53; Weber 1949, 23; GAW, 151; Weber 1949, 53). However, there is a clear implication in this account (though not logically entailed by it) that the dialectical movement of social-scientific clarification between ultimate values, subsidiary goals, political means, and foreseeable consequences and back to the choice of ultimate values will compel an agent to become conscious of the political limits on the realization of his or her political commitments. Thus ideal political commitments typically collide with 'developmental tendencies' (GAW, 53; Weber 1949, 23), such as the irreversibility of the expropriation of political means by the state and the modern bureaucratic political party, once politics becomes an autonomous business; the tendency for modern parliamentary politics to take either the form of leaderless democracy with competing party machines, or parties led by charismatic politicians; the necessity that both plebiscitary leaders and revolutionary leaders can be successful only if they demand blind obedience from their following, to name just a few (Weber 1994, 315, 339, 350–1, 357).[12] Weber rarely speaks of social-scientific clarification as opening up possibilities to realize political commitments that had seemed to be mere ideals. Indeed, one might even want to say that part of the authority of social science in clarifying political action, for Weber, rests on the fact that it chastens political expectations of the partisan – though, again, nothing about this argument requires it need do so.[13]

Clearly, in order for this circle of scientific clarification to occur, political sociology must at once provide an impartial account of the durable features of politics, the particular constellation of political structures in our historical moment, the logics impinging upon political action at the moment of political decision, and the roles available for individuals and collectivities seeking to engage in political action. And from this account, it must enable us to predict political outcomes with a high level of probability.

How can Weber claim for sociology such a high level of impartiality for the development of political structures and for prognostication? We have already seen that the ideal-type is not to be found in reality but merely gives us an entry into the causally intertwined reality of which we perceive only a minute part. We have also seen that the concepts used in the ideal-type constitute, as Weber said, a provisional 'utopia' made up of qualities of a thing but not identical with it. To understand this paradox, I now want to focus on the ways Weber uses the ideal-type to forge a notion of impartial political advice out of subjectively interpreted social relations.[14]

The Ideal-Type and Impartiality

We saw earlier that the ideal-type is a construct of the unique features of a socially significant, subjectively meaningful conduct. It is only in the backdrop of cultural values that social phenomena that are captured by the ideal-type are intelligible to us. And we select the distinctive features of a phenomenon – the state, political party, bureaucracy, or legitimate authority, the types of legitimate authority, the types of political party in different countries or under different developmental histories – from the vantage point of our fundamental practical values: the values that define our choice of life conduct within a constellation of cultural values. So for Weber the origin of the ideal-type seems doubly rooted in subjective interpretation: first, we find social phenomena intelligible only by dint of cultural values that we do not choose; and second, we understand them only in light of the stance we take to those cultural values. Thus any ideal-type construct or set of constructs used to understand a particular course of social action provides merely a perspective on an already culturally constituted object.

As we saw, Weber is able to claim that such subjectively constructed types can provide impartial understandings of world views, social forms, and streams of conduct by arguing that all rational people would agree with the process of the construction of the ideal-type, the concept of human action informing that construction, and the hypothetical reasoning behind the use of these types to predict social and political outcomes. Specifically, the ideal-type synthesizes a variety of constellations of activity into a consistent whole; therefore, although the ideal-type itself may not be found in empirical reality, it creates a coherent account of empirical conduct and its consequences (Weber 1978, 20–1).[15] Furthermore, the ideal-type is constructed with two features of human action in mind: it assumes that we act because the actions taken are valuable for their own sake (traditional or value-rational action) or because they are means to other ends (purposively rational action). Typologies of ideal-types can therefore be constructed in which some ideal-types view constellations of social activity as arising from the choice of means to given ends, and others are constructed as deviations from pure purposive (means-ends) reason. For example, Weber constructs an ideal-type of the state and of political association purely in terms of the means distinctive of them: legitimate domination backed by force. This construct enables him to examine how political actors motivated by different kinds of intrinsic values might fare in seeking to realize their ends using political means. Such typologies based on purposive rationality and its deviations can then be compared to a more complex empirical reality (GAW, 533; Weber 1949, 41; ES, 21). New ideal-types can then be used to account for significant deflections from the streams of conduct and their outcomes described by the original types. Types of this kind are recognizable to all rational persons because they embody purposive reason oriented toward means and deviations from such motives, which include all of the non-instrumental motives for social conduct. Finally, Weber can claim impartiality for his ideal-typical constructs for the paradoxical reason that they are purely hypothetical accounts (*Deutungs-Hypothesen*) of constellations of social action. That is, by showing how one ideal-type gives way to another, we can make general law-like statements of cause and effect from antecedent conditions. But these generalizations are probable rather than invariant, for they are constructed from unrealistic premises and designate possible – not empirically certain – outcomes of social action. Weber speaks of them as 'fictions' that are 'heuristically' useful 'in the interpretation of concrete events' (GAW, 529, 537, 130–1). They thus enable us to predict certain outcomes, given a particular constellation of historical or cultural features, on the assumption that empirical sequences of activity either approximate the course of events predicted by the ideal-type or are possible in light of the expectations the ideal-type sets before us (Brunn 1972, 235, 228, 223; Burger 1987, 165). Given, for example, the historical development of the modern political party, the modern state, and the modern professional politician we can expect that ordinary citizens will have great difficulties in dictating ends to the state. Depending on how we see the interlocking causal effects of the ideal-types of the party, state, and professional politician, we can say we have captured a significant tendency in modern politics. But we also know that there are counter-examples to this probabilistic judgment. Nonetheless, they do not invalidate the objectivity of this ideal-typical prognostication. They may simply qualify its reach or call forth a new set of ideal-types to explain the counter-tendency. In this sense, ideal-types may provide a set of counterfactual judgments of political possibility that may be at once objective, relative to the conditions in which they ideally apply, yet highly partial, relative both to the values informing their construction and to the empirical reality of subjectively motivated conduct to which they refer. In sum, through transparency in the concept construction of ideal-types, their alignment with the reasoning employed in methodically deploying means to chosen or imposed ends, and above all, by creating hypothetical constructs relating types to each other, Weber is able to provide apparently impartial – indeed he claims non-partisan – political advice on how various political commitments will fare once we decide to realize them through political action.

However, there is a danger in the deployment of hypothetical ideal-type constructs for the purpose of political prediction and practical clarification. Precisely because ideal-types forge unique historical and cultural circumstances into a consistent representation and combine them with general (purposively rational) features of human action, one is tempted to forget that the generalizations drawn from them are *only* hypothetical judgments regarding consequents, factual states, and antecedents. Once this temptation takes hold, one expands the reach of ideal-type constructs until one claims they provide general definitions and general laws of social and political action that are coextensive with empirical reality.[16] Weber is not immune to this temptation. Indeed, time and again he transforms a series of self-acknowledged partial hypothetical generalizations about the stream and outcome of unique social and political actions into general laws of society or politics. Hence his famous remark from the 'Objectivity' essay that a successful analysis of the internal logic of an ideal and 'the practical consequences' of pursuing it must be valid for a Chinese, that is, someone remote from our culture (GAW, 155; Weber, 1949, 59). So, for example, when he applies these generalizations to point out the ironies and paradoxes of political action within the modern 'business' of politics, for which a responsible political actor is accountable, he often treats them as if they were exhaustive of the possibilities for achieving political ends.

The question that arises then is why Weber can so easily forget the hypothetical, the as-if nature of his political sociological advice. I would like to argue that there are at least three reasons rooted paradoxically in the very fact that his ideal-types capture the unique dynamics of politics from multiple perspectives (*Gesichtspünkte*) rather than provide determinate causal laws. (Each of these reasons, as we shall see in a moment, will become the basis for Mannheim's criticism of Weber's notion of political clarification.) First, in his desire to claim impartiality for his political sociological types, Weber stops short of drawing out the full implications of his claim that these types are constructed from the viewpoint of our practical values and produce generalizations that are hypothetical conditionals. Judgments about possible outcomes of some action or series of actions are subjunctive or hypothetical conditionals and as such are not verifiable, although they are perfectly intelligible. Their typical form is, 'If p, then q,' where p is not a fact or an event but a condition. A typical statement of this sort is the following: if a political actor is not willing to use power backed by force, she or he will not achieve any fundamental goals in politics. Now, many such hypothetical conditional judgments can be replaced by general or particular causal statements. But frequently they are used in contexts where they cannot be, and more importantly, where we would not want them to be reduced in this way.[17] Historical, legal, and political judgments are of this kind. Such judgments are not ultimately decidable by reference to any general or specific causal law. In such cases, we seek plausible or reasonable judgments of possibility in light of the background conditions, rather than true or false ones. Weber's claim to provide a scientific clarification of political commitments by revealing possible outcomes in light of certain necessary means are precisely 'judgments' that cannot be reduced to general causal statements, but instead are plausible inferences from general tendencies (for example, the tendency for policies under modern conditions of formal legality to be carried out through administration that is based on formal hierarchal discipline) and certain background conditions (that the political community is characterized by its right to carry out its commands with the sanction of force). Some of these judgments have a close affinity to empirical statements of causality; others are strong hunches about what might happen in light of similar situations. Curiously, Weber himself wrote one of the major defences of the need for such counterfactual judgments in historical interpretation in his 'Critique of Eduard Meyer' (GAW, 266–90; Weber 1949, 164–88). Here he defended the need for constructing objective possibilities in light of background conditions that themselves rest on interpretation. As well, he argued that we need to exercise 'judgment' in imputing relevant causes to a phenomenon; that is, historical explanations require adequacy in 'causal imputation,' but such adequacy rests on a 'judgment' about the likelihood that a certain stream of events or structure could branch off from the ones under consideration. And yet, Weber's defence of the authority of sociology to provide a scientific clarification of partisan positions rests on a claim to provide judgments that can be reduced to causal generalizations that will serve as a reliable basis for us to determine the consequences of using political means to achieve our goals. Provisional judgments of probability slip into determinate claims about law-like causality.

We now come to the second reason that Weber was tempted to abandon the provisional nature of his ideal-type constructs in order to claim to provide impartial political advice. And this reason rests on his belief that although one could not rank values in social science, one could rank relevant causal sequences from a viewpoint outside of them. To be sure, Weber himself argued that the number of causes that have influenced any event are infinite, and therefore we can select only the relevant causes (and by the same token, the relevant consequences of any set of actions) according to the value concepts we bring to our inquiry (GAW, 177–8; Weber 1949, 178). Now, since these value concepts also form our political commitments in light of which we set political goals, it follows that different actors with different political beliefs would select different causal sequences in calculating the necessary means to a given end and the necessary consequences that would follow from realizing or trying to realize that end. To be sure, all of these actors may agree on certain general features of politics – for example, the need to acquire power – though they might disagree on the means that constitute power or even whether power is only a means and not a form of collective activity. In any case, in deliberating on the possible outcomes of political action, the socialist, the nationalist, the Realpolitiker, and the liberal will select a different range of causal influences and significant outcomes as relevant to making political judgments. Political actors holding each of these positions could obviously gain a certain systematic understanding of their political beliefs and the political conduct that follows from them by constructing their judgments using Weber's ideal-typical approach to making political predictions. However, given the different relevant causal sequences for each political belief, each political belief would construct the relation between values, the relevant means, and the range of relevant consequences differently as well. And each would see the range of possible actions differently: the conservative might see all breaks with custom to be self-defeating, while the socialist might see precisely such a break as necessary as well as possible in order to bring the direction of society under the control of its own members. The effect of such hypothetical constructs on the agent's commitments would also be different, for actors with different commitments would disagree about which courses of political action are self-defeating and which are not. Thus, it would seem that the very features of the ideal-type that lend it a certain impartiality – its transparency, its reliance on purposive reason, and its hypothetical rather than empirical nature – clarify the dynamic conditions for choosing one's political goals and the means of attaining them differently for different political beliefs. This means that ideal-typical clarification for partisan actors should provide a contested set of interpretations of political possibility, and it is the constellation of these different belief-driven accounts of the relation between long-run developments and the occasions for the exercise of political will that gives us a clue into how our own partisan political commitments might fare. Weber assumes that the construction of these sequences through the ideal-type will provide us with a synoptic view of the conditions for success and failure of competing prognostications, but it is unclear where such a viewpoint comes from.

We come now to our last reason: Weber does not account for the potential effect that the ideal-typical account will have on the very dynamic political context it constructs, were it to be taken up by the political participants it seeks to clarify. The advice it provides should explain whether or to what degree its translation into action would not alter just the long-run and contingent features of a situation, but also the background conditions and the law-like tendencies from which the particular advice is drawn. As we said, Weber wagers that such political-sociological advice would chasten political actors who see politics only from the viewpoint of their partisan commitments. But seen as emerging from the confrontation of different perspectives on political possibility – that is, from the expositioin of counterfactual judgments based on different assessments of antecedent conditions – such clarification may just as easily intensify conflict. Or it may teach political quiescence born of a belief that all outcomes are predetermined by forces beyond our control. In any case, Weber tries to avoid completing the circle that is at the foundation of his project of deploying hypothetical ideal-type constructs to provide political advice. That is, he seeks to escape the fact that the partisan political commitments of the scholar-theorist inform the construction of the sociological context constituting political reality from which the generalizations are derived and against which political commitments are tested. Weber makes us aware of the self-reflexivity built into his sociological notion of political advice only to try to transcend it by claiming an impartiality for his 'science' that his own account of the ideal-type serves to undermine.

In sum, if we accept Weber's account of the ideal-type, we find that it is far more partial than he claims it to be, and, as a consequence, the authority of his scientific claim to provide political education and self-clarification – first stated in the 'Objectivity' essay – turns out to be more partial as well. We might even want to say that its constructs provide not a political sociology that judges political convictions above the partisan fray, but rather a political sociology of one of the points of view within the fray itself. That is, the distance between scientific political clarification and partisanship becomes a matter of degree rather than kind. And there is good reason for this convergence, for in trying to find an equilibrium between distanced sociological clarification and engaged partisan attachment, Weber has come upon a problem that is fundamentally irresolvable. When we use sociological constructs to make sense of the possibilities for ordinary political actors, parties, states, or social movements to achieve their aims in light of tendencies at work that may shape political outcomes in a particular political situation, we at once claim a comprehensive view of the political field not perceived by the lay political actors; and yet our political sociological account is not completely distinct from the accounts that the actors themselves give about their ultimate goals and possible dynamics favouring or disadvantaging them. We oscillate, as it were, between distance and engagement. One can draw a parallel here with Weber's explicit argument throughout the 'Objectivity' essay that there always will remain a gulf, 'an unbridgeable gap' between our ideal-typical constructs and the social or historical practices they are meant to elucidate (GAW, 161; Weber, 1949, 63), and his further claim that social-scientific practice depends on it. Similarly, the separation between a distanced sociological clarification of political standpoints based on ideal-typical constructs and the politics that flows from realizing these positions in day-to-day practice is the condition for a constant readjustment of both.

Curiously, it is precisely the disjuncture between Weber's claim to provide an 'objective,' or better yet, 'impartial' account of political advice and the subjective and utopian features of his ideal-typical sociology that sets an agenda for a new kind of sociologically informed political judgment. It also stimulated other theorists to find a more coherent relation between sociology and political action.

Karl Mannheim and the Attempt to Find a Self-reflexive Political Science

At this point, I would like to discuss a theorist who made these paradoxes of impartial sociological advice and political action central to his theory: Karl Mannheim. In *Ideology and Utopia* Mannheim explicitly acknowledges Weber as the starting point – and model – for providing sociological political advice (Mannheim 1936; 1985).[18] But Mannheim puts the subjectivity of all ideal-typical constructs at the centre of his notion of political science. His answer to Weber's dilemma is his famous and controversial notion of political sociology as synthesis, which is to be a political science that is not merely a party science but a science of the whole political field of competing ideas. In seeking a synthesis of competing ideologies conceived as ideal-types, Mannheim claims that 'political sociology as the science of the coming in to being of the whole political field [*des gesamten politisches Feldes*] attains the stage of its actualization' (IuU, 130, 149; IU, 149, 171). This approach embraces rather than seeks to overcome the perspectival and partisan nature of our accounts of social and political 'reality' (IuU, 136; IU, 156). It also seeks to incorporate the testing of partisan positions for their ideological and utopian features against a dynamic historical and social reality. Like the party-centred approach to political science, this one also argues that we cannot find an impartial sociological account against which to test the feasibility of political projects. Political sociology as synthesis is aware that all attempts to assess what is possible in a given political situation are themselves informed by a partisan standpoint. But a synthetic political science does not see this limitation as a defect, because it assumes that all ideologies know something about the barriers and dynamic forces impinging on the realization of their ultimate aims. That is, all ideologies contain a sociology of their own realization and an evaluation of their opponents' capacity to thwart their aims. Thus Mannheim sees any political sociological evaluation of opposing partisan political positions as emerging directly out of the prudential sociological knowledge advanced by the contending political parties that constitute a particular historical political situation.

This new political science seeks to integrate the differing partisan positions – or more accurately, the differing political sociologies of each party – into a comprehensive view of the politics of a particular historical moment as it is dynamically constituted by the process of political conflict and routinization. It cobbles together this overview not by imposing a master political sociology but by using the sociology of knowledge to provide something like a phenomenology of politics at two levels. First, it seeks to understand the social origins of party positions. Second, it uses the particular political sociology of each of the positions themselves to fill in the blindness of each party to the insights of the opposing party into the conditions of political possibility. Because the conjuncture of modern politics is unique, this second move is something more than a mere bricolage, a fitting of bits and pieces from contending ideologies: the very origins of a sociology of knowledge – an increasing ability of all partisan positions to explain both the origin of their own concepts of thought and action and those of their opponents – creates an overlapping insight among the typical partisan positions of modernity. Thus the incommensurability of differing styles of thought, of the logic and concepts in each partisan position, is offset by their common attempt to explain their opponent's logic and concepts from within their own sociology.

The emblematic example for Mannheim is the modern conjuncture of political conflict among fundamental political world views consisting of historical conservatism, liberalism, and socialism. Bureaucratic conservatism and fascism represent the limiting cases on opposite ends of the continuum – pure formal rules on the one side, pure irrational will on the other. Without at this point going into Mannheim's revealing discussion of each of these positions, I would like briefly to discuss the way Mannheim demonstrates the intertwining of these ideologies in their assessments of the relation of political will to routine. Historical conservatism emphasizes the irrational moment of political will through its emphasis on historical prudence while finding the routine in the durability of custom and the organic development of society. Liberalism seeks a rational framework to reconcile all competing interests while extirpating all irrationality from politics. Marxism, by contrast, incorporates from the conservatives the organic notion of society as historically evolving but sees a logic of class conflict behind it, which it employs against liberalism in order to show the irrationality behind its claims to use reason to solve all conflicting claims (IuU, 102–32; IU, 117–46). Each of these positions finds politics somewhere else. But when we put their accounts of politics together, we get a comprehensive sense of the different possible loci of political action – in traditional prudence, in parliamentary discussion, in class conflict and revolution – and the different limitations on political action – in custom, in procedure and partial interest, and in the development of class structure and productive means (IuU, 130; IU, 150).

Political science as synthesis, then, makes explicit this incorporation of one's opponents into one's own world view and attached political standpoint and uses each partisan sociology to reveal features of the dynamics at work in the political field as a whole. Or to put it differently, by explaining the distortions of each contending position produced by social location, generation, and class and group affiliation, a political science can isolate an undistorted political understanding of the dynamics that inhibits or enables the exercise of political will and, much like Weber's ideal-types, create a temporary picture of political reality. From this description made up of political sociological insights from differing parties one can test individual positions against what is now a comprehensive construction of the dynamics impinging upon the exercise of political will.

In this way, Mannheim tries to find an equivalent to Weber's impartial sociological advice in a synthesis of contending world views in the political field. But Mannheim was aware that this attempt to incorporate the subjectivity of all sociologically informed political advice into a comprehensive view of the political field may itself react back on the situation being described. This reaction could take two directions. It could lead to a temporary reconciliation of conflicting partisan ideologies and greater perspicacity of the limits of one's own political world view – Mannheim hoped this would be the result, an aim analogous to Weber's dialectical advice. Or it could make the partisan political actors more aware of the points of conflict among them and give them an edge over their opponents. The result would be a sharpening of conflict.

This latter point was best captured by Antonio Gramsci – though unaware of Mannheim – when he argued that only by projecting a political will into a political situation can we assess the potential forces resisting our will and the possibility of organizing ourselves to realize it (Gramsci 1971, 123–205). Foresight – as Gramsci and his inspiration, Machiavelli, understood – cannot be attained by gaining a synoptic view of the political field but only by adopting the standpoint of a political agent within the situation being analysed. In this case, the durable element was not the struggle of political ideologies, each with its own account of the relation of political will and routine and long-range historical development, as Mannheim had argued, but rather the struggle of parties for hegemony over state, civil society, and economy. Once again, the attempt to find something akin to the impartial standpoint in using sociology to provide political advice leads us back to its implication in the struggle of partisan political wills. And each attempt to give a context for that struggle is implicated in the very political circumstances one is trying to account for. It is this irresolvable fact about sociological-political knowledge that Weber captures precisely in the way he mobilizes the ideal-type to aid in practical political advice, even though he seeks at times to transcend it. And it is this irresolvable fact that Mannheim puts front and centre in the hope that partisan reconciliation might follow, while aware that such reconciliation would at best be temporary.

Conclusion: Self-reflexivity and Impartial Political Advice

In closing I would like to draw upon Weber and Mannheim to address some of the features of a sociologically informed political judgment that takes the reflexive relation between the partisan principles being tested and the generalizations that provide the test. We have seen that from his 'Objectivity' article through his last lecture, 'Science as a Vocation,' Weber seeks to give an impartial 'scientific' clarification of the social and political dynamics constraining or enabling the realization of partisan commitments. We have also seen that such a practical clarification uses sociology to clarify for all the contending political partisans in a particular historical situation the prospects for success and the coherence of their commitments. Weber recognizes that sociologically informed political theories are subjectively constructed and irrevocably self-reflexive, but seeks to arrest the logic of his discovery. Mannheim presses this self-reflexivity to its logical conclusion, demonstrating that social science can inform political practice only by making explicit the mutual dependence of political ideas and the subjectively constructed sociological dynamics that describe the terrain in which these ideas are fought out. In short, Mannheim reveals that a sociologically informed political theory and political science are inexorably self-reflexive – and no worse for that.

To understand the sense in which this is so, I would like to make a distinction between two kinds of self-reflexivity in sociologically informed political theories. First, a theory can be self-reflexive in the sense that the political commitments of the theorist inform the construction of the sociological context constituting political reality from which the generalizations are derived and against which political commitments are tested. For example, my construction of the relations of state, power, and political parties to understand a political situation and my generalizations about political possibility that flow from these constructs are themselves constructed from one of the partisan perspectives that I am testing. Hence I am testing other political commitments using a construct derived from my own. Second, and this point has becomes something of a truism, sociologically informed theories of political possibility do not necessarily, but can, effect the very political reality whose general direction they are trying to understand. Thus my one-sided construct, which I am using both to advance my political commitments and test the possible realization of other political commitments, may create a new relation among the actors and structures I am trying to understand. It may educate actors and thus alter their concepts of what is possible, or it may lead them in directions that reveal forces unforeseen in my theory (Taylor 1985, 91–115). Now precisely because sociologically informed political theories are subject to the first kind of self-reflexivity, they often have a difficult time gauging whether or not they will be reflexive in the second sense. And even if they succeed in informing the deliberations of political actors, it becomes difficult to assess whether they will alter political situations in a productive or in a self-defeating manner. This means a sociologically informed political prudence of the kind Weber aimed to provide will at best alter the situations and the actors in unforeseen ways, possibly negating the political education to practical feasibility that it hopes to provide.

Thus, if political-sociological constructs are as one-sided as Weber demonstrates them to be, they will not be able to reliably predict their effects on the practical world should actors take them up as a guide to politics. The second kind of self-reflexivity means, as Mannheim revealed, that a sociologically informed political prudence has the potentiality of altering the situations and the actors in unforeseen ways, negating the political education to practical feasibility that our sociological constructs hope to provide. In this we reach the limits of political-sociological advice. And in discovering whether our principles and commitments are coherently connected to the political means that we deem necessary for their realization and the possible consequences these means may unleash, we have to rely on the projection of political will into the situation at hand. That is, at this point the discovery of what is politically possible and feasible depends on the exercise of political will itself. We are thus caught in the irresolvable tension – first articulated in Weber's 'Objectivity' essay – between distance and engagement: we construct our understanding of the social and political field from the vantage points of our own partisan interests and locations, and yet we seek a synoptic overview of the field separate from them. As Weber understood, despite his desire at times to resolve this tension in favour of the latter, we have to decide for ourselves the point at which these two forms of understanding are to inform both social-scientific and political practice. No methodology can help us here.

NOTES

1 The German version of Weber's methodological essays including the 'Objectivity' essay are collected in Weber (1982). I will refer to this collection as GAW.
2 One exception is Brunn (1972). Also see John Gunnell, 'The Paradox of Social Science,' in this volume.

3 I would argue that in the later work the distinction between generic and genetic concepts becomes rather murky. For example, the state as monopoly of legitimate violence over a territory is a historical genetic concept only by distinction from kinship systems that enforced discipline and punishment without a legitimate institution for that purpose. However, treated by itself, it tends to become a generic concept applicable to all states, whatever the historical context. That is, in *Economy and Society* seemingly generic concepts become genetic only in their contrasting concepts and ultimately in their application.

4 In the 'Rebuttal of the Critique of the "Spirit" of Capitalism,' Weber draws a distinction between ideal-types that are abstracted so as to emphasize features that are similar between apparently different social relations, and ideal-types that emphasize sharp distinctions in order to convey the unique qualities of social relations. While the former seems in danger of becoming the kind of generic concept that Weber rejects, one needs to remember that even concepts that draw together similarities, for example 'capitalism,' still point to unique historical features of the social relations they seek to understand. What defines both kinds of concepts as genetic ideal types is that they do not claim to provide a universal account of the phenomenon they describe (Weber 2002, 262)

5 I rely here on Breiner (2005) for my argument on Weber's use of the ideal-type.

6 It should be emphasized here that by utopia Weber does not mean a non-existent but desired model of society. Rather, the concept refers to the fact that the ideal-type is a perfect and coherent version of a social relation, concept of action, or world view that does not exist in that form in historical or social reality. It serves as a heuristic device to clarify that reality.

7 Viewed under this notion of constructed possibility we may view the famous statement at the end of *The Protestant Ethic* to the effect that 'it cannot, of course, be our purpose to replace a one-sided "materialist" causal interpretation of culture and history with an equally one-sided spiritual one. *Both are equally possible* [Weber's emphasis]' as expressing something beyond the debate over historical materialism. Weber is here saying that his thesis represents one possible construction of how rational capitalism could have occurred, and he emphasizes the '*preliminary*' nature of his inquiry (Weber 2002, 122). The materialist account is also a possible but preliminary approach, awaiting modification of the kind Weber provides.

8 Richard Ashcraft (1987, 307–14) takes Weber to task for claiming that there is no coherent historical reality outside of ideal-typical constructs and that ideal-types can be tested against historical reality. He suggests that Weber cannot defend his own ontological assumptions that reality is a vast sea

of particulars, and therefore we have just as good grounds for positing a brute set of historical facts in which to contextualize ideas as accepting Weber's absorption of reality into ideal-types. Without claiming that Weber was particularly interested in constructing a consistent ontology – he was not – one can respond that Weber was simply invoking the claim that what we call facts are already meaningful only under concepts and that ideal types as heuristic means of getting at these 'facts' are the best tool at our disposal for understanding relations about this conceptually constituted reality.

9 English version of 'Science as a Vocation' (Lassman et al. 1989) (hereafter SV).

10 It is also seldom recognized that Weber insists on his famous fact–value distinction primarily on moral and only secondarily on epistemological grounds. For example, he speaks of preserving 'the specific dignity' of both kinds of claims and the need to maintain this distinction to preserve 'intellectual integrity' (intellektule Rechtsschaffenheit) (GAW, 501, 502, 601–2). It is therefore not surprising that he would argue for separating science from political partisanship on the basis of moral duty as well.

11 One of the few works outside of the generation following Weber to appreciate this prudential aspect of Weber's methodology is the much neglected book of W.G. Runciman, *Social Science and Political Theory* (1965). Runciman makes the case that political arguments over the most fundamental ends of political thought can often be clarified and even settled by an appeal to sociological generalizations, for such 'sociological evidence,' broadly conceived, forces political agents to account for the sociological tendencies that would enable, frustrate, or redirect the achievement of their political goals. While he argues that such sociological clarification cannot compel us to support or abandon a fundamental political goal, it can require us to account for why we still adhere to a goal if its realization proves self-defeating or if the cost of achieving it is very high. By the same token, it can compel us to admit the validity of achieving a political end whose pursuit we have rejected because we falsely believed its realization was not feasible. Runciman explicitly finds the model for his account of sociology as aiding political theory in the work of Max Weber. The only problem with Runciman's use of Weber for this purpose is that he does not account for the construction of the sociological generalizations that are deployed for political clarification. Weber is all too aware of the reflexive nature of his account and seeks in his notion of 'objectivity' to escape it.

12 Weber's deployment of these developmental tendencies to test political arguments is discussed in Breiner (1996, 182–92).

13 There is a rhetorical reason, however, why Weber would insist on this:

were the typical consequence of such clarification a discovery process to help partisans realize their goals – that is, revealing the developmental tendencies and situations beneficial to one side or another – the distance between sociological clarification and partisan political judgment would narrow quite dramatically.

14 I cannot discuss the way the ideal-type aids Weber in combining explanation with understanding here. For a discussion of the uses of the ideal-type to solve the problems of explanatory understanding, see Burger (1987), Hekman (1983), and Oakes (1988). Interestingly, none of these works sees Weber's notion of practical clarification and his account of understanding and explanation as intertwined.

15 Hereafter called ES.

16 This point has been well made by Burger (1987, 165, 178) and Brunn (1972, 235). Brunn puts the problem nicely: 'Naturally the prognostic function of the ideal-type is of a *hypothetical* nature ... since the ideal type is by definition *unreal*: to the extent that conditions isolated in the type are met with in real life, we may expect real behaviour to conform more closely to the type. Since a great many conditions of behaviour *other* than those included in the type may be of importance to the actual chain of events, any such prognosis is *partial*. Now the danger of the ideal type ... is its tendency to make one forget this hypothetical restriction' (235). For a defence of Weber's claim to achieve impartiality through such 'technical criticism' see Ciaffa (1998, 114–25). Ciaffa argues that Weber's account is coherent once we agree that value judgments have a cognitive status. He does not, however, take up the subjectivity of the technical side of Weber's account.

17 In developing this criticism I have relied heavily on Hampshire (1971), Goodman (1983, 3–27), and Hawthorne (1991). Goodman points out that in counterfactual conditional statements, not just antecedent conditions require prior hypothetical judgments but also the selection of the consequents. Hawthorne adds to this criticism by arguing that as the number of causes of a social and historical occurrence expand, so do the number of alternative possibilities (10, 13, 157–8).

18 Since the German version and the English version of *Ideology and Utopia* differ markedly in style and vocabulary, I have often made my own translation of quoted passages. The German original tends to reflect more clearly the tradition of self-reflexivity of German sociology as well as the intense political debate over the relation between political theory and political practice taking place at the time of the writing. The English translation, in part directed by Mannheim, tends to downplay the political

passions in this work and instead seeks to establish the authority of the sociology of knowledge as method of inquiry. See Kettler and Meja (1995, 213–16) on discrepancies in the two translations. The German edition will be cited as IuU, the English translation as IU.

REFERENCES

Ashcraft, Richard. 1987. 'German Historicism and the History of Political Theory.' *History of Political Thought* 8, no. 2 (Summer): 289–324.
Breiner, Peter. 1996. *Max Weber and Democratic Politics*. Ithaca: Cornell University Press.
– 2005. 'Weber's *The Protestant Ethic* as Hypothetical Narrative of Original Accumulation.' *Journal of Classical Sociology* 5:11–30.
Brecht, Arnold. 1959. *Political Theory*. Princeton: Princeton University Press.
Brunn, H.H. 1972. *Science, Values and Politics in Max Weber's Methodology*. Copenhagen: Munksgaard.
Burger, Thomas. 1987. *Max Weber's Theory of Concept Formation*. 2nd ed. Durham: Duke University Press.
Ciaffa, Jay. 1998. *Max Weber and the Problems of Value-Free Social Science*. Lewisburg: Bucknell University Press.
Freeden, Michael. 1996. *Ideologies and Political Theory*. Oxford: Oxford University Press.
Goodman, Nelson. 1983. 'The Problem of Counterfactual Conditionals.' In *Fact, Fiction and Forecast*. Cambridge: Harvard University Press.
Gramsci, Antonio. 1971. 'The Modern Prince.' In *Selections from the Prison Notebooks*, edited by Q. Hoare and G.N. Smith. New York: International Publishers.
Gunnell, John G. 1993. *The Descent of Political Theory: An American Vocation*. Chicago: University of Chicago Press.
Hampshire, Stuart. 1971. 'Subjective Conditionals.' In *Freedom of the Mind*. Princeton: Princeton University Press.
Hawthorne, Geoffrey. 1991. *Plausible Worlds*. Cambridge: Cambridge University Press.
Hekman, Susan. 1983. *Weber, the Ideal Type and Contemporary Theory*. Notre Dame: University of Notre Dame Press.
Kettler, David, and Volker Meja. 1995. *Karl Mannheim and the Crises of Liberalism*. New Brunswick, NJ: Transaction.
Lassman, Peter, Irving Velody, and Hermino Martins, eds. 1989. *Max Weber's 'Science as a Vocation.'* London: Unwin Hyman.

Mannheim, Karl. 1936. *Ideology and Utopia*. Translated by L. Wirth and E. Shils. New York: Harcourt, Brace, and World.
– 1985. *Ideologie und Utopie*. 7th ed. Frankfurt a. M.: Vittoria Klostermann.
Oakes, Guy. 1988. *Weber and Rickert*. Cambridge, MA: MIT Press.
Runciman, W.G. 1965. *Social Science and Political Theory*. 2nd ed. Cambridge: Cambridge University Press.
Schmitt, Carl. 1996. *The Concept of the Political*. Translated by George Schwab. Chicago: University of Chicago Press.
Taylor, Charles. 1985. 'Social Theory as Practice.' In *Philosophy and the Human Sciences*. Cambridge: Cambridge University Press.
Weber, Max. 1949. '"Objectivity" in Social Science and Social Policy.' In *The Methodology of the Social Sciences*, edited by E. Shils and H. Finch. New York: Free Press.
– 1978. *Economy and Society*. Edited by G. Roth and C. Wittich. 2 vols. Berkeley: University of California Press.
– 1982. *Gesammelte Aufsätze zur Wissenschaftslehre*. Edited by J. Winckelmann. 5th ed. Tübingen: J.C.B. Mohr (Paul Siebeck).
– 1994. 'The Profession and Vocation of Politics.' In *Political Writings*, edited by P. Lassman and R. Speirs. Cambridge: Cambridge University Press.
– 2002. *The Protestant Ethic and the 'Spirit' of Capitalism and Other Writings*. Translated by P. Baehr and G.C. Wells. New York: Penguin.

4 Did Weber Practise the Objectivity He Preached?

MARIO BUNGE

To the memory of Robert K. Merton, great scientist, humanist, and friend

We are commemorating the first centenary of Weber's manifesto on objectivity in social studies (Weber 1988i).* This is a suitable occasion to celebrate because, as the dean of American philosophy put it recently, 'Objectivity has fallen on hard times. Among some because of a failure to understand its linkage to rationality. Among others, who understand this linkage only too well, because rationality itself is an object of repugnance' (Rescher 1997, 1). Indeed, objectivity calls for impersonal reason, and reason happens to be the *bête noire* of the New Age and postmodernism.

The central thesis of Weber's paper was that the cultural sciences, though radically different from the natural ones, have this in common with them: they seek objective truths, abstain from making value judgments, and avoid partisanship. Those sciences study what there is, instead of proposing what there ought to be. Thus Weber enjoined objectivity (or realism), value neutrality, and impartiality – three different concepts that he conflated.

My aims in this paper are (a) to clarify Weber's objectivity thesis, (b) to identify the uneasy place of objectivity in the neo-Kantian subjectivist credo that Weber professed, (c) to explore the extent to which he practised what he preached, and (d) to find out why Weber believed that objectivity had to be extolled particularly at that time, although it had been practised by all scientists from Thucydides to Durkheim. I

---

* See Editor's Note, p. 132.

will not discuss at length Weber's views on the fact–value gap, the value-neutrality of social science, and the alleged relativity of ethics, because these subjects have been treated at length by other authors (for example, Brecht 1959) as well as by myself (Bunge 1989).

The Ethos of Science: Weber and Merton

Weber started by correctly distinguishing basic social science from social technology (or policy science). Whereas the former is descriptive, the latter is prescriptive. And he added that the former, unlike the latter, must abide by objectivity, value-neutrality, and impartiality. Regrettably, Weber conflated these three categories, although the first one is epistemological, whereas the other two are meta-ethical.

There is no question but that objectivity – that is, respect for facts, regardless of personal interests – is of the essence of factual science, since its aim is to find facts and try to explain them. Whether Weber always attained objectivity will be discussed below. Here we shall discuss only briefly whether it is desirable, or even possible, to avoid value judgments and partisanship in social matters, as Weber claimed in 1904 and again in 1917, when the Great War was still raging (Weber 1988g).

Consider the following value judgments: 'War is the greatest crime,' 'Poverty is bad,' and 'Oppression is unfair.' Are they really subjective and therefore groundless, that is, matters of emotion or taste, as the intuitionists and positivists have been claiming? I submit that those and many other value judgments as well are perfectly objective, and moreover true. Consider: War is wrong because it involves murder, which is obviously bad for its victims and their relatives; poverty is bad because it prevents the poor from enjoying life; oppression is unfair because it creates unjustified privilege at the price of fear and misery; and all three are bad because they are divisive and wasteful.

To hold that social scientists should abstain from making objective value judgments is to restrict the reach of objectivity – or worse, to protect one's hide against witch-hunting. In any event, Weber (1988d, 156) broke his own rule when, in the midst of the 1914–18 carnage, he supported the German government against the criticism of some colleagues, 'because everyone knows that this war ... is necessary for our existence.' Stands such as Weber's on the Great War moved Julien Benda (1975) to write eloquently on the betrayal of the intellectuals at that time.

What is true is that the basic social scientist, unlike the social technologist, is not necessarily qualified to design policies and plans to solve social issues or to resolve social conflicts. Still, the social technologists, bureaucrats, and politicians won't be very effective unless they rely on scientific studies of social issues. For example, an effective plan to contain the coming flu pandemic should rely on epidemiological, demographic, and sociological studies of the propagation mechanisms of infectious diseases.

As for impartiality, contrary to Weber's opinion, it need not conflict with objectivity. As Rescher (1997, 43) states, 'Being objective about determining the facts does not demand being prepared to welcome them as is and refusing to try to change the conditions of things that they represent.' Partisanship is to be avoided only if it interferes with the search for truth, as when the free-trade mantra is sung as the panacea for national development even though the relevant statistics show that it favours only the economically and politically powerful, particularly those nations that practise protectionism at home.

Moreover, partisanship may suggest choosing good research problems. For instance, social scientists who disapprove of extreme economic, political, or cultural inequality are more likely to study income distribution than students who, like Weber, are unmoved by poverty, political marginality, political oppression, or cultural deprivation. In short, partisanship must not be allowed to misrepresent reality, but it may motivate fruitful research. In any event, social scientists do not 'go where the facts take them,' as a positivist would say, if only because any given mass of data is too bulky, unstructured, and confusing to be scientifically tractable without the help of some master ideas. Rather, scientists go where their hypotheses, intuitions, preferences, and ideological biases lead them.

It is instructive to compare Weber's objectivity–value neutrality–impartiality triad with the ethos of science as Merton (1968, 604–15) famously described it in 1942 in relation to its corruption by the Nazi scientists and pseudo-scientists. Merton asserted that the characteristics of basic science are: (a) universalism, because 'objectivity precludes particularism'; (b) epistemic communism, or the free sharing of scientific findings; (c) disinterestedness, that is, a passion for knowledge for its own sake; and (d) organized scepticism, that is, open rational debate about anything worth debating.

Interestingly, Merton did not quote Weber's famous paper in this connection. One reason may be that that Weber's demand for objectivity is only one of Merton's four conditions. An additional reason is that, unlike Weber, Merton goes beyond listing and justifying scientific mores: he also looks at their institutionalization – such as associations, congresses, and specialized journals – as well as the occasional conflicts between those norms and such extra-scientific interests as national loyalty and the wish to secure priority. After all, Merton fathered the scientific sociology of science and was a pioneer in the study of the conflicts among norms (for example, Merton 1976).

What Is New?

Weber's paper in question is usually regarded as an original and strictly methodological piece in support of epistemological and semantic realism, the doctrine encapsulated in the commandment *Thou shalt seek the truth*. However, this thesis was hardly original. In fact, it was what Thucydides and Aristotle had practised in antiquity, Ibn Khaldûn in the Middle Ages, Niccolò Machiavelli in the Renaissance, and Leopold von Ranke in the early nineteenth century. Besides, François Quesnay, Adam Smith, David Ricardo, John Stuart Mill, Alexis de Tocqueville, Karl Marx, Emile Durkheim, and Edward Westermarck had been no less committed to the search for truth even though each of them also had his own axe to grind – as Weber did.

So, where lies the novelty in Weber's paper? I submit that its novelty resides in that it is Weber's earliest and strongest attack upon the materialist view of history, particularly in Marx's economicist version. Note that I write 'attack,' not 'examination' or 'analysis.' The reason is that in the paper in question Weber does not argue convincingly that looking for the subjective 'meaning' (goal) of actions is more objective or important than investigating the so-called material conditions of human existence, such as the way our basic needs are satisfied or frustrated; he does not mention any of the damaging counter-examples to economic determinism, such as natural catastrophes, plagues, demographic explosions and implosions, political upheavals, or the many ideas that 'reflect' no relations of production; and he misses the opportunity to ridicule the fuzziness and fantasies of dialectical metaphysics (for which see Bunge 1981, 1998).

In short, though certainly flawed, Marxism is not dealt the fatal blow that Weber intended. Moreover, it is arguable that, despite all of its flaws, the materialist conception of history is far clearer, more plausible, and deeper than Weber's vague conception, which his star pupil characterized as 'psychologistic-realist subjectivism and individualism' (von Schelting 1934, 420) – hardly a flattery.

The only accusation that sticks is that the vast majority of Weber's Marxist contemporaries did not engage in serious social research. In fact, with the exception of Rosa Luxemburg, they were just popularizers, social critics, and propagandists. However, materialism, once purged from dialectics and radical economism, has been flourishing in anthropology, archaeology, and especially historiography over the past half century (see, for example, Barraclough 1979). In fact, it is practised every time a social researcher starts by asking how the people under study make a living, whereas his idealist counterpart is exclusively interested in the so-called symbolic features – which matter little when the people in question cannot feed or defend themselves.

Why did Weber launch an attack upon Marxism while rightly believing this view to be held at the time only by 'laymen and dilettanti'? And why was his attack far from ideologically neutral? Why did he abstain from attacking any of the numerous colleagues of his who, far from staying above the fray, defended the status quo or at least took it for granted, and many of whom – himself included – would justify the aggression of the central powers one decade later?

I submit that the reason for this tendentiousness on Weber's part is that Marxism had become, at least in words, the official philosophy of the German Social Democratic Party, which at the turn of the nineteenth century was growing at a pace that alarmed Weber. In other words, the Weber who wrote the paper in question was not the universally acclaimed objective and impartial scientist, but a right-of-centre liberal, chauvinist, and pro-imperialist (see Weber 1988d). In fact, this great socio-economist and defender of individual rights expressed no concern for basic human needs and no compassion for the downtrodden, hence no sympathy for the cause of social justice or for the welfare state, or even for human rights – which, incidentally, he called a manifestation of 'rationalist fanaticism' (Weber 1976, 2).

Idealism versus Materialism: Weber versus Durkheim and Marx

To better understand Weber's position, let us compare it with that of Emile Durkheim, his contemporary, rival, and fellow anti-Socialist. Durkheim too embraced and implemented epistemological realism. But, being unencumbered by German idealism, he expounded and defended the realist thesis in far clearer terms. He did this particularly in the preface to the second edition of his famous (and still inspiring) *Règles*. There he famously stated that 'social facts must be treated like things' (1988, 77), and moreover 'as external to individuals' (81). Durkheim's objectivism is thus tied to an ontology that is at the same time tacitly materialist, though not economicist, and explicitly holistic.

Durkheim's ontology is materialist to the extent that, contrary to the neo-Kantianism reigning in his time in France as well as in Germany, he asserts the independent existence and priority of concrete entities, whether physical, biological, or social. And being a materialist of sorts, objectivism or realism came naturally to Durkheim. By contrast, objectivism must have cost Weber quite an effort because his starting point is the individual's unobservable inner life. In fact, according to Weber, an individual's actions result not from external circumstances but from desires, beliefs, and decisions. And these are locked inside the actor's mind: they are not readily observable external facts. Hence they must be guessed. In Weber's hermeneutic jargon, an individual's observable actions must be 'interpreted,' thus, of course giving fantasy ample scope.

The philosophy that Weber preached was the version of neo-Kantianism introduced by Wilhelm Dilthey (1959). He learned it mainly from his friend Heinrich Rickert (see, for example, Oakes 1988). This doctrine, called variously historico-cultural, historicist, hermeneutic, interpretive, or *Verstehen* school, holds two main theses.

One of these principles is the ontological claim that everything social is spiritual (*geistig*) or cultural – whence the social sciences should be called *Geisteswissenschaften* or cultural sciences. These disciplines would be radically different from the natural sciences, not only in subject matter but also in method.

The second thesis of the school is the methodological rule that the way to approach social facts is through *Verstehen,* a slimy word variously translated as 'understanding,' 'comprehension,' or' interpretation.' Weber understood *Verstehen* as guessing the actor's goal or intention. In other words, *Verstehen* is no more and no less than forming a 'theory of mind,' or mind reading, as when a dog tries to guess whether his owner is in a mood for playing (see Premack and Woodruff 1978). Hence it is characteristic of ordinary knowledge rather than scientific research.

Even assuming that some individuals are better than others at *Verstehen,* there is no ground to believe that they will be able to detect and analyse such macro-social facts as inflation, jobs outsourcing, unemployment, protectionism, trade imbalance, war, or imperialism, by just speculating on what is in the minds of the actors in question. Only an objective study of the objective situation can bring about a scientific understanding of such facts. Once the objective situation has been studied, it may be worthwhile to go around and ask people what they feel about it. Hence Weber's advocacy of objectivity is inconsistent with his profession of faith in *Verstehen*.

In any event, the quaint idea of meaning or sense (*Sinn*, *Deutung*) of an action comes from ordinary language, in which one speaks loosely of actions that are meaningful or nonsensical, as when one says that it makes no sense to prevent a war by starting it. And the particular interpretation of 'interpretation,' as revealing the 'meaning' of an action, was an import from theological and literary hermeneutics, since only texts can be literally meaningful or meaningless. Obviously, the expression 'meaning of an action' makes sense only if one posits the absurd thesis that social facts are literally texts or text-like. (For a critical analysis see Bunge 1996, 1998.)

Weber (1988a) expounded both philosophical theses in the first few pages of his main work (Weber 1976), as well as in some of his methodological writings – which are the only ones that philosophers read. A goal of the present paper is to find out the extent to which Weber actually used those principles in his substantive work.

Impact of Idealism on Social Studies

The ontological thesis that everything social is basically spiritual leads straight to methodological individualism and the concomitant disregard for such supra-individual forces as climate changes, plagues, mass migrations, inflation, mass unemployment, tradition, and spontaneous social innovations. The idealist thesis that everything social is spiritual sounds particularly grotesque after two world wars, the Holocaust and other genocides, the Gulag, the Great Depression, the persistence of colonialism, the recurrence of oil and diamond wars, and the recent increases in economic and cultural inequalities among individuals and nations.

The effect of the idealist thesis in question on social studies is largely negative for two reasons. First because, in focusing on the subjective side of life, idealists underrate or even ignore the daily struggle for life of the vast majority of people, as well as the great anonymous natural and social forces, from global warming and epidemics to tradition, inflation, mass migration, and the corrosion of institutions for lack of democratic participation.

The second reason that idealism is bound to have a negative effect on social research is that it trivializes it, in decreeing that every event *must* have been someone's brainchild, even if no evidence for such link is available. Take, for instance, the 'ingenious [*geniale*] connection between the [Indian] caste legitimacy with the karma doctrine.' Weber (1988e, 131) assures us that this is 'absolutely only a product of rational ethical thought, not of any economic "conditions."' That is, that particular socio-theological order 'must have been ready as a mental representation' in some of the ruling Brahmins even before the Aryan invasion of the Indian subcontinent.

According to Weber, there would be no need, then, to try to trace the development of the caste system over the centuries and link it to such demographic, socio-economic, political, and cultural changes as the southward migration, the military conquest, the transformation of nomadic herdsmen and warriors into farmers settling in a foreign country, and the subjection of many of the conquered to the pariah condition. Instead of such painstaking research we are offered an instant explanation: whatever happened *must* have been someone's brainchild, even if we have no clue as to who that someone is, let alone how he got the clout required to implement his ideas.

(Compare this facile and fanciful 'interpretation' of social reality with the materialist view, even in its narrow economicist version. Whatever their flaws, Marx and Engels pioneered the scientific study of the so-called material conditions of people, in particular workers, on the strength of the old principle *Primum vivere, deinde philosophari*. For example, half a century before Weber, Engels [1973] conducted a firsthand investigation of the condition of the Manchester blue-collar workers. And Marx described in *Das Kapital* these conditions on the basis of the reports submitted by H.M.'s industrial inspectors, whose objectivity he praised warmly.)

The epistemological consequence of the idealist thesis is that the social sciences are decreed to be utterly disjointed from the natural ones. This claim was already obsolete even while Dilthey, Rickert, and Weber were writing. Indeed, geography, demography, epidemiology, anthropology, and neurolinguistics, all of which are bio-sociological sciences, had already emerged at that time; and a few other hybrid sciences, notably social psychology and social medicine, were soon to emerge (see Fox 1989). Thus the social/cultural dichotomy is wrong.

Since that dichotomy is wrong, it is not true that the scientific method, as practised in the natural sciences, is inapplicable in the social ones.

What are not portable across research fields are the special scientific techniques, such as microscopy and the interview. These special methods are not portable because they are topic-specific, whereas the scientific method is universal because it involves only general ideas: those of background knowledge, problem, guess, test ('reality check'), evaluation of the test's outcomes, and eventual enrichment or correction of the background knowledge.

That said, it must be admitted that the following mild version of the idealist thesis is true: social facts are perceived differently by different actors, as a consequence of which social relations pass through the heads of people, and social actions are partly motivated by mental processes. In sum, society is not ruled by ideas. But ideation, being a process in the brains of social actors, can have social consequences. Ideas are powerful to the extent that they are material rather than inmates of Plato's World of Ideas or its descendants, Hegel's absolute spirit, Dilthey's objective spirit, and Popper's world 3. This reconceptualization of the very concept of ideation saves both materialism and what can be salvaged of the idealist conception of society.

Did Weber Use *Verstehen* Consistently?

I submit that Weber did not always use the 'interpretive' or *Verstehen* approach. Moreover, it may be argued that he was ambiguous in everything, so he can be interpreted and reinterpreted without end, to the point of having given rise to an entire academic industry with a total of about 5,000 publications in English alone (Sica 2004).

More precisely, I suggest that in his best work Weber resorted to top-down (macro-micro) as well as to top-top (macro-macro) considerations, in addition to bottom-up (or micro-macro) ones. The following examples, drawn haphazardly from his vast oeuvre, should suffice to make this point, because they are quite important in Weber's own estimation.

Modern industry. Weber (1988b) described the modern factory as a machine that, once set in motion, proceeds automatically, regardless of the wishes of the workers chained to it. The factory acts overwhelmingly (*mit überwältingendem Zwange*) upon its workers and their lifestyles – a clear case of top-down action. Moreover, Weber (1988c) agreed with the claim of his brother Alfred that the industrial 'apparatus' is so rigid that it would not alter if capitalism were replaced with socialism. By contrast, such a macro-social change, involving a transition from individualism to solidarity, would radically change the 'spirit' of the firm, though in unpredictable ways (60) – yet another instance of top-down action.

Religion and capitalism. At the very beginning of his famous *Protestant Ethic and the Spirit of Capitalism* Weber (1988b, 19) admits that 'adherence to a religious confession is not the *cause* of economic phenomena but, to some extent, their *effect.*' This proposition, of course, contradicts his main thesis, which he proposed as a refutation of historical materialism – although at the end of the same book he disclaimed the 'doctrinaire' thesis that the Protestant ethic alone engendered the 'spirit' of capitalism (83). The Frugality → Savings → Investment mechanism was certainly fostered by Calvinist and Puritan asceticism. But the same mechanism has operated in many other cultures as well. After all, modern commercial capitalism was born (or rather reborn) in the Catholic cities of Florence, Pisa, Venice, and Genoa before it spread to the Low Countries, France, England, and Scotland. Besides, as Jere Cohen (2002, 272) concludes in his extraordinarily detailed study of Weber's thesis, 'religious legitimation is more critical to the survivability of a political regime than to an economic system. By comparison, religion has affected the economy quite moderately.' In sum, the Weber thesis is more famous than alive.

Decline of slavery. Weber (1976, 415) explained the decline of slavery in imperial Rome as a result of the 'pacification' of the frontiers: the slave market shrank as fewer wars supplied ever fewer prisoners of war. Thus, slavery disappeared not as a consequence of clever calculations and deliberate decisions by slaveholders, but as the automatic consequence of a supra-personal political movement. The Marxian flavour of this explanation of the top-top type has been noted before (for example, by Wright 2002).

Planning. According to Weber (1976, 35–6), planning is characteristic of the 'rational' (capitalist) economies. That is, the planner's goals and decisions are decisive: the rest of us must carry out the tasks assigned by the plan. But of course not even the planner is totally free: he or she must adjust the means-goal pairs to objective technological rules and economic situations. Weber was enough of a realist to emphasize that the free and rational utility-maximizer is only an ideal-type: he emphasized that we all dwell in what he called a steel cage and are moved by not only interests but also by passions and by tradition. Hence Weber can hardly be called a precursor of the rational choice approach (see Swedberg 2003).

Bureaucratization. The modern Western state, claimed Weber famously, is characterized by its bureaucracy. (How about the ancient Chinese, Ottoman, and Spanish empires?) And he characterized bureaucracy by the power of 'formalist *impersonality*: sine ira et studio, without hatred and passion' (Weber 1976, 129). Moreover, the bureaucracy, as a class, competes for power with all the other social classes. In particular, it stifles economic entrepreneurship – an instance of top-top interaction.

Socialization. Like everyone else, Weber conceived of socialization (*Vergesellschaftung*) as a top-down process rather than as a bottom-up one, if only because it starts at birth, when the individual is at the mercy of the environment he or she has inherited, and has no sophisticated mind to be 'interpreted.'

Exploitation. Contrary to Marx, Weber paid scant attention to exploitation. There is one exception, though: in 'Science as a Profession' he denounced in sarcastic terms the exploitation endured by the university assistant, who counted himself happy if he could lecture twelve hours a week, whereas his boss, the 'Ordinarius' (full professor), got by teaching only three (Weber 1998h). Weber likened this situation to that of the factory worker, and he even used Marx's expression 'separation of the worker from the means of production' – though without mentioning Marx. *Verstehen* cannot detect exploitation. By contrast, a look at balance sheets, payrolls, and work schedules – that is, at objective data about the objective situation – can.

Economic basis of culture. After ridiculing Marx's thesis that the cultural 'superstructure' rests upon an economic 'infrastructure,' Weber (1988f) states with a straight face that 'slavery became the economic bearer of ancient culture,' and even that 'the organization of slave work shapes the indispensable infrastructure of the Roman society.' To paraphrase an old German nursery rhyme: *Max, Du hast den Karl gestohlen / Gib ihn wieder her, gib ihn wieder her!*

In sum, Weber did not use the *Verstehen* approach in a consistent manner. However, this thesis is not new: it was first proposed by his student Alexander von Schelting (1934). Hans Albert (1994) goes further: he argues that, far from using *Verstehen* as an alternative to causal explanation, Weber combined both. I go even further: Weber's scientific level dropped precipitously when he resorted to *Verstehen*.

For better or for worse, inconsistency between science and philosophy is not uncommon. For instance, Marx praised dialectics at the beginning of *Das Kapital*, but fortunately forgot it in the sequel. And the creators of atomic and nuclear physics favoured an anthropocentric philosophy. As Einstein once remarked, to find out the philosophy that scientists practise one should look at their scientific work rather than at their philosophical essays.

Weber's Ambiguous Stand on Ideology

I suggested above that Weber was motivated to write the paper we commemorate by his worry that the social studies might be distorted and misused by leftist ideologues. However, this view does not negate his objectivity thesis: contrary to Weber's own opinion, good research has occasionally spurious motivations, as when contemporary scientists engage in excellent research more out of lust for research grants and prizes than out of sheer scientific curiosity.

Nor does Weber's warning against ideological contamination mean that he rejected all ideologies out of hand. In fact, he was an outspoken right-of-centre liberal, chauvinist, and pro-imperialist. As such, he criticized socialism more often and more vehemently than the right wing. For example, Weber's first empirical research, of 1892, the one on agricultural labour, originated in his participation in the Verein für Sozialpolitik. Now, this was no ordinary learned society. Indeed, its 'core was a group of university professors who were worried about the growing antagonism of German workers, organized in socialist unions, towards the German state. On the one hand they wanted to impress upon industrialists the need for social reforms, and on the other hand they wanted to minimize the influence of Marxist thinking on the workers ... The association's hope was that studies and discussions would lead to social legislation and what today we would call improved labor-management relations' (Lazarsfeld and Oberschall 1965, 185).

Thus, Weber was far more worried about the growing militancy of the trade unions and the Socialists than about the power of the Junkers, the big industrialists, and the military – the three main groups that ruled the German Reich at his time, and the ones that were preparing for the First World War and would eventually ally themselves with the Nazis and govern through them. (Yet he openly criticized those of his colleagues who proposed banning Socialists from the chair, and he gave a fair description of the tame social-democrats in wartime: see Weber 1988d.)

How did the Verein conduct the above-mentioned research on the working conditions of the agricultural workers? Was it thoroughly objective? Not quite. 'Somewhat more than 3,000 landowners received detailed questionnaires requiring a description of the situation within their particular areas' (Lazarsfeld and Oberschall 1965, 185). The fox was consulted about the chicken's welfare. Hardly a paragon of objectivity. True, Weber and others objected to this feature of the study. Nonetheless, he backed it up just by participating in it.

What worried Weber more than the biased choice of the sample was that the questionnaire put too much emphasis on the material conditions of the labourers. For him the problem was mainly subjective: whether 'he [the worker] and his employer are satisfied according to their own subjective evaluation' (Weber, in Lazarsfeld and Oberschall 1965, 186).

(But we know of course how misleading self-appraisals can be, particularly in a tradition of resignation. For instance, the contemporary American blue-collar worker, unlike his or her counterpart half a century ago, tends to regard himself or herself as a member of the middle class. And, as Amartya Sen [2003] reports, the inhabitants of the poorest Indian states, Bihar and Uttar Pradesh, do not complain about their health problems, whereas the Keralans, whose life expectancy at birth is nearly a dozen years longer than the Indian average, complain loudly.)

A year later Weber conducted, again at a distance, another survey of rural workers, this time on behalf of an evangelical organization. He had the choice of circulating questionnaires among rural ministers or doctors. He preferred the former not only because the evangelists kept a central register, but also because the parish ministers might be better acquainted with psychological problems. The doctors could 'only' report on such external and therefore superficial conditions as malnutrition, tuberculosis, injuries due to poor safety, and the way grievances were handled – or ignored. The state of the soul, in Weber's opinion just as in that of his informers, was far more important than the state of the body. Worse, he chose Protestant ministers as his informants about the state of mind of the Polish *Gastarbeiter*, who were mostly Catholic. Objectivity indeed!

In the 1907 study of workers in large industries, Weber shows the same concern with subjective attitudes to the exclusion of objective conditions. Whereas the trade unions and the Socialists emphasized the objective side of work and daily life, Weber focused on the subjective aspect. I submit that a really objective investigator would have examined both sides of the coin, though starting with the necessary condition for having an inner life, namely, a reasonably well-fed, well-clad, and well-lodged body.

So whether the workers were being fairly treated did not matter to Weber: what mattered to him was whether or not they were satisfied – that is, resigned. But the agricultural workers in East Prussia, which was Weber's chosen region of study, were likely to have felt rather satisfied by their working conditions and wages because most of them were imported from Poland, so that their reference group was that of the nearly starving landless peasants in their backward country of origin. Here is where considerations of fairness belong. But this is where Weber's value-neutrality allows him to skirt the important issue of fairness, which is psychological as well as moral, since being treated fairly is a basic human need, and thus one that should concern sociologists (Taylor 2003).

Worse, what really worried Weber about the *Gastarbeiter* in East Prussia was not that the landowners took advantage of them, that those labourers had hardly any rights, and that their competition depressed the wages of their German counterparts. He worried instead that the importation of Polish labourers was 'endangering the German character and the national security of this frontier of the German Reich' (Lazarsfeld and Oberschall 1965, 186).

Thus, from the start, Weber was more interested in the so-called national question than in the social question. Likewise, he went along with the great majority of the European professors everywhere in defending his government during the First World War. Only Albert Einstein, Bertrand Russell, and a few others condemned that enormous crime.

In short, Weber was *engagé* from start to finish: partial to industrialists, hostile to landowners, diffident of workers, respectful of stale academic philosophy, and loyal to his country even when in the wrong. Hardly an impartial, free, generous, and courageous spirit. This point should not be surprising, because the philosophical idealist is bound to be insensitive to large-scale suffering, just as the methodological individualist is bound to miss the big picture. The combination of idealism and individualism narrows down the scope of objectivity or even renders it impossible because it is egocentric (more in Bunge 1996).

Conclusion

Weber's substantive work may be thought of as composed of two halves: one scientific half and the other semi-scientific or even unscientific. The former is objective and therefore it owes nothing to neo-Kantian subjectivism, in particular to the *Verstehen* approach. Interestingly, fantasies of the second kind seldom occur in his posthumous magnum opus, the massive *Wirtschaft und Gesellschaft*, one of the earliest achievements of the emergent hybrid science of economic, political, and historical sociology. Here we read, for instance, that 'capitalists are interested in the expansion of the free market as long as one of them succeeds ... in attaining a monopoly and thus closing the market' (Weber 1976, 384). This sentence owes nothing to hermeneutics: it could have been written by Marx, or even Rosa Luxemburg.

Perhaps what happened in sociology since Weber's death in 1920 was the unfolding of the tension between idealism cum individualism, on the one hand, and materialism cum collectivism, on the other, a tension present in Weber's own work. Indeed, nowadays ideas, intentions, and agency are getting as much attention in social studies, even in neo-Marxist ones, as social structure, productive force, and political power. In any event, there are no longer pure Weberians left, any more than there are pure Marxists within sight. What we find instead are neo-Weberians and neo-Marxists.

Thus it may be argued that both great scholars made a lasting mark, to the extent that their followers replaced some of the original principles with new ones – notably a greater reliance on empirical data and the adoption of an approach midway between individualism and holism – and strived to be more objective and less beholden to ideology than their masters. In other words, both schools have survived through watering down, convergence, and abidance by the scientific method. As suggested above, Weber himself got sometimes close to his main rival.

To conclude, idealism impoverishes the social studies, because the autonomous mind and the objective spirit are figments of the metaphysical imagination of a Berkeley, a Kant, a Hegel, a Dilthey, or a Husserl. By contrast, materialism, once purged of dialectics and economism, has proved to be a viable and fertile general framework. Witness the *Annales* school in historiography (see, for example, Braudel 1976), and cultural materialism in both anthropology (for example, Harris 1979) and archaeology (for example, Trigger 2003).

The reason for these successes should be obvious: there are no such things as disembodied desires and thoughts. The subjective spring of social life dries up unless sustained by work that brings forth terrestrial nourishment. This is why Weber was objective to the extent that he failed to practise the idealist philosophy he preached. Blessed be the inconsistencies that allow one to break away from the cage of dogma!

ACKNOWLEDGMENT

I am grateful to Andreas Pickel for useful comments.

EDITOR'S NOTE

The inclusion of the present polemically critical chapter in a book that com-
memorates, if not celebrates, Max Weber's methodological contribution to
contemporary social science may seem to some readers inappropriate or a
provocation. It is indeed the author's as well as the editor's intention to
provoke. As one of the most widely published and cited contemporary philosophers of science, Mario Bunge has over the past decade devoted his
critical and fecund mind to the philosophy of the social sciences from a
perspective that he describes as scientific realism and non-dialectical materialism. Hailed by his admirers as a salutary iconoclast and decried by his critics
as a ruthless polemicist, Bunge has left few contemporary and classic social
theorists unscathed. Although the editor and his associates do not necessarily
share Bunge's appreciation of Weber, we include his chapter precisely because
it offers an ideal-typical illustration of Weber's reception among his critics –
ideal-typical in the Weberian sense of a self-conscious,
one-sided exaggeration in the interest of analytical clarity. Thus, when Bunge
takes Weber to task here for his neo-Kantian subjectivism borrowed from
Dilthey and Rickert, for example, he speaks not only for the vast majority of
contemporary social scientists, who associate Weber with the *Verstehen* approach of the *Geisteswissenschaften*, but also for expert Weber scholars such as
Guy Oakes, who contests the methodological tenability of Weber's epistemological reliance on Rickert. Similarly, when he attacks Weber's right-wing
nationalist political orientations, Bunge speaks not only for left-liberals',
social democrats', Marxists', and many Weberians' unease, if not disgust,
with the normative underpinnings of Weber's social science, but also echoes
the late great Wolfgang Mommsen's thesis, in which he accused Weber of
paving the way for Hitler (see our Introduction for more on Oakes and
Mommsen). Most importantly, however, Bunge does not throw the baby out
with the bathwater as he underscores the exemplary brilliance of Weber's
empirical work, despite his methodological and political shortcomings.

Laurence McFalls

REFERENCES

Albert, Hans. 1994. *Kritik der reinen Hermeneutik*. Tübingen: J.C.B. Mohr (Paul Siebeck).

Barraclough, G. 1979. *Main Trends in History*. London: Holmes & Meier.

Benda, Julien. 1975 [1927]. *La trahison des clercs*. Rev. ed. Paris: Bernard Grasset.

Braudel, Fernand, 1976 [1966]. *The Mediterranean*. 2 vols. New York: Harper & Row.

Brecht, Arnold. 1959. *Political Theory: The Foundations of Twentieth-Century Political Thought*. Princeton: Princeton University Press.

Bunge, Mario. 1981. *Scientific Materialism*. Dordrecht and Boston: D. Reidel [Kluwer].

– 1989. *Treatise on Basic Philosophy*. Vol. 8, *Ethics*. Dordrecht-Boston: Reidel [Kluwer].

– 1996. *Finding Philosophy in Social Science*. New Haven: Yale University Press.

– 1998. *Social Science under Debate*. Toronto: University of Toronto Press.

Cohen, Jere. 2002. *Protestantism and Capitalism: The Mechanisms of Influence*. New York: Aldine de Gruyter.

Dilthey, Wilhelm. 1959 [1883]. *Einleitung in die Geisteswissenschaften*. In *Gesammelte Schriften*, vol. 1. Stuttgart: Teubner; Göttingen: Vanderhoeck und Ruprecht.

Durkheim, Emile. 1988 [1895]. *Les règles de la méthode sociologique*. Introduction by J.-M. Berthelot. Paris: Flammarion.

Engels, Friedrich. 1973 [1845]. *The Condition of the Working Class in England*. Moscow: Progress.

Fox, Robin. 1989. *The Search for Society: Quest for a Biosocial Science and Morality*. New Brunswick, NJ: Rutgers University Press.

Harris, Marvin. 1979. *Cultural Materialism*. New York: Random House.

Lazarsfeld, Paul F., and Anthony R. Oberschall. 1965. 'Max Weber and Empirical Social Research.' *American Sociological Review* 30: 185–99.

Merton, Robert K. 1968. *Social Theory and Social Structure*. Enlarged ed. New York: Free Press.

– 1976. *Sociological Ambivalence and Other Essays*. New York: Free Press.

Oakes, Guy. 1988. *Weber and Rickert: Concept Formation in the Cultural Sciences*. Cambridge, MA: MIT Press.

Premack, David, and Guy Woodruff. 1978. 'Does the Chimpanzee Have a Theory of Mind?' *Behavioral and Brain Sciences* 1: 515–26.

Rescher, Nicholas. 1997. *Objectivity: The Obligations of Impersonal Reason*. Notre Dame: University of Notre Dame Press.

Sen, Amartya. 2003. *Rationality and Freedom*. Cambridge, MA: Belknap Press and Harvard University Press.

Sica, Alan. 2004. *Max Weber: A Comprehensive Bibliography*. New Brunswick, NJ: Transaction Publishers.

Swedberg, Richard. 2003. 'The Changing Picture of Max Weber's Sociology.' *Annual Review of Sociology* 29: 283–306.

Taylor, A.J.W. 2003. 'Justice as a Basic Human Need.' *New Ideas in Psychology* 21: 209–19.

Trigger, Bruce G. 2003. *Understanding Early Civilizations*. Cambridge: Cambridge University Press.

von Schelting, Alexander. 1934. *Max Webers Wissenschaftslehre*. Tübingen: J.C.B. Mohr (Paul Siebeck).

Weber, Max. 1976 [1922]. *Wirtschaft und Gesellschaft: Grundriss der verstehende Soziologie*. 5th ed. 3 vols. Tübingen: J.C.B. Mohr (Paul Siebeck).

– 1988a. *Gesammelte Aufsätze zur Wissenschaftslehre*. Tübingen: J.C.B. Mohr (Paul Siebeck).

– 1988b [1904–5]. *Die protestantische Ethik und der Geist des Kapitalismus*. In *Gesammelte Aufsätze zur Religionssoziologie*, vol. 1. Tübingen: J.C.B. Mohr (Paul Siebeck).

– 1988c [1908]. 'Methodologische Einleitung für die Erhebungen des Vereins für Sozialpolitik über Auslese und Anpassung (Berufswahlen und Berufsschicksal) der Arbeiterschaft der geschlossenen Grossindustrie.' In *Gesammelte Aufsätze zur Soziologie und Sozialpolitik*, 1–60. Tübingen: J.C.B. Mohr (Paul Siebeck).

– 1988d. *Gesammelte Politische Schriften*. Tübingen: J.C.B. Mohr (Paul Siebeck).

– 1988e. *Gesammelte Aufsätze zur Religionssoziologie*. Vol. 2. Tübingen: J.C.B. Mohr (Paul Siebeck).

– 1988f. *Gesammelte Aufsätze zur Wirtschafts-und Sozialgeschichte*. Tübingen: J.C.B. Mohr (Paul Siebeck).

– 1988g [1917]. 'Der Sinn der "Wertfreiheit" der soziologischen und ökonomischen Wissenschaften.' In Weber 1988a.

– 1988h [1919]. 'Wissenschaft als Beruf.' In Weber 1988a.

– 1988i [1904]. 'Die "Objektivität" sozialwissenschaftlicher und sozialpolitischer Erkenntnis.' In Weber 1988a: 146–214.

Wright, Erik Olin. 2002. 'The Shadow of Exploitation in Weber's Class Analysis.' *American Sociological Review* 67: 832–53.

PART TWO

'Objectivity' in Cross-cultural Translation

5 Speaking Past One Another: Durkheim, Weber, and Varying Modes of Sociological Explanation

CATHERINE COLLIOT-THÉLÈNE

Juxtaposing and opposing the works of Émile Durkheim and Max Weber have become ritual exercises of contemporary sociological training. The two authors themselves, however, never confronted one another's work, which may seem surprising, given that Durkheim (1858–1917) and Weber (1864–1920) were contemporaries whose most productive periods coincided during the final decade of the nineteenth century and the first of the twentieth. What is more, each was able to read the language of the other. It would seem, though, that Weber's knowledge of the French sociological literature of his time was extremely limited. The recurrent question of whether Weber ever read *The Rules of the Sociological Method* seems pointless to me: there is simply no trace of it anywhere. When Weber does cite sources in French, almost exclusively in his works on the sociology of religion, he refers to highly specialized articles.[1] Durkheim's ignorance of Weber is at first glance even more astonishing. After all, Durkheim spent a year in Germany (1885–6) and upon his return to France published a series of articles on German sociology and higher education, notably 'Positive Moral Science in Germany.'[2] He drew on German sources in *The Division of Labour in Society* as well as in *Elementary Forms of Religious Life*, while he also published reviews of works by German sociologists, psychologists, economists, and anthropologists, including Simmel and Tönnies as well as the economist Schaeffle.[3] The only time Durkheim even mentions Weber's name throughout his entire oeuvre is in a report on the First German Congress of Sociology of 1910, which appeared in 1913 in the *Année sociologique* (vol. 12).[4]

Nonetheless, if we consider the timing and forms in which Weber's work was published between 1890 and 1917, Durkheim's ignorance of his counterpart across the Rhine becomes more understandable. The great works to which Weber owes his reputation today, *Economy and Society* and *The Sociology of Religion*, were published after Durkheim's death: *Economy and Society* posthumously in 1922; and the *Essays on the Sociology of Religion*, prepared for publication by Weber himself but printed after his death in 1920. To be sure, the *Essays* were a collection of previously published (though partly revised) articles. With the exception of the *Protestant Ethic* (1904–5), however, they all originally came to print during the war, hardly a period favourable to Franco-German exchanges, even academic ones, and in any case they were available only after Durkheim had already written and published *Elementary Forms of Religious Life* (1912). Finally, Weber's methodological writings, which Durkheim might have known (at least those published between 1904 and 1917), were published in journals that Durkheim was not likely to have read, as they often addressed the methodology of the science of history. Indeed, whereas Weber considered that history and sociology, inasmuch as they are both 'empirical sciences of action,' faced identical methodological problems, Durkheim, as we shall see, argued that sociology had a scientific status entirely different from that of history. Thus, he would have had no reason to consult Weber's methodological work, even if he had had access to the relevant journals. In fact, with the exception of a passing note on the German anthropologist Vierkandt,[5] Durkheim's references in *The Rules of the Sociological Method* are all French (Comte, Tarde) or English (Spencer).

The failure of Weber and Durkheim to confront each other's work has been more than made up for by their successors. I am not entirely certain exactly when the comparison of these two authors became a mandatory rite of passage for students of sociology. The synthesis that Talcott Parsons proposed in *The Structure of Social Action* in 1937 no doubt played a decisive role in establishing the official pantheon of the discipline and, as a result, in elevating Weber and Durkheim (along with a few others) to the rank of founding fathers of sociology. This status made the confrontation of their respective conceptions of the discipline inevitable, whether this confrontation took the form of a reconciling synthesis or a systematic opposition. If the tendency to oppose Weber's and Durkheim's thought has predominated in France, this is no doubt due to the manner in which Weber first entered academic debate there, namely through the mediation of Raymond Aron, who introduced French readers to 'the German philosophy of history' (as represented, for him, by Rickert, Dilthey, Simmel, and Weber) in his second thesis, published in 1938.[6] Aron looked to these authors, Weber in particular, for epistemological grounds for calling French positivism into question. In order to offer a fuller picture of the French reception of Weber and interpretation of his position relative to Durkheim, which interests me here only insofar as I wish to propose a radical revision, it is necessary to mention the strategic function that some of his translators (notably Julien Freund) and interpreters (to a certain extent Aron) assigned to Weber's work in the context of the fight against Marxism in the 1960s and 1970s. It is more than likely that the obsession with the opposition between Weber's methodological individualism and Durkheim's holism owes much to this historical context in which methodological problems and political struggles were inextricably intertwined.[7]

Should we regret that Weber and Durkheim never read one another? Would that not have spared us endless, irresolvable discussions about the ultimate compatibility or irreconcilability of their methods and ontological premises? I would like to suggest here that their mutual ignorance about each other, though partly explicable by the timing of their publications, was in fact unavoidable. Putting it bluntly, I would argue that the two authors elaborated, under the common label 'sociology,' two entirely different projects of knowledge. To be sure, they both fought to assert the autonomy of this new discipline called sociology relative to other older disciplines that were well established within academia. They did so, however, within different contexts, to which we shall return, yet from the perspective of the history of sociology, we should recognize this similarity in their work despite the divergence of their objects and methods of study. The question remains, however, whether this common logic of carving out a distinct disciplinary space for sociology does not in fact conceal something much more decisive from an epistemological standpoint, namely the program of knowledge, that is, the fundamental questions underlying the set of problems that determine a scientific discipline's objects and methods. If we examine the *difference in style* of the two authors from this perspective, we realize that the collaborative links that they establish between sociology and other human sciences – in the case of Weber, primarily with history, especially legal and economic history, whereas in the case of Durkheim, with anthropology – owe nothing to chance. The questions that guide Weber's sociological undertaking are historical questions, even if he is careful to distinguish sociology from history, whereas for Durkheim these questions are anthropological, even if he did not formally encounter anthropology until he worked on the *Elementary Forms of Religious Life*.[8] The difficulty of combining Weber's and Durkheim's approaches – which always comes at the cost of violence to one, the other, or both – resides precisely in the fact that the same disciplinary label applies to two heterogeneous projects of knowledge. The elective affinities of these two types of sociology – if we insist on retaining this common label – with different human sciences are, in part, the cause of this heterogeneity (inasmuch as this difference originates from the particular training of each author), but above all, they are its symptom.

Many readers of Durkheim and Weber do not recognize that their differences in style conceal a fundamental divergence in the commonly labelled science they purported to practise, because both authors apparently addressed many of the same objects and themes, even drawing on the same source material. I shall point out only the most obvious similarities. Both produced a sociology of religion, and experts in that branch of sociology can legitimately place Durkheim's *Elementary Forms of Religious Life* and the three volumes of Weber's *Sociology of Religion* on the same shelf of their libraries. Both works include references to the same authors and the same books: Barth, Kern, and Oldenberg, for example. These common references, however, are more the exception than the norm, and we might ask whether the differences in citation are not more significant than the coincidences: Durkheim, for instance, cites Burnouf, whom Weber entirely neglects in *Hinduism and Buddhism*.[9] The same applies to our two authors' shared interest in law: Weber wrote a substantial sociology of law, which became a large section of *Economy and Society*, part 2, while Durkheim devoted considerable attention to the law in the argument of *The Division of Labour*, even drawing on numerous German sources (the originals or translations, when available).[10] With the exception of their references to Sumner Maine and to Gierke,[11] Weber and Durkheim cite entirely different sources. As we have seen, however, neither linguistic incompetence nor indifference to the cultural universe of the other (at least for the case of Durkheim) can explain the heterogeneity of their source material, even as they address apparently identical subjects.

One way to explain the diverging questions that guided Weber's and Durkheim's scientific enquiries would be to study in detail their choice of sources and, especially for the cases of convergence, the way they used them. I shall not take this long, tortuous route here. Instead, I shall adopt two other complementary approaches, for the time being in a schematic manner.

Boundaries between the Disciplines

The first approach examines the academic contexts within which Weber and Durkheim respectively staked out sociology's scientific turf. I do not intend to describe in detail the distribution of the disciplines, their institutional groundings, or their relative weight in turn-of-the-century Germany and France. Instead, I shall identify the features of these configurations to which Durkheim and Weber respectively attributed importance in the struggle each led to establish the autonomy of sociology. Four disciplines come into question with varying importance for each author: philosophy, psychology, history, and legal theory.[12] Putting it simply, we can say that Durkheim's efforts at demarcation were aimed at philosophy and psychology, whereas Weber tried to distinguish sociology both from psychology and from *Jurisprudenz*, that is, legal theory. For Weber, history and sociology are closely related (he subsumes both disciplines under the term 'empirical sciences of action' in opposition to the dogmatic disciplines),[13] while Durkheim pays little attention to history, aside from his disobliging remarks on the philosophy of history, which are aimed at philosophy (or at the philosophical elements of Comte's sociology) and not at the work of historians per se.

Philosophy

The relationship of the emerging science of sociology to philosophy is particularly stormy in France for institutionally strategic reasons that verge on the political.[14] Because it takes 'moral facts' (*les faits moraux*) as its object of study and claims to explain them, unlike philosophy, in a strictly positive manner, Durkheimian sociology calls into question the educational mission that philosophy was supposed to fulfil in the educational institutions of the Republic. Despite Durkheim's prudent claims in the preface to *The Division of Labour in Society* that his sociology was philosophically neutral,[15] his main thesis –according to which compulsion in general, and moral compulsion in particular, has its origins in the social realm and varies with its different forms – fundamentally challenged philosophy's claim that the moral education of individuals was the basis for socializing citizens. What is more, despite its claim to a purely positive status, Durkheim's sociology was not without practical – that is, ethical – consequences. After all, his positive moral science could on a factual basis, much like the experimental sciences, discover a society's inherent functional logic and observe empirical deviations from that logic. Durkheim could and did, in turn, propose social and political reforms aimed at restoring that functional logic converted, with positivist innocence, into an ethical norm.[16] Thus, sociology became a rival to philosophy. I cannot elaborate here on the different positions that Weber and Durkheim adopted on philosophy. To be sure, they both drew on Kant, but the different uses they made of the Kantian legacy merits a detailed study of its own. I shall thus limit myself to observing that Weber's relationship to philosophy could never have reached the level of conflict that has characterized the relationship between sociology and philosophy in France from the days of Durkheim to the present, for in Germany philosophy has never occupied the same privileged institutional position as was established for it by the educational system of the Third Republic. Even if philosophy had enjoyed such a status in Germany, it is unlikely that a sociology of the Weberian stripe would have sought to unseat it, since Weber rigorously respected the distinction between the *is* and the *ought*, a distinction that Durkheim acknowledged in principle but undermined by interpreting the relationship between the real and the ideal in a quasi-Hegelian manner.[17] In other words, Weber stressed that sociology could have no practical application (in the ethical sense of *practical philosophy*) except for the very modest one of making individuals aware of the axiological presuppositions of their actions and, possibly, of their rationally expected consequences.[18] As for the values that more or less clearly inspire action, from case to case, no empirical science can establish their validity. If Weber had caught wind of the normative pretensions that Durkheim ascribed to a 'moral science' that also aspired to 'positive' status,[19] he would have no doubt diagnosed that same paralogism of which he accused Stammler: the conflation of empirical analysis and normative interpretation.[20]

Legal Theory

If any discipline played for Weber a role analogous to that of philosophy for Durkheim, in the sense that sociology's claim to autonomy had to be formulated in opposition above all to that discipline, then surely it was legal theory. We know that Weber emphasized the difference between the 'empirical sciences of action' (sociology and history) and the 'dogmatic sciences,' among which he included metaphysics, aesthetics, logic, and legal theory.[21] In his 1913 essay 'Certain Categories of Interpretive Sociology,' a first draft of the methodological chapter that opens *Economy and Society*, Weber follows his characterization of 'interpretive' sociology with two sections elaborating on its relation to two apparently similar disciplines. The first section addresses the relationship of interpretive sociology to psychology, the second to legal dogmatics.[22] Although the second is shorter than the first, it is in this passage that Weber first articulates the famous propositions (which will be taken up with slight variations in *Economy and Society*) on the conditions for using collective categories – propositions that today prompt the classification of Weber as a methodological individualist. If we further consider these passages in light of those texts where Weber makes the distinction between the sociological and juridical meanings of the concepts of rule and of legal order, then we recognize how important it was for Weber to distinguish sociology from legal theory. This distinction, in fact, sometimes took on a polemical twist, notably in his scathing review of Rudolf Stammler's work.[23]

Weber thus makes the specificity of interpretive sociology explicit through a double demarcation – from psychology ('interpretive sociology is not a branch of "psychology"') and from legal theory respectively. It is important to stress the symmetry of this operation, especially since these passages have usually been cited for their critique of the reification of collective concepts: the structures that emerge from the interactions of individuals (the state, capitalism, feudalism, the nation, etc.) cannot explain socio-historical developments, for only individuals 'can be treated as agents in a course of subjectively understandable action.'[24] The citing of these passages to illustrate the stance of methodological individualism against the transcendence of the social, however, transforms Weber's elucidation of the specificity of sociology with respect to psychology and to law into an ontological debate. Granted, the individual constitutes the 'upper limit' of knowledge for interpretive sociology, but the individual is also the bottom limit. One can of course delve *into* the individual as a complex whole, a set of differentiated cells, a bundle of biochemical reactions, or an entity guided by psychic elements whose causal relations could be determined experimentally. Weber does not deny the value, for certain ends, of such potential bio-psychic knowledge, just as he admits the utility, for other ends, of treating social institutions as irreducible wholes, as legal theory can and does. What is at stake in Weber's well-known individualist statements is, in fact, the autonomy of the new, insecure discipline of sociology, threatened by the annexationist ambitions of neighbouring disciplines – and not, as the ritualistic opposition of Weber and Durkheim leads to believe, Weber's conception of the relationship between the individual and society.

Psychology

Our review of the disciplinary contexts within which the defence of sociology's independence took place on the two sides of the Rhine requires a more detailed examination of Weber's and Durkheim's respective positions vis-à-vis psychology. It would certainly be a mistake to assume that the two authors' common struggle against psychology compensates for their divergent fixations on legal theory or on philosophy as sociology's greatest nemesis, for they invoke radically opposed reasons for rejecting psychology's pretension to underlie and, hence, to subsume sociology. We hardly need to recall Durkheim's vehement affirmation of sociology's independence from psychology; it followed necessarily from his thesis that society has a *sui·generis* ontological status that it no way derives from the individuals who constitute it. Precisely because the essential characteristic of sociological phenomena 'resides in the power they have to exert pressure, from the outside, on individuals' consciousness, [those phenomena] do not derive from [consciousness], and hence sociology is not a corollary of psychology.'[25] As already noted, Weber is just as categorical that 'sociology is not a branch of "psychology."'[26] For Durkheim, however, sociology's autonomy from psychology does not impede analogous methodological premises. Thus, in chapter 2 of his *Rules*, he announces his intention to bring about for sociology a reform 'in all points identical to the one that has transformed psychology over the past thirty years.'[27] Durkheim is referring here to experimental psychology, which he considers methodologically exemplary for having abandoned introspection in favour of treating mental facts externally, that is, 'as *things*.' Sociology and psychology thus adopt the same scientific posture, but their objects are heterogeneous: states of collective consciousness, the objects of sociology, are certainly not reducible to states of individual consciousness, the objects of psychology. But positive sociology and experimental psychology both see these 'states,' collective or individual, only as facts whose existence and properties must be explained according to the exigencies of scientific rationality, which recognizes only relations of cause and effect. In either case, explanation does not take into account actors' proclaimed motives. By contrast, the sociology whose autonomy from psychology Weber seeks to establish is avowedly 'interpretive.' Such a sociology, unlike the positive science of society for which Durkheim sets the methodological 'rules,' seeks precisely to reconstruct the purposive structure of action (in this sense it is 'interpretive'), and it attributes all the virtues of authentic causal explanation to this reconstruction of motives. What is more, the branch of psychology whose potential founding role for sociology Weber most strongly opposes is experimental psychology,[28] precisely the kind of psychology whose methodology Durkheim seeks to emulate for positive sociology. And what Weber finds objectionable about experimental psychology Durkheim extols as exemplary, namely its objectification of states of consciousness, that is, its disqualification of conscious motives as possible explanations of social action.

It would be easy to characterize this difference of opinion as an expression of what is commonly seen as a sharp contrast between Durkheim's holism and Weber's atomism. Durkheim does after all assert the independence of sociology from psychology, on the grounds of the transcendence of the social, whereas Weber, in rejecting experimental psychology's objectivist bracketing of consciousness, opens the door to the derivation of social facts from the subjective intentions of actors, who in turn can be only individual. When Weber takes up the relations of interpretive sociology with legal dogmatism a few pages after considering its relations with psychology, he makes it unequivocal in the well-known formulations that have earned him recognition as one of the ancestors of 'methodological individualism': the individual is 'the only bearer of meaningful behaviour,' and sociology's task is to reduce collective categories (Weber mentions the notions of the 'state,' 'association,' and 'feudalism') to '"understandable" action, which without exception means the action of the participating individual human beings.'[29] Nonetheless, as we just saw when considering the different arguments that Durkheim and Weber adopted to justify the irreducibility of sociology to psychology, their differences do not primarily reside in divergent ontological presuppositions (who could think that Weber would deny the causal weight of the social realm?) but occur, rather, at the level of epistemology. Both of them conceive of sociology as a causal, and thus 'empirical' or 'positive,' science, but they disagree on the nature of those entities that can legitimately work as 'causes.' 'If there is one thing sociology must vehemently reject, it is the supposition that "understanding" and "causal explanation" have nothing to do with one another,' Weber remarks in his discussion of the relationship between interpretive sociology and psychology.[30] Precisely this supposition, however, underlies Durkheim's rejection of conscious motives as possible candidates for causality within the framework of his rationalist science. In Durkheim's debate with psychology, his enemy is introspection, and he thus takes pains to stress that the true causes of social phenomena can be found only at a level of reality that eludes social agents' consciousness. Hence, he must embrace the basic scientific posture of experimental psychology.[31] By contrast, Weber, in his essays *Roscher and Knies* (1904–5)[32] and 'Critical Studies in the Logic of the Cultural Sciences,'[33] pursues the debate introduced by Windelband and Rickert in attempting to liberate the cultural sciences from an exclusively nomothetic conception of scientific explanation. This debate affects his interpretation of sociology's relationship to psychology as well as of its relationship to history (a point to which we shall return). Although Weber hardly defends the introspective method (the ideal-typical reconstruction of the purposive logic of action has nothing to do with the recording of data acquired through introspection), he does not wish to establish the unconscious character of causal determinants but rather to defend the scientific validity of singular, non-generalizable interpretive explanations. Despite Durkheim's outstanding familiarity with the human sciences of late-nineteenth-century Germany, he seems not to have noticed one of their major cleavages: the vigorous debate over the possibility that causal explanation need not proceed by the subsumption of facts under covering laws.[34] It is precisely this debate and Weber's unqualified acceptance of such a possibility, however, that conditioned not only Weber's methodological positions but the cognitive objectives of his entire sociology.

History

I briefly mentioned that Durkheim, aside from the instrumental use he made of certain historians' work, made little effort to elaborate on the relationship of sociology to history, except perhaps in his polemical attacks addressed more to the philosophy of history than to history per se. In a review of a series of articles published in the *Rivista italiana di sociologica*, however, we can find a few comments that shed light on Durkheim's relative indifference to history. With regard to an article by Salvemini, Durkheim asserts essentially that history, which in a strict sense takes as its object only sequences of singular events, is constitutionally 'refractory to scientific form.'[35] He admits the possibility of another type of history that would rise to the study of 'social species' rather than individuals but adds that such a history would ultimately blend into sociology: 'History cannot become science until it rises above the singular; to be sure, it would then cease to be history and become a branch of sociology. It would become dynamic sociology.'[36] It does not matter which historiographic practice inspired this opinion; what is more important, from the perspective of Durkheim's confrontation with Weber, is his conviction that history cannot be a science unless it transforms itself into sociology. Weber, for his part, also thought that history and sociology were closely related, but he did so for the opposite reason: they both seek to make singular causal inferences, and thus the methodological problems of interpretive sociology are indistinguishable from those of the historical sciences in general. Even if Durkheim had read them, Weber's methodological essays could only have elicited his disdain. Weber, indeed, thought of sociology as a variety of the 'cultural sciences,' which in turn were historical sciences: they address the particularities of the phenomena they study as well as the unique causes that have lent these phenomena their specificity.[37] While, according to Durkheim, history must convert itself into sociology (and thereby abandon its status as an autonomous discipline)[38] in order to become scientific, Weber to the contrary held that sociology could be scientific only insofar as history was. This difference in the interpretation of the relationship between sociology and history derived from precisely the same methodological divergences that characterized Weber and Durkheim's understanding of the relations between sociology and psychology.

It bears repeating: Durkheim never read Weber, and vice versa. In 'Note on German Influences on French Sociology' published in the *Mercure de France* in 1902,[39] Durkheim, while admitting 'to owe much to the Germans,' relegates this influence to the past and goes on to state his impression that the German social sciences of his day were undergoing sclerosis. 'Saturated with its own production,' Germany was no longer interested in foreign products. This 'lack of curiosity,' he adds, indicates a state of self-absorption that probably prevents scientific progress. The heart of Weber's work was of course written in the following twenty years. Was Durkheim and Weber's mutual ignorance in that period really just a coincidence caused by the circumstances of war and of access to journals? But Weber's project of knowledge, including his conceptions of history and of the relations between the theoretical ('dogmatic') and the historical sciences, as well as between sociology on the one hand and psychology or history on the other, had taken form in the final years of the nineteenth century. Durkheim was familiar with many of the authors whose works had constituted the cultural environment within which Weber's project took shape. The very fact that Durkheim did not anticipate the possibility of such a project reveals the strength of his epistemological convictions. As we already remarked, he took no note of the discussion among philosophers and historians questioning the universality of the nomothetic model of explanation. His reading of the German historical school left out precisely those elements on which Weber drew. Weber often described himself as a disciple of the historical school of political economy (*die historische Nationalökonomie*), though he also allowed himself virulent critiques of some of its members. It would seem that Durkheim had a fairly deep understanding of this school, as attested to by his 1887 'Positive Moral Science in Germany' and by his article published jointly with Paul Fauconnet in the *Revue philosophique* in 1903.[40] In both texts, Durkheim credits the historical school in economics with having broken with the abstract assumptions (individualism and cosmopolitanism) of the Manchester, or 'liberal,' school. He mentions List, Roscher, Schmoller, and Bücher, as well as 'socialism of the chair.' The notion of *Volkswirtschaft*, which Durkheim translates as '*économie sociale*,' has for him the virtues of situating economic phenomena within the totality of society, of recognizing the links between the different dimensions of society, and hence of clearly establishing political economy as a moral science. In 1913, in the context of a polemic stirred up by an article by Simon Deploige,[41] Durkheim denies having borrowed from the Germans his fundamental thesis that society as a whole has properties that cannot be deduced from the sum of its parts and pays homage instead to Comte and to Renouvier. While Durkheim may not have first discovered this thesis among the German historical economists, he certainly met with it again among them and thus devoted them much more positive attention in his 1887 text than he later chose to admit. For Wagner and Schmoller in particular, he wrote in his 1887 text, 'Society is a veritable being, which without doubt is nothing in the absence of the individuals who make it up, but which nonetheless has its own nature and personality ... It is false to say that a whole is equal to the sum of its parts. By the very fact that its parts have defined relations among one another, are assembled in a certain manner, something new results from this assemblage, something that can under certain conditions become conscious of itself.'[42]

The shorter passage devoted to the historical school of political economy in his 1903 text again credits this school with having made political economy into a *social* science, and he also mentions that this orientation opened economics to comparison. Understanding economics as a social phenomenon means conceiving of it as essentially vari-able: Schmoller's or Roscher's interest in differences between societies contrasts sharply with the abstract universalism of liberal economics, which speaks of an imaginary economic world, 'the *Güterwelt*, an iso-lated world, everywhere the same.'[43] Thus, according to Durkheim, the historical school 'introduced some comparison into economic history' from Schmoller, who conceived of economic laws as inductive, to Bücher, who attempted a classification of economic regimes.[44]

Wilhelm Hennis has argued that the historicism practised by mem-bers of the historical school such as Schmoller, Roscher, or Knies (one member of the school whom Durkheim apparently did not read) paved the way for Weber's comparative project.[45] It would not seem, however, that the implications that Durkheim derived from these authors' com-parative forays were congruent with the scientific practice they inspired in Weber. Since for Weber sociology, like history, was a science of the particular, the primary purpose of comparison was, for him, to expose the differences between cultures, societies, and epochs. Thus, for ex-ample, in responding to criticisms of his best known work, *The Protes-tant Ethic and the Spirit of Capitalism*, Weber reiterated that he was not interested in capitalism in general but in 'the specificities of a particular historical system of this type,' his object of study having been 'the specific content of a development that had occurred only once.'[46] Still, one might be tempted to see in the typologies that Weber elaborated in the huge comparative project he undertook in *The Economic Ethics of the World Religions* and in *Economy and Society* a broadening of his scientific perspective, in which the recurrent traits that define 'types' suggest, despite Weber's claims to the contrary, a shift in interest from the particular to the general. Indeed, a passage in *Economy and Society* distinguishing sociology from history lends credence to such an inter-pretation. Sociology, Weber writes in this passage, 'seeks to formulate type concepts and generalized uniformities of empirical process,' whereas history 'is oriented to the causal analysis and explanation of individual actions, structures, and personalities possessing cultural sig-nificance.'[47] But this passage offers only a clumsy rendering of Weber's real comparative practice. Reading Weber's 1920 foreword, intended to open his entire work on the sociology of religion but often published and understood as an introduction only to *The Protestant Ethic*,[48] suffices to prove that the centre of gravity of his investigations always remained the specificity of Western culture and the particular historical develop-ment that gave this culture the traits that distinguish it from all others.

The 1916 introduction to the *Economic Ethics of the World Religions* already stressed that its efforts at typology did not intend to be systematic but rather sought above all to draw out contrasts, that is, to identify differences between religious ethics and economic mentalities 'to the neglect of everything else.'[49]

The historicism of the *historische Nationalökonomie* inspired Weber's comparative enterprise insofar as it emphasized the unique features of 'historical individualities.' By contrast, it is clear that Durkheim did not assign this particularizing function to comparison, despite the interest he claimed to have in the differences between 'social types.' Like Weber, he saw comparison as an ersatz for the social sciences' inability to experiment, as do the natural sciences. But in the texts where he explicitly defines the objectives of the comparative method, Durkheim remains faithful to the scientific ideal he articulated in his *Rules*. The objectivity of social facts resides in their constancy and regularity; the general nature of relations of cause and effect cannot be denied without at the same time denying 'the principle of causality' itself.[50] Sociology is a science only inasmuch as it seeks out the general, and comparison permits its discovery: 'To substitute for experimentation that is impossible, we need at least comparison, and comparison supposes that we abstract the particular from the particular to see only the general. The comparative method satisfies all the requirements of science, but it implies that science cannot take individual phenomena as its objects.'[51] Significantly, in the 1903 text already mentioned ('Sociologie et sciences sociales'), Durkheim identifies as the great innovation of the nineteenth century not the historicism of the new German school of economics, but the appearance of the new disciplines of anthropology and the science, or history, of civilizations. Referring to Humboldt and his 'fundamental axiom of the unity of the human spirit,' Durkheim cites the innovative contributions of Klemm's *Kulturgeschichte* and Pritchard's *History of Man* as well as the new research fields of German legal ethnology (notably that of Hermann Post), of comparative mythology (associated with Max Müller), and the ethnology of religion, which proves 'the uniformity of beliefs and religious practices among all of humanity.'[52] These comparative disciplines all reveal the constancy of causes and, hence, the existence of laws in human affairs just as there are in nature. The general nature of social phenomena 'shows that they derive from general causes, which, wherever they present themselves, always produce the same effects with a necessity equal to that of other natural causes.'[53] In short, the lesson that Durkheim drew from German historicism was less that of the variability of forms (of law, of economy, etc.) than that of the ubiquity of the social realm.

Ethnology

Durkheim became interested in ethnology when he began studying religious phenomena, as early as 1895, he claims.[54] In order to establish what he considers an appropriately sociological use of ethnology, he takes care to distinguish it from the 'anthropological school,' with which he notably associates Frazer. His arguments in favour of this distinction from anthropology, however, seem at first glance to contradict our conclusions about his assessment of the German historical school of economics, for what he finds at fault with the 'anthropological school' is precisely its universalism and its corollary: ignorance of the differences in form between societies. Disregarding the specific social milieus to which religions belong, the anthropological school seeks 'to establish, beyond national and historical differences, the universal and truly human bases of religious life.'[55] Durkheim objects to this view because the comparative method can proceed only on the basis of a differentiation of 'social types,' which precludes uncontrolled analogies between apparently similar social facts drawn from heterogeneous societies. Weber would no doubt have concurred with Durkheim on this point, but the methodological principle that Durkheim was defending would probably not have convinced him. What Durkheim proposes as an alternative to the anthropological school's across-the-board comparisons is in fact the study of one particular species of religion, the totemic, which he claims can reveal, by virtue of its simplicity and primitive form, the fundamental traits of the religious phenomenon in general. He thus invokes the difference between 'social types' only to justify the limits of his comparison to the case of clan societies that practise totemism. This difference, however, does not prevent him from drawing conclusions that extend to religious life in all forms of society.[56] Indeed, Durkheim is aware that his critique of the anthropological school does not address its universalism per se. He admits in a note, in fact, that he himself considers 'the principal goal of the science of religion is to come to grasp what constitutes the religious nature of mankind.' The critical difference, though, is that one should not look for this religious nature, as does the anthropological school, in the psycho-physiological constitution of the human being, but rather presume that it is 'a product of social causes.'[57]

A Difference of Grammars

The passage (cited above) in which Weber assigns to social science the task of 'understanding the characteristic uniqueness of the reality in which we move' as well as 'the causes of their being historically *so* and not *otherwise*' perfectly summarizes the central problem that orders his entire oeuvre. The guiding interest of sociology must be, according to him, the here-and-now, which is the particular character of modern Western civilization. Understanding what constitutes that particularity and identifying the causes that have conferred to our civilization these traits that distinguish it from others, past and present, are and should be, to Weber's mind, the primary goal and the ultimate justification of social science. Durkheim does not contest the view that sociological inquiry must address the here-and-now. He says as much on the very first page of *The Elementary Forms* just as he is about to inflict upon his readers some six hundred pages devoted to a form of religion that he himself calls 'very archaic.' At great pains to differentiate his study from those of ethnographers and historians, from whom he nonetheless borrows most of his material, he notes that the latter are interested in the 'bygone' forms of civilization for their own sake. This type of curiosity he adds, does not characterize sociology, which, 'like any positive science,' seeks above all to understand a present reality: that of man, 'especially man of today.'[58] Both authors thus seem to agree that the guiding interest of sociology is to be found in the present, and this is certainly a point upon which Weber's 'science of reality' and Durkheim's 'positive science' converge. Yet a confrontation of their positions demonstrates just how different two projects of knowledge that purport to have an 'interest in the here-and-now' as their determining motive of inquiry can be. In the case of Weber, this interest supports a discourse oriented to specificities and historical differences; in the case of Durkheim, it inspires a quest for the same and the unchanging.

Indeed, what emerges most clearly from *Elementary Forms of Religious Life* is that grasping human facts through the dimension of their social determinants does not necessarily lead to the recognition of differences between societies. Durkheim constantly repeats the methodological principle that 'when the existence of a law has been proven by a well-conducted experiment, this proof is universally valid,'[59] and on this basis he draws conclusions for all societies without exception from a case study (not precisely a monograph, but a 'social fact' such as religion analysed within the constraints of a single defined social type).

Thus, since he has succeeded in showing that the ideas of the sacred, of the soul, of divinities can be explained sociologically for the case of totemic religions, he presumes that this explanation must be valid 'for all peoples where the same ideas are found with same essential characteristics.'[60] In order to allow such extrapolation, though, this explanation can take on only a most general character. In fact, Durkheim's argument in *Elementary Forms* boils down to the demonstration that the objective cause of the religious experience is society. The epistemological significance of this thesis resides in its manner of opposition to other explanations of the religious, namely the conceptions of primitive religion that chapter 2 of *Elementary Forms* tries to refute: animism, naturalism, and the psychological approach taken by William James. In common to all of these theories is their situating the root of the religious in the relation of humankind to nature or to itself, in other words in an 'anthropological' trait as Durkheim understands the term, that is, beyond social determinants. For Weber, who never bothered to define the religious[61] and therefore never had to confront these alternative theories of the nature and the foundations of the religious experience, be they psychological or anthropological, the affirmation of religion's social character would be nothing but a truism and hence of little interest for guiding his studies of the sociology of religion.

One might object that Durkheim, in his earlier works, does not engage in such unilateral generalization: he constructs the *Division of Labour* around two totally different historical forms of social ties, and in the *Rules of Sociological Method* he devotes a chapter to the distinction between 'social types,' the task of an entire branch of sociology that he labels 'social morphology.'[62] According to some commentators, Durkheim fundamentally changed his modes of inquiry and explanation when he took up the problem of religion. To be sure, Durkheim's interests and approaches evolved over the course of his scientific career, but one can also posit that the theses of the *Elementary Forms of Religious Life* were foreshadowed in the role assigned to the morpheme 'society' already in *The Division of Labour* or *The Rules of the Sociological Method*, where Durkheim establishes the characteristic modes of sociological explanation. What I am getting at here is what I called above the second manner of trying to grasp the difference between Durkheim's and Weber's programs of knowledge. This manner requires a comparison of the two authors' grammars, by which I mean their semantics and their correlative rules of usage. Durkheim's inflationary use of 'the social' in the noun-form is well known. In 'The "Objectivity" of Knowledge,' by contrast, Weber denies that the notion of the social realm in general has any meaning, for in the absence of a particular accompanying predicate, the notion of the 'social' provides 'no specific *point of view*, from which the *significance* of given elements of culture can be analysed.'[63] This observation makes an appropriate starting point for elaborating on what I mean by a difference in 'grammars' between the two authors. This difference does not simply lie in their manners of expressing themselves, which would leave open the possibility of translating the theses of the one into the language of the other. The schematic contrast between Durkheim's holism and Weber's individualism rests in fact on the illusion that their languages are mutually convertible so that it appears possible to examine and to interpret Durkheim's propositions about social constraint and Weber's about the priority of the individual as symmetrically opposite positions. Such neat opposition can occur only across a common space. Yet what becomes clear from the different grammars of Durkheim and Weber is the heterogeneity of their universes, which makes it impossible to detect a common space. Each can equally well assert that sociology is an empirical, that is, causal, science,[64] but causality has a completely different meaning in their two oeuvres because the entities between which it comes into play are not of the same nature.

No matter how much Durkheim may have tried to distinguish sociological inquiry from the preoccupations of philosophy, his conceptual universe still bears the traces of his philosophical education. The difference between Durkheim and Weber does not reside in their more or less pronounced recognition of social constraint, but rather in the terms through which they describe this constraint's modes. Understood as moral obligation, constraint is still cast in philosophical terms. To be sure, Durkheim radically transformed the way to think of it, by comparison with the philosophy of his time, in looking for its causes in the social order, considered a *sui generis* reality that surpasses the individual and determines his or her rules of conduct. But it is also clear that this absorption of the moral by the social can also be read, inversely, as a reduction of the social to the moral: a peculiar morality, not very Kantian except in its anti-utilitarianism, which can be summarized at both the factual and the normative level, as the predominance of the group as unit over each of the individuals who make it up.[65] This coincidence of the social and the moral (thus understood) has consequences for the register in which Durkheim takes up phenomena of sociality: the terminological register of his causal explanations is that of expressiveness. Sociality is not explained but rather identified, under the label of the social, with membership in a collective, which makes itself felt in the constraint internalized by the individual's consciousness (which thus becomes divided into a strictly individual dimension and another one constituted by the presence of the collective within the individual). All phenomena with which sociology has to deal appear sufficiently explained when they have been recognized as *manifestations* or *expressions* of the social realm. Durkheim's mode of explanation operates in a universe of expressions that mirror one another indefinitely, to a point that verges on the tautological.[66] Thus, law becomes a 'visible symbol' of solidarity, that is, once again, of the cohesion of the group or of the social, which is why the different forms of law can reveal different forms of solidarity.[67] Similarly, religious life is 'the eminent form of, and like a shorthand expression for, collective life in its entirety.'[68] The use of 'the social' as a substantive, which Weber, as we noted, explicitly forbade himself from doing, is the cornerstone of all explanations that Durkheim's sociology offers. The presence of the social, as collective consciousness, within each individual allows the establishment of relations of inter-expressiveness between every instance of sociality (law, division of labour, morality, religion). This implies, naturally enough, the co-extensiveness of all forms of sociality. Thus, Durkheim says of law, for example, 'The general life of society cannot extend to a point without legal life extending there as well, and with the same relation. We can thus be certain to find all of the essential varieties of social solidarity reflected in the law.'[69] This co-extensiveness is also implicitly present in the thesis presented at the end of the *Elementary Forms*, according to which religion is the matrix from which all manifestations of the social originate;[70] even what seems to resist most being situated in the representational order, economic activity, can be reduced to the religious.[71]

I suggested above that the heart of the opposition between Durkheim's and Weber's attitudes towards psychology, notably, lies at the level of their grammars and what these allow or forbid as relevant for sociological explanation. In doing so, I did not want deny the importance that each attributes to the conscious motives of social agents: Durkheim simply and categorically excludes them from the realm of scientifically acceptable explanations of social facts, whereas Weber elevates them not only to the rank of perfectly legitimate modes of explanation but to the highest form of explanation to which sociology (as well as history) should aspire. The importance that Weber attributes to the interpretation of action (defined as human behaviour with which the agent associates 'subjective' meaning) is the corollary of his distrust of the abusive application of collective concepts, that is, of the method that he labels 'emanationist'[72] and of which he accuses the acolytes of the 'Volksgeist' and their various successors as well as the Marxists. But Weber also defended the interpretation of action out of the conviction that there is no reason to reject the scientific relevance of inquiry into the intelligibility of human action, for the fact that such action is at least potentially interpretable or understandable allows for a mode of explanation unavailable to the natural sciences. Far from considering that the historical sciences must neutralize this form of explanation as an obstacle to scientific objectivity, Weber to the contrary saw in it a potential for rationality superior to that of explanations in the natural sciences.[73] For Weber, this possibility of superior intelligibility is sacrificed by those who insist on imposing a conception of causality closely modelled on that of the natural sciences onto the historical sciences (including sociology, of course). Although Weber vehemently defended the objective character of the historical sciences and categorically rejected the idea that human phenomena were subject to modes of intelligibility radically foreign to those applied in the natural sciences, he nonetheless considered that the possibility of 'understanding' action justified a particular status for the historical sciences, but did not, however, abandon the goal of causal explanation.

Durkheim, by contrast, rejected any explanation of this type because scientific knowledge, for him, can proceed only from the known to the unknown, from the visible to the invisible. Treating social facts 'as things,' as the first rule that he proposed for sociology admonishes, means postulating that true knowledge can come only 'from the outside,' and not 'from the inside.' In other words, it means adopting 'a certain mental attitude' that presumes that the knowledge of individual states of consciousness is fundamentally suspect: consciousness cannot provide 'explanatory concepts.'[74] In place of the illusive familiarity of immediately apparent explanations, Durkheim proposes the surprise of laws whose discovery should destabilize us because they are most likely to contradict what we spontaneously believe.[75] This unknown that scientific inquiry seeks to uncover turns out, at the end of the *Elementary Forms of Religious Life*, to be 'the impersonal.' That the unknown within which sociology can find the only valid 'explanatory concepts' turns out to be the impersonal was already implicit in the inaugural act of a sociology, which rejects as suspect any explanation

that individuals might offer for their own behaviour. Durkheim could
have treated this suspicion as methodologically provisional and applicable above all to social agents' immediate self-explanations, but in
order to model the sociological method on that of all the positive sciences (and in assuming that real causes have the same 'foreignness' for
sociology as they do in general for the established sciences), Durkheim
from the very beginning had to locate the principle of sociality beyond
the reach of individual consciousness. His proposition that 'the impersonal is within us because the social is within us,'[76] which can also be
read the other way around, simply restates his situating of the social
realm, and hence the object of sociology, within a realm of causality
that, not provisionally but essentially, is beyond the reflexive knowledge of the protagonists of social action. Objective causality, according
to Durkheim, functions only at the level of what he calls the 'unconscious,' and the unconscious can only be impersonal.[77]

Durkheim does not seem able to envisage the possibility of an explanation following a purposive logic of action that nonetheless leaves
room for the unconscious, as does Weber. Careful to include within the
'understanding' sciences not only Jaspers's work in psychopathology
but Nietzsche's genealogical method as well as the Marxist theme of
'class interest,' Weber from time to time corrects the excessive intellectualism of his methodological principles by recognizing that the purposive structures through which sociology (and certain types of psychology)
explain the logic of social practice can be very different from the intended motives that agents themselves ascribe to their action. What
Weber calls 'pragmatic' explanation[78] includes 'very important branches
of interpretive psychology,'[79] which uncover connections that are understandable and objectively rational without being 'subjectively,' that
is, consciously, guided. Such connections include those identified by
psychoanalysis, historical materialism, and Nietzsche's theory of
ressentiment, including its 'interpretation that reveals, within the *pragma*
of a complex of interests, the objective rationality of internal or external
behaviour that until then had gone insufficiently noticed because, for
understandable reasons, it could not be admitted.'[80] To be sure, Weber's
acceptance of these kinds of explanation make the definition of interpretive sociology in the first lines of *Economy and Society* somewhat
problematic, since Weber there seems to identify the 'subjective meaning' that defines social action with the agent's self-consciously reflected
motives.[81] The comments that follow this definition, albeit somewhat
awkwardly, suggest nonetheless that Weber meant that explanation

need not reproduce conscious motives, but rather identify the 'reasons' for action whose structures are intentional and are 'subjective' reasons in that sense. One could, of course, equally say for Durkheim that causes need not be unconscious as long as they are impersonal in character. Still, it would be a mistake to try to reconcile them in this way. For Weber, the unconscious is the unconfessed (perhaps even what is not confessable), but it remains organized in a 'pragmatic' manner, that is, in terms of ends and means. For Durkheim, the unconscious is the impersonal. Weber's definition of the 'subjective meaning' of action, in the sense that I have just qualified it, makes it impossible to associate his sociology with the voluntaristic illusion that humans are the masters of their destiny. Durkheim more openly wages a battle against this illusion, though the importance that he grants the impersonal in the determination of behaviour does not seek to condemn us to fatalism. Despite such convergences, though, the tenor of their modes of sociological explanation remains irreducibly heterogeneous.

NOTES

Translated from the French by Laurence McFalls. (*Translator's Note*: I have translated citations of Durkheim directly from the original French sources cited here and have therefore not used published English translations of Durkheim's works when available. Since this volume addresses Weber's oeuvre primarily, which was of course not written in French, I have not translated the chapter author's French citations of Weber but have either sought out and cited existing English translations or else have cited and translated into English from the original German source.)

1 Thus, in *Confucianism and Taoism*, for example, he draws on the work of Edouard Biot (for example, an article on the Chinese monetary system), Edouard Chavannes (notably an article on the Ts'in engravings), and Louis-Charles Delamarre, among others.
2 'La science positive de la morale en Allemagne,' *Revue Philosophique* 24 (1887): 33–58; 113–42; 275–84, reprinted in Émile Durkheim, *Textes I* (Paris: Éditions de Minuit, 1975).
3 For example, 'Le programme économique de M. Schaeffle,' *Revue d'économie politique* 2 (1888): 3–7.
4 On the reception of Weber in the *Année sociologique*, see Philippe Steiner, 'L'*Année sociologique* et la réception de l'oeuvre de Max Weber,' *Archives européennes de sociologie* 33 (1992): 329–49.

5 At the end of chapter 4 of *Règles de la Méthode Sociologique [The Rules of the Sociological Method]* (Paris: PUF, 1967) (hereafter *Règles*), in a footnote Durkheim cites an article by Alfred Vierkandt (1867–1953), 'Die Kulturtypen der Menschheit,' published in the *Archiv für Anthropologie* in 1898. Durkheim also wrote a review of Vierkandt's *Das Kulturproblem* in the *Année sociologique* in 1901.

6 Raymond Aron, *La philosophie critique de l'histoire* (Paris: Vrin, 1938), republished with notes and revisions by Sylvie Mesure (Paris: Juillard, 1987).

7 For more on the opposition between holism and individualism, see my article 'Max Weber et la sociologie compréhensive allemande: critique d'un mythe historiographique' in Catherine Colliot-Thélène, *Études wébériennes*, 133–68 (Paris: PUF, 2001).

8 Émile Durkheim, *Formes élémentaires de la vie religieuse* (Paris: PUF, 1985). On Durkheim's encounter with ethnology, see Philippe Steiner, *La sociologie de Durkheim* (Paris: La Découverte, 1994), 23.

9 Durkeim cites the *Introduction à l'histoire du bouddhisme indien* (1845) by Eugène Burnouf (1801–52) in *Formes élémentaires*, notably 41–4.

10 For example, Binding's *Die Normen und ihre Übertretung* as well as several of his articles on Roman law; Walter's *Histoire de la procédure civile et du droit criminel chez les romains*; Rein's *Criminalrecht der Römer*; Mainz's 'Esquisse historique du droit criminel de l'ancienne Rome'; V. Post's *Bausteine für eine allgemeine Rechtswissenschaft*. The complete references for these works can be found in Émile Durkheim, *De la division du travail social* (Paris: PUF, 1991) (hereafter *DTS*) in the notes to pages 41, 42, 52, 53 ff.

11 Sir Henry Sumner Maine (1822–88), *Ancient Law* (1861); Otto von Gierke (1841–1921), *Das deutsche Genossenschaftsrecht* (4 vols., 1868–1913).

12 For the case of Weber, we should add political economy. Weber's relationship to theoretical political economy (he called himself a disciple of the historical school of political economy) is a chapter in itself. On this topic, see Hinnerk Bruhns, 'Max Weber, l'économie et l'histoire,' *Annales HSS* 51 (1996): 1259–87, and 'Max Weber: théorie économique et histoire de l'économie,' in *Histoire et économie politique en Allemagne de Gustav Schmoller à Max Weber*, ed. Hinnerk Bruhns (Paris: Ed. de la Maison des sciences de l'homme, 2004), 183–209. See also Catherine Colliot-Thélène, 'Entre économie, histoire et sociologie: les enjeux du "Methodenstreit,"' in *Wirtschaft und Wirtschaftstheorien in Rechtsgeschichte und Philosophie*, ed. Jean-François Kervégan and Heinz Mohnhaupt (Frankfurt/Main: Klostermann, 2004).

13 See *Economy and Society* (Berkeley: University of California Press, 1978) (hereafter *E&S*), 4.

14 On this subject see the outstanding work of Jean Louis Fabiani, *Les*

160   Catherine Colliot-Thélène

philosophes de la République (Paris: Editions de Minuit, 1988), and the
introductory presentation of Durkheim in Bruno Karsenti, *Sociologie et
philosophie* (Paris: PUF, 1996), v–lix.

15 See Durkheim, *DTS*, xxxviii: 'Thus understood, positive moral science is
not opposed to any kind of philosophy, for it is situated on an entirely
different plane.'

16 See, for example, the preface to the first edition of *DTS*, xl.

17 On Durkheim's 'Hegelianism' see Karsenti, *Sociologie et philosophie*, xxviii.

18 On the necessity of axiological abstinence in the empirical sciences, see
Max Weber, 'The Meaning of "Ethical Neutrality" in Sociology and Economics,' in *The Methodology of the Social Sciences*, 1–49 (New York: Free Press,
1949), as well as 'Science as a Vocation' in *From Max Weber*, ed. H.H. Gerth
and C. Wright Mills, 129–58 (New York: Oxford University Press, 1946).

19 See, for example, Durkheim, *DTS*, xli: 'What reconciles sciences and
morality is moral science; for at the same time as it teaches us to respect
moral reality, it provides the means to improve it'; or xxxix: 'We shall see
that science can help us to find the direction in which we should guide
our conduct, to determine the ideal towards which we move confusedly.
We shall rise to this ideal only after having observed reality, and we shall
derive it from that.'

20 See Max Weber, 'Rudolf Stammlers "Überwindung" der materialistischen
Geschichtsauffassung,' in *Gesammelte Aufsätze zur Wissenschaftslehre*
(Tübingen: Mohr, 1988), 331 (hereafter *Wissenschaftslehre*).

21 See note 13.

22 See 'Über einige Kategorien der verstehenden Soziologie,' in Weber,
Wissenschaftslehre, 427–42; s. 2, 'Verhältnis zur "Psychologie,"' 432–9; and
s. 3, 'Verhältnis zur Rechtdogmatik,' 439–41.

23 On Weber's critique of Stammler, see my article 'De l'autonomie de la
sociologie du droit: la norme et la règle,' *Études wébériennes*, 195–17. Also
see the detailed introduction by Michel Coutu, Dominique Leydet, Guy
Rocher, and Elke Winter to their French translation of Weber on Stammler,
Rudolf Stammler et le matérialisme historique (Quebec: Presses de l'Université
Laval, 2001).

24 Weber, *E&S*, 13.

25 Durkheim, *Règles*, 101.

26 Weber, *Wissenschaftslehre*, 432.

27 Durkheim, *Règles*, 29–30.

28 Weber confronts experimental psychology in greatest depth in his study
'Zur Psychophysik der industriellen Arbeit,' in Weber, *Gesammelte Aufsätze
zur Soziologie und Sozialpolitik*, 61–255 (Tübingen: Mohr, 1988).

29 Weber, *Wissenschaftslehre*, 439.

30 Ibid., 436.

31 His *Règles*, 4, are perfectly clear on this point: psychology as a science 'was not born ... until one finally arrived at the idea that states of consciousness can and must be considered from without, and not from the point of view of the mind that experiences them. This is the great revolution that this field of study has carried through. Sociology must still reach this state of progress. It must move from the subjective stage, which it has barely surpassed, to the objective phase.'

32 Max Weber, *Roscher and Knies* (New York: Free Press, 1975).

33 In Edward A. Shils and Henry A. Finch, eds., *The Methodology of the Social Sciences* (New York: Free Press, 1949), 113–88.

34 Durkheim did confront this problem but only through his discussion with Seignobos of his traditionalist conception of history, with the result that Durkheim associated the problem of singular causal imputation with what for him was the questionable scientific validity of the history of events. See 'Le débat sur l'explication en histoire et en sociologie' (1908) in Durkheim, *Textes I*, 199–217, notably the exchange between Durkheim and Seignobos, 203:

> DURKHEIM: It is true that you distinguish between and seem to oppose the terms cause and law. But what is a cause that is not a law? Any causal relation is a law.
> SEIGNOBOS: But no, there are events that have happened only once and for which one can determine the cause.

Durkheim did, of course, admit the possibility of another kind of history, closely related to sociology, provided its field of interest was institutions, but he could not imagine a history or sociology of this type that did not subscribe to a nomothetic conception of causality.

35 Durkheim, *Textes I*, 96.

36 Ibid.

37 See the well-known passage in the 'Objectivity' essay in which Weber (in Finch and Shils, *Methodology of the Social Sciences*, 72) defines the task of social sciences as the journal *Archiv für Sozialwissenschaft und Sozialpolitik* intends to practise them (this definition applies as well to the entirety of Weber's own sociological work): 'The type of social science in which we are interested is an *empirical science* of concrete *reality* [*Wirklichkeitswissenschaft*]. Our aim is the understanding of the characteristic uniqueness of the reality in which we move. We wish to understand on the one hand the relationships and the cultural significance of individual events in

their contemporary manifestations and on the other the causes of their being historically *so* and not *otherwise*.'

38 See the continuation of the passage cited in the text above: '[History] cannot remain its own discipline unless it limits itself to the study of national individualities taken in themselves and considered in their divers moments of evolution. But in that case it becomes nothing more than a narrative whose purpose is practical. Its function is to allow societies to remember their past; it is the eminent form of collective memory.' Durkheim, *Textes I*, 196–97.

39 Ibid., 400.

40 'La science positive de la morale en Allemagne' and 'Sociologie et sciences socials,' reprinted in Durkheim, *Textes I*, respectively 267–343 and 121–59.

41 See ibid., 401–7.

42 Ibid., 272.

43 Ibid., 149. We can thus understand why some contemporary economists (marginal ones, to be sure) have rediscovered the historical school and its interest in specificity; see Geoffrey M. Hodgson, *How Economics Forgot History* (New York: Routledge, 2001).

44 Ibid.

45 Wilhelm Hennis, 'A Science of Man: Max Weber and the Political Economy of the German Historical School,' in *Max Weber and His Contemporaries*, ed. Wolfgang J. Mommsen and Jürgen Osterhammel (London: Unwin Hyman, 1987).

46 Max Weber, 'Antikritisches zum "Geist" des Kapitalismus,' *Archiv für Sozialwissenschaft und Sozialpolitik* 30 (1910): 200.

47 Weber, *E&S*, 19.

48 Talcott Parsons's classic translation (New York: Charles Scribner, 1958 [1930]) presents the 'Vorbemerkung' as the 'Author's Introduction.'

49 Max Weber, *Gesammelte Aufsätze zur Religionssoziologie I* (Tübingen: Mohr, 1988), 265.

50 Durkheim, *Règles*, 42: 'Unless the principle of causality is an empty word, when certain characteristics are found to be identical without exception among all the phenomena of a certain order, one can be assured that they are intimately bound to their nature and are inseparable from it.' Further, Durkheim, *Formes élémentaires*, 593: 'It is inconceivable that, according to the circumstances, the same effect can have sometimes one cause and others times another, unless of course the two causes are in fact fundamentally the same.'

51 Durkheim, *Textes I*, 196.

52 Ibid., 151.

53 Ibid.
54 See ibid., 404.
55 Durkheim, *Formes élémentaires*, 132.
56 See the conclusion to ibid., 593, where Durkheim makes this extrapolation by virtue of the alleged principle that 'when the existence of a law has been proven by a well-conducted experiment, this proof is universally valid.'
57 Ibid., 132n5.
58 Ibid., 2.
59 Ibid., 593.
60 Ibid., 594.
61 At the very beginning of chap. 6 of *E&S*, 399, Weber writes, 'To define "religion," to say what it *is*, is not possible at the start of a presentation such as this. Definition can be attempted, if at all, only at the conclusion of the study.' Weber never does in fact offer such a definition.
62 Durkheim, *Règles*, chap. 4: 'Rules concerning the definition of social types.'
63 Weber in Shils and Finch, *Methodology of the Social Sciences*, 68.
64 See Durkheim, *DTS*, 139: 'All that [sociology] asks is that it be recognized that the principle of causality applies to social phenomena.' Weber, in his two essays on Roscher and Knies in particular, defended (notably in opposition to Münsterberger) the causal character of the historical sciences, among which he included sociology, of course.
65 A single citation among many other possible ones: 'If there is such a thing as morality, its only possible object can be the group formed by a number of associated individuals, i.e., society, assuming of course that society be considered an agent different from the individual actors who constitute it. Morality thus begins with the attachment to a group of any sort.' 'Détermination du fait moral' (lecture to the French Society of Philosophy), in Durkheim, *Sociologie et philosophie*, 52–3.
66 Thus, in a note at the end of *Formes élémentaires*, 630–1, Durkheim observes, after having identified the social with the totality of the group and situated the essence of religion in the expression of this totality in the form of rites and beliefs, 'Basically, the concepts of totality, society and divinity are probably only different aspects of one and the same notion.'
67 Durkheim, *DTS*, 28 ff.
68 Durkheim, *Formes élémentaires*, 598–9.
69 Durkheim, *DTS*, 30.
70 Durkheim, *Formes élémentaires*, 598.
71 See ibid., 598n2. Durkheim observes that, until now, economic activity has not been explicitly linked to religion. In evoking the magical (hence

religious) origin of productive techniques and the link between economic value and the notion of power (in the sense of effectiveness), he suggests the existence of a relationship between the ideas of economic value and religious value, whose exact nature remains to be established. Durkheim does not develop this idea, but it is interesting to note that Durkheim's interpretation of religion (precisely because what he calls its 'nature' is indistinguishable from its capacity to symbolize sociality in general) implies that all that is social must somehow be brought back to the religious.

72 Weber borrows the term from the neo-Kantian philosopher Emil Lask, *Fichtes Idealismus und die Geschichte* in *Werke, Band I* (Jena: Dietrich Scheglman Reprintverlag, 2002), whom Weber cites in his essays on Roscher and Knies, *Wissenschaftslehre*, 16n1.

73 See Weber, 'Roscher und Knies,' *Wissenschaftslehre*, 67: 'Our need to understand causes can find in the analysis of human behaviour a qualitative satisfaction of a different nature ... In other words, individual action is, because it is meaningfully interpretable (as long as the interpretation is sufficient), by principle specifically less "irrational" than an individual natural process.' Also, 69: '"Interpretability" here provides additional "calculability" in comparison with not "interpretable" natural processes.'

74 Durkheim, *Règles*, xiii.

75 Ibid., preface to the second edition, xiv: 'Upon entering into the social world, [the sociologist] must be aware that he is entering the unknown; he must feel himself to be in the presence of facts whose laws are as unsuspected as were those of life when the science of biology did not yet exist; he must be ready to make discoveries that will surprise and disconcert him.'

76 Durkheim, *Formes élémentaires*, 636.

77 See, for example, his remark in the debate with Seignobos, *Textes I*, 202: 'Every causal relationship is unconscious, it can be explained only after the fact.'

78 See Weber, 'Die Grenznutzlehre und das "psychophysische Grundgesetz,"' *Wissenschaftslehre*, 396.

79 Weber, 'Über einige Kategorien der verstehenden Soziologie,' *Wissenschaftslehre*, 434.

80 Ibid.

81 Weber, *E&S*, 4.

6 Talcott Parsons: A Critical Loyalty to Max Weber

GUY ROCHER

Max Weber's oeuvre first became known in Quebec's French- and English-language universities by way of Talcott Parsons. At least in this respect, Quebec was in no way different from the rest of postwar North America in the early 1950s, when the second, 1949 edition of Parsons's *The Structure of Social Action* had its impact.[1] Monumental and highly original in the context of American sociology of the time, Parsons's work compelled a rereading of Émile Durkheim's work and corrected the ambiguous if not false image from which Durkheim's sociology suffered in the United States, where one attributed a sort of 'collective animism,' or what was called 'collective mind,' to Durkheim's social theory. But more importantly, Parsons first exposed North American social science to Weber's oeuvre. To mostly Protestant North America, Parsons presented the first English translation of *The Protestant Ethic and the Spirit of Capitalism* in 1930.[2] Then, in *The Structure of Social Action*, Parsons devoted four chapters to Weber's sociology, of which two, both entitled 'Max Weber: Religion and Modern Capitalism,' dealt with Weber's sociology of religion in light of the *Protestant Ethic*.[3]

As a young student of sociology at Laval University in Quebec City at the end of the 1940s, I for my part first read Weber by way of and thanks to Talcott Parsons, through his translation of the *Protestant Ethic* but above all through his detailed presentation of Weber's sociology of religion in *The Structure of Social Action*. At a time when I found little intellectual stimulation in American sociology, this book by a Harvard sociologist who knowledgeably handled four European founders of social science was a veritable revelation for me. I was moved to reread Durkheim; I discovered Vilfredo Pareto, of whom I had never heard; and above all, I set out to read and to reread Max Weber, following in the footsteps of Talcott Parsons.

I allow myself to be personal, even autobiographical here, for I happen to have played a role in the reception of Weber in Quebec, where I was among the first to read and to teach his work. I first studied social sciences at Laval University between 1947 and 1950 and received an MA in sociology. During my studies I wanted to enter into the subject matter of sociology by 'conversing' with those whom my professors had presented to me as the great masters. The first of these was Durkheim. Thus I set out to read his principal works and the entire collection of the *Année sociologique*. At the time, Laval was a Catholic university, run by priests from the Seminary of Quebec. But the Faculty of Social Sciences, founded by the Dominican Father Georges-Henri Lévesque, constituted, thanks to its founder, an enclave within the University by virtue of its political and social orientations as well as of its intellectual freedom. Whereas the Seminary of Quebec considered Durkheim a dangerous anti-clerical and anti-Catholic who preached a dogmatic secularism unacceptable to practising Catholics, this was not the case in the Faculty of Social Sciences. There Durkheim was embraced without any reservation as the founder and grand master of sociology in the French language, whom we had not only the right but the duty to read.

So I read Durkheim. While I understood *Suicide* to be the first great empirical work in sociology and gleaned the lessons to be learned from *The Rules of the Sociological Method*, I was not sure to have perfectly understood *The Division of Social Labor* and even less *Elementary Forms of Religious Life*. I thus felt that I needed help better to read and to reread Durkheim. I no longer know who it was who first exposed me to Parsons's *Structure of Social Action*, which had first been published in 1937 but had just come out again in a second edition in 1949. I do not hesitate to admit that at the time that book opened whole new horizons for me. Until then, the empiricism of the Chicago School had put me off, but now an American sociologist had opened my eyes to the European theoretical founders of contemporary sociology while U.S. sociology was – and to this day largely remains – self-absorbed. Parsons's approach provided me with an overview of Durkheim's oeuvre, making clear to me its many internal linkages and consequences, even as he added critical insights into its errors and limits.

Beyond his treatment of Durkheim, however, what fascinated me in Parsons's book were his obvious intentions. Parsons's intellectual journey showed me for the first time that sociology could perhaps be a cumulative science, that is. like Parsons, one could read the works of disciplinary predecessors and look for their convergences and their contributions to the construction of a general theory of sociology. While others have seen Parsons's integrative theoretical ambitions as his great fault, for me it revealed and confirmed the existence of an emergent science.

But reading *The Structure of Social Action* brought another revelation, that of a German author whom I did not yet know: Max Weber. In fact, it struck me that while Parsons covered Durkheim's work in 170 pages, he devoted 220 to Weber's. If only physically, Parsons showed me that Weber, in his eyes, was at least as important as Durkheim, maybe even more. In his book Parsons paid particular attention to Weber's sociology of religion, summarizing the *Protestant Ethic* in detail as well as Weber's writings on the religions of China and India. Immersed in a society in which religious festivals, rituals, and the clergy still occupied so much space, I was intrigued by this dominant element of Quebec's social and cultural environment. I was thus drawn to the sociology of religion. Indeed, I had written my master's thesis on Herbert Spencer's sociology of religion. One can thus readily imagine how deeply impressed I was with the two chapters that Parsons devoted to Max Weber's sociology of religion.

At the end of the 1940s, Weber's oeuvre was accessible to us only in English. Thus, I first read *Die protestantische Ethik und der 'Geist' des Kapitalismus* in Talcott Parsons's translation. In 1947 Parsons and Henderson had also made part of *Wirtschaft und Gesellschaft* available under the title *The Theory of Social and Economic Organization*.[4] About the same time, Gerth and Mills proposed translations of other sections of *Wirtschaft und Gesellschaft* as well as of the two lectures on science and politics as vocations.[5] Although Parsons's presentation of Weber in *The Structure of Social Action* is better known, his introduction to *The Theory of Social and Economic Organization* is at least as remarkable; I learned much about Weber from it, as I also did from the rich introduction to the Gerth and Mills translations. Fortunately, Raymond Aron was there as well. Thanks to his *Sociologie allemande contemporaine*, I could read yet another introduction to Weber, this time in my own language.[6] More clearly than Parsons or Gerth and Mills, Aron helped me situate Weber's thought in its historical context of German thought in the human sciences. What is more, Aron seemed to me to be more in tune with Weber's political sociology than Parsons was, or even Gerth and Mills were.

I must, however, admit that I had the greatest respect for Talcott

Parsons, who seemed to me to be the most authoritative translator and interpreter of Max Weber. Thus, I took up my doctoral studies at Harvard University under the supervision of Parsons with the intention of deepening my knowledge of the founders, Durkheim and especially Weber, whose work I had only begun to explore. In a large course that Parsons taught on the sociology of religion, I recognized how Weber's thought inspired and structured the entire course. But I was soon in for a big shock: in his doctoral seminar, Parsons assigned, chapter by chapter, the manuscript of *The Social System*, which would be published a few months later, in 1951. He invited us to comment on and even to criticize his work, in which to my surprise I found hardly a trace of Durkheim or Weber. I could not understand how this new work, which Parsons deemed so important, related to *The Structure of Social Action*. I shall come back to this problem later, for it is fundamental for explaining the intellectual relationship between Parsons and Weber. For now, though, let us step back in time and see how Parsons first encountered Weber's oeuvre and became its interpreter.

In an autobiographical lecture that he gave to the Eastern Sociological Society of the United States on 31 March 1978, a year before his death, Parsons recounted what he called 'the circumstances of my encounter with Max Weber.'[7] There he recalls how, before he began his doctoral studies at the University of Heidelberg in 1925, he had never even heard of the name of Max Weber, neither in his studies in the United States nor during his year at the London School of Economics, where his teachers had included Morris Ginsberg as well as R.H. Tawney, who at the time was working on his *Religion and the Rise of Capitalism*. Upon his arrival in Heidelberg at the age of twenty-three, he first read *The Protestant Ethic*. 'I don't think it was mere chance that the first of Weber's works which I read was his study, *The Protestant Ethic and the Spirit of Capitalism*. I don't know how surprising it will be for others, however, that this reading had an immediate and powerful impact on me. It gripped my intense interest immediately and I read it straight through ... as if it were a detective story.'[8] Like love at first sight, this experience marked his entire intellectual life and career track, allowing him to say in retrospect, 'I am quite sure that without exposure to Weber's work, which occurred from the beginning of my Heidelberg experience, I would never have undertaken anything like *The Structure of Social Action* ... It was that book, of course, which established something of a position for me personally. Had I not written it, heaven knows what kind of career I might or might not have had.'[9] Parsons adds, 'My personal concern with Max Weber's work thus extended well over fifty years,'[10] and 'Indeed, given the course on which I had embarked, it did not seem likely that, as long as I remained intellectually active, I would ever cease to be concerned with Weber's work.'[11] Parsons could not have said it better: the following year, in early May 1979, he was invited to Heidelberg for a conference that the Faculty of Social Sciences organized in honour of the fiftieth anniversary of his doctorate. Before an audience including the likes of Habermas, Luhmann, Lepsius, and Schluchter, he gave a paper entitled, 'On the Relation of the Theory of Action to Max Weber's *Verstehende Soziologie.*' Parsons died in Munich two days later during the night of 7–8 May.

In the 1960s and 1970s, and later as well, I read nearly every one of the numerous critiques of Parsons, of his theory, of his ideology, and, clearly, of the supposedly erroneous presentation and use that he made of Durkheim's and Weber's thought in elaborating his own theory. While some of these criticisms were valid, I have found most of them to be partial (in both senses of the word), carried away with and by the anti-Parsonian wave that swept sociology in the United States during the late 1960s and 1970s and whose effects continue to be felt today. More than any other, the sociological theory of Talcott Parsons has divided the profession between those who reject it and those who still find inspiration in it. In the last few years, however, Parsons's sociology has met with a more serene and positive evaluation than in the 1970s in a series of books on his work that have taken into account all the dimensions of a complex thinker and of his evolution over fifty years.[12] It is not my intention to enter into this debate here. Instead, I wish to re-examine Talcott Parsons's treatment of Max Weber's methodology and how he both criticized and distanced himself from it. I am thus interested in only one very particular aspect of Parsons's intellectual relationship with Weber. Exploring this theme is especially relevant for a volume such as this centennial celebration of Weber's 'Objectivity' essay, for a major part of Parsons's work makes sense only in light of his ongoing attempt to investigate if not 'the spirit of science,' then the purpose, the requirements, and the limits of scientific knowledge. Like Weber, and in response to him, Parsons devoted considerable attention to the methodology of science and of the social sciences in particular.

In 1964, on the occasion of the German Sociological Association's famous congress marking the centennial of Weber's birth, Talcott Parsons read a paper in German, subsequently published in French and in English.[13] The organizers of the congress had asked Parsons to address the theme of Weber's contribution to social-scientific objectivity and evaluation. He begins his paper with a disclaimer: 'I am not a Max Weber scholar; in particular, a scholar of the intricate details of his methodology of science and its relation to the currents of German philosophy of his time.'[14] This surprising act of humility probably had something to do with the fact that Parsons was addressing an audience of German specialists on Weber. Thirty years earlier, however, Parsons had devoted many pages of *The Structure of Social Action* to the method-ology of the social sciences, not only with reference to Pareto and to Durkheim, but especially to Weber. What's more, in the final part of the book, in which he presents the conclusions of his lengthy effort, he devotes his final chapter to what he calls 'Tentative Methodological Implications,' underscoring at the chapter's beginning that 'certain meth-odological questions have run through the study as a whole.'[15] Among the numerous commentaries and criticisms that Parsons's first major work elicited, few if any have taken up let alone analysed the method-ological thread running through the book. Yet this early methodological preoccupation casts light on the scientific project that guided Parsons's career over the subsequent forty-two years until his death.

From 1937 onwards, Parsons's scientific project was clearly directed against the empiricism and empirical methodology that, under the influence of the Chicago School, dominated American sociology. This empiricism consisted of gathering of facts and then of letting them speak for themselves, as if they were transparent and eloquent, requir-ing little if any conceptual or theoretical translation. In the opening pages of *The Structure of Social Action*, Parsons denounces 'what lies at the basis of many deep-rooted errors, especially in social science. It is the fallacy which Professor Whitehead has so beautifully exposed un-der the name of the 'fallacy of misplaced concreteness.' This raises methodological issues which will be of fundamental importance through-out the later discussion.'[16] This reference to Whitehead's felicitous phrase, which Parsons held dear throughout his life, recurs on two more occa-sions in *The Structure*.[17] For Parsons, the fundamental error of positivist empiricism, as practised in American sociology at the time, resides in a confusion between knowledge of an object and the object itself, that is, in the reification of knowledge.

In adopting this anti-positivist position, the publication of *The Struc-ture* in 1937 went radically against the tide of American sociology. Indeed, not a single American sociologist of the Chicago tradition mer-its even the scantest citation in the book. Perhaps for this reason the book received little attention when it first appeared; only after the war did the book become widely read in its second edition, published in 1949.[18] At that time a 'Harvard school' of American sociology emerged around Parsons and his book as a theoretical counterweight to the empiricism of the Chicago School. Although *The Structure* represented a break with the dominant orientations of American sociology because it drew on only European thinkers – Marshall, Pareto, Durkheim, and Weber – and completely ignored American social 'scientists,' it did so primarily through its methodological position. Parsons summarizes this position: 'It has been necessary to criticize, in terms of their unfortunate empirical implications, a group of views which had been brought together under the term empiricism,'[19] adding a few pages later, 'In opposition to ... these untenable views may be set the epistemological position that seems to be supplied throughout this study – analytical realism.'[20] For Parsons, what is 'realistic' about his position is that it assumes, in an epistemological and philosophical sense, that the world outside of the thinking subject is an empirical reality, not a creation of the mind nor reducible to an ideal order.[21] This realism is at the same time 'analytical' in that it approaches reality, the object of scientific research, by way of 'a frame of reference,' a term that Parsons uses often. This frame of reference belongs to the realm of abstraction: it neither is reality nor directly reflects reality. Instead, it isolates certain aspects of reality and reconstructs them according to a structure of knowledge and interpretation that makes sense. Scientists do observe facts, but they require, to this end, an intellectual procedure and a preexisting universe of interpretation that allows for the categorization, comparison, and dissection of facts. Above all, as will become a central theme in all of Parsons's thought, the analytical task is possible only insofar as scientific knowledge takes on the form of a 'system,' which does not correspond to reality but is a construct that extracts the elements of reality best suited for understanding it. Parsons thus situates his 'analytical realism' at equal distances between positivist empiricism and idealism. Establishing this middle ground, both theoretically and epistemologically, is the task Parsons set for himself in *The Structure of Social Action*.

Parsons owes this methodological position to Weber, from whom he borrowed and adapted it. This debt, however, brings us back to the question of Parsons's apparent timidity vis-à-vis Weber's epistemology and methodology. Indeed, for his presentation of them in *The Structure*, Parsons relies on the authority of a scholar whom he completely trusts:

Alexander von Schelting, whom he had met in Heidelberg, where he appeared to Parsons to be one of the most brilliant representatives of the new generation of scholars in Germany. By contrast, Parsons quickly found himself in profound disagreement with another leading light of that generation, namely Karl Mannheim, whose very first seminar Parsons attended. Parsons cultivated his disagreement with Mannheim, which he shared with von Schelting, for the rest of his life. In 1934, von Schelting published *Max Webers Wissenschaftslehre*, a book in which he presented, analysed, and commented on Weber's methodology. Parsons held great store in this book, writing a long, praising review of it in the *American Sociological Review* in 1936, the first year of this journal's publication by the American Sociological Association.[22] It was probably no coincidence that Parsons's review of von Schelting's book was preceded, in the same issue, by an even longer and highly critical review of Karl Mannheim's new book by none other than von Schelting.[23] In any case, Parsons drew heavily on von Schelting's work in his chapter on Weber's methodology in his book published the following year. This reliance on von Schelting suggests that Parsons's claim in 1964 not to be an expert on Weber or his methodology may not just have been false modesty. Parsons never felt quite as much at ease with Weber's methodology as he did with the rest of his thought. Thus, Parsons must have been happy to have von Schelting's work to turn to, as he admits in a footnote at the beginning of his methodological chapter in *The Structure*: 'It is indeed fortunate that there is available for the purposes of this chapter the excellent secondary study, already referred to, by Dr. Alexander Von Schelting, *Max Webers Wissenschaftslehre* ... The present writer is greatly indebted to Dr. Von Schelting's treatment at many points and will follow him closely.'[24]

Despite this timidity, be it feigned or genuine, Talcott Parsons seized numerous occasions throughout his career to revisit Weber's methodology, and I would argue that he adopted three different attitudes towards it. The first is that of the attentive pupil: Parsons spent many years on the benches of the school of Weber and took great pains to understand the diverse parts of Weber's oeuvre and of the methodology, both explicit and implicit, that underpinned Weber's research on religion, law, economics, etc. At different points in his life, Parsons took it upon himself to explain and to make explicit to Anglo-American audiences Weber's contributions to the new methodology of the social sciences destined to break out of the ruts of idealism, positivism, and historicism.

Parsons's second attitude, of particular interest to us here, is critical of Weber's methodology. The point of departure for Parsons's critique is his reproach to Weber for having too radically distinguished and opposed the natural sciences and the social sciences. According to Parsons, Weber did not clearly enough see that these two orders of knowledge may be distinctive in their substantive contents, but not in their logic, which is identical. 'The natural and the social sciences,' Parsons writes, '... belong to the strict logic of empirical science in general in which ... the two groups of sciences do not differ at all. Weber's failure to clarify the distinctions and their consequences for general theory and its empirical application seems to have been largely due to the rigidity of the methodological line that he attempted to draw between the two groups.'[25] From a methodological standpoint – that of the canonical requirements for the intellectual construction of reality – the social sciences do not differ from the natural sciences, according to Parsons. They both have the obligation to represent and to explain reality according to ever greater and higher degrees of conceptual and theoretical generalization. To be sure, the object of research in social science differs in certain respects from that in the physical and natural sciences, if only by virtue of the subjectivity and consciousness of actors, but it is important, as Parsons argues against Weber, not to confuse, as Weber does, the 'substantive' differences between the two orders of science and the methodological requirements that unite them. Weber had not gone far enough in saving the social sciences from subjectivism, according to Parsons: 'What Weber did was to take an enormous step in the direction of bridging the gap between the two types of science, and to make possible the treatment of social material in a systematic scientific manner rather than as an art. But he failed to complete the process, and the nature of the half-way point at which he stopped helps to account for many of the difficulties of his position.'[26]

In *The Structure of Social Action*, Parsons explains what he means by 'the difficulties of his position' as a consequence of Weber's too-radical distinction between the two scientific universes. 'It is in the natural sciences that generalized theory ... has been most highly developed in the past, and his rigid separation prevented him from making the fullest possible use of the methodological achievements in that field. In this respect Pareto had a distinct advantage over Weber.'[27] Parsons of course does not accuse Weber of being an empiricist of either the positivist or historicist ilk. To his great credit, in Parsons's view, Weber had distanced himself from both of these schools of thought, dominant in his age. Notably against historicism, Weber demonstrated the need for abstract and general conceptualizations.

Weber's polemical orientation was directed against a methodological position according to which such categories (subjective categories) could be used only to formulate individually unique complexes of meaning and sequences of motivation. Weber fully agreed with the proponents of this position that concrete phenomena were individually unique, but disputed the relevance of this fact to his problems. Scientific conceptualization is, he said, in the nature of the case abstract and never fully exhausts or reflects concrete reality.[28]

To escape from historicist empiricism, Weber developed an original concept, the ideal-type, which he was able to use, Parsons recognizes, both empirically and in an abstract or general manner. Certain ideal-types are historically singular, such as the prophet in Judaism; others are general, such as bureaucracy. This methodological innovation is associated with Weber and generally considered his principal methodological contribution. As early as 1937, however, Parsons was no doubt the first sociologist to formulate a critical analysis of the Weberian ideal-type. He makes two major criticisms. The first concerns Weber's use of rationality as the starting point for his ideal-typical constructs. Parsons questions Weber's dichotomous opposition of rationality and irrationality, finding it excessively simple. For Weber, any deviation from rationality falls into the category of the irrational, whereas for Parsons many of these deviations are the product of particular value orientations. Moreover, irrationality is much more complex than Weber acknowledges, Parsons claims, especially since many actions are inspired more by the non-rational than by the irrational or the rational, Parsons adds with reference to Pareto.[29] Although Parsons recognizes that the ideal-typical dichotomization of rationality versus irrationality is a 'useful fiction,'[30] it is of limited utility, because rationality thus narrowly defined does not apply very widely. Consequently, Weber's analysis of action remains almost exclusively at the level of individual acts as the unit of analysis; it fails, Parsons claims, to address the social actor as a 'total functional system,' a concept whose complexity escapes Weber's methodology, especially when the actor, as is usually the case, is situated within an equally complex social system. The rationality of ideal-typical action for Weber leads Parsons to consider his methodology faulty because of its excessive conceptual polarization: Weber's ideal-types are always limiting, extreme cases. Thus they do not lend themselves well to the analysis of complex social reality in which the researcher generally faces what Parsons calls 'relative degrees of social integration and disorganisation' within systems characterized by an equilibrium of forces.[31] To be sure, Parsons admits that Weber's ideal-types are not supposed to correspond to empirical reality, but he faults Weber for offering precisely such an impoverished perspective on social reality. He labels Weber's ideal-types 'atomistic' because they are so remote from the elements that constitute the complex reality of social action. The ideal-type thus offers only limited utility for research.

Parsons's second methodological critique of Weber follows from his critique of the excessive rationality of his ideal-typical constructs, which impeded Weber from articulating a complete sociological theory. Weber succeeded in surpassing historicism by stressing the need for abstract concept construction, but Parsons regrets that Weber stopped at the threshold of a general sociological theory because he got stuck at the level of generalization of the ideal-type. In *The Structure of Social Action*, Parsons is very explicit:

> Weber did not set out to build up a generalized theoretical system in the social field. Indeed there is little evidence that he had any clear conception either of the possibility of doing so or of its usefulness if it could be done. He was, rather, deeply absorbed in specific empirical problems and conceived theory directly as an aid to empirical research, never to be pursued for its own sake, only as a means of forging tools for the empirical tasks directly in view ... General theory, properly understood, is not sterile dialectical argument, but of the utmost consequence for the interpretation of empirical problems.[32]

Weber understood the importance of theory and engaged abstract conceptualization, but, Parsons regrets, he stopped halfway.

At this point Parsons adopts his third attitude towards Weber: having learned from the master and criticized him, he sets out to surpass him. He takes on the mission to complete the theoretical edifice that Weber left unfinished. This mission leads him to elaborate a general theory of human and social action, including a theory of the social system. He devotes himself to this task with the publication of *The Social System* in 1951 and of the *Working Papers in the Theory of Action* in 1953, two books that will determine his work for the remainder of his life.[33] Despite claims to the contrary,[34] these works do not constitute a rupture within Parsons's oeuvre: their contents were foreseen in *The Structure of Social Action* of 1937 and in Parsons's lengthy introduction to his translation of part of *Wirtschaft und Gesellschaft* published in 1947 under the title *Max Weber: The Theory of Social and Economic Organization*. In Parsonian thought, the theory of the social system is simply one element of his general theory of action, the latter being the foundation of his entire theoretical and conceptual model, as anticipated throughout *The Structure of Social Action*.

The most common criticism of Parsons is that he 'parsonized' Max Weber, and Émile Durkheim as well. I do not intend systematically to defend Parsons here but would like to make one point. Those who attack Parsons do not usually distinguish sufficiently between Parsons's presentation of the works of Weber, Durkheim, and Pareto and his use of them in the elaboration of his own theory on the basis of various elements belonging to the intellectual and scientific legacy of these three foundational thinkers (to whom we should not forget to add Marshall). With regard to Weber alone, Parsons's presentation of his work in some two hundred pages of *The Structure of Social Action* offers a very close reading of much of Weber's sociology of religion and remains a useful synthesis to this day. It is thus more relevant to ask precisely how Parsons made use of Weber, Durkheim, and Pareto in articulating his action and systems theory. Throughout his career Parsons remained loyal to Durkheim, as Edward Tiryakian has demonstrated,[35] and to Weber as well, as William Buxton and David Rehorik have shown.[36] At the same time, however, Weber and Durkheim's continued influence on Parsons's thought did not occupy a central position in the grand systems-theoretical model of action and social system that Parsons elaborated without their input, or at least without any obvious direct theoretical influence on their parts.

Parsons sought inspiration in the work of his three great predecessors, who perhaps presaged a general social theory, but it remained up to him alone to formulate it in all its dimensions. Parsons's ambition was clear already in *The Social System* and became more evident as he developed his theoretical oeuvre. Nonetheless, in one of his final writings, 'A Paradigm of the Human Condition,' where Parsons affirms that his theoretical enterprise has taken another great step forward in addressing the entire 'human condition' (a notion explicitly inspired by André Malraux's novel of the same name), Parsons claims to have been 'especially influenced by repeated revisits to Weber's work.'[37] In particular, Parsons refers to Weber's treatment of 'problems of meaning' in his sociology of religion. This appeal to Weber allows Parsons to introduce what he calls 'the residual category of the cognitively non-empirical,' something he admits having never dared to take up in his systemic theory, namely religious faith, beliefs in the Beyond, which he now can incorporate as the 'telic system' within his general system of the human condition. On closer observation, though, aside from this Weberian influence, Parsons's overall system of the human condition is hardly Weberian in inspiration. It flows from many sources and answers to a theoretical ambition that is Parsons's alone and which he pursued throughout his career ever since the publication of *The Structure of Social Action*.

As Bryan Turner rightly observes, Parsons drew on diverse sources in order to develop his general systemic theory of action and of the social system.[38] Among these sources is one that is rarely recognized but is explicitly present in his work as of 1947, namely biology and biological theory, in which Parsons, who originally wanted to pursue a career in medicine, had cultivated an interest since his youth[39] and to which he returned after *The Structure of Social Action*. Indeed, his interest in biology underlay one of his major criticisms of Weber:

> One of the sources of Weber's failure to think explicitly in terms of a theoretically generalized social system lies in certain features of the biological thought of his time ... The important feature of this thought for present purposes is the tendency to attempt to simplify dynamic problems by attributing as many as possible of the features of the organism to the necessities imposed upon it by the environment if it or its species is to survive. This has tended to divert attention from the functional analysis of the organism as a going concern to the external conditions of the survival of organisms. To a certain extent it is a result of the preoccupation in biological theory with problems of evolution rather than of physiology.[40]

For Parsons, recent progress in physiology and biochemistry were a major inspiration for his conception of systemic function. He was notably influenced directly by the work of the biochemist Lawrence J. Henderson, of the biologist Walter Cannon, and, by way of the latter two, by the French physiologist Claude Bernard and his experimental method.

Parsons was particularly interested in the convergence between biological and sociological theory after attending an interdisciplinary conference in Bellagio in 1969 and pursued this interest until his death. He co-organized two further conferences on the subject with the historian of science A. Hunter Dupree, with whom he published a short article in

1976 in which they expressed the hope that 'serious theoretical work on the borderlines between biological and socio-cultural systems may make an important contribution to their eventual synthesis, understandable in terms of a wider conceptual framework acceptable both to biologists and social scientists.'[41] Parsons will himself attempt to achieve such a synthesis at a higher level of generalization in one of his last writings, 'A Paradigm of the Human Condition,' mentioned already above.

Other sources of inspiration and influence also contributed to the constant evolution of Parsons's quest for a grand theory. We might mention his reading and rereading of Freud, of Chomsky's linguistics, of Norbert Wiener's cybernetics, of information theory, of T.H. Marshall's analysis of the evolution of the concept of citizenship, and of Charles H. Cooley and George H. Mead's theory of symbolic interaction. By Parsons's own admission, these diverse influences helped to broaden his systemic perspective to include all fields of knowledge, to which the notion of the system applies as it takes on an increasingly general and universalizable abstract form. Parsons expressed this conviction in commenting upon one of his final articles on social systems, in which he claimed to go farther and in much greater depth than he had in his 1951 book, *The Social System*: 'There is an even stronger emphasis than before on the necessary abstractness of what is treated as a system in scientific theory, a development from the earlier influence on me of Whitehead and Henderson and of Max Weber.'[42]

On several occasions, Parsons reiterated that he thought that he had always remained faithful to the first sources of the evolution of his thought and that this allegiance expressed itself in continuities throughout his whole oeuvre. In 1977, not long before his death, he wrote, 'There has been essential continuity over the forty-years period since *The Structure of Social Action*. This continuity has centered above all on the "mining" of the theoretical richness of the works of Emile Durkheim and Max Weber, attempting not only to understand them but to use them constructively for further theoretical development ... The completion of that study was followed almost immediately by intensive study of the writings of Sigmund Freud. Those three have stayed with me as fundamental anchor points ever since.'[43]

This continuity cannot be denied, but it also cannot be denied that Parsons constructed his vast theoretical system of action and, ultimately, of the human condition, by drawing on numerous and highly diverse new sources and, in so doing, reduced the relative influence of his earlier inspirations. This point becomes all the more obvious when one attempts to follow the ever-growing complexity of his theoretical model. Thus one can observe the paradox of an avowed and no doubt real continuity in his work and a certain disjuncture. There is continuity, on the one hand, because Parsons spent his entire life developing and refining the theoretical work that, in his eyes, Weber had failed to produce. On the other hand, there is a disjuncture because the totality of the grand, global systemic theory that Parsons elaborated, from its conception to its overall architecture, is essentially Parsonian. Weber's contribution is at most partial and highly localized (for example, the 'telic system' in the paradigm of the human condition).

In my opinion, the rupture in Parsons's relationship to Weber grew out of his early critique of Weberian methodology. It is especially clear that, as avowedly Weberian as he may have been, his critique of the ideal-typical method and its practical limitations meant that he never adopted it. Parsons was convinced that this method had thwarted Weber's theoretical élan and that therefore he himself had to abandon it and surpass it in order to elaborate the general sociological theory that Weber probably never could have undertaken in the scientific and intellectual context of his time. For other reasons, in particular his analysis of capitalism, his comparative sociology of religions and of their economic ethics, and his sociology of law, Parsons held Weber to have had one of the most brilliant minds of the twentieth century and to be an eminent – if not the most eminent – founder of modern social science, and of sociology in particular. I have wanted to demonstrate here, however, how Parsons's critique of Weber's methodology explains that, despite his frequent claims to continuity, Talcott Parsons constructed his theoretical lifework in rupture with Weber as well as with Durkheim and Pareto.

Finally, it seems that the criticisms that the young Parsons made, especially in the 1930s and 1940s, of Weber's methodology were motivated already then by his deep-seated and unshakeable conviction, which guided him throughout his life, that the progress of social science depended on a sophisticated, complex, and highly abstract conceptual and theoretical apparatus. To this end, he very early on reached the conclusion that such a theoretical apparatus had to go beyond the sciences of society to include them in a general theory of human action whose bases were necessarily biological, psychological, social, and cultural. Parsons intimates this belief in his earliest writings, loudly proclaims it in *The Structure of Social Action* of 1937, and never wavers from it for the rest of his life. It is what made him describe himself, in the dedication of *The Social System* to his wife, as an 'incurable theorist.'[44] His steadfast conviction and his manner of living it certainly distinguished him within sociology in the United States and beyond. It was also the cause for the many criticisms he and his work had to suffer. Even his closest disciples had to express their doubts about some part or another of his grand theory. And Parsons had to face the same criticism that he had made of Weber, namely that this theory was of limited use for empirical research.[45] Despite these criticisms, Parsons's reputation and influence did not decline – as is sometimes claimed – in the 1960s and 1970s. Bibliographies of the writings about his oeuvre testify to the remarkable consistency in the commentary that his work has generated since the early 1940s up to the present.[46]

Still, another discontinuity or rupture characterizes the evolution of Parsons's uninterrupted effort at theorization. In writing his first great book, his youthful work *The Structure of Social Action*, often considered his best, Parsons drew on European sources only, without a single tip of the hat to American thinkers. Subsequently, however, Parsons sought no inspiration from contemporary European thinkers. Almost without exception, he turns to research and studies in psychology, biology, linguistics, or cybernetics produced in the United States, as if postwar Europe had nothing to offer him intellectually. Perhaps it served Parsons right that discussion and debate of his work hardly escaped the confines of the sociological community in the United States – with two very notable exceptions, however. Jürgen Habermas and his theory of communicative action in particular clearly bear the marks of Parsons's influence, while Niklas Luhmann, who sought inspiration in Parsons only subsequently to distance himself from him, subjected Parsons to the same treatment the latter had given Weber, namely using his work as a springboard for leaping to a higher level of abstraction and of complexity. Parsons, however, died too soon to have any knowledge of Habermas's *Theory of Communicative Action* (1982) or of Luhmann's *Social System* (1984). In Luhmann in particular he might have recognized a dissident disciple who even more than Parsons himself was an 'incurable theorist.'

NOTES

Translated from the French by Laurence McFalls.

1 Talcott Parsons, *The Structure of Social Action* (New York: McGraw-Hill Books, 1937; 2nd ed., New York: Free Press, 1949; 3rd ed., New York: Free Press, 1968).

2 Max Weber, *The Protestant Ethic and the Spirit of Capitalism* (London: Allen and Unwin, 1930; paperback edition, New York: Scribners, 1958).

3 Parsons, *Structure of Social Action*, chap. 14 and 15.

4 Max Weber, *The Theory of Social and Economic Organization*, trans. A.M. Henderson and Talcott Parsons, introduction by Talcott Parsons (New York: Oxford University Press, 1947).

5 *From Max Weber: Essays in Sociology*, trans. Hans H. Gerth and C. Wright Mills (New York: Oxford University Press, 1946).

6 Raymond Aron, *La sociologie allemande contemporaine* (Paris: Vrin, 1935; 2nd ed., Paris: Presses Universitaires de France, 1950).

7 Talcott Parsons, 'The Circumstances of My Encounter with Max Weber,' in *Sociological Traditions from Generation to Generation*, ed. Robert K. Merton and Matilda White Riley, 37–43 (Norwood, NJ: Ablex Publishing, 1980).

8 Ibid., 39.

9 Ibid., 41.

10 Ibid., 43.

11 Ibid., 42.

12 In the 1970s three books appeared in French with an aim to familiarize francophone readers with the work of Parsons: Guy Rocher, *Talcott Parsons et la sociologie américaine* (Paris: Presses universitaires de France, 1972), in English translation, *Talcott Parsons and American Sociology*, trans. Barbara Mennell and Stephen Mennell (London: Nelson, 1974); François Chazel, *La théorie analytique de la société dans l'oeuvre de Talcott Parsons* (Paris: Mouton, 1974); François Bourricaud, *L'individualisme institutionnel: Essai sur la soci-ologie de Talcott Parsons* (Paris: Presses universitaires de France, 1977), in English translation, *The Sociology of Talcott Parsons*, trans. Arthur Gold-hammer (Chicago: University of Chicago Press, 1981). In recent years most of the 'revisionary' work on Parsons has been in English. I have in mind Jeffrey C. Alexander, *Theoretical Logic in Sociology*, vol. 4, *The Modern Reconstruction of Classical Thought: Talcott Parsons* (Berkeley: University of California Press, 1983); Pat N. Lackey, *Invitation to Talcott Parsons' Theory* (Houston: Cap and Gown, 1987); Roland Robertson and Bryan S. Turner, *Talcott Parsons: Theorist of Modernity* (London: Sage Publications, 1991); A. Javier Trevino, ed., *Talcott Parsons Today: His Theory and Legacy in Contemporary Sociology* (New York: Rowman and Littlefield, 2001); Uta Gerhardt, *Talcott Parsons: An Intellectual Biography* (Cambridge: Cambridge University Press, 2002).

13 Talcott Parsons, 'Evaluation and Objectivity in Social Science: An Interpretation of Max Weber's Contribution,' *International Social Science Journal* 17, no. 1 (1965): 46–63.

14 Ibid., 46.

15 Parsons, *Structure of Social Action*, 3rd ed., 728.
16 Ibid., 29.
17 Ibid., 589, 753.
18 Gerhardt, *Talcott Parsons*, 1 ff., analyses the difference between the book's lukewarm reception in 1937 and its widespread influence after 1949. She contends that it was only after the war that other sociologists recognized Parsons's intention to contrast democracy with Nazism. 'Not when it first appeared, but when it became a success after 1949, was the aim of *Structure* recognized, if indirectly. Parsons' intent in this book I wish to maintain, was to make understandable why, from a scientific point of view, National Socialism was the adverse of democratic structure of social action … When its second edition became successful, it provided sociologists in the post–World War II era with an answer to the question how a regime of terror could be conceptualized within a theory of the structure of social action.' Although Gerhardt probably correctly interprets Parsons's intentions, she does not prove that the sociologists of the time read Parsons in the manner that she assumes.
19 Parsons, *Structure of Social Action*, 728.
20 Ibid., 730.
21 Ibid., 753.
22 Talcott Parsons, 'Review of *Max Webers Wissenschaftslehre* by Alexander von Schelting,' *American Sociological Review* 1, no. 4 (1936): 675–81.
23 Alexander von Schelting, 'Review of *Ideology and Utopia* by Karl Mannheim,' *American Sociological Review* 1, no. 4 (1936): 663–74.
24 Parsons, *Structure of Social Action*, 579n1.
25 Ibid., 622–3.
26 Talcott Parsons, 'Introduction,' in *Max Weber: The Theory of Social and Economic Organization* (New York: Oxford University Press, 1947), 10–11.
27 Parsons, *Structure of Social Action*, 623.
28 Parsons, 'Introduction,' 11.
29 Ibid., 17.
30 Parsons, *Structure of Social Action*, 730.
31 Parsons, 'Introduction,' 26.
32 Parsons, *Structure of Social Action*, 686.
33 Talcott Parsons, *The Social System* (New York: Free Press, 1951); Talcott Parsons with Robert F. Bales and Edward A. Shils, *Working Papers in the Theory of Action* (New York: Free Press, 1953).
34 Bernard Barber, one of the principal commentators on Parsons's oeuvre, calls *The Social System* a 'second project,' yet its origins are evident in *The Structure of Social Action*. See Bernard Barber, 'Parsons' Second Project: The

Social System – Sources, Development, and Limitations,' in Trevino, *Talcott Parsons Today*, chap. 4.

35 Edward Tiryakian, 'Parsons' Emergent Durkheims,' *Sociological Theory* 18, no. 1 (March 2000): 60–83.

36 William J. Buxton and David Rehorick, 'The Place of Max Weber in the Post-Structure Writings of Talcott Parsons,' in Trevino, *Talcott Parsons Today*, chap. 2.

37 Talcott Parsons, 'A Paradigm of the Human Condition,' in Talcott Parsons, *Action Theory and the Human Condition* (New York: Free Press, 1978), 355.

38 Bryan S. Turner, 'Social Systems and Complexity Theory,' in Trevino, *Talcott Parsons Today*, chap. 5, p. 57, in particular.

39 On this subject, see Charles Camic, 'Introduction: Talcott Parsons before *The Structure of Social Action*,' in *Talcott Parsons: The Early Essays*, ed. Charles Camic (Chicago: University of Chicago Press, 1991), xiv–xv.

40 Parsons, 'Introduction,' 19.

41 Talcott Parsons, 'The Relations between Biological and Socio-Cultural Theory,' *Bulletin of the American Academy of Arts and Sciences* 29, no. 8 (May 1976), reprinted in Talcott Parsons, *Social Systems and the Evolution of Action Theory* (New York: Free Press, 1977), chap. 5.

42 Parsons, *Social Systems*, 146.

43 Ibid., 2.

44 The dedication reads, 'To Helen whose healthy and practical empiricism has long been an indispensable balance-wheel for an incurable theorist.'

45 See, for example, Barber, 'Parsons' Second Project.'

46 See Lackey, *Invitation to Talcott Parsons' Theory*; and Guy Rocher, 'Bibliographie des écrits sur l'oeuvre de Talcott Parsons,' *Sociologie et sociétés* 21, no. 1 (1989): 187–203.

7 Weberianism, Modernity, and the Fall of the Wall

ROBERTO MOTTA

Der Massstab also, mit dem Weber gemessen sein wird und den der Spezialist gerechterweise an seine Forschungen wird anlegen müssen, ist nicht derjenige der Richtigkeit im einzelnen, sondern die Fruchtbarkeit seiner Fragestellungen und Deutungen. (The yardstick by which Weber will be measured and which specialists building on his work will have to apply is not that of the correctness of details but that of the fecundity of his formulations and interpretations.)

Günter Abramowski

Introduction

A primary assumption of this chapter is that the attraction exerted by Max Weber's historical sociology is related to the importance he attributes to the process of rationalization. Thus it begins with 'Hegel, Weber, and the Theme of Rationality.' An attempt is made to show how the two authors converge (but do not merge) on the universal significance and value of the concept of rationality, in spite of the fact that, according to Hegelian metaphysics,[1] history is the process whereby the world-mind develops through time, while Weber considers rationality as a contingency of history.[2] This concern with historical contingency constitutes the specific topic of section 2, 'Weber's Two-Front War,' in which an attempt is made to show how the Weberian thesis of the Protestant ethic corresponds to some pressing political issues of Wilhelmine Germany. Section 3, 'Before and after the Fall of the Wall,' stresses the transformation (or the amplification), largely under the influence of Talcott Parsons, of that thesis into a general theory of economic development, allegedly capable of being applied, mainly after the Second World War, to the issue of the modernization of the countries of the Third World (and, in a special way, of Latin America, with its Catholic past but also with some meaningful Protestant inroads). In another twist of history, the end of 'real-existing socialism' and the breakup of the Soviet Union and its empire entailed the discredit of the Marxist paradigm of development and a shift, in Eastern Europe and Latin America (and perhaps other areas), to some version of 'Weberianism.' Hence a warning: the Protestant ethic thesis, in sheer Weberian terms or in secularized versions allegedly derived from it, should not be treated as ersatz Marxism, keeping the methodological rigidity and the dogmatism of this system.[3] If studies on social change, inspired by Max Weber, are not to remain part of the mist-enveloped attitude that used to be associated with the quasi-religious treatment of Marxism, there is no other way but to follow the methodological suggestions of Karl Popper.[4] From Weber's questions and interpretations, hypotheses susceptible to empirical verification or 'falsification' should be deduced and tested empirically. This conclusion is stated and illustrated, in section 4, 'Calling and the Spirit of Capitalism,' with several examples or suggestions concerning the testing of some Weber-derived or Weber-related hypotheses. This is the guiding thread throughout the whole chapter. Weber himself dealt with a contingent history. His theories therefore are unfit to replace, indeed to 're-enchant,' a philosophy of history directly or indirectly[5] based on Hegel's metaphysical core. Very much to the contrary – and this applies especially to the Protestant ethic thesis – they are to be viewed as permanently open to contestation. For what is science, after all, if not unending quest and unending revision?

1. Hegel, Weber, and the Theme of Rationality

The literature on Max Weber's interpretation of society and history keeps increasing, in many countries and languages, especially after the fall of the Berlin Wall and the 'end of history,' which implied the failure of Marxism, once considered the 'unsurpassable philosophy of our century.'[6] Weber is now being used as a kind of second line of defence of a certain conception of modernity and progress that had been threatened by not only the 'end of history' but also by the rise of the theories of postmodernism, which seemed to imply the exhaustion of the historical project that resulted from the Enlightenment. It is largely his latent affinity with Hegel that accounts for the increasing acceptance at this moment of his model of historical interpretation.

Yet the very existence of a relationship between our sociologist and the philosopher is not altogether clear. Hegel is not mentioned in *The Protestant Ethic*, and Weber never admits to any kind of intellectual debt vis-à-vis the author of *Lessons on the Philosophy of History*. To the contrary, he criticizes Roscher and the so-called German historical school for what he considers their Hegelianism and deductivism.[7] Yet Weber, like Hegel, places rationality at the summit of history.

Concerning Weber, we have only to be reminded of the opening paragraphs of the introduction to the *Gesammelte Aufsätze zur Religionssoziologie*,[8] in which he asks himself about 'what combination of circumstances the fact should be attributed that in Western civilization, and in Western civilization only, cultural phenomena have appeared which (as we like to think) lie in a line of development having *universal* significance and value' (emphasis added).[9] And he goes on to make it clear that it is the rationality of science, systematic theology, astronomy, medicine, chemistry, music, architecture, administration, and, finally, economy, that gives universal value to Western civilization. For Hegel, it is also in the West, and in the West only, that the spirit reaches rationality, by becoming conscious of itself in clarity, reflection, and freedom, which is but the consequence of the coincidence of its existing in itself and for itself. 'What makes the grandeur of our time is the recognition of freedom, the possession of the spirit by itself, that fact that it is in itself and for itself.'[10]

Weber and Hegel appear to converge, despite their different intellectual premises. Weber did not propose a metaphysical[11] system to account for the rise of rationality, yet he says that, in the West, cultural phenomena have gained universal meaning, thanks to their impregnation with rationality. This point does not imply a system of metaphysics, but rather that, situated as he is *'am Spitze der Geschichte,'*[12] Weber is committed, as a sociologist, to the understanding of a major tendency of the history of his time.

On the other hand, Hegel carries a heavy metaphysical load. He is wedded to a conviction about reason as the 'substance' of both nature and spirit and hence of history. Nonetheless Hegel is also an interpreter of his time. His metaphysical system does not preclude a keen sensibility to contingent historical trends of his period and thus to some of the basic tendencies of modernity – among them, or even chief among them, the tendency toward rationality, or, as German authors often say, the *Rationalisierungsprozess*. This view of Hegelianism coincides with that of one of his major French interpreters, Jean Hyppolite, who says that 'Hegel discovers, beyond the morality [*Moralität*],[13] which, in Kant and Fichte expresses only the point of view of the individual, the living reality of customs and institutions [*Sittlichkeit*].'[14] Hypolitte also says that 'what concerns Hegel is to discover the spirit of a religion, the spirit of a people, he wants to forge new concepts capable of expressing man's historical life, his existence within a people and a history.'[15] Hegel was thus, in spite of his own avowed metaphysical principles, a kind of sociologist[16] '*avant la lettre.*'

The relationship between Weber[17] and Hegel has been commented upon by several major commentators, like Jürgen Habermas, Karl Loewith, Günter Abramowski, A. Müller-Armack, D. Henrich, Wolfgang Schluchter, Catherine Colliot-Thélène, and many others.[18] At least at this stage there is little to be added to their conclusions. Let us now turn to a problem that *at first sight* is quite a different one. It concerns the attraction that Weber's thought – mainly as expressed in *The Protestant Ethic and the Spirit of Capitalism* – continues to exert, indeed that it exerts more than ever. This attraction often derives less from Weber's descriptions and analyses than from the model of society he implicitly formulates, that is, from a conception of modernity alternative both to historical materialism and to reactionism impregnated with Roman Catholicism, which refuses the full deployment of rationalization, comprising the abstraction and impersonality of nearly every kind of social relationship.[19]

2. Weber's Two-Front War

In order to understand the birth of Weber's sociology of religion, one should adopt a methodology like that adopted by Weber himself in the sixth chapter of *Economy and Society* entitled 'Sociology of Religion.' One should look for the material interests, of a social and political kind, that leave their imprint on all kinds of religious and philosophical preferences, although one need not in the least infer that the latter are but mere epiphenomena of the former. One therefore should first of all study the *Sitz im Leben*[20] of Max Weber himself, his social, political, and historical context, which will certainly help us understand why the great sociologist and historian veered toward certain theoretical choices rather than to others. It is well known that Weber was linked to a certain tradition that, during the heyday of Wilhelmine Germany, that is, during the three decades previous to the First World War, was threatened by pressures from both left and right.

To the left that threat was represented by the rise of the Social Democratic party, which based its program on the tenets of Marxist historical materialism. To the right was the counteroffensive of Roman Catholicism, which was abhorrent, indeed very abhorrent, to a liberal like Weber, who had his deepest roots in the Protestant tradition. Let us not forget the *Kulturkampf* with all of its implications. That counteroffensive was well represented by the growth of the *Zentrum* (Catholic party) in the Reichstag.[21]

Wolfgang Mommsen, in *Max Weber und die Deutsche Politik, 1890–1920,*[22] deals in several passages with the influence of the *Kulturkampf* on Weber. I will here limit myself to a single quotation:

> [Germany's] internal political situation during the 90s gave Weber an extremely pessimistic vision of the future. Liberalism was in bad shape, with many divisions and dominated by an outdated ideology. The left was disunited and largely dominated by a severe dogmatism; the National-Liberals, obsessed by the problem of military security, became, in Prussia at least, the allies of the Conservatives headed by Miquel. The Reichstag was dominated by the Zentrum, but Weber, faithful to his liberal origins, was clearly opposed to this tendency. For Weber never forswore the spirit of the Kulturkampf, the fight against Ultramontanism, a fight to which he had passionately adhered in his youth.[23]

To this Mommsen adds the following passage from one of Weber's own letters: 'According to my estimation, two powers, the State bureaucracy and the virtuous machinery of the Catholic Church ... have the clearest chances to stamp all the rest under their feet. However limited the strength (but even so and just because of this) I may still have, I hold it as a command of human dignity to engage in the fight against those powers.'[24]

Weber, above all in *The Protestant Ethic*, was thus engaged in a two-front war. Against historical materialism, he wanted to show how rationality and – as one of its consequences – economic rationalism actually preceded the development of capitalism as an economic system. According to him, the spirit of capitalism, which, in spite of some qualifications, derives from the Protestant ethic, would be a necessary condition (altogether different from a sufficient condition) for the rise of modern capitalism, that is, the rise of capitalism in the proper sense of the word, different – as he claims in his polemical point against the Werner Sombart of *Die Juden und das Wirtschaftsleben*[25] –from the vulgar capitalism based on no other motivation but 'the impulse to acquisition, pursuit of gain, of money, of the greatest possible amount of money ... common to all sorts and conditions of men at all times and in all countries of the earth,'[26] which leads straight to 'the capitalism of promoters, large-scale speculators, concession hunters, and much modern financial capitalism even in peace time ... and some, but only some, parts of large-scale international trade are closely related to it, today as always.'[27]

Against the right, Weber renews an old theme of Protestant apologetics, about the beneficial impact of the Protestant churches on the economic, social, and intellectual progress of some nations and regions. In Brazil (or concerning Brazil), a most interesting polemical literature had been produced on this subject, even prior to the publication or the diffusion of Max Weber's essays.[28] The hypothesis of a correlation or 'affinity' between modernity, with its economic, social, cultural, and political concomitants, and the 'Protestant ethic,' with its secularized equivalents, also looms very large in Brazilian social science, whose basic query, although seldom explicitly formulated, is 'why are we not the United States?' Prominent authors such as Sérgio Buarque de Holanda, Vianna Moog, and Roberto da Matta,[29] thinking that the Protestant ethic lies right at the source of American greatness,[30] have articulated the need for a kind of cultural conversion if Brazil is ever to become a fully modern country.[31]

3. Before and after the Fall of the Wall

To the extent that Weber has been made the standard-bearer of a certain moral community,[32] French sociologist Michel Maffesoli may be right in claiming that Weber's ideal-types, among them such basic concepts as inner-worldly asceticism, rationality, modern capitalism, etc., are equivalent to totemic symbols in that they express the identity and the interests of certain groups.[33] Or, to put it in a different vocabulary, as suggested by an earlier French interpreter, Augustin Cochin,[34] Max Weber's sociological system, in spite of its valid claims to accurately describe and interpret a concrete historical reality, could also be used as a *fiction nécessaire*, the expression of a certain community of thought (*société de pensée*).

Whether or not one agrees with this reading of Weberianism, it is nonetheless of great interest, for students of the history of social science, to study how Weber was received in different countries, and by different groups – often in conflict with one another – in the same countries.[35] Let us remember the writings of Talcott Parsons, who was, among other things, the first translator of the *Protestant Ethic* into English and who, more than anyone, contributed to the diffusion of Weber's ideas in the United States. Let us also remember the work of some of his disciples, like Everett Hagen, David McClelland, who explicitly applied concepts of Weberian inspiration to the sociology of development.[36] It is well known that after the Second World War, great importance was attributed to the modernization of the so-called underdeveloped countries in Asia, Africa, Latin America, and even Southern Europe. Once again, Weber supplied the weapons for the fight against the reactionary right, including, at least in Latin America, the fight against feudalism and traditionalism intertwined with aspects of Catholicism. But he also supplied the intellectual weapons needed for the fight against the competing ideology of historical materialism, fully supported by the parties of the extreme left.

Yet by the end of the 1960s, Weberianism was increasingly viewed as out of fashion in this field of study, as shown, among others, by the devastating critique of Andre Gunder Frank.[37] Can we associate this latter trend to the actual failure of the model of modernization, allegedly deduced from Weber's writings and believed to apply to practically all the countries of the Third World?

But whatever did happen, or did not happen, in the countries of the Third World, whether or not they developed according to principles and recipes claiming descent from *The Protestant Ethic and the Spirit of Capitalism*, the Weberian paradigm seems to have won the day as the result of events that took place right in the heart of Europe: all that has been represented by, and associated with, the fall of the Berlin Wall, the end of 'real-existing socialism' and the breakup of the Soviet Union and its empire, which could not, and did not fail to, entail a radical loss of credibility in the rival Marxist paradigm.

Very much in the same way that, after the fall of the Wall and subsequent events, only one superpower was left, of the two previously contending paradigms of development only the Weberian[38] was left, at least for those who did not want to accept the idea of the 'end of history,' such as expressed, for instance, in Jean-François Lyotard's analysis of '*la fin des grands récits*,' leading ultimately to the meaninglessness of history and to the collapse of the notion of progress.[39] This is why adhesion to Weberianism may be considered as a second line of defence of progressivist thought, such as derived or influenced by Hegel, who shares with Weber (in spite of different philosophical premises) the treatment of rationality as the summit of history, giving universal significance to the culture of the West.

This tendency seems to affect scholars and researchers of many countries, and to deal with it in detail is of course a task well beyond the possibilities of this paper, which will be limited to a few examples and suggestions. The author of this paper remembers how much he was impressed, in September 1994, by the international conference 'Religion, Civilization and Modernity,' organized by the Babes-Bolyai University of Cluj-Napoca, Romania.[40] Just a few years after the official end of socialism, it was possible to realize – even among some who had ranked high in the intellectual *nomenklatura* of the previous regime – an anxious quest for new solutions to development problems and new theoretical principles of historical interpretation.

Only specialized research could follow the process of 'Weberianization' in Eastern Europe, the Cluj-Napoca conference of 1994 and its proceedings being only one among many events of a similar kind.[41] Brazil did not change from socialism to capitalism, but the events of Eastern Europe and the near demise of Marxism did not fail to deeply affect its intellectuals. The Weberian paradigm (concerning the religious and ethical origins of the spirit of capitalism) had already been influential, as previously mentioned in this paper, among some of the most respected interpreters of Brazilian history and society. However, it was Marxism (in more than one variety) that used to dominate departments of social sciences all over the country in the 1960s and 70s. After the fall of the Wall, one witnesses a multiplication of conferences and collections of essays bearing on Max Weber and his ideas. In Brazil, not wholly unlike Eastern Europe, Weberianism also replaced Marxism among leading sectors of the intelligentsia.[42]

Besides being likely to include papers by Wolfgang Schluchter, the collections from Eastern Europe and Brazil have a few other things in common.[43] Their full analysis lies, as previously stated, beyond the scope of this paper. Let us just remark on some striking similarities and parallelisms (in spite of different terminologies) between the Brazilian Jessé Souza and the Bulgarian Dimitri Guinev. To the former,

The Protestant Ethic and the Spirit of Capitalism mirrors the attempt to understand the genesis of this revolution of conscience, this genesis that would be tantamount to the greatest transformation of human history.

The reader who conceives of the Protestant ethic as interfering only in the work ethic, that is, as restricted to the economic sphere of society, does not grasp the full dimension of the Weberian oeuvre. For it implies a 'recreation' of the world in the strongest, widest and deepest meaning of the term: it is the production of a new rationalism. A cultural rationalism for Weber means that all spheres of society, as well as all individual actions that take place in the context of those spheres, will follow a new frame of reference... The Protestant Ethic favors not only a 'spirit of capitalism,' but, in a broader way, it leads to a 'spirit of reification.'[44]

The latter writes, 'Weber begins his reflections on Luther stressing a philological fact: the specific meaning of the German word Beruf as well as of the English word calling derive from the Lutheran translation of the Bible ... The Reformation was able, by giving a positive value to everyday practice and to inner-worldly work, to beget a new language in agreement with a new social reality. The Reformation leads to a "philological reform." The Reformation would not have been possible without the "philological act" constituted by Luther's translation.'[45]

Guinev, in other words, wishes, as he says, 'to emphasize a) the philosophical presuppositions of the development of the hermeneutics of old Protestantism as the cultural rationalization of the practical interpretation as the modern attitude toward the world; and b) the agreement between the *sola fide* principle with the consequences of the principle *sola structura*, whose solution is the main task of the *hermeneutica generalis*.'[46]

Let us remark that the reasoning of both the Brazilian and the Bulgarian – at times more explicitly, at times in a rather implicit way – hinges on the supposition of a Protestant 'semantic' or, as Guinev puts it, 'philological' revolution: the new concept of vocation – *Beruf*, 'calling' – introduced by Luther's Bible and unique to Protestantism. This issue will loom large in the following and last section of this paper.

4. Calling and the Spirit of Capitalism

Max Weber's ideas, which represent a grandiose moment in the evolution of historical and sociological thought, have not – in spite of all qualifications and restrictions that later research may have added to it – lost their youth and their strength. In fact, Max Weber is situated right at the summit of history, '*am Spitze der Geschichte*,' according, as already quoted in this paper, to the felicitous expression of Nikolaus Sombart.[47] Or following Jaspers,[48] let us see him as the clearest consciousness of our time by itself.[49] As stressed, among others, by Günter Abramowski, 'Weber is not to be judged by the details of his research, but by the fecundity of his questions and interpretations.'[50] Following these commentators, it is also my view that Max Weber's historical sociology is a supreme interpretation of our time. Weber perfectly seized what is essential: the rationality, indeed even the iron cage of rationality, that penetrates and permeates every aspect of the society, the culture, and the economy of the leading countries of the Western world,[51] which have led, influenced, challenged, and changed the rest of the world.[52]

However, granted the validity and the fecundity of Weber's general conception of historical development, some conditions concerning the details of research should be met if studies on, and inspired by, Max Weber are not to remain part of the metaphysical or quasi-religious attitude often associated with the problem of modernity. Here the only solution seems to be the one suggested by Karl Popper.[53] From Weber's questions and interpretations, from his *Fragestellungen und Deutungen*, hypotheses susceptible to empirical verification or 'falsification' should be deduced and tested. Let us try to illustrate this by a concrete example of a concept generally viewed as central to the reasoning of *The Protestant Ethic*: the concept of *calling*. We tend to accept with an almost religious awe Weber's statements on the matter. Thus he says,

> If we trace the history of the word through the civilized languages, it appears that neither the predominantly Catholic peoples nor those of classical antiquity have possessed any expression of similar connotation for what we know as a calling (in the sense of a life-task, a definite field in which to work), while one has existed for all predominantly Protestant peoples.[54]

> In the Romance languages only the Spanish *vocación* in the sense of an inner call to something, from the analogy of a clerical office, has a connotation partly corresponding to that of the German word, but it is never used to mean calling in the external sense.[55]

> All the languages that were fundamentally influenced by the Protestant Bible translation have the word, and all languages for which this is not the case (like the Romance languages) do not, or at least not in its modern meaning.[56]

Critiques have been addressed to Weber, bearing on this theme or closely related ones, by authors such as Lujo Brentano, Werner Sombart,

H.M. Robertson, Amintore Fanfani, Kurt Samuelsson, Herbert Lüthy,[57] and others. Indeed, the more recent research by Tatsuro Hanyu[58] seems to have shown that the concept of 'vocation,' such as expressed by the word *Beruf*, with the meaning of 'a religious conception, that of a task set by God'[59] ('*eine religiöse Vorstellung: – die einer von Gott gestellten Aufgabe*'),[60] is simply not found in Luther's own translation of the Bible.[61] Hanyu's criticism seems to be devastating.[62] He says that Luther, contrary to Weber's claim on the matter, never used *Beruf*, but rather *Ruff*, in the decisive passage of I Corinthians 7:20.[63] Luther, notwithstanding the adoption of *Beruf* in the translation of Sirach 11:20–21, did not attach to the word *Beruf* the meaning that Weber claims he did, since the far more decisive passage of Proverbs 22:29[64] – revised by Luther, according to Hanyu's detailed demonstration, *after* the last revision of Sirach that can be attributed to him or to the committee of translators that he chaired – has not *Beruf* but *Geschefft* (*Geschäft* in a modernized spelling). Hanyu claims that Weber's failings in textual criticism and in the conclusions he tried to draw from it are due to the simple fact that Weber did not use 'the true Luther's Bible' and, even more regrettably, he was aware that he did not. In the *Protestant Ethic*, the expression '*Bei Luther (in den üblichen modernen Ausgaben)*' shows that he was aware that, in order to discuss Luther's terminological usage, he did not use the original Luther Bible, but rather the 'usual modern' edition, many times revised since Luther's death, such as usually available around 1904.[65]

Weber might have spared himself and his commentators this incursion on the slippery soil of philology and textual criticism if he had stood on the more solid historical, social, and theological ground of the revolution that the Reformation *did indeed entail* simply by proscribing otherworldly asceticism.[66] He is aware of this when, for instance, he says that 'in the conception of *industria*, which comes from monastic asceticism and was developed by monastic writers, lies the seed of the *ethos* that was fully developed later in the Protestant worldly asceticism.'[67]

Hence his conclusion at the end of chapter 4: 'Christian asceticism, at first fleeing from the world into solitude, had already ruled the world which it had renounced from the monastery and through the Church. But it had, on the whole left the naturally spontaneous character of daily life in the world untouched. Now it strode into the market-place of life, slammed the door of the monastery behind it, and undertook to penetrate just that daily routine of life with its methodicalness to fashion it into a life in the world, but neither of nor for this world.'[68]

Let us also remark that the concept of vocation understood, as Weber himself puts it, as a religious conception, namely that of a task set by God, is clearly to be found in Spanish and French, to name but two Romance languages, and from the pen of Catholic authors. In the *Spiritual Exercises* (first published in 1548) of Ignatius of Loyola[69] the concepts of divine calling and election (choice)[70] play essential roles. Indeed, the *Exercises* have no other aim but to lead the faithful 'to become perfect in whatever state or condition God our Lord will inspire us to choose.'[71] Teresa of Ávila uses the word *llamamiento* (calling) at least three times in the opening chapters of her *Camino de Perfección* (originally written in 1566),[72] with exactly the meaning of 'a religious conception, that of a task set by God,' but it is not clear whether she means to extend the scope of *llamamiento* to plain worldly, non-monastic asceticism.

The concept and the very word of *vocation* – understood, let us reiterate, in the Weberian sense of '*eine religiöse Vorstellung: – die einer von Gott gestellten Aufgabe*' – are clearly found in the writings of François de Sales (1567–1622), some passages of which I shall quote. What I suggest here is that, if we trust François de Sales (and Bernard Groethuysen), even in Catholicism 'the naturally spontaneous character of daily life in the world' *was not left untouched* but was also subject, at least in some countries and periods, to religious rationalization. These quotations are drawn from a chapter of François de Sales's *Introduction to a Devout Life*,[73] which has as its title nothing less than 'How Devotion Is Convenient to All Kinds of Vocations and Professions.' Indeed, it is the very notion of worldly asceticism which is upheld *avant la lettre* by François:

> God commanded in the creation the plants to bear fruit, each according to its kind. On the same way he commanded the Christians, who are the living plant of his church, to bear fruits of devotion, each according to its quality and state [*vacation*]. Devotion should be differently exercised by the gentleman, the valet, the prince, the widow, the maid, the married woman.[74]

> Devotion spoils nothing when it is authentic. If it becomes detrimental to the legitimate state of life of some person, then it is undoubtedly false. It is an error, indeed a heresy, to wish to exclude a devout life from the company of soldiers, from the shop of the artisan, from the court of the princes, and from the household of married people. It is true ... that a purely contemplative, monastical or religious devotion ... cannot be exercised in these occupations; yet, beside those three kinds of devotion, there

are several other, appropriate to bring to perfection those who live in a worldly [séculier] state ... Wherever we are, we can and we must aspire to a perfect life.[75]

It is certainly regrettable that even Bernard Groethuysen, whose *Les origines de l'esprit bourgeois en France*[76] represents one of the most pertinent critiques of Weber's theory on the rise of capitalism, fails to mention – as he only purports to study the period between the reign of Louis XIV and the French Revolution (1643–1789) – François de Sales's concept of inner-worldly devotion.[77] Yet he mentions Louis Bourdaloue's[78] *Sermon pour la fête de François de Sales* and quotes from it: 'Do not think that in order to save us God requires from us great austerities or extraordinary deeds. Each of you, within your own state, can easily find salvation. The duties that you must fulfill, the obligations you must acquit, are enough to make you walk on the path of the saints.'[79]

Groethuysen is to be read with caution by Weberian-minded scholars, because there are some tricky specificities in the meaning he attributes to some key words. He draws attention to the opposition of the Catholic Church 'to the very spirit of rising capitalism, which disturbs the established order,'[80] this opposition, however, being specifically directed toward the impulse for acquisition, *la soif d'acquérir*. Now, according to Weber, 'The impulse for acquisition, pursuit of gain, of money, of the greatest possible amount of money, has in itself nothing to do with capitalism ... Unlimited greed for gain is not in the least identical with capitalism, and is still less its spirit. Capitalism may even be identical with the restraint, or at least a rational tempering [*Bändigung*], of this irrational impulse.'[81]

Thus, Groethuysen uses the expression *spirit of capitalism* in a sense quite different from Weber's. However, both authors share the idea that it is essentially through the principles of a *Berufsethik* that the churches – Protestant for Weber, Catholic[82] for Groethuysen (and at that, both Jesuit and Jansenist)[83] – contributed to the ascent of capitalism.

The question can now be raised whether post-Reformation Catholic authors, like the ones mentioned in this paper, have not themselves been influenced by the Reformation in the matter that concerns us in this section: their conception of inner-worldly asceticism. This issue, which requires monographic studies about each of those authors,[84] cannot be elucidated within the limits of this chapter, whose more modest aim is to show that *vocation* or similar words that have meaning equivalent to the Weberian *eine von Gott gestellte Aufagbe,* are found to have been written by relevant Catholic authors.[85]

In spite of these caveats, a few remarks can be safely made. Whereas Luther, Lutherans, and other Protestants are hardly mentioned in Ignatius of Loyola's exercises, Teresa of Ávila (who, however, hardly, if ever, deals with inner-worldly asceticism) had as a stated aim of her monasteries a kind of counter-reformation consisting of prayer and penance. François de Sales – a titular bishop of Geneva – was certainly highly cognizant of the tenets of the Reformation, including the Calvinist Reformation, and his writings cannot be understood outside the context of the Catholic reaction against Protestantism. It is in his *Introduction à la vie dévote* that one of the first[86] full-fledged presentations of a doctrine of inner-worldly asceticism is to be found. But let us keep in mind one or two basic points. The idea of the priesthood of all believers – and hence the abolition of a clerical state in the Catholic sense of the term – is a basic aspect of the Reformation. And the Reformers very soon proscribed monasticism and all forms of non-worldly asceticism. Nevertheless, it would be erroneous to conclude, without further evidence, that the old forms were automatically replaced by a new, inner-worldly asceticism, which might be as detracting to the *sola fide* principle – salvation situated well beyond the merits acquired by any human work and flowing only from the grace of God accepted through faith – as the old one.[87]

Let us also take note of the fact that the issue of a Protestant versus a Catholic influence upon the growth of a work ethic compatible with the requirements of a modern capitalism (in the Weberian or Sombartian meaning of the term) only gains the urgency it has had for very nearly 140 years, after the publication of Émile de Laveleye's *Le protestantisme et le catholicisme dans leurs rapports avec la liberté et la prospérité des peuples,* published in Belgium in 1875. In other words, it becomes a central issue for the social sciences after the defeat – soon interpreted as far more than simply military – of traditionally Catholic Austria and traditionally Catholic France by traditionally Protestant Prussia (leading to the foundation of the Wilhelmine Reich), soon to be followed by the defeat of another central Catholic country in the Spanish-American war.[88]

If a conclusion can now be reached, it is that the theses of *The Protestant Ethic and the Spirit of Capitalism* are not to be treated as self-evident. To the contrary, they have to be empirically validated with the aid of sociological and historical methods. Similarly, nothing precludes the search for, or the recognition of, other sources, indeed religious sources, of modern rationality beside the Protestant ethic. Jean-Paul Sartre, in his *Critique de la raison dialectique*, used to say of Marxism that it represented the 'unsurpassable philosophy of our century.' And, for him, that was all, the rest being reduced to the rank of mere commentary or *idéologie*, including, modestly, his own existentialism. Following the *Entzauberung* of Marxism as a viable political movement, this attitude has been transferred to Weberianism, however little of a 'Weberian' Weber himself can be considered to have been. Now, if Weber's historical sociology is placed *am Spitze der Geschichte*, and if his theories, whose spell binds us are not to be reduced to a collection of some certainly exciting but purely speculative considerations about the essence of modernity, then his concepts should constantly be challenged by empirical research trying to test – indeed to falsify – some of the most cherished and established notions and postulates we have taken from him.

NOTES

The author wishes to express his gratitude to Laurence McFalls, editor of this volume, and to two anonymous readers of the University of Toronto Press, for their pertinent queries and suggestions, which were very much taken into account by the author in the preparation of the final version of this paper.

1 This word is being used in a very broad sense.
2 There is in Weber no equivalent to the opening lines of Hegel's *Lectures on the Philosophy of History*, according to which Reason rules the world and, therefore, the whole of History has followed Reason. (I am here using a Spanish translation of the *Vorlesungen über die Philosophie der Geschichte*, written in 1830, *Lecciones sobre la Filosofía de la Historia Universal* [Madrid: Alianza Editorial, 1982].)
3 Although there were (or there are) several kinds of Marxism, some of them claiming to be less rigid and less dogmatic than others.
4 Karl Popper, *The Logic of Scientific Discovery* (London: Hutchinson, 1959). However, I do not mean to imply that Popper was the only or the first philosopher of science to suggest the use of this kind of heuristic strategy.
5 Let us not forget that Marx was a 'left-wing Hegelian.'
6 This quotation is drawn from the introduction of Jean-Paul Sartre's *Critique de la raison dialectique* (Paris: Gallimard, 1960).
7 Max Weber, 'Roscher und Knies und die logischen Probleme des histori-

schen Nationaloekonomie,' in *Gesammelte Aufsätze zur Wissenschaftslehre* (Tübingen: J.C.B. Moor [Paul Siebeck], 1968).

8 Max Weber, *Gesammelte Aufsätze zur Religionssoziologie* (Tübingen: J.C.B. Mohr [Paul Siebeck], 1972).

9 Max Weber, *The Protestant Ethic and the Spirit of Capitalism*, trans. Talcott Parsons (New York: Scribner's, 1958), 13. Unless otherwise stated, all quotations from the *Protestant Ethic* are drawn from this edition.

10 G.W.F. Hegel, *Vorlesungen über die Geschichte der Philosophie*, vol. 3, Werke, Frankfurt, b. XX, s. 329, as quoted by Jürgen Habermas, *Le discours philosophique de la modernité* (Paris: Gallimard, 1988), 3.

11 This word is being used in a very broad sense.

12 Nicolaus Sombart, 'Einige Entscheidende Theoretiker,' in *Einführung in die Soziologie*, ed. Alfred Weber (Munich: Pipper Verlag, 1958), 43.

13 Hyppolite, basing himself on some passages by Hegel himself, translates into French *Moralität* as *moralité* and *Sittlichkeit* as *monde éthique*.

14 Jean Hyppolite, *Introduction à la philosophie de l'histoire de Hegel* (Paris: Seuil, 1983), 20.

15 Ibid., 13.

16 Inasmuch as cultural anthropology is the science of 'customs and institutions' it might even be claimed that Hegel was also an anthropologist. Although he does not necessarily follow Hypollite's line of interpretation (adopted into this paper), a distinguished anthropologist of the middle of the twentieth century wrote a major essay on Hegel's bearing on cultural anthropology. I refer to Robert F. Murphy, *The Dialectics of Social Life: Alarms and Excursions in Anthropological Theory* (New York: Basic Books, 1971).

17 Two fallacies should be carefully avoided in this rapprochement: to take a part for the whole and, conversely, the whole for a part. If Weber and Hegel converge (but do not merge) in their treatment of rationality, we need not jump to the conclusion that they converge in metaphysics. In a way, Hegel, who, as a result of the attention, and in spite of his system of idealistic metaphysics, did not fail to give to the concrete and contingent character of historical tendencies, was a forerunner of Weber's sociology.

18 Habermas, *Le discours philosophique*; Karl Loewith, 'Max Weber und Karl Marx,' in *Gesammelte Abhandlungen* (Stuttgart: Kohlhammer, 1960), 1–67; Günter Abramowski, *Das Geschichtsbild Max Webers: Universalgeschichte am Leitfaden des okzidentalen Rationalisierungsprozesses* (Stuttgart: Ernst Klett Verlag, 1966); A. Müller-Armack, *Religion und Wirtschaft: Geistesgeschichtliche Hintergründe unserer Europäischer Lebensform* (Stuttgart: Kohlhammer, 1959); D. Henrich, *Die Einheit der Wissenschaftslehre Max Webers* (Tübingen:

J.C.B. Mohr [Paul Siebeck], 1952); Wolfgang Schluchter, *Die Entwicklung des okzidentalen Razionalismus* (Tübingen: J.C.B. Mohr, 1979); C. Colliot-Thélène, *Le désenchantement de l'état: de Hegel à Max Weber* (Paris: Les Editions de Minuit, 1992).

19 Concerning this point, see Paul Ladrière, 'La fonction rationalisatrice de l'ethique religieuse dans la théorie wéberienne de la modernité,' *Archives des sciences sociales de la Religion* 61, no. 1 (1986): 105–25.

20 Using this expression with the meaning it has in R. Bultmann's essays on New Testament theology. 'This task supposes the idea that the literature in which the life of a community is expressed … has its source in the manifestations and in the needs of this community' (quoted from Rudolf Bultman, *L'histoire de la tradition synoptique* [Paris: Seuil, 1979], 18–19).

21 For a somewhat similar approach to some concepts of Weber's sociology of religion, see Gary A. Abraham, *Max Weber and the Jewish Question: A Study of the Social Outlook of His Sociology* (Urbana: University of Illinois Press, 1992).

22 Wolfgang J. Mommsen, *Max Weber und die Deutsche Politik, 1890–1920* (Tübingen, J.C.B. Mohr [Paul Siebeck], 1959), here quoted after its French translation, *Max Weber et la politique allemande* (Paris: PUF, 1985).

23 Ibid., 164.

24 Ibid., 165.

25 Leipzig: Duncker und Humblot, 1911.

26 Weber, *Protestant Ethic*, 17.

27 Ibid., 21.

28 See, among others, Zachary Taylor, *The Rise and Progress of Baptist Mission in Brazil* (Arkadelphia, AK: Ouachita Baptist University, 1969) (original ca. 1890); E. Carlos Pereira, *O Problema Religioso da América Latina: Estudo Dogmático-Histórico* (São Paulo: Empresa Editora Brasileira, 1920); Leonel Franca, *A Igreja, a Reforma e a Civilização* (Rio de Janeiro: Agir, 1948) (original 1922).

29 Sérgio Buarque de Holanda, *Raizes do Brasil* (Rio de Janeiro: José Olympio, 1956) (original 1936); Vianna Moog, *Bandeirantes e Pioneiros: Paralelo entre Duas Culturas* (Porto Alegre: Editora Globo, 1955); Roberto da Matta, *Carnavais, Malandros e Heróis: Para uma Sociologia do Dilema Brasileiro* (Rio de Janeiro: Zahar, 1979).

30 On the other hand, the writings of Gilberto Freyre, which enjoy an unequalled prestige in Brazil, represent an uncompromising vindication of the 'Luso-Tropical' and Catholic (also in secularized forms) values, which presided over Brazil's historical development. Freyre's best-known book is

The Masters and the Slaves (Berkeley: University of California Press, 1986) (Brazilian first edition 1933).

31 This should take the form of a 'liquidation of roots,' such as suggested by Antônio Cândido commenting on Sérgio Buarque de Holanda: 'Considering that our past is an obstacle ... the liquidation of roots is an imperative of our historical development ... entailing an increasing loss of Iberian characteristics to the benefit of the paths open by the urban and cosmopolitan culture.' Antônio Cândido, 'O Significado de Raízes do Brasil,' in Sérgio Buarque de Holanda, *Raízes do Brasil,* 26th ed. (Rio de Janeiro: José Olympio, 1994), xxxix–1.

32 The author of this paper wishes to make it clear that he is very far from thinking that Max Weber can be reduced or interpreted to be only the standard-bearer of a moral community.

33 Michel Maffesoli, *La connaissance ordinaire* (Paris: Méridien-Klincksieck, 1985).

34 Augustin Cochin, *La révolution et la libre pensée* (Paris: Copernic, 1979); François Furet, *Penser la révolution française* (Paris: Gallimard, 1978).

35 Concerning Weber's reception in France, see Michaël Pollak, *Max Weber en France: L'itinéraire d'une oeuvre*, issue 3, de l'Institut d'Histoire du Temps Présent (Paris: Centre National de la Recherche Scientifique, 1986); Monique Hirschhorn, *Max Weber et la sociologie française* (Paris: L'Harmattan, 1988).

36 Talcott Parsons, *The Structure of Social Action* (New York: McGraw-Hill, 1938), *Societies: Evolutionary and Comparative Perspectives* (Englewood Cliffs: Prentice Hall, 1966), *The System of Modern Societies* (Englewood Cliffs: Prentice Hall, 1971); Everett Hagen, *On the Theory of Social Change* (Homewood: Dorset, 1962); David McClelland, *The Achieving Society* (Princeton: Van Nostrand, 1961).

37 Andre Gunder Frank, *Latin America: Underdevelopment or Revolution* (New York: Monthly Review, 1969).

38 This term understood in a very broad sense.

39 Jean-François Lyotard, *La condition postmoderne* (Paris: Les Éditions de Minuit, 1979).

40 The proceedings of this conference were published as *Studi Weberiene*, ed. Traian Rotaru, Andrei Roth, Rudolf Poledna (Cluj-Napoca, Romania: Clusium, 1995). My contribution (originally delivered in English) was included as 'Note asupra Conceptului de Vocatie la Weber si Sfântul François de Sales,' 149–60.

41 Let us here be limited to pointing to just another collection of essays on

the theme (beside the proceedings of Cluj-Napoca): Ivaylo Znepolski, ed., *Max Weber: relectures à l'Ouest, relectures à l'Est – Actes du Colloques de Sofia, 28–30 novembre 1998* (Sofia: Maison des Sciences de l'Homme et de la Société, 1999). Another collection, Richard H. Roberts, ed., *Religion and the Transformations of Capitalism: Comparative Approaches* (London: Routledge, 1995), though it does not bear only, or even mainly, on Eastern Europe or Latin America, is nevertheless a good example of post-Wall revivalist Weberianism.

42 The following essays or collections of essays are good examples of this tendency: Edmundo Lima de Arruda Jr, ed., *Max Weber: Direito e Modernidade* (Florianópolis: Letras Contemporâneas, 1996); Maria Francisca Pinheiro Coelho, Lourdes Bandeira, and Maria Loiola de Menezes, eds., *Política, Ciência e Cultura em Max Weber* (Brasília: Editora Universidade de Brasília, 2000); Jessé Souza, ed., *A Atualidade de Max Weber* (Brasília: Editora da Universidade de Brasília, 2000); Jessé Souza, *A Modernização Seletiva: Uma Reinterpretação do Dilema Brasileiro* (Brasília: Editora da Universidade de Brasília, 2000); Jessé Souza, ed., *O Malandro e o Protestante* (Brasília: Editora Universidade de Brasília, 1999).

43 Wolfgang Schluchter, 'Religion et Conduite de Vie' in Znepolski, *Relectures*, 186–202; 'As Origens do Racionalismo Ocidental' and 'A Origem do Modo de Vida Burguês,' in Souza, *O Malandro e o Protestante*, 55–120 and 121–36; 'Politeísmo dos Valores' in Souza, *A Atualidade de Max Weber*, 13–48.

44 Jessé Souza, 'A Ética Protestante e a Ideologia do Atraso Brasileiro,' in Souza, *O Malandro e o Protestante*, 43–4. Souza does not explain what he means by *reification* in this context, referring instead to Schluchter's *Die Entwicklung des Okzidentalen Razionalismus.*

45 Dimitri Guinev, 'L'Approche Wébérienne de la Conception Luthérienne de la Vocation à la Lumière de l'Herméneutique du Portestantisme Ancien,' in Znepolski, *Max Weber: Relectures*, 105–6.

46 Ibid., 115.

47 Sombart, 'Einige Entscheidende Theoretiker,' 43.

48 Jaspers's words seem to imply that Max Weber is the outstanding representative of Hegel's Absolute Spirit in our time.

49 Quoted by Abramowski, *Die Geschichtsbild Max Webers*, 9.

50 Ibid., 12.

51 This is not tantamount to saying that only Max Weber dealt with rationality. Even apart from earlier forms of this concept in the writings of Hegel and of Marx, it also plays leading roles, to give but two eminent examples, in Ferdinand Tönnies, *Gemeinschaft und Gesellschaft* (1887) and Werner Sombart, *Der Moderne Kapitalismus* (1916–27).

52 This, of course, does not imply the successful Westernization or modernization of the whole world, but it does imply that no country failed to be
affected by the diffusion of rationality.

53 Popper, *Scientific Discovery*.

54 Weber, *Protestant Ethic*, 79.

55 Ibid., 205.

56 Ibid., 207. (I have slightly changed Parsons's rather complex reading of
this passage.)

57 Lujo Brentano, *Der wirtschaftende Mensch in der Geschichte* (Leipzig: F.
Meiner, 1923); Werner Sombart, *Der Bourgeois: Zur Geistesgeschichte des
modernen Wirtschaftsmenschen* (Leipzig: Duncker und Humblot, 1913);
Amintore Fanfani, *Catolicesimo e Protestantesimo nella Formazione Storica del
Capitalismo* (Milan: Vita e Pensiero, 1933); H.M. Robertson, *Aspects of the
Rise of Economic Individualism: A Criticism of Max Weber and His School*
(London: Cambridge University Press, 1933); Kurt Samuelsson, *Religion
and Economic Action* (New York: Basic Books, 1961); Herbert Lüthy, *Le passé
présent* (Monaco: Éditions du Rocher, 1965).

58 Tatsuro Hanyu, 'Max Webers Quellenbehandlung in der Protestantischen
Ethik: Der Berufs-begriff,' *Archives Européennes de Sociologie* 35, no. 1
(1994): 72–103.

59 Weber, *Protestant Ethic*, 79.

60 Weber, *Gesammelte Aufsätze sur Religionssoziologie*, 63.

61 If Hanyu is right, the lofty considerations of the Brazilian Souza and of
the Bulgarain Guinev, concerning a 'revolution of conscience,' indeed a
'philological reform,' are very much weakened inasmuch as they claim to
be based on Luther's use of *Beruf*.

62 At least to one who is not a specialist in biblical studies.

63 'Let every man abide in the same calling wherein he was called,' according to my copy of the King James version, printed in 1934.

64 'Seest thou a man diligent in his business? He shall stand before kings; he
shall not stand before mean men,' according to my King James copy.

65 Hanyu, 'Max Webers Quellenbehandlung,' 101.

66 Let us not, however, until further proof, draw from this statement the
conclusion that only the Reformation, in the West itself or elsewhere, did
entail an attitude of worldly asceticism.

67 Weber, *Protestant Ethic*, 196.

68 Ibid., 154.

69 There are many editions of the *Spiritual Exercises*. I have here mainly used
a recent French translation, edited, with an introduction, by Jean-Claude
Guy (Paris: Seuil, 1982).

70   On the issue of election, see Mario Perniola, 'L'Elezione della Differenza in Ignazio di Loyola,' *Conoscenza Religiosa* 3 (1980): 217–45.

71   *Spiritual Exercises*, para. 135.

72   A standard edition of *Camino de Perfección* is found in Santa Teresa de Jesus, *Obras Completas* (Madrid: Biblioteca de Autores Cristianos, 1962), 181–320.

73   Quoted here according to the text of Saint François de Sales, *Introduction à la vie dévote*, in *Oeuvres*, ed. André Ravier (Paris: Gallimard, Bibliothèque de La Pléiade, 1969).

74   Ibid., 36.

75   Ibid., 37.

76   Bernard Groethuysen, *Les origines de l'esprit bourgeois en France* (Paris: Gallimard, 1927).

77   I have previously dealt with some aspects of this issue in 'L'ethique catholique et l'esprit du capitalisme: la vocation chez François de Sales,' *Sociétés* 49 (1995): 303–11.

78   A prominent Jesuit preacher and writer (1632–1704).

79   Quoted by Groethuysen, *Les origines de l'esprit bourgeois*, 205. The full text of Bourdaloue's sermon, the 'Panégyrique de Saint François de Sales,' of great interest to students of the history of inner-worldly asceticism, can be found in Saint François de Sales, *Oeuvres complètes* (Paris: G. Martin, 1846), 5:S399–414.

80   Groethuysen, *Les origines de l'esprit bourgeois*, 234.

81   Weber, *Protestant Ethic*, 17.

82   It is not that Groethuysen denies the Protestant influence on the rise of capitalism. But he deals only, at least explicitly, with the theme of 'the [Catholic] Church and the Bourgeoisie.'

83   The Duke of Saint-Simon (not mentioned by Groethuysen) bears witness, in his memoirs to this 'éthique du devoir' in early eighteenth-century France. A Catholic, and at that neither a Jansenist nor a Jesuit, he says of the Duke of Burgundy (heir to the French crown) that the prince 'finally understood the meaning of leaving God for God and that one's faithful practice of the duties of the state to which one has been assigned by God [nothing less, it seems, than *die von Gott gestellte Aufgabe*,' so dear to Weber] is the solid piety that pleases Him most.' *Mémoires* (Paris: Gallimard, Bibliothèque de la Pléiade, 1985 [originally written ca. 1750]), 4:416.

84   However, because a large number of scholars in many countries have often been working on those topics without the awareness of one another, preliminary monographic research may also consist of research on what has already been done.

85 Let us not lose of sight that, when he speaks about *vocation* (precisely with the meaning of *eine von Gott gestelltne Aufagbe*), in passages that have already been quoted, Weber is saying that, by the time of his (not Luther's) writing, it is simply not found in Romance languages.

86 If not the very first.

87 Thus, returning to previous quotations, 'the conception of *industria* ... the *ethos*, which was fully developed later, now strode into the market-place of life ... and undertook to penetrate just that daily routine of life with its methodicalness to fashion it into a life in the world,' would belong rather, to use another Weberianism, to the realm of the 'unintended consequences of the Reformation.'

88 The gap in overall social and economic development between Anglo-Saxon America and Latin America has also played a role in the awakening of this issue, as Herbet Lüthy points out in *Le passé présent*, mentioned earlier in this paper.

8 Rethinking Weber's Ideal-Types of Development, Politics, and Scientific Knowledge

NAOSHI YAMAWAKI

In this chapter, I would like to consider to what extent Max Weber's ideal-types of development, politics, and scientific knowledge are still valid today. His studies ranged from the methodology of social science and the comparative sociology of world religions based upon his view of modernity to theories of politics as well as of scientific knowledge (*Wissenschaft*). There is no denying the historical fact that Weber, whose achievements are still influential today, won the debate with the ethico-historical school of his time represented by Gustav von Schmoller (1838–1917), whose achievements have now been almost forgotten. In my view, however, this fact does not mean that Weber's social theory is convincing enough to be able to replace today's normative social theory. Rather, I would like to point out that – by contextualizing and relativizing Weber's grand theory from a non-Weberian viewpoint – despite his great macro-sociological achievements on world religions, some aspects of his thought are now obsolete, especially when we try to address the serious social problems of our contemporary world in an age of unstable globalization.

To argue these theses, I shall begin in the first section by revisiting the controversy between Schmoller and Weber on the methodology of social science, focusing on their different ideas of socio-historical development. I shall try to clarify the main issues between them and to highlight a fatal weakness of Schmoller's theory as well as the merits of Weber's methodology. After that, I shall point out that Weber did *not entirely* overcome Schmoller from today's perspective. Introducing a new 'normative' economic theory advanced by Amartya Sen (1933–), I shall address a serious weak point of Weber's social theory.

In the second section, I shall deal with Weber's 'non-progressive' theory of modernization based upon his ideal-type of development, which can be regarded as one of Weber's greatest contributions to Western social thought. After evaluating his attempts as a Western scholar, I shall take a critical look at typical receptions of Weber in the Japanese-speaking as well as the Chinese-speaking world and point out Weber's misunderstanding of Confucianism. In my view, this problem requires that Weber's Eurocentric view, which inevitably derived from what Catherine Colliot-Thélène calls his 'methodologically founded ethnocentrism,' must be radically modified in order to understand the world religions in their relationship with modernization. In the last part of this section, I shall suggest that, if this modification is made, Weber's macro-sociology can offer a promising starting point for comparative studies of religions and modernity.

On the basis of these two sections, in the third section I shall reflect on his understanding of politics and scientific knowledge with regard to our contemporary situation. I shall first criticize his one-sided under-standing of politics, which derived from the situations of his time but nowadays hinders those wanting to make use of his comparative macro-sociology. And then, I shall try to combine some post-Weberian norma-tive viewpoints with Weber's understanding of politics. After that, I shall characterize his understanding of scientific knowledge as a repre-sentative product of the 'time of specialization of sciences,' to which Weber contributed in his era. Instead of the one-sided understanding presented by Weber, which hinders normative and interdisciplinary social studies on development and inter-cultural dialogue in the con-temporary world, I would like to make an appeal for an alternative social theory, which is able to deal with contemporary global issues, in what I call the 'time of post-specialization of sciences.'

1. Reflections on Weber's Theory of Socio-Historical Development in Comparison with Schmoller's

I would like to start from the controversy between Weber and Schmoller, which took place about a hundred years ago, because it is precisely in this controversy that Weber's theory of development can be well char-acterized in distinction from Schmoller's ethico-historical school. In my view, this controversy points to a serious issue, which cannot be re-duced to a generational conflict between them: the question of socio-historical development.

As is well known, the so-called *Methodenstreit*, in which Weber was later engaged, began in the 1880s as a controversy between Gustav von Schmoller and Carl Menger (1840–1921) over the nature of economics. While Schmoller, a prominent leader of the German Association of Social Policy, thought that economic theory cannot be separated from historical research and social policy, Menger, a prominent professor of the University of Vienna, advanced economic theory as an exact science independent from historical research and social policy.[1] Both criticized the other's misconception about the study of economics. According to Schmoller, Menger confined himself to 'a corner of the largest house that represents our science and took it for the whole house or the best and fanciest salon in the house.'[2] Menger answered this criticism by saying that 'Schmoller's view is like that of a navvy who wants to be regarded as an architect because he carried some stones and sand to a construction site.'[3]

Thus, the controversy had an emotional feature from the start and continued for more than a decade without resolution. It was in this context that Weber's '"Objectivity" of Knowledge in Social Science and Social Policy' was published in 1904. Although Weber, unlike Menger but like Schmoller, had been much interested in the topic of socio-historical development, Weber's target in this essay was not Menger but Schmoller. Weber emphasized the distinction between social-scientific knowledge and value judgments. He criticized Schmoller's ethical-historical economics since it neglected this distinction, confused the two categories, and instead, derived ideals from its subject matter and produced concrete norms by applying general ethical imperatives.[4]

In Weber's view, cultural values cannot be unambiguously derived as being normatively desirable. An empirical social science cannot tell anyone what to do, but rather what one can do. Value judgments belong to the matter of personal individual decision based upon each person's world view, while social-scientific knowledge belongs to the sphere of academic research based upon what Weber calls 'ideal-types.'[5] Inspired by neo-Kantian epistemology about the validity of cultural science, Weber introduced the ideal-type as an intersubjectively valid framework to recognize culturally significant social events. The ideal-type is not a description of social reality itself, but it aims to give unambiguous means of expression to such a description. For example, the concept of 'city economy' is constructed as not an average of the economic structure actually existing in all the cities observed but as an ideal-type. Similarly, the 'handicraft system' or 'capitalistic productive system' can be constructed as an ideal-type. The stage theory, which Schmoller's historical school has in common with Marxism, should be replaced by the theory of ideal-type of development. Social scientists must be free from their own values and understand culturally significant social events by intersubjectively valid ideal-types. This also means that they should be conscious of their commitment to the concrete recognition of historical values. That alone confers objectivity to social science.[6]

Advancing his methodology of social science in this way, Weber criticized Schmoller's ethico-historical economics. Schmoller made his counter-argument to Weber in the last parts of the third edition of his *Volkswirtschaft, Volkswirtschftslehre und -methode* published in 1911.[7] In order to do justice to both disputants, I would like to take up this largely unknown counter-argument.

In his essay, Schmoller stressed that value judgments are indispensable to social science because they belong not to the private concerns of individuals but to the publicly objective sphere. They could be recognized as social facts and could indicate to social researchers the orientation of society toward ethico-historical progress, which should not be neglected. Therefore, value judgments such as progress have to be understood not as a matter extraneous to social science but 'within' social science. In particular, when discussing social institutions concerning social welfare, insurance systems, trade unions etc., the questions of 'to be' (*Sein*), 'ought to be' (*Sollen*), and 'to become' (*Werden*) cannot be isolated. Thus, social researchers' knowledge of and practical commitment to improve the social welfare of people are also inseparable from each other in their contribution to socio-ethical progress. Indeed, Schmoller was a *Kathedersozialist* in this sense.

In Schmoller's view, Weber's methodology insists that social researchers should pursue empirical inquiries into 'what exists' without any ethical value judgments or without any perspective of 'what ought to be' or 'what will become.' Instead he demands that they treat these practical problems on a level other than social science. Such a demand is, for Schmoller, unacceptable, because it means that 'each social researcher had to speak with two tongues and to write with two colors of ink.'[8]

In answer, Weber attacked Schmoller again in his 'The Meaning of Ethical-Neutrality [*Wertfreiheit*] in Sociology and Economics,' published in 1917.[9] Weber repeatedly emphasized that the validity of a practical imperative as a norm and the truth value of an empirical proposition are absolutely heterogeneous. According to Weber, Schmoller's methodology makes a fatal error, because it implies that ethical imperatives are identical to cultural values. For Weber, understanding cultural values does not mean agreeing with them but leads to the acknowledgement of what J.S. Mill once called 'the absolute polytheism of values.' In this respect, Schmoller's belief in the harmony of social knowledge with ethical judgment is anachronistic and wrong.[10]

What conclusion should be drawn now from this century-old controversy? First of all, I would like to say that Weber's polytheistic insight exceeded Schmoller's in that the social situation in their age had invalidated the quasi-teleological belief in the harmony of 'socio-historical development' and 'socio-ethical progress' in the sense of increase in values, a view that Schmoller held in common with Herbert Spencer.[11] The catastrophe of the First World War, in which technological development had destroyed the social welfare of the people and caused carnage on a massive scale, was enough to endorse this reality. In this regard, Schmoller's belief in the harmony between socio-historical development and socio-ethical progress displayed a fatal error, and Weber proved himself much more realistic than Schmoller.

A second strength of Weber's methodology lies in its avoiding the danger of academic paternalism as well as sectarianism. While Schmoller, as a leader of the German historical school, tended to force his stage theory of historical development on his disciples, Weber's methodological individualism and polytheism of values made such an academic paternalism impossible.[12] That is one of the reasons why the German ethical-historical school of economics declined after the death of Schmoller and passed gradually into oblivion, while Weber's sociology has been influential until today.

The third strength of Weber's methodology is that it was open to the macro-sociological study of world religions, which Schmoller's was not. I shall take up this strength in a broader context of social thought at the beginning of the next section.

Despite these strengths of his argument, I would hesitate to say that Weber overcame Schmoller in every respect, especially if we pay attention to the fact that Weber decided not to develop the normative theory of social policy on the ground that it does not belong to empirical social science. Weber largely rejected the normative concept of justice as an elusive postulate of any social policy and instead emphasized the ethic of responsibility for the predictable consequences of socio-political action. Indeed, he regarded the orientation of socio-economic policy by a normative concept such as justice as obsolete.[13]

Is this view still valid for today's social theorists? I do not think it is, for the following reasons. To be sure, Weber was right to think that the meaning of development should be distinguished from that of progress.[14] His view of development as a value-free ideal-type could avoid the modern progressive bias of history. His view, however, has the problem of blindness or indifference to the question of what kind of development is or is not desirable. Although this normative question now has little to do with the progressive bias of history, the historical reality of capitalist development in Europe and its global diffusion means that the question of development has become the central normative stake of politics in the non-Western world since no later than the Second World War. It has even taken a front seat today, as 'Human Development Reports' published by the United Nations Development Program since 1990 show.[15] Without some intersubjectively valid normative theory of justice and freedom, we cannot today discuss the problem of socio-historical development: the fact of 'development' is inextricably linked to the normative discourses of 'developmentalism.'

To clarify this matter in an academic way, I would like to introduce a theory of development advanced by Amartya Sen, the 1998 Nobel laureate for economics. With a critical look at John Rawls's theory of justice, Sen tries to reintroduce ethics into economics and to lay the ethical foundations for the concept of development. For him, values such as freedom, justice, democracy, human rights, and well-being are indispensable when thinking about the development of societies. In particular, freedoms should be regarded as the primary ends of development.[16] Supporting a view of development as an integrated expansion of substantive and interrelated freedoms, Sen concludes his recent book with the following remark: 'Development is indeed a momentous engagement with freedom's possibilities.'[17]

In comparison with this normative socio-economic theory advanced by Sen, Weber's view of value-free social policy would seem to be out of date. Because Weber neglected to lay the normative foundation of social policy as an alternative to Schmoller's teleological evolutionism, his theory of social policy remained too scant to treat the normative problem of development in the contemporary world. In this regard, we have to re-evaluate the forgotten heritage of Schmoller's ethical-historical economics, without falling into naive teleological evolutionism. As I mentioned above, Schmoller regarded the three questions of 'to be,' 'ought to be,' and 'to become' as inseparable when discussing social institutions. This viewpoint almost coincides with that of Sen. In addition, Schmoller's historical approach, if it discards its teleological evolutionism, could even make up a desideratum in Sen's rational social choice approach, which seems to me not to be able to adequately take the historical dimensions of development into consideration.[18]

I will address this problem again in the third section in my critical remark on Weber's understanding of politics and scientific knowledge. In the following section, however, I would like to critically appreciate Weber's theory of modernization based upon his ideal-type of socio-historical development, which could still offer us a positive legacy today.

2. Critical Appreciation of Weber's Theory of Modernization from a Non-Western Viewpoint

For Weber, the methodology of social science was merely a formal presupposition to studying (understanding) concrete socio-historical facts and changes, especially the modernization of Europe. Weber tried to understand the modernization of Europe with his sociological study of the world religions, as his *Gesammmelte Aufsätze zur Religionssoziologie* shows.[19] Undoubtedly, he surpasses Schmoller's historical school in the scope of study. It must be pointed out that his theory of modernization was, unlike that of Hegel and Marx, characterized by the non-progressive view of history. As was pointed out above, Weber distinguished the value-free concept of development from the ethical concept of progress and adopted the former to understand modernization. By doing so, he intended to avoid confusing the historical development called modernization with historical progress, to which both Hegel and Marx attached so much importance.[20] Indeed, he was not so much influenced by Hegel and Marx as by Nietzsche in this respect.

Instead of referring to the freedom or emancipation of humankind, Weber referred to the rationalization of the world to characterize modernization and introduced an ideal-type to describe it, that is, 'goal-oriented rational action' (*zweckrationale Handlung*), as distinct from value-rational, traditional, merely emotional actions. According to Weber, goal-oriented rational action is action by anyone who expects some benefits from the results it will cause and acts in consideration of its conditions and effects.[21] It is precisely a marked increase in this goal-oriented rational action in society that characterizes modernization. Rationalization in this sense necessarily increases bureaucracy and spoils any romantic picture of the world, replacing it with a sense of the meaninglessness of the world. As is widely known, Weber called this process the 'disenchantment' (*Entzauberung*) of the world.[22]

Thus, Weber described modernization as neither progress nor as regress but as a socio-development understood in terms of a value-free ideal-type. Evidently, this ambivalent theory of modernization differs from not only that of Hegel and Marx but also that of Nietzsche and Heidegger, who regarded the modernization of Europe rather as a regress of thought (*Verfallensgeschichte*).[23] Although Weber agreed with Nietzsche in that he did not believe in teleological evolutionism and the progress of history, he did not agree with Nietzsche's prophetic diagnoses such as that of the *Übermensch*.[24] Indeed, Weber was not a philosopher, but a historical sociologist. Without philosophically speculating on Europe's modernization, he enlarged his scope of inquiry in connection with a study of the comparative sociology of world religions. Starting with the question of why such a rationalization or modernization took place only in Europe, Weber investigated world religions such as Protestantism, Judaism, Buddhism, Hinduism, Taoism, and Confucianism.[25] To that extent, he seems not to have shared Hegel's, Marx's, and Nietzsche's Euro-centrism. One could regard this broad view of Weber as unique, epoch-making as well as ahead of his time, a positive legacy for a non-Eurocentric study of world religion.

Yet it has to be pointed out that a Eurocentric as well as Protestant-centric view in Weber's study of religions still remains. To be sure, in the *Vorbemerkung* (preface) of his *Gesammmelte Aufsätze der Religionsoziologie* Weber declares that all his arguments are based on his particular and limited viewpoints of the modern Europe in which he lives.[26] This acknowledgment of the particular value orientations that underlie his concept formation can be called 'methodologically founded ethnocentrism,' and in recognizing the spatial and temporal boundedness of his ideal-types, Weber distinguishes himself from any progressive, teleological Eurocentrism.[27] Nevertheless, it is precisely in this 'methodologically founded ethnocentrism' that his non-progressive Eurocentrism paradoxically appears. I will illustrate this with the help of the example of Weber's non-Western reception.

Since he derived the ethos of capitalistic development of the economy from the worldly ascetic ethic of Calvinism in his famous monograph *Die protestantische Ethik und der 'Geist' des Kapitalismus* first published in 1904–5, Weber tried to show that no equivalent ethic could be found in any religion besides Protestantism.[28] One very important criterion for making such a judgment was whether a religion was captured by magic or not. According to Weber, almost all religions except Calvinism (Puritanism) had failed to get rid of magic. Only Puritanism succeeded in banishing magic, promoting worldly asceticism, motivating people to accumulate capital and generating modernization in the process.[29] Irrespective of scholarly controversies surrounding the *Protestant Ethic*, Weber's thesis has lost its historical significance in light of the firm social fact of worldwide economic development, especially since the Second World War. Today it even seems anachronistic to rely upon Weber's thesis on the comparative study of religions to explain the reasons for modern economic developments.

Indeed, the reception of Weber in postwar Japan well illustrates the relativization of his thesis. After the collapse of the Japanese imperial system in 1945, it became imperative for many Japanese social theorists to think about the modernization of Japan. It was in this context that Weber's works were read and studied. Hisao Otsuka (1907–96), a prominent scholar on European history of socio-economy, proposed that the Japanese people need a new ethos like Protestantism in order to achieve modernization.[30] This quasi-Hegelian interpretation of Weber, which is no more tenable today than it was then, was dominant for a long time among postwar Japanese intellectuals. Indeed, it was not until in the 1980s that Japanese scholars were freed from this interpretation of Weber. At that time, Japanese scholars began to notice that Weber's theory of modernization was not a progressive one. Instead, some scholars began to emphasize the great influence of Nietzsche on Weber.[31]

It is a little curious, however, that very few Japanese scholars are interested in Weber's misinterpretation of Confucianism, although Confucianism had greatly influenced early modern Japanese intellectuals. Although it did not occur in Japan, a remarkable critique of Weber's one-sided interpretation of Confucianism was made in the Chinese-speaking world. Yu Yung-shi (1930–), a former professor at Princeton University, published a stimulating book titled *Religious Ethic and Mercantile Spirit in Early Modern China* in 1987.[32] According to Yu, Weber was wrong to believe that Confucianism lacks a worldly ascetic ethic. Neo-Confucianism, which was advanced mainly by Chu Hsi (1130–1200), developed a kind of worldly ascetic ethics through the metaphysical thought of the Learning of Principle (*li-hšéh*) and of the Learning of the Mind and Heart (*hsin-hšeh*). This kind of ethics transformed the behaviour of Chinese merchants in early modern China, yet Weber's study based upon old Confucianism completely overlooked this trait of neo-Confucianism.[33]

Although Yu reserves judgment upon whether this trait contributed to the success of capitalistic production in East or Southeast Asia, we cannot ignore Yu's criticism of Weber's misunderstanding of Confucianism and Weber's one-sided theory of modernization. Furthermore, it is worth mentioning that Robert Bellah (1927–), an eminent sociologist and an author of *The Habits of Hearts* and *The Good Society*, published *Religions in the Tokugawa Period* (1967), which studied the considerable influence of an early modern religious ascetic ethos on the economic ethics as well as endogenous development in eighteenth-century early modern Japan. According to him, there was a Japanese tradition of social thought equivalent to Protestantism in Europe.[34] This hypothesis was both admired and criticized by Japanese scholars.[35]

What conclusions should be drawn when considering these studies, which can in no way match Weber's large scale of macro-sociology, but can offer some non-Eurocentric views? First, it would be safe at least to say that Weber's Eurocentric as well as Protestant-centric view should be recognized and discarded, and the relationship between modernization and the world religions should be reconsidered from another perspective. It is obvious that there are spiritual traditions other than Calvinism capable of promoting modernization, as the history of Asian countries after the Second World War shows. Weber's thesis seems no longer tenable in this regard.

Second, it would be too severe, however, to lay the blame on Weber for Eurocentric bias. As is emphasized above, Weber was conscious of his 'methodologically founded ethnocentrism' and therefore did not share a progressive Eurocentrism with Hegel. While Hegel thought that Europe stood at the top of world history,[36] Weber's Eurocentrism had nothing to do with such a triumphalism of history, which is partly found in Marxism too. Furthermore, although Weber made Calvinism pivotal to his argument on the comparative sociology of religions, he did not insist on its superiority to other religions. He tried to distinguish Calvinism from other religions mainly in terms of goal-oriented rational actions, which caused the development of capitalism but also 'the iron cage.' Weber thus should not be condemned for his Eurocentrism: it is only necessary to acknowledge and discard his limited viewpoint.

Third, amid contemporary globalization, the comparative study of the world religions, especially in its relationship to modernization as well as globalization studies, should be recognized much more as a positive legacy of Weber's sociology. Although modernization and globalization studies are becoming more and more active today, the study of world religions seems to lag behind the study of economy and politics. Neither the 'theory of the World Economic System' (Wallerstein)[37] nor 'the theory of reflexive modernity' (Giddens),[38] for example, can match Weber's study of modernity, because both ignore the social role of religions in the age of globalization.[39] In this respect, Weber's comparative macro-sociology offers a promising vantage point (*Ansatz*) from which to view and understand world religions in the age of globalization, only if his Eurocentric and Protestant-centric perspectives are discarded. To be sure, the contemporary works of Wolfgang Schluchter as a sociologist or Richard Swedberg as a socio-economist have been developing this positive legacy.[40]

Nevertheless, I cannot but point out that Weber's understanding of politics and scientific knowledge, which was presented in parallel to his macro-sociology, has to be criticized in order just to salvage this vantage point. In the next section, I will argue this point.

3. Weber's Understanding of Politics and Scientific Knowledge from a Contemporary Viewpoint, or Post-Weberian Desiderata

It is important to note that Weber's theory of modernization was also connected with his understanding of politics and scientific knowledge as his last two lectures, 'Politics as a Vocation' and 'Science as a Vocation' showed. But today how should we evaluate his understanding of eighty-five years ago? Indeed, it is absolutely necessary to contextualize and relativize them from the contemporary viewpoint. In this section, I would like to make some critical remarks on each of these questions and suggest some post-Weberian desiderata in order to make use of the above-mentioned vantage point.

As is well known, Weber's understanding of politics is characterized as power politics. Indeed, Weber attached little importance to traditional ideas such as natural law or justice. Instead, he regarded the essentials of politics as 'power and rule' (*Herrschaft*), defining them as 'the chance of having an order with a specific content obeyed by specifiable persons.'[41] He saw the ethic of inner conviction (*Gesinnungsethik*) as not only invalid but also misleading for politics, and he limited political norms to the 'ethic of responsibility' (*Verantwortungsethik*) for the consequences of political actions.[42] Instead of referring to the traditional classification of the six forms of constitution since Aristotle,[43] he introduced 'three ideal-types of legitimate rule' to understand political systems: traditional rule, charismatic rule, and legal rule.[44]

To be sure, such an understanding of 'power politics' may be regarded as a product of the catastrophic time in which Weber lived. They were, as a matter of fact, valid around the time of the Second World War as well as of the Cold War, and even today.[45] His insight that bureaucracy[46] plays an important role, whether in capitalism or socialism, seems to be ever truer today. The ethics of responsibility are also increasingly relevant to political leaders acting in an unstable age of globalization. Thus, it would be a mistake to think that Weber's view of politics has lost its validity.

Still, one very important question arises. Is it enough to discuss the nature of politics solely in terms of power politics, especially in our contemporary world? As was pointed out in the first section, Weber's disregard for the normative theory of social policy is no longer tenable today. In my view, the same can be said about his one-sided view of politics. By that I mean that Weber's combination of power politics on one hand and polytheism of values on the other hand cannot do justice to contemporary serious topics such as 'dialogue among civilizations or religions' and 'human development,' which have, for example, become serious agenda items at UNESCO and the UN for the twenty-first century.[47] In many respects, Weber's conflict-ridden real-political thought reflected and participated in the high-modern European political world that came to an end with the conflagration of the First World War. In our contemporary intellectual environment, Weber's political thought as well as his comparative sociology of religions (and cultures) need to be reconciled with normative political theory.

Indeed, it seems to have become an essential task for today's political theorists as well as comparative sociologists to seek a way toward mutual understanding of cultures or religions in order to escape from what Samuel Huntington calls 'the clash of civilizations.'[48] In this regard, it would be interesting to try to combine the comparative sociological legacy of Weber with the contemporary multiculturalism advanced by Charles Taylor, Will Kymlicka, Bhikuh Parekh, and others, as well as with the contemporary ethical economics advanced by Amartya Sen.[49] As a matter of fact, Human Development Reports of UNDP show that the concept of development has become a serious issue to be discussed together with human, political, and cultural freedom, which Weber's understanding of politics lacks. Therefore, it is necessary to introduce some post-Weberian normative political theories, which discuss social justice, multiculturalism, and so on.

To sum up, Weber's understanding of politics retains its validity in terms of power politics but it is insufficient in terms of normative theory in an unstable age of globalization. Therefore, it would be desirable to try to integrate the comparative macro-sociology of world religions or cultures with the normative theories of justice, multiculturalism, as well as development, from a post-Weberian perspective.

Just as Weber's political thought needs to be brought up to date, so too does his understanding of scientific knowledge as summarized in his celebrated lecture 'Science as a Vocation.' Weber's understanding in this lecture presented a marked contrast to that of W. Humboldt (1767–1835) a century before. While Humboldt as a founder of the University of Berlin emphasized that the knowledge to be acquired in the university should be combined with philosophical insight as well as formation of human character (*Selbstbildung*),[50] Weber regarded such a combination as anachronistic and instead regarded the specialization of scientific knowledge as a historically irreversible destiny. For him, the scientific division of labour was an inevitable tendency of time, which should be accepted by all scholars,[51] though in practice he excepted himself from this necessity.

Certainly, Weber's characterization of modern science has been valid until now, especially his admonishment that the autonomy of scientific research should be respected. However, we should not forget that, at the end of his essay 'Objectivity' in 1904, Weber attached much importance to the value consciousness of each scholar in the age of specialization of sciences and suggested that the understanding of sciences could be changed in the future.[52] He also criticized the specialist without spirit in the last part of his *Protestant Ethic* in 1905.[53] Nevertheless, this viewpoint seems to have faded away in his 'Science as a Vocation' in 1919.

As a matter of fact, it does not now seem possible to reconcile this understanding with the contemporary need for interdisciplinary social studies, which transcend the limits of each individual discipline. Therefore, Weber's rigid argument for the specialization of scientific knowledge in 1919 must be historically relativized and modified in favour of interdisciplinary or trans-disciplinary social studies, and the position of social philosophy, which Weber so underestimated, must be restored.

I would like to call the time until Wilhelm von Humboldt, in which philosophy played an important role for social theory, the 'time of pre-specialization of science.' In opposition to this time, I call the time in which social sciences separated into individual disciplines, and philosophy played a very small role in social theory, the 'time of specialization.' Indeed, Weber lived in this time and explicitly named it a *Zeit der Spezialisierung* in his 'Objectivity' essay.[54] Yet, in my view, we live in another time in which social sciences and philosophy should cooperate with one another to tackle the global problems faced by humankind. I would like to call this present time the 'time of post-specialization of sciences.' I think that by using this concept we can overcome Weber's obsolete understanding of science and politics.[55]

As was argued above, Weber's positive legacy, which we can appreciate, is his non-progressive as well as broad view of history and world religions. This positive legacy, however, was accompanied by negative legacies such as an impoverished theory of normative social policy and politics, a Protestant-centric view of religion, and a one-sided understanding of scientific knowledge. These negative legacies should be now discarded in favour of his positive legacy. To do so, I would like here to outline an alternative social theory, which fits well in what I call the time of post-specialization of sciences from a post-Weberian viewpoint.

What I mean by the time of post-specialization is the academic environment in which social sciences, humanities, and natural sciences cooperate with one another to tackle serious problems of our time such as development, human rights, peace-building, dialogue among religions, and so on. This idea forms a striking contrast to the academic ideology, according to which each science should be isolated and performed separately, but must not be, however, confused with an academic dilettantism. In my view, Weber was right to distinguish scientific knowledge from dilettantism.[56] But his understanding of science as a vocation was not favourable to interdisciplinary studies, although his study of modernization and world religions had considerable interdisciplinary features. Undoubtedly, Weber's attitude here is closely tied to his neglect of normative social theory.

Accepting Weber's broad view of history and cultures *and* at the same time rejecting his narrow view of science, I believe that social theory – in what I call the time of post-specialization – should try to combine empirical studies with normative theory. Indeed, Sen's theory might provide a good model for this, but unlike Weber's theories, it still lacks the broad view of history and cultures, including religions. In order to overcome both weaknesses, social theory of today and in the future has to work hard to do justice to the historical, cultural, and normative dimensions of social realities all over the world. Such a step may require a *glocal viewpoint* instead of a merely global or a merely local viewpoint. By a 'glocal' viewpoint I mean a mixture of a global viewpoint, which requires a universal thinking, and of local viewpoints, which require their own particular thinking according to their situations.[57] I hope that this glocal viewpoint can overcome the dichotomy of methodological universalism and ethnocentrism.

The global issues of today such as human development, dialogue among civilizations or religions, peace-building, etc., should be studied from both interdisciplinary and glocal viewpoints. Normative political theory, economic and environmental ethics, social and public policy, cultural anthropology, and historical sociology must cooperate with one another in order to tackle serious social problems in the world. It is through this cooperation that we can offer a genuine alternative to Weber's theory yet avoid falling into pre-Weberian, blindly normative teleology or dilettantism.[58]

NOTES

1 See Carl Menger, *Untersuchungen über die Methode der Sozialwissenschaften, und die politische Ökonomie insbesondere* (Leipzig: Dunker and Hunblot, 1883).

2 See Gustav von Schmoller, 'Die Schriften von C. Menger und W. Dilthey zur Methdologie der Staats-Sozialwissenschaften,' in *Zur Literaturgeschichte der Staats-und Sozialwissenschaften* (Leipzig: Dunker und Humblot, 1888), 293–4.

3 See Carl Menger, *Die Irrtümer des Historismus in der deutschen Nationalökonomie* (Vienna: Alfred Hoelder, 1884), 46.

4 Max Weber, *Gesammelte Aufsätze zur Wissenschaftslehre* (hereafter *WL*) (Tübingen: Mohr, 1968), 146–214. Although there are excellent previous works on this topic, such as Wilhelm Hennis, 'Eine Wissenschaft vom Menschen: Max Weber und die deutsche Nationalökonomie der historischen Schule,' in *Max Weber und Seine Zeitgenossen*, ed. Wolfgang J. Mommsen and Wolfgang Schwenker (Göttingen: Vandenhoeck und Ruprecht, 1988), 41–83; Manfred Schon, 'Guatav Schmoller und Max Weber,' ibid., 84–118; Wilhelm Hennis, 'Die volle Nüchternheit des Urteils: Max Weber zwischen Carl Menger und Gustav von Schmoller: Zum hochschulpolitischen Hintergrund des Wertfreiheitspostulats,' in his book *Max Webers Wissenschaft vom Menschen: Neue Studien zur Biographie des Werkes* (Tubingen: Mohr, 1996); 114–151, Richard Swedberg, 'The Evolution of Weber's Thoughts on Economics,' in his book *Max Weber and the Idea of Economic Sociology*, 173–206 (Princeton: Princeton University Press, 1998), I would like to reconsider this controversy not from a retrospective interest, but from my own perspective in connection with contemporary issues. It

is regrettable that these works do not address themselves to the contemporary issues of development studies, for which normative theory and ethics are indispensable. Even if Swedberg points out at the end of the last chapter of his above-mentioned book that 'economic ethics, which is not to be found in today's economic sociology, raised a host of interesting research questions,' he concludes only with his appraisal of Weber's individualistic attitude and avoids entering into contemporary normative debates on socio-historical development (see 172). I appreciate, however, his efforts to reformulate Weber's achivement from the perspective of socio-economics. See note 40 below.

5 Weber, *WL*, 148–61.

6 Ibid., 190–214.

7 Gustav von Schmoller, *Volkswirtschaft, Volkswirtschaftslehre und methode*, in *Handwörterbuch der Staatswissenschaften*, ed. J. Conrad, L. Elster, and E. Loening, 3rd ed. (Jena: Gustav Fisher, 1911), 8:426–501.

8 Ibid., 490–8.

9 Weber, *WL*, 489–540.

10 Ibid., 501–8.

11 See Herbert Spencer, *The Evolution of Society* (Chicago: University of Chicago Press, 1967). Although Spenser's laissez-faire policy is incompatible with Schmoller's interventionism, both had in common a belief in harmony between evolution and ethical progress of society.

12 One of the reasons that Weber, as well as Werner Sombart, had been so hostile to Schmoller lay precisely in this paternalistic tendency of Schmoller's.

13 See Weber, *WL*, 505–9.

14 See ibid., 518–30.

15 See United Nations Development Program, *Human Development Reports* (New York: Oxford University Press, 1990–2005).

16 See Amartya Sen, *Development as Freedom* (New York: Anchor Books, 2000), 3–84, 282–98.

17 Ibid., 298.

18 For the appraisal of Schmoller's ethico-historical school from a contemporary viewpoint, see Yuichi Shionoya, 'A Methodological Appraisal of Schmoller's Research Program,' in *The Theory of Ethical Economy in the Historical School*, ed. Peter Koslowski (Berlin: Spranger, 1995), 57–78, and 'Rational Reconstruction of the German Historical School,' in *The German Historical School: The Historical and Ethical Approach to Economics*, ed. Yuich Shionoya (London: Routledge, 2001), 7–18. A desideratum of the historical approach in Sen's theory can be found in his *Rationality and Freedom*

(Cambridge, MA: Harvard University Press, 2002), published after *Development as Freedom*.

19 Max Weber, *Gesammelte Aufsätze zur Religionssoziologie* (hereafter cited as *RS*), 3 vols. (Tübingen: Mohr, 1920).

20 See Georg Wilhelm Friedrich Hegel, *Vorlesungen über die Philosophie der Geschichte* (Frankfurt am Main: Suhrkamp, 1970); Karl Marx, 'Formen, die der kapitalistischen Produktion vorausgehen,' in *Grundrisse der Kritik der politischen Ökonomie* (Berlin: Dietz, 1953), 375–415.

21 See Max Weber, *Wirtschaft und Gesellschaft* (hereafter cited as *WG*) (Tübingen: Mohr, 1972), 12–13.

22 See Weber, *WL*, 594.

23 See Martin Heidegger, *Nietzsche, der europäische Nihilismus* (Frankfurt am Main: V. Klostermann, 1968).

24 Thus, Weber's stance on Nietzsche has been ambivalent. On this point, see Wolfgang Mommsen's *Max Weber: Gesellschaft, Politik und Geschichte* (Frankfurt am Main: Suhrkamp, 1974), 97–142, 260–3.

25 See Weber, *RS*, 1:237–573.

26 Ibid., 1–16.

27 On this point, I am inspired by Laurence McFalls in his essay 'Entre ethnocentrism et histoire universelle: Max Weber et le dépassement des *area studies*,' *Lendemains* 31, nos. 122/123 (2006): 31–40. The term *methodologically founded ethnocentrism* derives from Catherine Colliot-Thélène, *Max Weber et l'histoire* (Paris: PUF, 1990), 57.

28 See Weber *RS*, 1:17–206.

29 Ibid., 1–16.

30 Otsuka's progressive view of Weber was closely connected with his intention to compete with contemporary Marxism over Japanese modernization. See Otuka's *Collected Work* (in Japanese) vol. 9 (Tokyo: Iwanami, 1969).

31 I have not mentioned here the names of Japanese scholars who emphasize Nietzsche's influence on Weber. Instead, I only point out that this switch from Hegelian to Nietzschean interpretation of Weber would have been unthinkable without a translation of Mommsen's aforementioned book into Japanese in 1977. However, it would also be necessary to mention here that there are a few remarkable works written by Japanese scholars who tried to refute Mommsen's thesis.

32 To my knowledge and regret, this remarkable book of Yu Yung-si, though he taught at Princeton University, is not yet translated into English.

33 This fault in Weber's understanding of Confucianism has also been admitted by an eminent German Weberian, Wolfgang Schluchter. See his *Religion und Lebensführung* (Frankfurt am Main: Suhrkamp, 1988), 2:54–61.

Schluchter referred to a pioneering study of Thomas Metzger, *Escape from Predicament* (New York: Columbia University Press, 1977).

34 Robert Bellah, *Tokugawa Religion: The Cultural Roots of Modern Japan* (New York: Free Press, 1985).

35 Among the critics of Bellah's study of Japanese modernity, I mention here the name of Masao Maruyama (1914–96), the most influential Japanese political theorist after the Second World War and an enthusiastic supporter of radical democracy, and the name of Hiroshi Orihara (1935–) as my former honourable colleague as well as an enthusiastic Weberian who translated Weber's 'Objectivity of Knowledge in Social Science and Social Policy' into Japanese, with excellent comments.

36 Recently, this Hegelian view of history was misleadingly rehabilitated by Francis Fukuyama. See his *The End of History and the Last Man* (New York: International Creative Management, 1992).

37 See Immanuel Wallerstein, *The Modern World System*, 3 vols. (New York: Academic Press, 1974–89).

38 See Anthony Giddens, *The Consequences of Modernity* (Stanford: Stanford University Press, 1990).

39 For an example of a social theory that attaches much importance to the role of religions in the age of globalization, see Roland Robertson, *Globalization: Social Theory and Global Culture* (London: Sage, 1992).

40 See Wolfgang Schluchter, *Religion und Lebensführung*, 2 vols. (Frankfurt am Main: Suhrkamp, 1988), Richard Swedberg, *Max Weber and the Idea of Economic Sociology* (Princeton: Princeton University Press, 1998). What I am still missing in these books, however, are the *normative issues* on the global level that go beyond the scope of sociology and socio-economics.

41 See Weber, *WG*, 541–50.

42 See Max Weber, 'Politik als Beruf,' *Gesammelte politische Schriften* (Tübingen: Mohr, 1981), 505–60.

43 See Aristotle, *Politics* (New York: Modern Library, 1943).

44 See Weber, *WG*, 122–76.

45 As is well known, Weber's understanding of politics has influenced so-called political realism, which mistrusts normative ideas such as justice.

46 See Weber, *WG*, 551–79.

47 See UNESCO's home page, http://portal.unesco.org, and UNDP, *Human Development Reports*.

48 See Samuel Huntington, *The Clash of Civilizations and the Remaking of World Order* (New York: Touchstone, 1997).

49 See Charles Taylor, Amy Guttmann, et al., *Multiculturalism: Examining the Politics of Recognition* (Princeton: Princeton University Press, 1994); Will Kymlicka, *Politics in the Vernacular: Nationalism, Multiculturalism and*

Citizenship (New York: Oxford University Press, 2000); Bhikuh Parekh, *Rethinking Multiculturalism: Cultural Diversity and Political Theory* (Cambridge, MA: Harvard University Press, 2000); Amartya Sen, *Development as Freedom* (New York: Anchor Books, 2002).

50 See Wilhelm Humboldt, 'Über die innere und äussere Organisation der höheren wissenschaftlichen Anstalten in Berlin,' in *Gesammelte Schriften* (Berlin: Gruyter, 1968 [1810]), 10:250–60. It was according to this idea of Humboldt that.Hegel, Schleiermacher, and others developed their social theories.

51 Weber, *WL*, 582–613.

52 Ibid., 211–13.

53 Weber, *RS*, 1:204.

54 Weber, *WL*, 214.

55 I first introduced this historical perspective of *Wissenschaft* in terms of the categories of pre-specialization, specialization, and post-specialization in *Manifesto of a New Trans-Disciplinary Social Philosophy* (in Japanese) (Tokyo: Sobunsya, 1999), and since then I have been emphasizing it in a number of my books and papers in order to highlight the historical particularity of our contemporary environment of social sciences.

56 See Weber, *WL*, 590.

57 This term *glocalization* has been used by the above-mentioned Robertson. See Roland Robertson, 'Globalization or Glocalization,' in *Globalization: Critical Concepts of Sociology*, ed. Roland Robertson and Kathleen White (London: Routledge, 2001), 3:31–59, and 'Globalization Theory 2000+: Major Problematics,' in *Handbook of Social Theory*, ed. George Ritter and Barry Smart (London: Sage, 2001), 456–71. Quite independently of this sociological study, I have been engaged with 'a glocal public philosophy,' which is trans-disciplinary as well as internationally conceived. See Naoshi Yamawaki, 'The Idea of Glocal Public Philosophy in the Unstable Age of Globalization,' *International Journal of Public Affaires* 2 (2006): 65–9; 'Pour une philosopie glocal de l'espace public,' trans. Jacques Joly, *DARUMA – Revue internationale d'études japonaises*, forthcoming 2007; 'Toward a Glocal Philosophy and Comparative Study of Philosophical Thoughts for the Interregional Dialogue,' presented to a UNESCO Congress, Paris, 16–17 November 2004.

58 In this, my viewpoint is distinct from an anachronistic viewpoint represented by so-called Strausians, see Leo Strauss, *Natural Right and History* (Chicago: University of Chicago, 1999); Allan Bloom, *Closing of the American Mind* (New York: Touchstone Books, 1988).

9 Weber, Braudel, and Objectivity in Comparative Research

JACK GOODY

Weber's '"Objectivity" of Knowledge in Social Science and Social Policy' constituted the introductory remarks of a new editorial board for the journal *Archiv für Sozialwissenschaft und Sozialpolitik* (1904). He explains that the difference he perceived between the natural and the cultural sciences lies in the fact that 'the significance of cultural events presupposes a *value-orientation* towards these events. The concept of culture is a *value-concept*. Empirical reality becomes "culture" to us because and insofar as we relate it to value ideas' (Weber 1949, 76). His argument is based on the need to make an 'unbridgeable distinction' between 'empirical knowledge' and 'value judgements.' Both are recognized as important topics for reflection and 'those highest "values" underlying the practical interest are and always will be decisively significant in determining the focus of attention of analytical activity in the sphere of the cultural sciences' (Weber 1949, 58). Nevertheless what is valid for us 'must also be valid for the Chinese,' although he saw the development of the scientific spirit as more significant in the West. Take the process of the disenchantment of the human mind, which marked the growth of meaningful scientific knowledge by the process of intellectualization. This process has, he argues, 'continued to exist in Occidental culture for millennia' and constitutes progress. That notion of progress, of 'continuous enrichment of life,' is the key to civilized man.

Weber writes at one point that 'an "objective" analysis of cultural events, which proceeds according to the thesis that the ideal of science is the reduction of empirical reality to "laws," is meaningless' (1949, 80). It is meaningless for a variety of reasons. One reason lies in his definition of culture, which is 'a finite segment of the meaningless infinity of the world process, a segment on which *human beings* confer meaning and significance' (1949, 81). This definition is very different from the classical definition of the British anthropologist E.B. Tylor (1881), which embraces all human action and beliefs. It is one that was essential to the schema of Talcott Parsons, now largely abandoned, and to the many American anthropologists who followed him. I myself cling firmly to the wider definition of Tylor's in which culture covers all human action, material and spiritual, and would set aside this concept of Weber's, on which his discussion of objectivity depends, because in practice it is impossible to establish a field of enquiry that centres upon the values of the observer (that he rightly considers important in the selection of topic) or indeed those of actors (in the way most sociologists understand the proposition). In any case, few scholars would wish to limit their analyses in this way, in spite of those anthropologists who claim to try to follow Parsons's view that their entire discipline is concerned only with beliefs and values, the domain of 'cultural science.'

It is difficult to dispute Weber's overall aim of objectivity. What he failed to appreciate were the difficulties in achieving it, in separating 'fact' and 'values' and in the extent of their interpenetration, determining a good deal more than 'the focus of attention.' The difficulty is to be seen in his own work. I do not want to argue that Weber was wrong in his programmatic pronouncement, only that he did not fully realize what was involved. And if he did so 'theoretically,' he did not do so 'analytically.' He makes great efforts to be 'objective' when considering the nature of the 'economic ethic' in different religions (in ancient Israel, India, and China, as well as in Europe) mainly in relation to the rise of capitalism, but he then comes down firmly in favour of the Protestant variety, which was indeed his starting point. That focus has been firmly rejected by many other historians, but principally by Fernand Braudel, the French historian of the Mediterranean. However, when Braudel turned his attention to capitalism, he accepted an important number of Western propositions about East-West differences and their relevance for the rise of capitalism, including those concerning some features of daily life and above all the nature of the European city, beginning with the north Italian commune of the tenth century.

I shall not comment directly on Weber's own original attempts at global comparison; I am interested in him as a model for others. He was of course concerned primarily with the economic and cultural dominance of the West in recent times, and his acute analyses of India and China always have the growth of capitalism as their background. In practice he does not limit himself to the development of industrial capitalism in eighteenth-century Europe but understandably looks back to the preconditions, specifically to the Reformation (the Protestant ethic), to the Renaissance, and to the 'Age of Exploration,' and even further back, as I have suggested, to the 'unique' nature of the European city.[1] That route has been followed by many commentators on the situation. Both Marx and Wallerstein go back at least to the Age of Exploration, pushing Europe's advantage backwards in time. In his comparative work Weber has been ambitiously followed by Braudel (and he in turn by Wallerstein). In this paper I want to concentrate upon Braudel's contribution and comment indirectly on the way in which all these writers, coming from the same Eurocentric starting point, have deviated from 'objectivity,' despite their best intentions. That applies both to nineteenth-century authors like Marx and Weber, living at the time of full flush of European industrial advancement, as well as many more recent historians such as Braudel, living in a more sceptical period.

Braudel was a historian of the very first rank. His *Structures of Everyday Life* (1981) is described by his colleague Zeldin as 'brilliant' and by Plumb as 'a masterpiece.' I want to review one aspect of his work both admiringly and critically, from the standpoint of later developments in world history that attempt to modify certain Eurocentric biases. These any Western scholar inevitably has. Braudel certainly displays less tendency in this direction than, say, Weber or Marx and gives consideration to a wide range of comparative material on everyday life.

He is in general much subtler about the question of European advantage than earlier writers. Nevertheless his sources are inevitably largely European and partake of some of those prejudices. Some of these are minor, some major. Let me begin with the first, with domestic mores, before dealing with the problem of towns. Braudel considers that Europe had a 'privileged position' regarding the consumption of meat (1981, 199); but equally, of course, we could take a different standpoint and assert that China and India were privileged with regard to the consumption of fruit and vegetables. One of his sources, Labat, remarks of the Arabs that they didn't know the use of tables; one might equally claim that Europe did not have the divan or the carpet until they came from the East. His section on 'the slow adoption of good manners' (206) seems to show a similar kind of bias as Elias towards European behaviour, for it is widely thought by others that the Far East had more elaborate and exacting etiquette at an earlier period. Not everything was straight progress. The West, according to Braudel, suffered a 'significant regression' (329) from the point of view of body baths and bodily cleanliness from the fifteenth to the seventeenth centuries. Baths, 'an invention from Rome' (!), were found throughout medieval Europe, private as well as public, with both sexes bathing naked together. They were even subject to seigniorial dues (Cabanès 1900, 8, who sees their origin as Asian). In fact there was a great deal of ambivalence about the luxury of warm baths, even before Christianity, which became more apparent afterwards. 'C'est ce caractère de luxe et de plaisir qui obligea les premiers chrétiens à proscrivre les bains, au même titre que les théâtres' (Cabanès 1900, 119). They were finally condemned by St John Chrisostom, patriarch of Constantinople at the end of the fourth century, for their licentious reputation, for their luxury, and for the dangers of nudity (de Bonneville 1998, 33). Roman public baths closed, the steam baths disappeared, but baths were permitted in religious establishments and, at the time of the Crusades and possibly as the result of Arabic influences, they became more widespread (Cabanès 1900, 174). After the sixteenth century, bathing became rarer, partly from the fear of disease, partly from the influence of preachers, both Catholic and Calvinist, who fulminated against the moral dangers and 'ignominy of the baths' (Braudel 1981, 330). Ambivalence remained. There was not a single bathing establishment in London in 1800. Soap production was low, though said to be lower still in China, which was without the benefit of underwear (which appeared in Europe in the second half of the eighteenth century). However, the Chinese had toilet paper a thousand years before Europe – a fact that Braudel does not mention; it is discussed only in connection with printing and money, the presence of which redeemed China's backwardness, mysteriously seen as a result of living near primitive countries 'in their infancy' (1981, 452). When baths were reintroduced they were known as 'Chinese baths' and Turkish baths (330). Cleanliness was certainly not the sole prerogative of Europeans, and the importance of the Chinese invention of paper for hygiene as well as communication was fundamental (but long absent in Europe, which he does not mention).

It was not only baths but cleanliness more generally that was problematic. In Rabelais, Gargantua was visited by his father, who asked if he had kept clean while he was away. Yes, the son replied, none cleaner, because he had invented a special ass wiper (chapter 13). He had used various pieces of cloth, including his mother's gloves – 'nicely scented with cunt flavour.'

'Then I wiped myself with sage, with fennel, with dill and anise, with sweet marjoram, with roses, pumpkins, with squash leaves, and cabbage, and beets, with vine leaves, and mallow, and *Verbascum thapsus* (that's mullein, and it's as red as my asshole), and lettuce and spinach leaves – and a lot of good it all did me! – and mercury weed, and purslane, and nettle leaves, and larkspur and comfrey. But then I got Lombardy dysentery, which I cured by wiping myself with my codpiece.

Then I wiped myself with the bedclothes, the blankets, the bed curtains, with a cushion, a tablecloth (and then another, a green one), a dishcloth, a napkin, a handkerchief, and with a dressing gown. And I relished it all like mangy dogs when you rub them down.'

'To be sure,' said Grandgousier, 'but which ass wipe did you find the best?'

'I'm getting there,' said Gargantua. 'In just a minute you'll hear the *tu autem*, the real heart of it. I wiped myself with hay, with straw, with all sorts of fluffy junk, with tag wool, with real wool, with paper. But:

Wipe your dirty ass with paper

And you'll need to clean your ass with a scraper.' (Rabelais 1990, 35)

By the sixteenth century when he was writing, paper had come into Europe from the Arab world and had made an enormous difference in so many ways, not only for communication. Earlier in the fourteenth century Langland in *Piers Plowman* describes how people cleansed themselves with leaves.

And seten [sat] so til evensong, and songen umwhile [from time to time],
Til Glotoun hadde yglubbed [guzzled] a galon and a gille.
His guttes bigonne to gothelen [rumble] as two gredy sowes;
He pissed a potel [pot full] in a Paternoster-while [the time it takes to say the Paternoster],
And blewe his rounde ruwet [horn] at his ruggebones [backbone's] ende,
That alle that herde that horn helde hir nose after,
And wisshed it hadde ben wexed [scoured] with a wispe of firses [furze].
(B version, Passus 5, ll. 339–45)

This 'primitive' aspect of European life in the Middle Ages, and indeed until much later, is quite neglected by these writers, especially by the sociologist Elias, but Braudel too displays a lack of 'objectivity' in seeing the 'civilizing process' as primarily a European affair. It was not (Goody 2002, 2003).

Braudel continues his comparison as follows. Seen as 'the great innovation, the revolution in Europe' was 'alcohol,' distilled liquor, though the name like alembic clearly indicates its Islamic provenance. Nevertheless, referring to the rest of the world, he asks 'Did the still give Europe the advantage over these people?' In fact Europe was slow to adopt alcohol. In any case, why is it always Europeans who were seen to have the advantage? Other drinks are treated from the same perspective. At nearly the same time as the 'discovery' of alcohol, Europe, considered to be at the centre of the innovations of the world, 'discovered' new drinks, stimulants, and tonics; coffee, tea, and chocolate. But all three came from abroad: coffee was Arab (originally Ethiopian); tea, Chinese; chocolate, Mexican (1981, 249). Clearly the sense in which Europe discovered or innovated these beverages is very limited indeed. In the same way, New Guinea too can be said to have discovered or innovated all these foods somewhat later. The idea that Europe was ('always'?) at the centre of innovations is bizarre in the context of food, as elsewhere, since Braudel recognizes that 'there was no real luxury or sophistication of eating habits in Europe before the fifteenth or sixteenth centuries. In this respect Europe lagged behind the other Old World civilisations' (187). That seems to be correct. Wherein, therefore, lies the European advantage in this sphere?

In other words, there are biases of which the reader should be aware. We have seen that Braudel speaks of the slow adoption of manners in Europe, as if the same process did not happen elsewhere. He seems particularly Eurocentric about matters to do with the house. Tables and chairs we have mentioned. He quotes one European observer as saying the Christians do not sit on the ground 'like animals' (1981, 285); others did. The consumption of meat poses another problem of this kind. Europe had 'a privileged position' relative to other societies (199). So too, of course, did hunters and gatherers. Preferences for a vegetarian diet are given no weight at all, whether based on taste, religion, or morality. The spread of beverages round the world – coffee, tea, chocolate, beer, alcohol – as well as sugar and spices are dealt with primarily from a European point of view. But all were discovered by others. Table and chair 'implied a whole way of life' (288) and were not present in early China until after the sixth century. 'It was probably European in origin,' for the sitting up position was not found in non-European countries and represented 'a new art of living.' That was certainly not true of 'sitting up': many people had stools, though few with backs. In any case, to give that difference such an importance (a change in 'lifestyles') after the sixth century is hardly compatible with the view that Chinese society 'stood still' (312), a conclusion he derives from the consideration of one feature, clothing. But it was certainly not a general characteristic (see Bray 2000). Changing fashion he thinks indicates a dynamic society, along with Say (1828), who wrote disparagingly about 'the unchanging fashions of the Turks and other Eastern peoples,' that 'their fashions tend to preserve their stupid despotism' (314). However, similar statements could have been made about our own villagers, who wore the same clothes and rarely changed them; and consider all those men who dress up in an unchanging evening costume on special occasions. 'Fashionable whims' affected only a small number of people, Braudel claims, and even then only became 'all-powerful' after 1700, when Europe broke away from 'the still waters of ancient situations like those we described in India, China and Islam' (1981, 316). Change was on the side of the privileged few. Hence, in his view, fashion is not frivolous but 'an indication of deeper phenomena' (323). The future belonged to societies that were prepared 'to break with their traditions,' in fact to Europe.

The notion that some societies are more prepared to change than others may be correct for specific periods and for specific contexts, but it is manifestly an error to cast all Asia in the same mould. At least until the sixteenth century, China was probably more 'dynamic' (supposing there is a satisfactory measure). Braudel's concept of 'civilization' and 'culture' tend to suggest that such differences characterized 'la longue durée'; I would place them more at the 'historical' level of 'events,' of the 'conjunctural' rather than the 'civilizational.' To do otherwise seems to project Europe's undoubted differences (and in some respects, advantages) in the nineteenth century right back in time. Why should we not be equally prepared to do the same for the convergences of the twentieth?

However, the recourse to fashion is at the same time seen to be the result of 'material progress' (324) rather than a profound societal characteristic. One example he takes is the way the silk merchants of Lyons exploited 'the tyranny of French fashion' in the eighteenth century by employing 'silk illustrators' who changed the patterns every year, too quickly for the Italians to copy them, as Poni had pointed out (2001). By this time silk production had been present in Sicily and Andalusia for almost seven hundred years, spreading in the sixteenth century, together with the mulberry, to Tuscany, Veneto, and down the Rhone Valley. Venice imported raw silk from the Near East as well as cotton in the form of yarn or raw bales; the former had been the basis of the weaving of silk at Lucca since the 1250s (Inalcik 1994, 219).

Braudel is somewhat contradictory on the subject of change. He argues convincingly for the rapid spread of American crops, such as tobacco, throughout the world. Coffee, tea, and cocoa followed similar worldwide trajectories at roughly the same time. Nevertheless, Europe is said to have 'discovered' them (1981, 249), whereas in fact it is clear that others did. The same is true of buildings. Yet Braudel comes out with the notion that outside Europe there are 'static, inward-looking' – that is, poor – civilizations. Only the West is distinguished by uninterrupted change. 'In the West,' he writes, 'everything was constantly changing' (293). He sees this as a longstanding feature. Furniture varied by country, witness to a 'broad economic and cultural movement carrying Europe towards what itself christened the Enlightenment, progress' (294). And a few lines later: 'If it is established for Europe, the richest civilisation and the one most ready to change, it will apply *a fortiori* to the rest.' While it is true that Europe may have been more ready to change in recent times (some would say after the Industrial Revolution, others would insist since the Renaissance), there is no evidence that Europe was more likely to change in earlier periods. Yet this formulation of Braudel's, whatever qualifications he introduces elsewhere, whatever contradictory evidence he produces, makes the contrast between dynamic Europe and 'static' Asia seem longstanding, if not permanent.

Let us turn to the second point. The major substantive issue on which Braudel shares the Eurocentric prejudices of many of his fellow European historians is the supposedly unique nature of Western towns and their relation to the growth of capitalism and to the rise of the bourgeoisie. He asks if Western towns would have been able to subsist if the 'absurd Chinese-type village had been the rule instead of the exception' (338). That tillage (for rice production) was carried out with hand tools rather than the plough. But that 'absurdity' was the mark of a very intensive, very 'advanced' agriculture that allowed higher population densities and larger towns than in Europe, partly because it did not devote space to the larger domestic livestock needed to pull the ploughs. It is perverse to wonder whether Western towns could 'subsist under such conditions' (338). But in any case, the rice agriculture of Asia demanded more intensive techniques of planting and transplanting; it was not simply the case that mechanisation was 'blocked by cheap labour' (339). Indeed the wheelbarrow was Chinese, and the bridle probably Mongol (*pace* Lynn White). Water mills were certainly not confined to Europe; windmills may have come from China or Iran. In non-agricultural activities, the Chinese were far ahead in the production of iron and the use of coal, though Braudel refers to China's 'stagnation after the thirteenth century,' especially with regard to the use of coke (375). His comment is that earlier 'the Chinese advance is hard to explain' (376). But that is surely the case only if one takes a Eurocentric standpoint. In many areas, the advantage was theirs.

Braudel does not have the same problem with Europe's technology: 'the conquest of the high seas' produced 'a world supremacy that lasted for centuries' (402). That uniqueness was puzzling, he suggests, because 'the maritime civilizations had always known about each other.' The Mediterranean and the Indian Ocean formed 'a single stretch of sea,' the 'route to the Indies,' which had earlier included a connection between the two, known as Nechao's Canal, later to disappear. But it was the conquest of the high seas that gave Europe the advantage. Indeed, 'a long period of pressure after the thirteenth century' 'raised the level of its material life' (415) as a result of 'a hunger to conquer the world,' 'a hunger for gold' or spices, accompanied by a growth in utilitarian knowledge.

One of China's problems, according to Braudel, was that it did not possess 'a complicated monetary system' (440), which was required for production and exchange; only 'medieval Europe finally perfected its money,' because it had to meet the challenge of the Muslim world – a curious proposition. This perfection was due to 'its urban progress in the seventeenth century and the growth of a "truly bourgeois civilization" in privileged towns.' The nature of towns and their inhabitants is discussed below. However, long-distance trade, large-scale commercial capitalism, he importantly observes, depended upon the ability to speak a common 'language of world trade,' inducing 'constructive change' and rapid accumulation. So trade involved reciprocal exchange between equals. Nevertheless, Europe had always to be distinguished from the halfway economies of Asia. India used precious metals and experienced 'an enormous burst of industrialization' in cotton in the sixteenth century, but the economy was marked by 'monetary chaos' (450). Equally China can be understood only 'in the context of the primitive neighbouring economies' (452), which account for both 'the backwardness of China itself' and 'at the same time a certain strength of its "dominant" monetary system.' That strength, it should be noted, included the invention of paper money long before the West even had paper, though it was used extensively only in the fourteenth century. Despite China's 'backwardness' under the Ming (1368–1644), 'a monetary and capitalist economy was coming to life, developing and extending its interests and services,' leading to the rush on the Chinese coal mines in 1596 (454). That development must lead us to qualify its backwardness and makes it difficult to take Braudel's word, as he asks us, that 'in monetary matters China was more primitive and less sophisticated than in India' (457). Or than in Europe? For we need to ask at what period did Europe 'stand alone' with regard to other civilizations. He admits that 'these [monetary] operations were not confined to Europe' but were 'extended and introduced over the whole world like a vast net thrown over the wealth of other continents.' Nevertheless, with the import of American treasures, 'Europe was beginning to devour, to digest the world.' At the same time 'all the currencies of the world were enmeshed in the same net,' suggesting communication of a kind. If China was indeed backward, why were precious metals leaving the Western circuits for Asia (462)? Clearly not only Europe had 'a hunger for gold.' The East knew what it wanted and how to get it by peaceful means – by trade.

The core of Braudel's analysis is centred upon towns and cities, which he compares to electric transformers, constantly recharging human life, beginning – following Marx (and Morgan) – with the transition from barbarism to civilization, that is, with the Bronze Age. Towns were already associated with the coming of the written word, but Braudel among others sees them as reviving Europe in the eleventh century, marking 'the beginning of the continent's rise to eminence' (479). Braudel asserts that 'a town is always a town,' characterized by 'an ever-changing division of labour.' He also writes in general terms of the problem of recruiting the inhabitants of towns because they failed to reproduce themselves (490), and of their self-consciousness that resulted from the need for secure walls (and the dangers that artillery brought in the West from the fifteenth century [497]), of urban communication and of the hierarchies among them. But despite a recognition of these common features and of Bronze Age transformation, his main point has to do with 'the originality of Western towns,' a topic on which he follows Max Weber. They displayed, he argues, 'an unparalleled freedom' (510) developing in opposition to the state and ruling 'autocratically' over the surrounding countryside. Their evolution was 'turbulent' compared with the static nature of cities in other parts of the world; change was encouraged.

After the decay of the urban framework of the Roman Empire, Western towns revived only in the eleventh century, by which time there had already been 'a rise in rural vigour' (510), bringing together there both nobles and churchmen. That shift was possible because of the improving economy and the growing use of money. 'Merchants, craft guilds, industries, long-distance trade and banks were quick to appear there, as well as a certain kind of bourgeoisie and some sort of capitalism' (511). But that was also largely true of towns elsewhere. In Italy and Germany they outgrew the state, forming city states. So too Larsen (1976) writes of city states in Mesopotamia, and others of similar regimes in the Near East. 'The miracle of the West,' according to Braudel, was that when towns revived they displayed great autonomy. On the basis of this 'liberty,' 'a distinctive civilisation' was built up. The towns organized taxation, invented public loans, organized industry and accountancy, becoming the scene of 'class struggles' and 'the focus for patriotism' (512). In other forms, those features too were found widely enough – not only in Europe.

Nevertheless, these European towns were seen as developing bour-geois society, characterized according to Sombart by a new state of mind that appeared in Florence at the end of the fourteenth century (after the textile revolution). 'A new state of mind was established, broadly that of an early, still faltering, Western capitalism' accomplished in 'the art both of getting rich and of living.' Its characteristics also included 'gambling and risk'; 'the merchant ... calculated his expendi-ture according to his returns' (1911, 514). Of course, all merchants have to do that, otherwise they would not survive. They also had to calculate risks, which made them particularly committed to games of chance and gambling, as in China.

While he praises the particular 'freedom' of European towns, Braudel proposes a developmental scheme that runs from classical towns – open to and equal to the surrounding countryside, in which 'industry was rudimentary' (1981, 515) – to the 'closed city' of the medieval period, populated by peasants who had freed themselves from one servitude only to be subjected to another, and finally to the 'subjugated towns of early modern times' (519). However, the state everywhere 'disciplined the towns,' the Hapsburgs and German princes just as much as the popes and the Medicis. 'Except in the Netherlands and England, obedience was imposed.' Given the fact that the last two countries had centralized monarchies and that the 'free' city states of the medieval period in Germany and Italy are now listed as 'subju-gated,' the concept of the 'free' Western town certainly needs to be qualified. That does not prevent Braudel, like Weber and Marx (to-gether with many classicists) before him, from claiming a dramatic contrast with the 'imperial towns' of the East. In the West we do find some towns of a similar kind, but they are 'marginal,' like Cordoba or

Oran. (But why were these to be considered 'marginal'?) 'The usual pattern [in the East] was the huge city under the rule of a prince or Caliph, a Baghdad or a Cairo' (524). In 'distant' Asia too, imperial cities were 'enormous, parasitical, soft and luxurious.' They were 'incapable of taking over the artisanal trades from the countryside,' not because of the nature of authority but because 'society was prematurely fixed, crystallized in a certain mould' again – static, unchanging. In India the problem lay with the castes, in China with the clans. The Weberian notion about their role in impeding capitalism has been largely set aside by modern scholarship (Goody 1996). In China, he claims, there was no authority to represent the town against state or countryside; 'the rural areas were the real heart of living, active and thinking China' (Braudel 1981, 524). However, government officials certainly represented the towns where they lived, as well as the countryside, and much activity took place in the urban centres: artisanal, administrative, judicial, literary, and artistic. Indeed, Braudel elsewhere insists that towns and capitalism in a general way developed together, that the Eastern variety was not much of an impediment. However, capitalist activity also takes place in the villages, especially when the latter provide water power for the mills and labour power to run them, as demonstrated so frequently in the nineteenth century in southern France or in the eastern United States, as well as in China for both paper production and textiles.

What remains problematic in the work of Braudel and other Westerners is the characterization of the Eastern – and by contrast the Western – towns. In general then, his view of Eastern towns was that they were 'enormous, parasitical, soft,' they did not take over artisanal trades from the countryside, and they were the residences of officials and nobles rather than the property of the guilds or merchants. But Western towns too provided residences for nobles and officials and were not *owned* by guilds or merchants, though these often played an important role in governance. It may be that the towns became somewhat 'freer' in parts of the West, but many would dispute the absence of wider governmental control for many regimes other than city states. 'Freedom' was seen as critical to the effective role (indeed, often to the emergence) of a 'bourgeoisie,' who were intrinsic to the changes needed for the development of capitalism. While the bourgeoisie are usually considered by Western scholars as a uniquely European feature, like the incessant change that Wallerstein considers as the key to 'the spirit of capitalism,' Braudel admits that at times the Chinese state 'nodded' at the end of the sixteenth century, allowing the emergence of a bourgeoisie 'with a taste for business enterprise' (524). The features to which he calls attention in the 'free markets' of the West – organized industry, guilds, long-distance trade, bills of exchange, trading companies, accountancy (512) – were also present in China and India, as recent historians such as Pomeranz and Habib have pointed out. Not only were they present, but they were so *before* the birth of towns in eleventh-century Europe. Braudel is prepared to admit such developments, but in his view they did not constitute 'a distinctive civilization,' a concept that is essential to his notion of the genesis of capitalism, real capitalism with its 'mighty networks' in contrast to the more widespread 'micro-capitalism' (562). The contention seems circular.

There is also some confusion here. 'Mighty networks' of this kind arrived only with industrial capitalism. But Braudel has throughout emphasized earlier developments in mercantile capitalism between the fifteenth and eighteenth centuries. This is the period when the question of the 'free worlds' of towns was relevant. The insistence of Western scholars has been about both their 'freedom' and that of their inhabitants. Indeed, classical scholars often see this freedom as an inheritance of slave labour (Finley 1970). But freedom for the town is not the same as freedom for the inhabitants. The latter always gain a measure of 'liberty' when they move to its relative anonymity from the more 'solitary' experience in the countryside. The towns too always seem to have a measure of freedom because of their command of resources, especially money and manufacture, but the degree of constraint from any central authority, secular or religious, clearly varies everywhere, as it did in Europe. Obviously in city states, whether in Europe or in Western Asia, the towns as such had more liberty of action, although mercantile activity itself might suffer restrictions; however, those were not imposed by an external authority, as in some state systems, but internally. By the nineteenth century, Western towns were firmly part of a nation state. It is clear that the degree of 'freedom' of towns varied in different societies, and it may be the case that in the West it was generally greater than elsewhere. European societies certainly had *villes franches*, which were partially 'freed' from government taxation with the aim of encouraging commerce. But Braudel certainly does not definitively demonstrate that in other parts of the world pre-industrial towns were less free. If it is a measure of freedom, many others seem just as 'turbulent' as European ones, in some cases more so.

That East and West should have run broadly parallel courses in the growth and nature of towns, as in mercantile capitalism, is quite understandable. As Braudel often insists, no town was an island; they did not stand alone but were part of a much wider set of relationships, largely reciprocal, necessarily so, as one of their common characteristics was engagement in long-distance trade. Such trade involved a plurality of partners from different 'civilizations' who exchanged not only 'material products' but ways of creating them, in the course of which there was a transfer of other ideas. In this way we can account not simply for 'distinctive' civilizations but for the parallelism between them, such as the emergence of towns throughout Eurasia, with the creation of a bourgeoisie, and of roughly parallel kinds of literary, scientific, and artistic development. Take painting, take literature, take indeed religion. Christianity travels from the Near East to Europe and to Asia. So does Islam. Buddhism goes from India to China and Japan, as well as briefly to the Near East. The movements of these great religious ideologies, often carried by merchants, would not have been possible unless there was some common ground at the time. Urbanization, writes Braudel, is 'the sign of modern man' (1981, 556). If so, modernity began a long way back, at least in the Bronze Age, though humankind has been growing more modern ever since.[2]

The importance of correcting this discussion of the uniqueness of the Western town is this: towns were central to the classical civilizations of the Mediterranean, but they were also important wherever the 'urban revolution,' in Childe's terms, had taken root. In parts of Western Europe, towns virtually disappeared with the fall of the Roman Empire. In the eastern Mediterranean, as well as in Asia, where there was no such collapse, towns continued to operate. 'A town,' as Braudel remarked, 'is always a town.' That did not stop him (or, for that matter, Goitein, Finley, and many others) from following Max Weber in drawing a radical distinction between the Western town with its 'freedoms' (which led to 'capitalism') and Asian cities without them (which did not). Obviously there were some general differences within Eurasia, but these authors locate them on the ideological level, because they are all interested in the teleological result: the advent of capitalism. It was the same story with the family (Goody 1990, 1996). When the economy and urban life of Western Europe began to pick up in the eleventh century, what was important was the renewed trading activity and cultural connections with the existing towns of the eastern Mediterranean, especially Constantinople and Alexandria – towns that had continued to maintain their active connections with the East, with Iran, with China, with India.

If one sees a generalized capitalism, as Braudel does, as a feature of all towns and their commerce, then that insistence on radical East-West difference loses its force. Later towns and their activities can be seen as developments of earlier ones in all their various facets, that is, not only commercial and manufacturing, but even to a greater extent adminis- trative, artistic, and educational – all activities related to the uses of literacy and the growth of learning. As with other facets, communica- tion was subject to a process of social development (or 'evolution') over time, for it was the towns that were the centre of most educational and learning activity, including the production of literature, of written reli- gion, and of textual knowledge – the last of which was essential to the emergence of industrial capitalism in its successive forms. The town was much more than a centre for merchants and their commerce, criti- cal as they were to its economic well-being.

In conclusion, Weber, and following him Braudel, as well as many other lesser sociologists and historians, have failed to live up to expec- tations of objectivity, not so much by over-stressing the comparative advantages of Europe in the nineteenth century, which were consider- able, but by searching for deep-seated reasons for that advantage in the features of earlier societies, a search in which teleology and ethnocen- trism has often led them astray. That position is possibly a result of reading back from the European achievement of the nineteenth and twentieth centuries, partly as the result of an egocentricism built into the human situation. But the search for 'objectivity,' never ultimately obtainable, requires that we try to set these tendencies aside in a more resolute manner than these authors have succeeded in doing.

NOTES

1 He also discussed Rome, in an early work translated as *The Agrarian Sociol- ogy of Ancient Civilizations*.
2 The problem with the interactionist explanation of social evolution is that it neglects the parallel developments in the comparatively isolated New World, which also achieved its urban civilization. While interaction cannot be completely ruled out, there we have to turn to an explanation in terms of the logic of internal developments.

REFERENCES

Braudel, F. 1981. *The Structures of Everyday Life: Civilization and Capitalism, 15th–18th Century*. Vol. 1. Trans. S. Reynolds. London.
– 1992. *The Mediterranean and the Mediterranean World in the Age of Philip II*. Trans. S. Reynolds. London.

Bray, F. 2000. *Technology and Society in Ming China (1368–1644)*. Washington, DC.

Cabanès, A. 1900. *Moeurs intimes du passé*. 2ᵉ série. *La vie aux bains*. Paris.

de Bonneville, F. 1998 [1997]. *The Book of the Bath*. New York.

Elias, N. 1978. *The Civilizing Process*. Oxford.

Goody, J.R. 1970. *Early Greece: The Bronze and Archaic Age*. London.

– 1990. *The Oriental, the Ancient and the Primitive*. Cambridge.

– 1996. *The East in the West*. Cambridge.

– 2002. 'Elias and the Anthropological Tradition.' *Theoretical Anthropology* 2: 401–12.

– 2003. 'The "Civilizing Process" in Ghana.' *European Archives of Sociology* 44: 61–73.

Habib, I. 1990. Merchant Communities in Precolonial India. In *The Rise of Merchant Empires*. Ed. J.D. Tracy. Cambridge.

Inalick, H., with D. Quataert. 1994. *An Economic and Social History of the Ottoman Empire, 1300–1914*. Cambridge.

Larsen, M.T. 1976. *The Old Assyrian City State and Its Colonies*. Copenhagen.

Pomeranz, K. 2000. *The Great Divergence: China, Europe and the Making of the Modern World Economy*. Princeton.

Poni, C. 2001. 'Comparing Two Urban Industrial Districts: Bologna and Lyon in the Early Modern Period. In *Knowledge, Social Institutions and the Division of Labour*. Ed. P.L. Porta, R. Scazzeri and A. Skinner. Cheltenham.

Rabelais, F. 1990 (1542). *Gargantua and Pantagruel*, trans. B. Raffel. New York.

Say, J. 1828. *Cours complet d'économie politique practique*. Paris.

Sombart, W. 1911. *The Jews and Modern Capitalism*. Leipzig (Engl. trans. 1993, London).

Tylor, E.B. 1881. *Primitive Culture*. London.

Weber, M. 1949. *The Methodology of the Social Sciences*. Trans. E.A. Shils and H.A. Finch. Glencoe, IL.

White, L. 1962. *Medieval Technology and Social Change*. Oxford.

10 An Empirical Assessment of Weber's 'Objectivity of Social Science Knowledge'

ANTHONY OBERSCHALL

Weber's Methodology

The objectivity of social science knowledge has vocal critics. On the conservative right it is claimed that Western values like tolerance and free inquiry are unique to Western civilization, as are analytic and probing rationality. Those steeped in non-Western cultures acquire different values, learn a different mode of rationality, and lack the capacity for understanding Western culture. On the political left, muticulturalists, postmodernists, and deconstructionists claim that values and knowledge are a product of a strategic contention for power between rivals. Facts, truth, discourse, and interpretation are valid only for particular local consensus. An objective method and standard for truth value in social science, such as Weber sought to establish, is a misguided intellectual enterprise. Boudon (1995) critiques both such viewpoints from a philosophic standpoint. I offer an empirical assessment of these claims and of Weber's method for achieving objective knowledge in the cultural sciences. My conclusion is that Weber's methodological writings are a robust and valid argument for truth value in the social sciences, which today is still a compelling answer to deniers of objectivity. ·

Weber's methodological essays were written for historians and social scientists, not for philosophers. Weber was an outstanding, practising comparative historian and social scientist. His reach spanned all cultural sciences; today we would term it multidisciplinary. His theoretical inclination was tempered by commitment to empirical work. In *Wirtschaft und Gesellschaft* (*WuG*), the sections devoted to basic concepts and categories of social science are filled with historical and contemporary illustrations. For instance, the section on group relations/solidarity based on language, culture, and ethnicity (*ethnische Gemeinschaftsbezie-hungen*) discusses how the following people and groups view their identities, loyalty, and state affiliation: Swiss, Belgians, Alsatians, Baltic Germans, Prussians, Poles in Upper Silesia, Serbs and Croats, French Canadians, Afro-Americans, with some mention of citizens of Luxembourg and Lichtenstein. That is vintage Weber. He participated in several social surveys, engaged in fieldwork in a textile factory for a whole summer in preparation for a *Verein fur Sozialpolitik* collaborative research on industrial labour, and sought, unsuccessfully to be sure, to found an institute for social research (Oberschall, 1965). In this connection, he told students in his well-known address 'Science as a Vocation,' 'No sociologist ... should think himself, too good, even in his old age, to make tens of thousands of quite trivial computations in his head, and perhaps for months at a time' (Gerth and Mills 1958, 135).

Weber's methodology dealt not with the techniques of research such as sampling and statistical analysis but with establishing the truth value of explanations of human actions and institutions, using *Verstehen* (translated in English as 'understanding'). *Verstehen* is the attempt and capacity of humankind to make sense of one's own and others' actions (choices, beliefs, values, moral prescriptions, motivations, goals, intentions, dispositions, emotions) by introspection and social monitoring, that is, by observing the reaction of other humans to one's own and their own actions. This mode of establishing truth value is referred to as 'interpretative,' and Weber referred to interpretive social science as *verstehende Soziologie*.[1]

Verstehen

The centrality of *Verstehen* in Weber's methodology justifies his frequently misunderstood methodological individualism: '*Verstehen* is at bottom the reason that interpretive sociology [*verstehende Soziologie*] views the concept of individual action as its fundamental building bloc, as its atom ... concepts like state, association, feudalism and similar concepts are categories for specific individual interactions and ... have to be reduced [analytically] to the actions of individual persons in these institutions' (Weber 1958, 110, hereafter *Essays*). He warns about 'the great misunderstanding that an "individualistic" method implies valuing "individualism" over social values, and the mistaken notion that the inevitably rationalist character of concept formation implies that rational motives predominate in human action' (*WuG* 1:9).[2]

An interpretive method can be challenged on 'objectivity' since it is based on mental operations and personal knowledge that are 'subjective,' thus variable from person to person.[3] Yet Weber set high standards for social science truth value: 'Scientific truth can only be that which is valid for all' (*Essays*, 227). Just because cultural knowledge (*Kulturwissenschaftliche Erkenntnis*) is linked to subjective assumptions, it does not follow that the researches and findings in the cultural sciences 'are valid for one but not for the other.' He claimed intersubjectivity for his methodology, or as he put it, 'One does not have to be Caesar for understanding Caesar, or else all history writing is meaningless' (*Essays*, 98). He claimed transcultural truth value when he repeatedly writes that a valid social science should be recognized as true 'even by the Chinese' (*Essays*, 194), Weber's personification of conventional and rigid way of thinking different from European modes of inquiry.

Weber concedes that establishing truth value is more difficult in the cultural sciences than in the natural sciences. Both establish empirical regularities whose 'lawfulness' has to be explained with a causal mechanism. Since human action is not impersonal like nature, only social science introduces cognitive and dispositional mechanisms into causation, and these mental phenomena (*geistige Vorgänge*) have to be explained introspectively (*nacherlebend zu verstehen*).

How does a *Verstehen* methodology for 'mental phenomena' achieve intersubjective and transcultural truth value? In the physical sciences, there are clear definitions of basic concepts and uniformity in measurement, an experimental method for establishing causation, replication to remove subjectivity (personal attributes of the scientists, differences in skill, fame seeking, and other subjective variables). These operations make science public and valid. Weber describes them to students in 'Science as a Vocation' (Gerth and Mills 1958, 141–3). It makes cumulative knowledge possible. Measurement can be made more precise; the causal mechanism can be refined using the comparative method to explain more variation in the observations and experimental findings; replication is made under a wider range of initial conditions.

The Ideal-Type

In *Wirtschaft und Gesellschaft* and *Soziologie, Analysen, Politik*, Weber creates a similar logic of inquiry for the cultural sciences. He starts with a set of precise concepts, categories, and classifications, for example, types of authority, starting with and then building on the elementary concept of 'human action.' Concept formation ranges from the genetic type of the German historical school for unique events and institutions (for example, European capitalism), to the generic type of the Austrian school for repetitive actions (for example, economic exchange in markets). Weber takes a further step with the concept of 'ideal-type,' a key term in his methodology, 'which refers to the construction of certain elements of reality into a logically precise conception' (Gerth and Mills 1958, 59). It is an abstraction from the bewildering variety of concrete instances, not hypothesis or description or statistical average, but a unified mental construct (*einheitliches Gedankenbild*, also, *gedankliche Gestalt*) that links several elementary concepts into a cultural representation of action, institution, and process (*Essays*, 234–6). For instance, if the elementary concept 'exchange' is combined with money economy, free competition, and means-ends rationality for choice, one obtains the theory of choice in the Austrian school of political economy as an ideal-type.

Weber's concept formation is value free. Market exchange is an ideal-type and makes no claim to moral superiority over other forms of economic exchange. Nor is there a rational bias in concept formation. The principles of market exchange are derived from assuming diminishing marginal utility and rationality of buyers and sellers. Yet individual dispositions and capacities need not adhere to these assumptions. Those who consistently ignore the laws of supply and demand in market exchange will be driven out of business, and those who conform to market pricing by imitation of competitors or by intuition rather than rational calculation will compete successfully.

Applying an ideal-type is only the start of an explanation. In ancient Rome, Weber notes, economic exchange had the same properties as in the contemporary world, for price was determined by supply and demand and not the personal attributes of buyers and sellers, yet some things that were bought and sold, like slaves and tax-farming, are no longer so, whereas intellectual property rights did not exist, though they are marketable today. The cultural scientist seeks to explain how from modest beginnings market exchange grew into capitalism and why and how marketable commodities are not the same. To do so necessitates the concrete historical knowledge produced by the historical school. But one has to have a clear understanding of what exchange and its associated concepts like market exchange are, as the Austrian school views them. Combining the two in the ideal-type solves the concept formation issue in the cultural sciences, and lays the groundwork for explanation.

How are ideal-types used in causal explanation of cultural change? A typical Weberian causal sequence finds that a cultural configuration (an ideal-type) is changed into another one with greater opportunities for social change (a second ideal-type) under the impact of a religious belief system (a third ideal-type). As an example, Weber writes that neighbours within kinship groups, tribes, and villages tend to conform to an in-group morality of generalized reciprocity but transact with outsiders using instrumental, short-term, self-interest calculations. How is the narrow circle for in-group morality breached to encompass larger populations recruited from out-groups? Prophecies of salvation in religious movements attract adherents to a charismatic leader from diverse groups and backgrounds, and to his adherents he preaches a religious ethic of brotherliness modelled on in-group morality. In this religious community, the affluent are obligated to give alms to the poor, provide loans free of the threat of enslavement for debts, support the needy with charitable foundations, and the like: 'The religiosity of the congregation transferred this ancient economic ethic of neighborliness to the relations among the brethren of the faith' (Gerth and Mills 1958, 329). Thus private motivations for religious salvation among adherents are channelled by a religious entrepreneur to mould an expanded community of the faithful. Its cultural consequences, unintended by the converts, is a moral code of reciprocity and impersonal trust binding larger populations of non-kin and non-neighbours. A similar process in a secular era is initiated by political leaders and intellectuals on behalf of political movements and state building. Following Weber, much social science has gone into elaborating processes of group formation and collective action, based on the social construction of categories, boundaries, identities and solidarities.

The cultural scientist's work is still not finished. A process formulated as an ideal-type has to be tested against real world data and alternative explanations. Truth value is not based on guesses, uninformed opinion, and idiosyncratic attributes, but on knowledge. Although it is true that we don't have to be Caesar to understand Caesar, we have to know a great deal about Roman history, military organization, the state, the ruling elite (the Senate), etc. before we can understand him.

Discovery and Proof

Contemporary methodology makes a useful distinction between the logic of discovery, when subjective dimensions of social inquiry are prominent, and the logic of proof, when objective criteria for truth value transcend the subjective dimension. In discovery, the values of social scientists direct their choice of topic, their skills influence their choice of subject matter, and their personal experiences inspire their hypotheses. During proof, however, the truth value of observations and hypotheses, the logic of the argument, and the validity of inferences are opened to the scrutiny of the 'invisible college' of scholars, and as in the natural sciences they are tested by replication. For Weber, *Verstehen* bridged the gap between the logic of discovery and of proof. The social scientist formulates hypotheses and explanations subjectively, and then evaluates their truth value with *Verstehen*. Since Weber, there have been important advances on studying attitudes, beliefs, intentions, and dispositions with objective methods, such as survey research. Their use narrows but does not eliminate the scope of *Verstehen* in social science. It is interesting that when Weber developed plans for a large study of German industrial workers, he did not think it was possible to measure attitudes, beliefs, and motivations in face-to-face interviews with a standardized questionnaire, or in a self-administered questionnaire. When a self-educated worker, Adolf Levenstein, actually did exactly that for several thousand workers and was willing to share his findings, Weber was quite enthusiastic about the results and advised Levenstein on how to analyse the results (Oberschall 1965).

Thus Weber has four requirements of method for claiming objectivity in the cultural sciences and achieving truth value: (1) value-free concept formation based on methodological individualism and a precise vocabulary, (2) ideal-types, (3) *Verstehen* based on introspection informed and disciplined by mastery of the subject matter, and (4) systematic ruling out of alternative hypotheses and explanations. Is that a strong enough claim to assure intersubjective and transcultural knowledge?

My contribution to the question is to assess Weber's method and its claims to truth value in an empirical manner, and not with philosophic argument. I will do so in three ways. First, there are empirical studies on the transcultural reach of Weber's ideal-types. Second, my transcultural professional experiences and observations from living and lecturing and researching in Uganda, Zaïre, and Zambia (two and a half years), China (one year), Hungary (one year), France (one year), and shorter spells in other places provided me with insights about *Verstehen* and objectivity. Third, I have studied the first encounters between European explorers and indigenous people, especially in the eighteenth-century voyages of discovery in the South Pacific, and they tell an interesting story about transcultural understanding and objectivity in the cultural sciences.

An Empirical Assessment of the Transcultural Reach of Ideal-Types

Weber stated that the ideal-type market exchange modelled by economists applied to Roman market exchange, which he had studied. There are empirical studies of market exchange in non-Western countries. The neo-classical economist Gary Becker in 1960 told me about a student of his who had tested key assumptions of market exchange in Malawi and Eastern Zambia, then called Nyasaland and Northern Rhodesia. Edwin Dean, the student, had conducted a series of randomized experiments, based on hundreds of economic transactions in marketplaces, on whether or not prices varied with the attributes of buyers and sellers, such as age, gender, tribe/language. These African marketplaces turned out to be similar to markets elsewhere: supply and demand determined price, not the attributes of the transactors (Dean 1962).

Twelve years later I was in some of the same marketplaces researching small African businesses that had sprung up in the intervening decade following independence. I found that success had no correlation with tribe/language, gender, or other ascribed characteristics (Beveridge and Oberschall 1979). The strongest correlation was with innovation, precisely what the economist Schumpeter had emphasized in his analysis of capitalism. Schumpeter described innovative entrepreneurs in nineteenth-century small town Austria, and I found parallel instances in small-town twentieth-century Zambia. Market exchange as defined by Weber in his ideal-type had demonstrated its truth value as far as I was concerned.

In the 1980s and 1990s I studied the change from collective farms to privatized agriculture in China and in Hungary, and read the research on these countries and others undergoing similar change (Oberschall and Hanto 2002). On the whole, all researchers found similar problems in collective farming. Lack of incentives, free riding, under-utilization of labour, politically motivated capital investment and pricing policies, were the causes of failure, as predicted by neo-classical and transaction cost economics. There were huge variations in the ratio of land per household, crops grown and farm animals raised, irrigation, farm machinery, marketing opportunities, literacy, standard of life, peasant traditions, etc. from country to country (and regions within the same

248 Anthony Oberschall

country). Nevertheless, abstract models with a few pivotal variables describing economic organization – what Weber referred to as ideal-types – were suitable for an understanding of failures and occasional successes. In Hungary I interviewed collective farm managers on their insider assessment of success and failure, and by and large their analysis matched that of the academic experts. In fact, over the years they had introduced market incentives and rational pricing to the limit of what was politically allowed, but the blending of socialist and capitalist economic organization became the victim of contradictions. The ideal-type had both transcultural truth value and intersubjective validity inasmuch as researchers and farm managers fully understood one another, despite the fact that some managers were personally and ideologically committed to socialism whereas others could not wait for its demise. The usefulness of Weber's ideal-types was confirmed during my fieldwork.

Experiences with Transcultural Understanding

To Weber's Chinese test for an objective social science – namely, whether even the Chinese have to understand it and accept it as valid – I can literally answer, 'Yes, they do.' In 1985, at the Foreign Studies University in Beijing, I taught graduate students the contemporary version of Weber's theory of action (called rational choice and the new institutional economics). They thrived on it. All had been taught a Marxist/Leninist/Maoist mode of social science, which by the 1980s was simply a ritualistic formula that had to be memorized for passing entrance examinations (there was one correct answer to every question) and could thereafter be ignored and was. The reason I did not assign from Weber's own writings was simple. Although his formulation of many fundamental intellectual questions and his methodology of inquiry are sound and useful, his information base of late-nineteenth-century scholarship has been improved upon, and some of his causal explanations have since been found incomplete and unsatisfactory. Thus on the issue of the uniqueness of Western rationalism, one would assign Eric Jones, David Landes, and Douglass North, rather than the *Protestant Ethic* and the *General Economic History*; on Chinese Confucianism and socioeconomic change one would assign Ezra Vogel; on the political economy of capitalism, Oliver Williamson; on the theory of action, Mancur Olson and James Coleman, to name but a few obvious choices. Many prominent topics in today's world, such as democracy, human rights, nationalism and multinational states, revolution and insurgencies, Weber touched upon only briefly. But there is nothing unusual or surprising about it. Weber himself expected social change and scholarship to supersede his work.

For my Chinese students, Weberian social science filled the vacuum for making sense of the social and cultural world. They wrote little essays applying newly learned models to familiar experiences, such as why no one took the initiative to break up a dangerous icy patch just outside the university back gate through which hundreds passed and slipped throughout January and which Olson's free-rider dilemma fitted perfectly. Similarly the Congolese students in Lumumbashi in 1982 and the Hungarians in Budapest in 1990 applied these models to such topics as corruption in authoritarian regimes, with which they were familiar.

Do 'outsider' accounts of indigenous people, like Tocqueville's of the Americans, possess truth value to the subjects themselves? In my experience they do. When I did fieldwork in Luapula province in 1971 I made a courtesy call to the paramount Lunda chief to ask his permission for research among his people (which I did not actually need but requested as a sign of respect), and I asked him about a British anthropologist's (Cunnison 1959) account of the Lunda written about a decade earlier. The chief said he remembered Cunnison and got a copy of Cunnison's book out of his library. He volunteered that Cunnison had 'understood' them well and that the book was valuable because the Lunda way of life was changing and that people tended to forget the customs of earlier generations.[4]

During my year in China, since I was not a China expert and did not speak Chinese or read Chinese characters, communication beyond my English-speaking students and American studies colleagues was at times roundabout but not insurmountable for meaningful understanding. When I gave a talk in Xian about U.S. culture and society, at one point I could tell that the audience became puzzled. I had a brief tête-à-tête with my interpreter. It turned out that *individualism* has no Chinese equivalent, and he used the Chinese word for *selfishness*, thus their astonishment that what I positively valued came across as a negative to them. But I explained the difference between *selfishness* and *individualism* from my vantage point, and from the questions at the end I could tell that some at least had understood my meanings. Another concept, *privacy*, which the Chinese translated as 'secretiveness,' had to be explicated by analysis and example on another occasion when I talked about a civic culture. By such explication meanings can be conveyed across cultures.

First Encounters between Europeans and Pacific Islanders in the Eighteenth Century

My research on cooperation and conflict in the state of nature started in order to gain insight and test some hypotheses from the 'evolution of cooperation' theory (Axelrod 1984). The theory models transactions in the absence of authority to enforce agreements and rules as a Prisoner's Dilemma (PD) and studies the conditions and strategies under which cooperation and conflict emerge.[5] I decided to find the closest historical approximation to the 'state of nature' postulates of the theory, and chose European–non-European encounters that were not motivated by conquest (which is a zero-sum game, not a PD).

Such encounters occurred frequently during the sixteenth to eighteenth centuries, when Europeans undertook voyages of exploration and discovery, by sea and by land, in Asia, Africa, and the Americas (Oberschall 2001). The record of these encounters is preserved in journals, naval logs, and diaries, the best of which provide a day-by-day running account of events and transactions, for example, canoes came to meet the ship anchored in the bay and the natives traded coconuts and other foodstuffs for bells, trinkets, and nails.[6]

Europeans and the Tahitians managed to cooperate by and large, without a shared language and despite some misconceptions of one another. Findings from content analysis of records of these encounters leaves no doubt that Europeans and indigenous people shared many understandings. Laying down weapons on the ground, in contrast to brandishing them menacingly, was signalling friendship. Waving a palm frond meant peaceful intent. Holding up coconuts and other foodstuffs, or cloth, ship nails, axes, etc., meant trade. Fresh water and fish in the bay were free goods, but to cut a tree near a village the Europeans asked permission and paid compensation. Acts of war were different from individual aggression and crime. Justice required proportionality of punishment to offence, even though the mode of punishment differed. Both sides understood hierarchy and rank signalled by clothing and adornment, and the deference of inferiors to superiors. Both understood supernatural beliefs and ritual and identified who were religious leaders. The Europeans understood the concept of taboo (for example, when places or relationships were forbidden), and the Islanders understood the Europeans' designation of boundaries with sticks and stones around their encampment and Captain Cook drawing a line in the sand on the beach. Shared ritual and ceremonies for cementing solidarity were well understood and enjoyed by both: banquets, group dancing, soldiers marching in formation and presenting arms, joint wrestling matches, fireworks from naval cannons, music all around. Although the Europeans were not used to the permissive sexual mores of the unmarried Polynesian women, and delighted when they discovered them, they did not confuse the sex-for-nails trade with promiscuous free-for-all, or with prostitution; the tendency was for couples to form stable pairs (the girls were called sweethearts), and it was not uncommon for sailors to jump ship to stay on the island with their sweetheart. A shared understanding facilitated trade: it was voluntary, both parties were equal (each could make an offer, each refuse), it was a permanent transfer of possession, it was reciprocal (one gives, the other takes, and vice versa), price was set by bargaining, and some goods and services were not traded (Europeans didn't trade their weapons, married women didn't engage in the sex trade). Both sides understood that price responded to changing supply and demand. Hogs and sex fetched a higher price in ship nails as the Islanders acquired more nails. Captain Cook sent food-buying parties in small vessels to nearby islands and bays when he noticed that the supply was drying up at his anchorage and prices were rising.

Misunderstandings and conflict did take place. Most started with theft, especially of objects that were important for European survival like major ship-repair and timber-working tools, boats, and weapons, rather than the more common pilfering of hats, eating utensils, small tools, and contents of pockets. The most common response of Europeans was to demand restitution from the chief who seemed to be in charge of the local people. Failing that, they would seize boats and even take hostages in expectation of restitution.

Was this a transcultural misunderstanding between Europeans and the islanders? In my view the deadly quarrel was inherent in the paradox of collective punishment when agency and responsibility are not clearly defined. When governments face anonymous insurgents and terrorists, and the indigenous leaders cannot or will not control and punish the offenders (French in Algeria, British in Northern Ireland, Israelis in the West Bank), they hold the entire collectivity responsible and resort to collective punishment. And frequently the strategy fails to apprehend offenders and deter further offences, and leads instead to escalation of aggression. The paradox is inherent in collective punishment as a mode of conflict management, and is not contingent on a European/non-European (or some other transcultural) distinction. The 'first encounters' study demonstrated to me empirically the transcultural validity of *Verstehen*. Not only did Europeans and Islanders communicate meanings successfully, but a social scientist 250 years later made sense of why and how they shared meanings.

Transcultural Understanding: How Is *Verstehen* Achieved?

In Karamoja, Northern Uganda, I happened to attend skits put on by boarding school students in 1966. I did not understand a word of what was said, but the story was plain enough. The two younger wives of an older husband were making fools of him behind his back while maintaining a facade of submission and compliance. It was very funny. I immediately thought of Molière and Mozart's comedies of manners on gender relations and on servants outsmarting their masters and mistresses, with their domestic settings, and social criticism. In China in 1986 I was visiting a primary school and looked at children's drawings fastened on a wall. One caught my attention: Mao, the Great Helmsman, standing on the top deck, steering a ship filled with passengers below on a stormy sea. The ship was the Communist Party and the passengers were the Chinese people. I recalled a drawing I had made as a seven-year-old in catechism class of the 'Pope, the Great Helmsman,' steering on the top deck a ship called the Church filled with passengers called Faithful Catholics through turbulent seas filled with sharks marked 'deadly sins,' just like Mao navigating his people across the perils of capitalism to the safe shore of socialism. Both stories and metaphors had the same symbolic structure. If one were familiar with either, one would recognize and understand the other. Transcultural understanding is conveyed with stories, metaphors, and analogies, mapping the unfamiliar onto the familiar.

How was mutual understanding possible in these encounters? Culture refers to a socially constructed, cognitive, normative, and affective meaning system that creates an objective, shared reality for a people such that 'they inhabit the world they imagine' (D'Andrade 1984, 115). Culture is an information system encoded in human minds and their extensions: language, books, ritual, architecture, cooking recipes, flower gardens, conventions, norms, collective representations, beliefs, mathematical theorems, computer programs, sports, the Geneva Conventions. Its cognitive dimension consists of classifications like gender and descent, and conceptions about causality and time, what Durkheim referred to as collective representations. Alport (1958, 19) wrote that 'the human mind must think with the aid of categories ... We cannot possibly avoid this process. Orderly living depends on it.' Culture's moral dimensions are convictions about what is right and wrong, honourable and cowardly, and what is just and unjust, and these guide moral choices and value judgments. On the moral dimension, Fortes (1983, 6) wrote, 'The capacity and the need to have, to make, and to follow and to enforce rules are of cardinal importance for human social existence ... for without rules there can be neither society nor culture.' The emotional dimension of culture orients our likes and dislikes, attraction and fear, gratitude, pity, and other affects.

Any information system is composed of symbolic elements that are selected, sorted, redirected, joined, processed, and encoded according to a structure. Simon (1969) has demonstrated that perception, cognition, and communication are not possible without structure. Without structure, information is a random, meaningless sequence and jumble of sense perceptions, what Weber referred to as the 'endless variety of sequential and coincidental, past and present, internal [mental] and external events' (Essays, 212).

Simon (1969), Dumont (1977), Leach (1976), and others have shown that the structure of information systems consists of hierarchy, symmetry, opposition, balance, repetition, and the like. In combination, simple structures become complex structures. A Karamajong skit and a Molière comedy had the same structure, as did the domestic experience of the audience. The children's drawing of Mao and of the pope, both Great Helsmen, have the same structure, 'the ship of state,' a symbol for societal authority. Duality is the simplest structure. In duality, opposites are complementary: right and left, male and female, good and evil, lord and peasant, 'us' and 'them,' cause and effect, reward and punishment, sacred and secular. More complex structures are built from elementary relationships: virtue and vice may be joined to reward and punishment, and one has the germ of a cosmology.

The complementarity of right and left hand is analogous to that of male and female. No physical or social body can operate properly without both, but one has to be in charge of coordinating lest, as the saying goes, the right hand does not know what the left hand is doing. Hierarchy added to duality solves the problem. The mind rules both hands, and the intellect tames the body's passions, just as Mao and the pope maintain order with command. Cognitive structures are aligned to moral prescription with metaphor. A complex social unit such as a religious organization is symbolized by military metaphors that convey order, power, and success, and thus the Church Triumphant is conveyed through 'Onward Christian Soldiers,' 'Rock of Ages,' 'A Mighty Fortress Is Our God,' Christ the Lord, the heavenly host. Douglas (1986) describes how the uncertain, unfamiliar, and arbitrary – what does not fit into structure – is mapped to the familiar and conventional by means of analogy and metaphor, and thus acquires meaning. Random events not comprehensible in terms of conventional notions of causality are given structure by socially constructed beliefs about luck and good fortune, witchcraft, divine intervention, and more recently the law of large numbers in the theory of probability, and are thus explained and become meaningful.

The acquisition of goods has structure. Bilateral exchange is symmetrical (both parties are equal, they can initiate and refuse a transaction), and reciprocal (both consent). Add many buyers, and you get an auction. Add many sellers, and you get a market. Add repetition, and you get a marketplace. But if you have hierarchy and remove consent, goods acquisition becomes robbery and warfare. Transcultural understanding in eighteenth-century encounters results from mapping other people's culture (authority, rank, property, exchange, justice) on structures familiar from one's own culture (hierarchy, opposition, duality, etc.). However much variation exists in the details, both Europeans and Islanders were familiar with property, goods acquisition by exchange, theft and robbery as a coercive mode of property acquisition, the right to defend property against theft, the victim's right to demand justice against an offender. There may have been disputes over the identity of the thief, the severity of the offence, the mode of punishment, but there was mutual understanding and agreement about what was legitimate and what was consensual goods acquisition and what was theft and robbery.

The structure of the human mind, an information systems of great complexity and subtlety, was called by the Greeks and Romans 'rational faculty.' The mental operation that Weber designated *Verstehen* consists of imposing such structure on cultural phenomena, and that is also what the historical actors themselves do. In the great debates among sixteenth-century Spaniards on what degree of humanity to assign to Native Americans, those arguing for their full humanity pointed to similarity with human institutions and culture elsewhere: 'There is a certain method in their affairs, for they have polities which are orderly arranged and they have definite marriage and magistrates and over-lords, laws and workshops, and a system of exchange, all of which call for the use of reason; they also have a kind of religion' (Elliott 1970, 45). On the basis of these similarities, the Puritans and Quakers framed the Native Americans into their familiar classification for varieties of hu-mankind derived from the Bible: they were descendants of one of the ten tribes of Israel that had been taken captive by the Assyrians (Bitterli 1989, 170). The Spanish philosophers and English colonists turned the question of transcultural understanding on its head: since we Europe-ans comprehend the natives, they must be human beings like us. If we didn't comprehend them, they would be inferior to us. The postmodernist reasons differently. We are both human beings and we both possess reason. We do not agree with one another on values and truth, therefore there cannot be an objective standard for values and truth and cultural understanding.

Are these structures universal? Not likely. We create categories for those who do not conform, be they called psychotic, autistic, mentally retarded, or savages. In the encounters I studied, the Europeans occa-sionally ran into people with only a rudimentary technology and mate-rial level of living (as on the north coast of Australia and on Easter Island), who did not seem to understand economic exchange, simply grabbing what the Europeans offered and not reciprocating. Mostly they fled and hid when strangers were sighted. In the total range and volume of European encounters, they are but a small fraction of the record. Weber himself did not claim universal applicability for his method (he mentions young children who are incompletely socialized and psychotics who are deficiently socialized), but that does not detract from the Weberian method of establishing intersubjective and transcultural truth value in the cultural sciences.

Conclusion: What Remains of Weber's Methodology?

Methodology consists of an assemblage of techniques, nowadays heavily weighted to the analysis of large quantitative data sets, and the logic of inquiry that Weber presented in his now hundred-year-old essay. The logic of inquiry contends with the truth value or objectivity of knowl-edge, and what Weber formulated with his four principles (value-free concept formation combining genetic and generic concepts, ideal-types, *Verstehen*, and the comparative method for testing inferences) is sound

and justifies a universal social science. The denial by conservative sceptics as well as postmodernists and deconstructionists of the Weberian
conception and method in the cultural science is an empirical issue, not
a logical one. In my experience, and that of many others, and in my
historical and comparative researches, and those of many others including Weber, intersubjective and transcultural understanding is the rule
rather than the exception. It results from hard work, study, research,
and discipline. It cannot be left to opinion, intuition, and dilettantism.
Truth value of facts and causation can be established on a valid, shared,
non-arbitrary standard for social inquiry. As in the natural sciences,
new facts will be uncovered and some accepted facts will be shown not
to be so. Some causal mechanisms will be exposed as spurious and new
mechanisms discovered. Completely new intellectual puzzles and questions about culture will be asked. Knowledge and understanding change,
but not in an arbitrary manner. And they will keep changing because
culture and institutions change, necessitating additional knowledge
and understanding.

NOTES

1 *Verstehen* was widely practised by the English philosophers and the Scottish
Enlightenment thinkers, who anchored it in the faculty of sympathy (we
would now use the word *empathy*) between humans, and who explicated it
with the image of a mirror or looking glass. Hobbes in *Leviathan* (part 1)
writes that 'whoever looketh into himself, and considereth what he doth,
when he does think, opine, reason, hope fear, etc., and upon what grounds;
he shall thereby read and know what are the thoughts and passions of all
other men upon the like occasions,' and Hume writes in *An Inquiry Concerning Human Understanding* that 'the minds of men are mirrors to one
another.'
2 Individualism and rationality in concept formation and modelling explains
emotional and irrational collective actions, like destructive crowd behaviour and speculative crazes in the stock market (Oberschall, 1993, chap.
1). As Schelling (1978) has shown, the aggregate properties of collectivities
derived from methodological individualism are not simply individual
behaviour magnified (for example, war results from many aggressive individuals). To the contrary, the method can show why war occurs despite
the fact that most people want peace. Rationality is defined from the point
of view of the actor, not of the outside observer. Given their conception of

human agency in the causality of natural events, it is not 'irrational' for
natives to perform rain rituals to hasten the onset of rain at the start of the
rainy season. What would be irrational would be for the ritual to be performed in the middle of the dry season when it never rains.

3 Leach (1976, 6) writes that 'the central puzzle is to determine how "meaning" which is conveyed to the listener is the same as that which was intended by the originator.'

4 This was not a unique experience. In Lusaka I studied a Shona religious
sect whose leader owned a copy of a book written by a nineteenth-century
missionary on the Shona and which the sect elders consulted on their
traditions.

5 For instance, how did British and German soldiers facing each other across
trenches in the First World War manage to tacitly agree on local ceasefires
and maintain them for weeks against the explicit orders of their higher
command? Much of the theory was elaborated using computer simulation
and experiments with undergraduate subjects.

6 Each transaction was characterized as cooperation C, non-cooperation D,
or avoidance A. Under C were subcategories like trade, gift-giving, hosting
ceremonies, and other such actions; under D were theft, physical aggression, and war. I distinguished verbal from non-verbal symbolic signallings
that were meant to influence actions, such as warnings, threats, peace
gestures, and which side initiated a transaction sequence. I also distinguished individual action from agency action, such as an interpersonal
dispute between a European and a non-European over a private matter
from the actions of a guard protecting ship property as an agent of his
superiors.

There is a huge literature on encounters in the age of discovery. It differs
from my approach inasmuch as I analyse entire transaction chains according to the properties of transactions in strategic interaction, whereas many
historians and anthropologists select particular incidents that they believe
are typical of the European mentality, that is, what they reveal about European culture rather than the dynamic of transacting in the state of nature.

REFERENCES

Alport, Gordon. 1958. *The Nature of Prejudice.* New York: Doubleday.
Axelrod, Robert. 1984. *The Evolution of Cooperation.* New York: Basic Books.
Beveridge, Andrew, and Anthony Oberschall. 1979. *African Businessmen and
Development in Zambia.* Princeton, NJ: Princeton University Press.

Bitterli, Urs. 1989. *Cultures in Conflict*. Stanford, CA: Stanford University Press.

Boudon, Raymond. 1995. *Le juste et le vrai*. Paris: Fayard.

Cunnison, Ian. 1959. *The Luapula Peoples of Northern Rhodesia*. Manchester: Manchester University Press.

D'Andrade, Roy. 1984. 'Culture Meaning Systems,' in *Culture Theory*. Ed. Richard Schweder and Robert Levine. Cambridge: Cambridge University Press, 88–121.

Dean, Edwin. 1962. 'Studies in Price Formation in African Markets.' *Rhodes-Livingstone Journal* 31: 1–20.

Douglas, Mary. 1986. *How Institutions Think*. Syracuse, NY: Syracuse University Press.

Dumont, Louis. 1977. *Homo Aequalis I*. Paris: Gallimard.

Elliott, J.H. 1970. *The Old World and the New, 1492–1650*. Cambridge: Cambridge University Press.

Fortes, Mayer. 1983. *Rules and the Emergence of Society*. London: Royal Anthropological Society, Occasional Papers 39.

Gerth, Hans. and C. Wright Mills. 1958. *From Max Weber*. New York: Oxford University Press.

Leach, Edmund. 1976. *Culture and Communication*. Cambridge: Cambridge University Press.

Oberschall, Anthony. 1965. *Empirical Social Research in Germany, 1848–1914*. The Hague: Mouton.

– 1993. *Social Movements: Ideologies, Interests and Identities*. New Brunswick, NJ: Transaction Books.

– 2001. 'Cooperation in the State of Nature: Encounters of Europeans and Non-Europeans during the Voyages of Discovery.' Presented at Public Choice Society, San Antonio, March 2001.

Oberschall, Anthony, and Zsuzsa Hanto. 2002. 'Birth of a Market Economy: Hungarian Agriculture after Socialism.' *Research in Social Stratification and Mobility* 19: 77–102.

Schelling, Thomas. 1978. *Micromotives and Macrobehavior*. New York: Norton.

Simon, Herbert. 1969. *The Sciences of the Artificial*. Cambridge, MA: MIT Press.

Weber Max. 1956. *Wirtschaft und Gesellschaft*. Tubingen: Mohr.

– 1958. *Soziologie, Analysen, Politik*. Stuttgart: Kroner.

PART THREE

Weber and Contemporary Social Science:
An Opportunity Missed?

11 On Being a Weberian (after Spain's 11–14 March): Notes on the Continuing Relevance of the Methodological Perspective Proposed by Weber

ROBERT M. FISHMAN

I take as constitutive of the distinctively Weberian approach to social science the recognition, indeed embrace, of (at least)[1] two more-or-less interrelated tensions: (1) the effort to delineate and account for what is *specific*, and thus historically individual, in given empirical realities balanced against the attempt to formulate – and then apply in explanatory endeavours – *generalizing concepts and theories*; (2) the pursuit of types of knowledge, and thus the posing of questions, that are *meaningful* from the value perspective of the investigator (but less so from other value perspectives) alongside the commitment to both *impartiality and rigour* in addressing those questions so that the answers may be seen as objective. In this essay I discuss these tensions, elaborating upon their place in Weberian methodology and in contemporary social science practice. Given this emphasis on tensions, such as the Weberian opposition between formulations he understood to be strictly *intellectual* or *scholarly* and the exploration of the empirical world as it actually *is*, I complement my discussion of methodology with the examination of an empirical problem, one that I claim cannot be adequately accounted for without the benefit of the Weberian approach as I outline it here. Undoubtedly, some readers will find in this juxtaposition of a theoretically oriented methodological discussion and a case-sensitive empirical examination – focusing on Spain's experience with elections in the aftermath of terrorism – a certain tension, but that is precisely what I argue to constitute the social science practice defended by Weber.

What I present above as the *second* tension – Weber's dual commitment to objectivity *and* subjectivity in the social science enterprise – has likely received the greatest sustained attention in the secondary literature on the Objectivity essay, as classically reflected in Sheldon Wolin's influential discussion that precisely accentuates Weber's synthesis of objectivist and subjectivist perspectives on methodology.[2] Indeed, debate over the place of objectivity and subjectivity in scholarly work remains lively and important within a wide variety of fields.[3] Yet I emphasize in this chapter another constitutive tension that is perhaps even more relevant for the work of empirical social scientists: the conflict between the effort to build generalizing theory and the commitment (of Weber and those who follow his lead, but *not* of many other contemporary scholars) to know empirical reality as it really *is*. Weber struggles with and embraces these tensions with a clarity that continues to speak powerfully to many practising social scientists at the dawn of the twenty-first century, and he offers what continues to be the strongest rationale for scholarship that refuses to renounce either the allure of generalizing theorization or the frequent explanatory emphasis on case-specific nuance and detail.

Despite the differences between them, I suggest here that these two tensions (and others closely related to them) – most clearly and memorably formulated by Weber in his methodological masterpiece, '"Objectivity" of Knowledge in Social Science and Social Policy' (hereinafter 'Objectivity' essay) – impel the social scientists who embrace them to look simultaneously toward the world we live in *and* the scholarly community to which we contribute, for the meaning and validation of our scientific endeavours. In making this claim I borrow loosely from Theda Skocpol's recent formulation of comparative historical scholarship as a 'double engagement' oriented toward both the academy and the larger world.[4] I contend here that it is exactly such a simultaneous preoccupation with the world *and* the academy that thoroughly informs the Weberian perspective – and its constitutive tensions. Social scientists uncomfortable with the embrace of these intellectual oppositions are free to concentrate exclusively on the specialized scholarly arena, with its distinctive exigencies, preoccupations, and rewards, but they – unlike the Weberians – risk losing touch with the ever-changing complexities, challenges, and meanings with which the empirical world is imbued.

Weber's approach addresses a concern that remains quite relevant for empirical social science one hundred years hence: the issue that Peter Hall has recently formulated as the fit (or misfit) between our scholarly *ontologies* and our *methodologies*, our sense of how the world *is* and how we should *study* it.[5] For Hall, writing in 2003, contemporary social science has all too often elaborated upon and deployed methodologies that ill fit the most prevalent scholarly wisdom on how the empirical world actually *is*. In the face of this disjuncture, Hall calls for a convergence of *methodology* and *ontology*. For Weber, the effort to theorize in generalizing terms and to search for probabilistic regularities is meritorious, but – if taken in isolation – inherently flawed. It was precisely Weber's *ontological assumptions* that led him to that conclusion.

Indeed for Weber, methodological discussion is constantly interwoven with ontological claims: Weber's ontology assumed the world to be more complex and (within any given empirical setting) more historically singular than any general theory or concept can fully capture, yet he also insisted that it was precisely the world's infinite complexity that made empirical reality unintelligible without a methodology that used generalizing concepts and theories to organize our understandings. His methodology, with firm roots in his ontology, offers an approach that insists on the virtue – indeed indispensability – of the tension between generalizing theory and case-specific nuance.

The dual focus of Weberian social science invigorates and renews the work of those who pursue it, but (in ways that Weber himself made at least somewhat explicit in the 'Objectivity' essay) those benefits come at a certain cost; to be more precise, they rub against the grain of views, practices, and incentives that often predominate within the social science scholarly world to which the Weberians are nonetheless fully committed. Weberians – in my understanding[6] – are strongly devoted to conventional social science disciplines, but they are at the same time somewhat skeptical of much that goes on – and achieves widespread acceptance – within those disciplines. Following the call of the 'Objectivity' essay, they see generalizing concepts and theories – which conventional social science almost invariably values more highly than nuanced analysis highlighting the singularity of historical configurations and the inadequacy of existing general theories – as intellectual *tools that may be useful*, indeed necessary, in the course of empirical analysis *but that nonetheless stand as a highly inadequate representation of empirical reality*. Scholars who adopt the approach of Weber look with keen interest not only toward their own disciplines but also toward *extra-disciplinary sources of knowledge and insight*, thus often casting their academic production in a mould that departs from the most prevalent professional norms within their home disciplines.

It is worth noting that, for many scholars, the Weberian perspective may be taken to mean something quite different: adherence to a *particular* set of theoretical claims, the use of a *fixed set* of conceptual and definitional tools, a given approach to the collection and analysis of

empirical material, and so forth. Yet I argue that none of those understandings captures the true essence of the Weberian legacy, given the
eclectic and diverse range of themes, arguments, theoretical devices,
and evidence to be found in Weber's extraordinary corpus of writings.
Indeed 'template Weberianism' that seeks to reduce Weber's scholarly
legacy to the use of a fixed set of conceptual tools and explanatory
hypotheses can be seen from this essay's perspective as simply one
more example of what I refer to as conventional social science. Contemporary social scientists who adopt the Weberian perspective as it is here
understood are highly quantitative, thoroughly qualitative, or some
combination of these two possibilities. They constantly search for useful
theoretical claims in existing scholarship, but clearly they do not defend
one unique or unchanging set of general causal propositions. They do
seek to develop generalizing concepts and theorizations where that
proves fruitful in their own work, but they also incorporate within that
work case-specific nuance and complexity as often as required by the
evidence they encounter. *They are distinguished not by their research techniques or specific theoretical claims but instead by their dual intellectual devotion to both the specialized scholarly community and the larger world within
which it is set.* As suggested above, this dual intellectual devotion is
manifested above all in the embrace of a series of interrelated tensions.

Weber's most eloquent and carefully formulated methodological statement – the great 'Objectivity' essay of 1904 – represents the centrepiece
of his perspective, but standing alone it clearly assigns *priority* to what
he formulates as the intrinsic complexity of the 'infinite causal web,' the
inescapable singularity of all historically given realities and the inadequacy to reality of conceptual and theoretical formulations. The 1904
essay unambiguously places at the core of the social scientist's mission
the effort to determine why empirical reality is 'historically *so* and not
otherwise' (72). With this primary objective in mind, he argues that
generalizing concepts and theories 'are obviously of great value as
heuristic means but only as such' (76). From this perspective, generalizing laws are only a tool, a necessary but inadequate one, in that 'the
reality to which the laws apply always remains equally *individual*, equally
undeducible from laws' (73). Reality is historically and contextually singular and 'it is these individual configurations which are significant for
us' (73). Thus even though the 'Objectivity' essay formulates as *necessary* and as *constitutive* of social science the tension between generalizing theorizations and the actual empirical singularities of all given
cases, it does so in a fashion that presents theorization as a mere *tool*

while nuanced case-sensitive analysis is clearly presented as the *objective* of scholarly analysis. However, given Weber's extraordinary efforts elsewhere at conceptual and theoretical generalization – especially in his monumental achievement, *Economy and Society* – I take much of what is argued in the 1904 essay as simply an accentuation of one side of the characteristically Weberian tension.

Although at different places in his enormous corpus of writings Weber (temporarily) prioritizes *either* generalizing theorization *or* case-specific singularities, the constant thread one encounters is his reminder that the tension between the two is essential for the advance of knowledge. Whichever of these two primary objectives one gives priority, the other is *equally necessary* for Weberian social science. It is this perspective that leads to what anthropologist James Boon (this volume) persuasively formulates as the constant *point and counterpoint* of Weber's exposition. The seeming priority within Weberian work may be placed primarily on case-based singularity or generalizing theorization, but neither pole of this characteristic tension can be avoided if scholarship is to be persuasively Weberian. Thus I take the 'Objectivity' essay as the basis for a social science resting on the embrace of certain tensions.

Much follows from the Weberian embrace of *both* poles characterizing such fundamental tensions – and the contrasting *rejection of one side* of these interrelated oppositions that today predominates within much (high-quality) conventional social science. For many conventional social scientists, existing theorizations and scholarly debates are seen as the preferred – or for some, the *only appropriate* – point of departure for posing research questions. For Weberians, changes in the empirical world (including its cultural currents) may lead the researcher to pose questions that had not been highlighted or identified as meaningful in pre-existing theorizations, but in posing *new* questions, the Weberian researcher seeks to enter and address scholarly debates with a commitment to theorization and rigour second to none.

The primacy that many conventional social scientists afford to a priori causal propositions and conceptualizations – rather than allowing for the usefulness of empirically based theorization, case-derived insights, and the formulation of genuinely new questions – may carry many disabling consequences if we assume, as Weberians do, that *our goal is to understand and explain those aspects of the world that we find meaningful.* The Weberian is as interested in generalizing theory and concepts as any social scientist, but is *also* bound to study the history and cultural specificities of contexts under examination, and always allows the possibility of introducing case-specific explanations where they prove useful. Thus, the Weberian is devoted to the advance of generalizing theories *and* the understanding of individual cases, which, it is assumed, such theories will never fully illuminate. Moreover, the Weberian will never shy away from posing intellectually new questions that the researcher finds meaningful, even if their relevance has yet to be fully enshrined by the existing literature. In the 'Objectivity' essay, Weber formulated the matter quite emphatically: 'The points of departure of the cultural sciences remain changeable throughout the limitless future as long as a Chinese ossification of intellectual life does not render mankind incapable of setting new questions to the eternally inexhaustible flow of life' (84).

Many conventional social scientists see such an approach as unacceptably ad hoc or even atheoretical. Indeed, many non-Weberians see any reliance on case-specific explanations (or the posing of fresh questions emerging from one's reading of the world) as scientifically inferior to the exclusive explanatory use of generalizing theories devoid of any case-specific referents and consecrated in prominent scholarly debates. The point at issue concerns not *how many* cases one studies, but rather *how* one studies them.[7] The Weberian may study many cases or just one, but in doing so seriously examines complex case-specific histories and potentially distinctive causal configurations.[8] The non-Weberian often studies multiple cases but just as easily may limit an investigation to one case (as is exemplified by the exclusive focus of many American social scientists on the United States), typically *avoiding* any serious consideration of its specificities, or its particular claim to interest. For the extreme non-Weberian, cases offer nothing but an opportunity to collect data. If their specificities cannot be easily captured by variables that have been carefully theorized and operationalized prior to the beginning of research, they are assumed to be without scientific relevance. Non-Weberians are disinclined toward the demanding search for *causal configurations* that may be, indeed likely are, somewhat distinctive to particular cases.

Conventional social scientists are heavily oriented toward the use of currently fashionable concepts and techniques; a concept that is frequently used within the specialized scholarly community is typically assumed to be important and often treated as if it were *as real* as the empirical world itself. Such fashionable concepts are routinely invoked by researchers seeking to place their own work within the framework of specialized professional discourse, and doubts over the actual correspondence of such concepts to underlying empirical reality may be seen as secondary in importance or even inconvenient. Weberians, in contrast, answering the eloquent and unmistakable call of the 'Objectivity' essay, look to the empirical world itself to *assess the validity and usefulness* of prevailing scholarly approaches. Whereas conventional social scientists may come to take for granted that a concept widely in use effectively captures underlying empirical reality, Weberians always look carefully to the empirical world to assess the utility of conceptual approaches and related operationalizations, thus leading them to treat with some skepticism the usefulness of many fashionable concepts.[9]

One can easily overstate the contrast between the tendencies currently prevailing in conventional social science and those encouraged by Weber's methodological writings. Many Weberian ideas have been more or less thoroughly incorporated within contemporary social science at its mainstream best.[10] Weber's formulation of causality as an *infinite causal web* has been at least partially taken to heart through the reigning concern over endogeneity, spuriousness, unmeasured variables, interaction effects, and so on. The Weberian emphasis on the *distinctiveness* of cases – and indeed of individuals – is partially, if imperfectly, reflected in the conventional concern over selection bias. And the Weberian understanding of causality as probabilistic is the currently dominant view. Despite all of these points, the Weberian embrace of a series of interrelated tensions is most definitely *not* the norm in contemporary social science. The pressures and predispositions found within the specialized scholarly world of professional social scientists lead largely toward one pole of each of the oppositions that the Weberian perspective instead embraces in whole.

This is not to say that the Weberian perspective has been marginalized in the contemporary social sciences. It is hardly necessary to point out that self-consciously Weberian scholars have attained great interdisciplinary prominence, as in the case of Juan Linz,[11] and others – such as Philippe Schmitter,[12] Guillermo O'Donnell,[13] and Linz's frequent collaborator Alfred Stepan[14] – who share an ability to formulate new approaches and conceptualizations for the study of a constantly changing world. At its best, much of contemporary social science *is* essentially Weberian – especially in the case of those scholars who work simultaneously within more than one discipline.

Indeed, even among social scientists who were not initially seen as self-conscious followers of Weber, some of the most widely acclaimed recent scholarship does successfully work *within* what I present here as characteristically Weberian tensions: using and developing generalizing theorizations while carefully examining all available knowledge on case-specific dynamics; offering strong and highly focused analytical claims while also identifying more complex and historically contingent causal patterns and configurations; addressing questions of unmistakable value relevance to the authors while offering answers of impeccable rigour and objectivity; building from the existing literature with utmost care while offering ideas, understandings, *and new questions* extending well beyond the pre-existing theorizations to be found in the literature. Strikingly, both qualitatively oriented social scientists – such as Theda Skocpol[15] – and highly quantitative social scientists – such as Gosta Esping-Andersen[16] – fit this description. Moreover, Donald P. Green and Ian Shapiro's important critical examination of the connection between theory and empirical evidence in contemporary political science[17] can also be seen as a defence of such an approach.

Yet in saying that the de facto Weberians are engaged in work that seeks its direction and validation simultaneously from the professional scholarly arena and the world that – in all its complexity and dynamism – surrounds us, it should be clear that *much contemporary scholarship does not fit this description* and that *the purely professional pressures and biases lead elsewhere*, namely toward work that is geared toward *internal* professional controversies – at times without an accompanying concern for underlying empirical reality. Prior theorization is taken as superior to empirically driven nuance and complexity; generalization as superior to specificity and contingency in explanation; literature-driven hypotheses as superior to real world–based questions. These views, and others, are the new orthodoxies that Weberian scholars constantly encounter in the professional social science arena. At the risk of tedious redundancy, allow me to add that *Weberians most emphatically do not reject the perspectives preferred within conventional social science. Rather, they combine those preferences with others that are fundamentally dissimilar, thus affording the Weberians a broader repertoire of scholarly approaches and explanatory devices* than the range of possibilities routinely employed by their more conventional counterparts. To underscore this point: *some social scientists adopt neither the Weberian nor the conventional perspective* and instead seek virtually all their validation and orientation in the public role of their intellectual production and the resonance of that product with their value-derived priorities. *Unlike this third group, the Weberians insist on validation of scholarship through scientific debate in the professional arena.*

As should be clear by now, I believe that the Weberian perspective alone allows scholars to (1) refine and validate the tools of social science by using them in the analysis of questions that the researcher delineates following value-based observation of the world (rather than purely internal academic controversies), (2) address such questions with all the explanatory rigour, impartiality, and technical or interpretive firepower made available by the accumulation of scientific knowledge, and (3) fully incorporate within our explanations all the relevant available knowledge, regardless of whether that knowledge responds directly to a priori theoretically derived hypotheses and without regard to its case-specific or general quality. Thus I contend that the Weberian approach generates a social science superior to any of its alternatives, both in its explanatory power and in its ability to fully address themes of genuine human concern. This claim may well strike some readers as mistaken or, at a minimum, excessively strong.

Below, I attempt to offer support for this claim through a rather tentative and incomplete analysis of the Spanish election of 14 March 2004 held just three days after the 11 March terrorist attack in Madrid.[18] My intention is to offer validation for the Weberian approach by using it (however incompletely and inadequately) in the examination of a question of extraordinary current interest at the time of this writing. In analysing Spain's experience with an election in the aftermath of terrorism, I take up a question that holds meaning for not only this author but also for others in the contemporary world. I offer an interpretation that emphasizes case-specific historical antecedents of the election, the interconnection among numerous events and processes, and the complexity of processes some of which existing conceptualizations would fail to fully capture. *I offer an explanation that relies on both generalizing and case-specific thinking, on existing concepts and a sensitivity to their limitations, on the delineation of complex configurations and unintended consequences.* I offer an analysis that I could not conceive of as social-scientific in its inspiration without the guidance of Weber's Objectivity Essay and subsequent work carried on in its spirit.

Spain's 11–14 March: Voting in the Aftermath of Massive Terrorism

The brutal terrorist attack on Madrid's working-class commuter rail lines on the morning of 11 March 2004 occurred roughly seventy-two hours prior to the scheduled opening of the polls on 14 March, the day of a crucial national election, the ninth of the post-Franco period.[19] For countless Spaniards, the immense shock and sadness generated by the massacre were immediately interwoven with questions about the event's likely impact on the impending elections. The campaign, which was in its final two days, given the prohibition on electioneering during the 'day of reflection' prior to voting, was immediately halted and never formally resumed. The outcome had been in some doubt – as I shall discuss below – although the available polls all coincided in suggesting that the governing conservative Partido Popular (PP) was likely to be returned to power, albeit by an uncertain and possibly rather narrow margin. The victory on 14 March of the opposition Socialist Party (PSOE) by a rather substantial margin – exactly 5 per cent of the votes cast – came as a surprise to some (but not others) and quickly raised questions within Spain and well beyond its borders over the possible impact of the terrorist incident on the electorate's verdict.

In a sense the issue at hand can be taken as a purely 'academic' question – perhaps even as a *generalizing theoretical query* – on the way that voting decisions are likely to be shaped by terrorist incidents. Politicians, journalists, scholars,[20] and others all came to see the election results – and the effort to establish their greater or lesser connection to the prior terrorist incident – as a matter of considerable importance. As newspaper headlines throughout the world attested at the time, the PSOE victory was interpreted by some as a de facto victory for terrorism, a charge that took several forms that I will not elaborate on here. In fact, the PSOE had been consistently opposed to the presence of Spanish troops in Iraq well prior to the events of March 2004 and included in its electoral program a pledge to remove those troops unless the United Nations assumed command over all foreign troops present. Indeed, this position was an integral part of the public appeal for votes offered by PSOE candidate for prime minister,[21] José Luís Rodríguez Zapatero. In some of his most enthusiastically applauded lines of the abbreviated campaign, during a campaign rally in Valencia, Zapatero replied to a PP charge that he lacked principles by declaring that two of his fundamental principles were 'thou shalt not kill ... thou shalt not lie,' which he then presented as the basis for the PSOE's position on Iraq.[22] Given that the large majority of the Spanish public had opposed the war, this pledge to withdraw troops was seen throughout the campaign, and its antecedents, as a major source of strength for the Socialists – well prior to the events of 11–14 March.

The general theoretical query over the extent to which terrorism may alter election outcomes – perhaps, as a result, attaining its aims – is a reasonable and useful device to begin our analysis, but just as Weber leads us to expect, the use of a general theoretical query cannot, in this case, begin to *fully answer* the broader question at stake. We will need to introduce numerous case-specific causal observations in order to understand the dynamics of Spain's 11–14 March, and some of those observations, in turn, may prove useful for generalizing theoretical and conceptual endeavours. In the absence of a rigorous comparative political sociology on the general question of terrorism and elections, it is difficult to offer a definitive judgement on that broad query, but it appears to be evident and easily demonstrable that terrorism does hold an ability to reshape voter sentiments – *although most certainly not in ways fully anticipated or intended* by those responsible for such deeds. Voter sentiments and decisions in the United States (for example, the 2002 congressional elections), Israel (especially in 1996), and other countries appear to offer clear evidence that terrorism *can indeed* change mass opinion. But as a general matter, on average, the direction of that change is likely to favour the most right-wing and militaristic political forces in the electoral arena rather than the advocates of international law, peace, and negotiations. If taken in isolation from more specific questions and forms of evidence, the *general theoretical question* – and the evidence one could surely assemble in a rigorous *comparative* effort to address it – appears to offer no support whatsoever for politically motivated claims that Spanish voters bowed to terrorism in supporting the Socialists. Yet regardless of what one makes of the contemporary political critiques of Spain's 2004 electoral outcome, the general theoretical query, and the evidence it would generate, clearly offer unsatisfying proof, even for those predisposed against the charge that has been made. Neither critics nor supporters of the Socialists' victory on 14 March would be induced to change their view of the electoral outcome by virtue of general theoretical arguments resting on the analysis of terrorism and electoral politics in Israel and the United States. Clearly, if the 11 March attack contributed to the PSOE's victory, it did so in ways that run counter to the most probable or generalizable effects of terrorism on electorates. Unusual or possibly case-specific aspects of Spain's experience with an election after terrorism need to be examined – unless one wishes to drop the entire matter. Weber's charge to explain why the world is 'so and not otherwise' cannot be answered without a careful examination of the case.

The most straightforward question that one must confront is virtually impossible to answer with absolute certainty: would the Socialists have won were it not for 11 March (and its extraordinary aftermath of governmental misinformation and popular mobilization)? A simple, if inadequate, approximation to this issue lies in examining the available public opinion polling. Opinion polls may not be published in Spain during the final six days prior to an election. Polls released early on the morning of 8 March offer us the last pre-electoral public evidence on this matter. The most recently conducted poll released at that time was the radio network Cadena Ser's tracking poll, the Pulsómetro.[23] That tracking poll indicated that as of Sunday evening, one week in advance of election day, the PP led the Socialists by 2.5 per cent, a margin smaller than that reported at the beginning of the campaign and somewhat lesser than the margin reported in other surveys reported at the same time (but conducted earlier). Thus the available survey evidence suggests that the PSOE was gaining increased support during the campaign, and that the PP would likely win by a relatively small margin – thus losing the absolute majority it had enjoyed in Spain's parliament since the elections of March 2000. Given the narrow margin of difference reported in this and other pre-election surveys, neither a more substantial margin of victory for the PP nor a narrow margin of victory for the PSOE could be excluded.

However, just below the surface, publicly available polling data offered a more troubling message for the governing conservatives, a more hopeful message for the PSOE. In the final Pulsómetro tracking poll (completed, as noted above, one week prior to the March 14 election), an extraordinary 59.3 per cent of respondents expressed their belief that the country 'needed a change of party in government.' Only 30.7 per cent of respondents replied that the country did *not* need a change in the party of government. This distribution was the most unfavourable to the PP of the entire campaign, and it raised the very real possibility that last-minute voting decisions could easily generate a final, if unenthusiastic, groundswell of support for the PSOE just as the electorate went to the polls. Three very distinct sectors of the electorate held the possibility to produce such an outcome, providing the PSOE with a last-minute surge at the campaign's close. (1) Relatively anti-government non-voters, or to be more precise, voters who had failed to participate in the most recent national election of March 2000, could decide to go the polls, thus raising the level of electoral participation and providing the PSOE with much additional, albeit soft, support. (2) Supporters of a variety of small or minor parties, including the post-communist United Left (IU) and others, could strategically switch to the Socialists at the last minute in order to increase the odds of defeating the PP. (3) Soft supporters of the PP could decide at the last minute to switch their allegiance to the Socialists. Lest one minimize the magnitude of this final possibility, it is useful to note that the Pulsómetro released on 8 March reported 40.5 per cent of the electorate planning to vote for the PP, but only 30.7 per cent willing to clearly affirm that the country did not need a change in the party of government. *It is evident that prior to the terrorist attacks many Spaniards contemplated the approaching 14 March election day with ambivalence and uncertainty.* What was the nature of that ambivalence and uncertainty? Post-election survey work[24] will help us address that question more fully than is now possible, but rudimentary ecological analysis and a more qualitative macro-level examination can help us make sense out of this question.

(The first significant post-election poll to be published, the Pulsómetro released on 22 March 2004[25] offered highly suggestive findings. Although the large majority of those surveyed reported that they had settled on their vote prior to the terrorist attack, 8.2 per cent of the sample reported that it decided how to vote after the attack took place. A large majority of those interviewed, 64.7 per cent, believed that information was manipulated or hidden from the public in those final days – when the government and state television initially insisted that the attack had been carried out by ETA. Subsequent survey work has reported that a higher percentage of the population presents its voting decision as being influenced by the attack, but in most such cases it is likely that the influence of the attack merely *strengthened and reinforced prior preferences*.)

It must be said that on several occasions during the two years prior to the 2004 election *the PSOE had led the PP*, in publicly available poll results, at times by a significant margin. It is instructive to briefly review the evidence. During the spring of 2003, when the Iraq war was in its most active phase, the PSOE led the PP by 6 per cent in the 21 March Pulsómetro and by 6.5 per cent on April 4. Clearly the Iraq war had pushed ambivalent sectors of the Spanish electorate toward the Socialists and away from the PP by a margin even greater than that ultimately recorded on 14 March 2004. Spaniards knew what they thought of this war – and of its implications for Spanish politics – well before the brutal attack on 11 March 2004, but those attitudes rooted in war were inter-meshed (in Weberian multi-causal fashion) with attitudes formed in many other issue arenas. The strong anti-war majority during 2003 was no guarantee of Socialist victory one year later, and the

PP had various strong cards to play in its effort to retain plurality support. (It is also worth mentioning that the first moment, over the four years between national elections, in which the PSOE surpassed the PP in professed voter intent occurred well before the Iraq war. During the summer of 2002, a PP plan to restrict unemployment benefits and to eliminate a public employment program for under-employed farm workers in Andalucía and Extremadura led to a successful general strike accompanied by large anti-government demonstrations on 20 June 2002.[26] In the aftermath of that general strike the PSOE established a temporary lead over the PP in opinion polling. The factors that were capable of leading Spaniards toward the Socialists and away from the PP were never limited to foreign policy.) The evidence examined thus far produces no certain conclusion: many Spanish voters were ambivalent, and serious examination of public opinion data shows that prior to 11 March there was some doubt about the election outcome. The similarity between the actual 14 March outcome and the distribution of electoral opinion at the time of the invasion of Iraq, roughly one year earlier, suggests that the terrorist attack may have activated a latent anti-war vote, but this is far from clear; other political controversies during the two final years prior to the elections had generated similar distributions of opinion.

A highly useful way to address the questions we face is by examining the geographic distribution of votes. The approach I take is a simple one, asking the following question: where did the greatest movement of votes take place? *Was it a uniform process experienced equally throughout Spain? Did the shift in votes occur with greatest intensity close to the direct impact of the terrorist attack in Madrid? Or did the greatest shift occur elsewhere?* Three types of change deserve attention: (1) the electoral participation of previous non-voters, (2) the strategic decision of small and minor party supporters to vote Socialist, and (3) the movement to the PSOE of some voters who had supported the PP in the elections of March 2000. It is certain that all three processes took place to some extent, but the relative magnitude of each is more difficult to determine with precision. Given limitations of time and space, I shall concentrate on the first and the third of these shifts: the increase in voting participation and the movement of some voters from the PP to the PSOE. In absolute terms the latter process – the direct shift by some voters from the governing party to the opposition – is likely the least important of the three electoral movements, but in *political* terms it is in some ways the most interesting, and it would appear to be the place to look for evidence that the attack itself led some voters to change allegiance – perhaps, to follow the arguments of some – in the calculation that a PSOE victory would reduce the danger of further terrorist incidents in Spain.

Much of the dramatic difference between the election results of 2000, when the PP won 44.52 per cent of the nationwide vote and an absolute majority of the seats in parliament, and 2004, when they won 37.64 per cent of the vote and fell twenty-eight seats short of a parliamentary absolute majority, can be accounted for by the enormous increase in voting turnout. Neither election is a complete outlier in the pattern observed to date in Spain's post-Franco democracy,[27] but they represent two substantially different points in the distribution of voting turnout. In 2000, 68.71 per cent of the electorate voted, whereas 77.21 per cent of the voters deposited ballots at polling stations in March 2004. Nationwide voting turnout increased by 8.5 per cent. Was this increase, widely thought to have benefited the PSOE, the *direct and exclusive* result of 11 March, as some might have us believe? The data suggest otherwise – although the complex aftermath of the attack was not without its impact. In Madrid, where the attack took place, the increase in participation, at 8.59 per cent, was ever so slightly higher than the national average. The most pronounced increase in voting participation was experienced in the country's periphery, especially in the (more or less) pluri-national autonomous communities of Catalonia, the Basque country, Navarra, and Galicia. In Catalonia, electoral participation increased by a dramatic 12.95 per cent over the figure recorded four years earlier, and in the Basque country the increase was only slightly lower, with Galicia and Navarra following closely behind. In addition to the aftermath of the attack, two other factors – (1) disagreements over the government's rhetoric and policies on Spain's complex set of pluri-national identities,[28] and (2) the intrinsic interest and uncertainty generated by the election campaign – helped to encourage electoral participation. The PP government's apparent electoral calculation[29] that its stance highly critical of peripheral nationalism would win votes in the country's unilingual and unambiguously Spanish-identifying heartland must be weighed against this evidence that the PP unintentionally activated massive opposition in much of the pluri-national periphery. *This fundamental component of Spanish politics stands as a far more important piece of the 11–14 March puzzle than an uninformed external observer, or a social scientist armed only with generalizing theoretical queries, might initially perceive.* Moreover, the interconnection of factors in complex causal configurations – a hallmark of the Weberian approach – is evidenced by the intertwining of this history of political antagonism between the PP and the pluri-national periphery with the highly charged events of 11–14 March.

If we focus on the loss of votes by the PP since the previous national election in 2000, the empirical evidence offers additional pieces of the overall puzzle. Nationwide, the absolute number of Spaniards voting for the PP (9,630,512 in 2004 versus 10,321,178 four years earlier) was 6.70 per cent lower in the 2004 election. *Yet the decline in Madrid and in adjoining regions was less than that experienced in much (but not all) of the country's periphery.* In Madrid the PP lost 4.11 per cent of its 2000 electorate, a figure slightly higher than that of Castilla–La Mancha just to the south and slightly lower than in Castilla y León just to the north. The most dramatic declines in voting support for the Partido Popular were the Basque country where the loss of votes represented 28.05 per cent of those won by that party four years earlier, Catalonia where the decline represented 19.26 per cent of the party's 2000 electorate, Aragón where the loss was 17.17 per cent of the earlier figure, Navarra with a loss of 16.58 per cent by the PP in number of votes, Galicia where the decline was 8.53 per cent, and Andalucía with a loss by the PP of 8.15 per cent of its electorate from four years earlier.

Clearly, in Spain, *the political – or more precisely, the electoral – shock of 11 March and its aftermath was felt primarily not in the epicentre of the tragedy but hundreds of kilometres away in much of the country's periphery.* Yet the pattern we can observe is in no sense a primarily spatial one. Parts of the geographic periphery – such as Cantabria and Asturias on the northern coast – saw no decline in the PP vote, and in Mediterranean Murcia the vote for the Partido Popular was in absolute numbers significantly higher in 2004 than it had been four years earlier. The fault lines determining *where and how* the shock of 11 March would be felt at the ballot box three days later were largely political and they existed well before the attack occurred, thus underscoring the continuing usefulness of the Weberian approach to explanation, with its concern for historical antecedents and complex multi-causal configurations. The lines of division in the Spanish electorate involved issues of national identity – Spanish, Basque, and Catalan – alongside policies meant to deal with the terrorism of ETA; economic and social policy; and – in the case of Aragón and Murcia – disagreements over a national plan to redirect water from the Ebro River.

The severe deterioration in relations between pluri-national Spain and the PP government[30] represents a large part of this overall picture, but this identity-based phenomenon does not explain all that requires an accounting. Economic and social policies, such as the government's curtailment of support for the unemployed, also played a crucial role as is manifested by the large drop-off in votes for the PP in Andalucía, where under-employment and unemployment represent extraordinarily important issues. The government's national water redistribution plan was taken by the electorate to be good for some regions and bad for others; in relatively arid and agricultural Murcia, which anticipated receiving new water from the Ebro to the north, the absolute number of voters supporting the PP *increased* 5.8 per cent over the number recorded four years earlier (although this increase is masked by the fact that the PP's *percentage* of the overall vote declined marginally because the total number of voters in Murcia increased by a larger proportion than the PP vote itself); in Aragón, where the Ebro provides vital irrigation, the drop-off in support for the PP was almost as pronounced as in pluri-national Spain. Political disagreements and cleavages predating 11 March best explain this complex pattern of variation by region in the evolution of votes for the PP.

Yet despite the unmistakable importance of pre-existing political opinions and cleavages, the terrorist attack did fundamentally alter the political atmosphere and the array of actors surrounding the electorate's trip to the polls on 14 March. However, it did so in a way that was *indirect, extraordinarily complex, and not designed or knowable in advance.* Neither prior theoretical work nor the political actors themselves could have fully predicted this complex constellation of causality. Terrorism *had* been a major theme of political debate during the Spanish election campaign, but it was ETA, rather than Al-Qaeda, that much political discourse had emphasized.

The PP's campaign heavily emphasized its hard line on ETA terrorism and on pro-independence or pro-sovereignty peripheral nationalists in the Basque country and Catalonia. Moreover, the conservative governing party was harshly and incessantly critical of the Socialists for their coalition government in the Catalan autonomous community in alliance with Esquerra Republicana de Catalunya (ERC), a pro-independence left-of-centre party, and Iniciativa per Catalunya, a post-communist formation. The initially secret meeting of ERC leader Carod Rovira (hereinafter, Carod, the first of Carod Rovira's two last names) with ETA representatives in early January (discovered and reported by a conservative Madrid daily, *ABC*) was repeatedly used by the PP as illustrative support for its claim that the PSOE could not be trusted with governmental power in Madrid. The conservatives insinuated that Carod had negotiated a separate peace for Catalonia, a claim he emphatically denied while defending his meeting to listeners by reminding them that years earlier *he had* persuaded a small Catalan terrorist group, Terra Lliure, to abandon armed struggle in favour of the peaceful and legal pursuit of independence.[31] In the controversy surrounding this incident, Carod was forced to resign his number two position in the Catalan regional government, but the alliance of ERC with the Socialists remained in force.

Critics of the PP hoped that would be the last of the matter, notwithstanding the unceasing criticism emanating from the PP, but days later a video appeared in which two masked men, speaking below an ETA emblem, announced that their pro-independence terrorist group had declared a truce in Catalonia – but not in the rest of Spain. This announcement proved highly embarrassing for both the PSOE and ERC. The Socialists insisted that their opposition to ETA terrorism was as unflinching as that of any other political party – as attested to by the fact that several prominent Socialists had been killed by the terrorist organization – and they argued that ETA should not be permitted to determine the agenda of Spain's national election campaign. Carod reiterated his insistence that he had not negotiated a separate peace for Catalonia. However, the PP seized on the circumstance as an opportunity to argue that ERC was thoroughly disloyal and that the PSOE was untrustworthy, given its Catalan alliance with Esquerra. One PP government minister went so far as to state in public that the Socialists were allied with murderers – a charge that deeply angered Catalans who thought of Carod Rovira in decidedly different terms, regardless of whether they had ever voted for his party.

When Spaniards learned of the horrendous bombing early on 11 March, most quickly assumed that ETA had chosen to prove its ability to launch a massive attack in Madrid, while respecting its declared truce in Catalonia. Catalans cringed at the thought that truce in their territory might be linked to massacre in Madrid. Black sashes began to appear on balconies throughout Barcelona, as Catalans in massive numbers hung these visible symbols of mourning, striving in that manner to show that their grief and sense of horror were as deep as the shock and sadness to be found in Madrid. To the extent that Spaniards thought of the election during the very immediate aftermath of the explosions, most of them probably concluded that the PP would be swept to a decisive victory in a collective repudiation of the Socialists and their Catalan ally Carod.

Government officials and top-level representatives of the PP quickly spoke out, declaring not only their sense of profound outrage at the attack and solidarity with the victims but also indicating their firm conviction that ETA was responsible for the attack and that the election campaign could not continue under such circumstances. All significant parties shared in the declaration of outrage, in the affirmation of solidarity with the victims and their families, in their rededication to the effort to overcome terrorism, and so forth. Election campaigning was formally suspended by all political parties. In a decision that PP leaders may have later regretted, the government called for massive nationwide demonstrations on Friday afternoon to permit citizens the opportunity to express their shared sense of outrage. Government officials, including Prime Minister Aznar himself, contacted newspaper editors and other opinion leaders to present the case that ETA was responsible for the outrage.

From some point on Thursday itself, only hours after the attack took place, evidence began to emerge that Al Qaeda rather than ETA was guilty of the atrocity. A prominent Basque politician close to the pro-independence terrorists insisted that they were not the authors of the deed. Police quickly found a van near the railway station in which the bombs were planted on trains and in which detonators and other materials were found. Among the materials police encountered in the vehicle were tapes with koranic verses in Arabic. Later that same day Al Qaeda claimed responsibility. The chain of evidence was to grow longer rather quickly. ETA explicitly denied responsibility. A second claim of responsibility by Al Qaeda was made. And more importantly, on Saturday the police made their first arrests of Islamic militants believed responsible. By the time of nationwide demonstrations on Friday afternoon,[32] many Spaniards had concluded that Al Qaeda was responsible, but others continued to believe that ETA had carried out the attack – *as the government and state television continued to argue.*[33] Granted, a note of uncertainty was introduced into official declarations on Friday, but as late as Saturday morning, during the official 'day of reflection' prior to voting on Sunday, Mariano Rajoy, the PP candidate to succeed Aznar as prime minister, indicated publicly his 'moral conviction' that ETA was responsible.

The state of public opinion was tellingly illustrated by perhaps the most commonly chanted slogan during the massive demonstration in

Madrid: '¿Quién ha sido?' (Who did it?). The stark contrast between the growing public realization that the evidence pointed to Al Qaeda and governmental claims blaming ETA was neatly captured on Saturday morning, 13 March, by the headlines in Barcelona's relatively conservative establishment daily newspaper, *La Vanguardia*: 'The Evidence Points to Al Qaeda, But the Government Insists It Was ETA.' The deep incongruity between official declarations, on the one hand, and on the other, the growing realization that Al Qaeda had carried out the attack, gained added meaning for Spaniards for at least two reasons: (1) state television, widely watched in many parts of the country, continued on Saturday to insist that the evidence pointed toward ETA, and (2) no one could tell with certainty what most Spaniards believed on this matter or how those beliefs might affect the casting of votes. One could speculate that an attribution of the attack to ETA would help the PP by reminding voters of the truce declared in Catalonia following (but not necessarily negotiated during) Carod's secret meeting, whereas an attribution to Al Qaeda could help the opposition by reminding voters of the PP's highly unpopular support for the invasion of Iraq. Yet no one knew with any certainty what most Spaniards believed or how their vote might be influenced by these extraordinary events.

It is highly likely that many Spaniards – especially in the country's pluri-national periphery – interpreted the government's inaccurate attribution of the attack to ETA as simply the extreme culmination of a policy that had harshly criticized regional nationalists and their allies as allegedly soft on terrorism, or worse. Thus, in its electoral impact, the PP's attempt to blame ETA interacted with its previous policies and campaign strategy on matters of national identity. The fact that the greatest erosion of PP electoral support in March 2004 took place in the pluri-national periphery underscores this point.

In this setting, the arena of politically relevant actors was drastically and unexpectedly transformed, reducing the salience of institutionalized actors such as political parties and increasing the role of the news media, social movements, spontaneously organized demonstrations, and micro-contextual phenomena such as conversations among friends, fellow workers, students, and family members attempting to make sense out of the events.[34] The abrupt end to the campaign prevented political parties and their leaders from channelling public expressions of support (or other opinions) in conventional ways during the final three days prior to balloting. Yet this closing down of the conventional political arena was not accompanied by a decline in public interest. A number of factors – the attack itself, the massive demonstrations on Friday afternoon, and the combination of controversy and confusion over the identity of the terrorists responsible for the explosions – combined to heighten public interest *and outrage*. As should by now be clear, the extraordinarily multi-causal (and case-specific) nature of this configuration of factors influencing the election is quintessentially Weberian.

The massive demonstrations held throughout Spain on Friday deserve special attention, and they help to underscore the indispensability of the Weberian tool kit, with its tendency not only to use generalizing concepts (such as 'demonstrations,' 'political mobilization,' or 'social movement') but also to look beyond conventional conceptualization toward underlying empirical reality in all its complexity. Although each major Spanish city was the site, in principle, of only one *officially sponsored demonstration*, in practice the millions of people who participated generated countless *micro-demonstrations* within the larger crowds assembled. Signs denouncing the news media and the government for allegedly hiding the truth, banners opposing the war in Iraq, denunciations of terrorism in general, chants demanding the full truth about the incident, insults directed toward the governing party or others, simple expressions of grief – these sentiments, and others, were communicated by Spaniards in their uninstitutionalized encounter with one another in the streets where millions demonstrated.

One cannot understand this phenomenon without appreciating the massive level of participation generated by the country's collective sense of grief and the institutional sponsorship initiated by the government and quickly seconded by the opposition. *Yet neither that official sponsorship nor a conventional conceptualization of demonstrations can fully capture the complex nature of what happened on the streets of Spain that Friday afternoon.* A huge proportion of the public – perhaps a third of the adult population – engaged in this enormous collective encounter two days before the election. A characteristic feature of the Spanish political arena, well before these events took place, was the relative weakness of parties juxtaposed against the prevalence of protests, and crucially, *the predisposition of many Spaniards to demonstrate publicly in often spontaneous or improvised ways*.[35] The demonstrations of Friday afternoon permitted those Spaniards most sceptical of the government's claim of ETA responsibility to reach a cross-section of their fellow citizens with banners and chants transmitting their views. The trip to the polls two days later was to become as much a social movement event as a routine and institutionalized political episode.

By Saturday many of those Spaniards who were convinced that Al Qaeda had authored the massacre had grown increasingly angry at the government's declarations (which did begin in the course of that day to allow some possibility that the terrorists responsible for the attack might be Moroccan extremists rather than ETA) as well as the coverage on state television. Their anger was accompanied by concern over what other Spaniards – especially those who learn of news only from state television – knew or believed. With the elections set to take place the following day, Spaniards witnessed an extraordinary and thoroughly unpredictable 'day of reflection.' Repeated television appearances by the minister of the interior and representatives of the major parties were only some of the departures from the norm for the day before voting. Concerned citizens began to contact one another through Internet postings and mobile phone messages, conveying their sense of concern at the information being provided by the government and calling for action. The micro-contextual conversations and debates among friends and family over the vote to be cast the next day inevitably came to focus on the simple question, 'Who did it?' Those with access to satellite or cable television and who knew foreign languages quickly reported to their conversational circles that foreign news media had attributed the attacks to Al Qaeda.

In this setting, spontaneous demonstrations broke out in front of PP headquarters in Madrid and other cities[36] denouncing the government's information policy and, in the case of some demonstrators, placing at least some responsibility for the 11 March massacre on the government in the view that the attack had been a consequence of the PP's highly unpopular decision to support the Iraq war. For some of these spontaneous demonstrators the critique of the official handling of the incident blended into an anti-war critique of earlier (and continuing) PP policies. The demonstrations, reported in some news media, quickly spread. In Madrid, the central Puerta del Sol was the scene of a continuous protest from Saturday afternoon through early Sunday morning. In Barcelona spontaneous *caceroladas* broke out throughout the city as a cross-section of residents went to the streets, banging on pots and pans, to denounce the government. Others blacked out their lights at 10 pm in protest against the information being provided by state television and official spokespersons. The next day, as Spaniards went to the polls in massive numbers, several PP leaders were unexpectedly met by hecklers at their polling stations.

The space that parties typically occupy in channelling public sentiment at the close of a campaign had been obliterated by the tragic end of the campaign, and in its stead – partly encouraged by the dynamic intrinsic to the demonstrations on Friday, the confusion created by official attempts to blame ETA, and the pre-existing Spanish predisposition toward spontaneous protest – social movements and improvised expressions of opinion set the backdrop for the trip to the polls. What may have begun (and what was perceived by many) as a governmental effort to use the terrorist incident to remind voters of ETA's truce in Catalonia (and the alleged role of PSOE ally Carod Rovira in that regard), ended up backfiring, so to speak, as it seriously diminished the government's credibility and instead reminded many voters of the massive anti-war protests one year earlier. Some voters surely did see their vote as an opportunity to express opposition to the war, but that opposition was not new, nor had it been generated by the 11 March attack.

It seems clear that the massacre on 11 March did drastically change the backdrop to the elections of 14 March, but it did so in ways that could not have been predicted. No single political actor can be seen as uniquely responsible for the ultimate electoral outcome, or for the way in which terrorism shaped it. A complex and inherently unpredictable dynamic, in which spontaneous protest and perceived governmental dishonesty played a large role, helped to guide the collective sense of grief toward the ultimate electoral verdict rejecting the PP at the ballot box. *Yet that outcome rests also on prior political cleavages and sentiments.* The most important new sentiment generated by 11 March and its aftermath was outrage, an outrage that likely increased voting participation. In this environment the PSOE benefited from the synergy between its institutional form of expression and the social movement-like protests in the streets.[37] For many Spaniards, voting Socialist on 14 March became a de facto social movement event. Yet when the Socialist victory became apparent late on Sunday, virtually no public celebration took place. The feeling of collective grief and exhaustion lingered – although for many Spaniards it was now qualified by an accompanying sense of relief.

A Weberian searching for validation of the emphasis on complexity and multi-causality might find in the Spanish experience the basis for an appealing general proposition: that the impact of terrorism on voting is shaped by a complex process involving multiple actors and pre-existing cleavages. Yet even this conclusion could be dangerously absolute if taken as a universally applicable causal law. One cannot easily dismiss the possibility that a future terrorist incident occurring shortly before elections *could* massively shift an *entire* electorate in a way far less mediated by micro-level and meso-level actors and their interactions, far less conditioned by prior political preferences. Indeed, if ETA had been responsible for 11 March, the outcome analysed in this essay would have been drastically different, and if the attack had hit another country, the story would likely have been highly dissimilar. The superiority of the Weberian perspective lies not in an unchanging (or for that matter, in a *new*) set of causal propositions this school can call its own but instead in its ability to look toward the world that matters to us with open eyes and toward the scholarly arena with a dedication to rigour second to none (even if constraints of time or resources – especially in the case of the early work on a topic such as is evident in this essay – may often leave scholars short of the full Weberian objective). Yet this is not to say that Weberians are uninterested in the formulation of new concepts and theories of a generalizing nature. Far from it. Many works by latter-day Weberians concentrate more on the search for generalizing propositions than does this essay – just as Weber in some of his works prioritized the search for generalizing concepts to a greater extent than in his 'Objectivity' essay. But the generalizing ideas that Weberians formulate and deploy are developed in constant tension with the effort to make sense of empirical reality in all its complexity and historical singularity. The concepts, arguments, and causal assertions to be found in this examination of Spain's experience in March 2004 do not in any sense represent an unchanging core of presumed Weberian 'truths,' but they would not have been developed or effectively deployed without the benefit of Weber's methodology and its embrace of tensions. Without the benefit of the approach eloquently articulated by Weber in the 'Objectivity' essay, the search for an adequate understanding of the Spanish March – or any equally meaningful and challenging political episode – would be left entirely to amateurs or journalists, with their characteristic shortcomings, rather than professional social scientists.

NOTES

I am deeply indebted to the great Weberian Juan Linz for his extraordinary intellectual guidance and inspiration since first introducing me to the study of political sociology. I wish to thank Julián Casanova, Gosta Esping-Andersen,

Jeff Goodwin, David Hachen, Jacint Jordana, Juan Linz, Julia Lopez, Jim McAdams, Laurence McFalls, Guillermo O'Donnell, Luís Ortiz, Francesc Pallares, Richard Snyder, Mariano Torcal, Samuel Valenzuela, and Ruben Vega Garcia for their comments on this analysis written immediately after the Madrid bombing. I mention these debts with some reservation, given the limitations the reader will encounter in this text.

1 One can easily list other fundamental tensions that the Weberian approach embraces, rather than attempting to wish them away. These overlapping tensions include the interest in motivations and intentionality balanced against the assumption of – and search for – *unintended* consequences of action; the commitment to disciplinary communities and approaches coupled with the eclectic embrace of multi-disciplinary approaches and sources; the emphasis on the partial *autonomy* of given institutional spheres such as politics, religion, and the economy, juxtaposed against the constant search for causal interconnections among institutional spheres; the adherence in principle to methodological individualism combined with the constant conceptual and explanatory use of macro-level concepts; the assumption that empirical reality is infinitely complex and inescapably specific in its manifestations alongside the constant search for conceptual generalization; the impulse to theorize juxtaposed against the claim that theories are all simplifications and that reality cannot be deduced from them. A final if more debatable tension consists of the conflict between scientific precision and esthetic appeal in scholarly expression. Although Weber does not embrace this last tension, he does appear to *experience* it in his own writing. One could easily continue, but all of these tensions – along with the embrace of both the value-oriented question *and* the objective response – can be understood to form part of the Weberian approach that seeks validation (in different ways) and/or direction for the social scientist within the specialized scholarly community and outside it in the larger world that we observe, experience, and find meaningful.

2 Sheldon Wolin, 'Max Weber: Legitimation, Method, and the Politics of Theory,' *Political Theory* 9, no. 3 (August 1981): 401–24.

3 For a recent discussion in the field of legal studies and the philosophy of law see José Juan Moreso, 'Putting Legal Objectivity in Its Place,' *Analisi e Diritto* (2004): 243–52.

4 See Theda Skocpol, 'Doubly Engaged Social Science: The Promise of Comparative Historical Analysis,' in *Comparative Historical Analysis in the Social Sciences*, ed. James Mahoney and Dietrich Rueschemeyer (Cambridge: Cambridge University Press, 2003), 407–28.

5 See Peter A. Hall, 'Aligning Ontology and Methodology in Comparative Research' in Mahoney and Rueschemeyer, *Comparative Historical Analysis,* 373–404.

6 Readers may wish to take my characterization of Weberians as an ideal-type.

7 For stimulating essays offering differing perspectives on how one may conceive of cases and case studies, see Charles C. Ragin and Howard S. Becker, eds., *What Is a Case? Exploring the Foundations of Social Inquiry* (Cambridge: Cambridge University Press, 1992).

8 The methodological writings of Charles C. Ragin, most prominently *The Comparative Method: Moving beyond Qualitative and Quantitative Strategies* (Berkeley: University of California Press, 1987), and the work on comparative methodology of Samuel Valenzuela, 'Macro Comparisons without the Pitfalls: A Protocol for Comparative Research,' in *Politics, Society and Democracy: Latin America; Essays in Honor of Juan Linz,* ed. Scott Mainwaring and Arturo Valenzuela (Boulder, CO: Westview, 1998), 237–66, offer important recent arguments on the need to search for causal configurations that may take case-specific forms.

9 In this spirit I offer a strong critique of the concept of social capital in chapter 4 of *Democracy's Voices: Social Ties and the Quality of Public Life in Spain* (Ithaca: Cornell University Press, 2004).

10 One can see this in some – although not all – of the arguments found in Gary King, Robert Keohane, and Sidney Verba, *Designing Social Inquiry: Scientific Inference in Qualitative Research* (Princeton: Princeton University Press, 1994).

11 Among his important Weberian works, in addition to his classic typology of regime types, see Juan Linz, *The Breakdown of Democratic Regimes: Crisis, Breakdown and Reequilibration* (Baltimore: Johns Hopkins University Press, 1978), and with his frequent collaborator Alfred Stepan, *Problems of Democratic Transition and Consolidation: Southern Europe, South America and Post-Communist Europe* (Baltimore: Johns Hopkins University Press, 1996).

12 In addition to his now classic work on neo-corporatism, see Philippe Schmitter, *How to Democratize the European Union and Why Bother?* (Lanham, MD: Rowman and Littlefield, 2000), as well as his important collaborative work on transitions to democracy (see note 13).

13 See Guillermo O'Donnell, *Modernization and Bureaucratic Authoritarianism: Studies in South American Politics* (Berkeley: Institute of International Studies, University of California, 1973); and in collaboration with Philippe Schmitter, *Transitions from Authoritarian Rule: Tentative Conclusions about Uncertain Democracies* (Baltimore: Johns Hopkins University Press, 1986).

14 In addition to his numerous collaborative works with Linz, see, for example, Alfred Stepan, *Rethinking Military Politics: Brazil and the Southern Cone* (Princeton: Princeton University Press, 1988).

15 See, for example, Theda Skocpol, *Protecting Soldiers and Mothers: The Political Origins of Social Policy in the United States* (Cambridge: Harvard University Press, 1992), and Theda Skocpol and Morris Fiorina, eds., *Civic Engagement in American Democracy* (Washington, DC: Brookings, 1999).

16 See, for example, Gosta Esping-Andersen, *Social Foundations of Post-industrial Economies* (Oxford: Oxford University Press, 1999), and Gosta Esping-Andersen and Marino Regini, *Why Deregulate Labour Markets?* (Oxford: Oxford University Press, 2000).

17 Donald P. Green and Ian Shapiro, *Pathologies of Rational Choice Analysis: A Critique of Its Applications in Political Science* (New Haven: Yale University Press, 1994).

18 As a part-time resident of Spain (who was in Barcelona at the time of the events here analysed) and as a scholar devoted in part to the study of that country, I have followed these events with a level of interest that made it impossible for me to choose a different empirical focus in March 2004, when I wrote the first draft of this essay.

19 The most important work on the emergence of a democratic party system in Spain's post-Franco democracy is Richard Gunther, Giacomo Sani, and Goldie Shabad, *Spain after Franco: The Making of a Competitive Party System* (Berkeley: University of California Press, 1986).

20 Spanish political scientists quickly wrote on the election. See Mariano Torcal and Guillem Rico, 'The Spanish General Election: In the Shadow of Al-Qaeda?' *South European Society and Politics* 9, no. 3 (2004): 107–21; Josep M. Colomer, 'The General Election in Spain, March 2004,' in *Electoral Studies* 24, no. 1 (2005): 149–56; and Francesc Pallares, 'La Influencia de'l 11-M,' in *El Periódico*, 21 March 2004, 32–3.

21 In Spanish politics the prime minister is typically known as 'the president of government,' thus leading to some uncertainty in rendering this term in other languages, but given that the political system is a parliamentary monarchy lacking a president, for comparative purposes any translation other than 'prime minister' can only create confusion.

22 See *El País*, 29 February 2004, 23.

23 Much useful data from this regular survey of the Spanish public is available at www.cadenaser.es

24 Richard Gunther, José Ramón Montero, and Mariano Torcal are currently engaged in such work, as is the Centro de Investigaciones Sociológicas.

25 As with all Pulsómetro polling, this is available at www.cadenaser.es

26 For extensive coverage, see *El País*, 21 June 2002.
27 On voting participation and exceptional elections in Spain, see José Ramón Montero, 'Elecciones normales y elecciones excepcionales: algunos datos y factores de la movilización electoral de 1982,' *Estudis Electorals* 8 (1986): 173–95.
28 See the excellent discussion on the importance of such issues for Spanish politics in Linz and Stepan, *Problems of Democratic Transition and Consolidation*, and the comparative analysis of Basque and Catalan nationalism in Juan Diez Medrano, *Divided Nations: Class, Politics and Nationalism in the Basque Country and Catalonia* (Ithaca: Cornell University Press, 1995).
29 In the absence of monographic work on the Aznar government's motivation for its policy toward peripheral nationalism, my inference that the policy was motivated by an electoral (mis)calculation should be seen as quite tentative – although it does fit the theoretical image many scholars hold of governmental decision making.
30 One of the most surprising episodes in the broader pattern of increasingly bitter relations between the Aznar government and the pluri-national periphery was the sharp confrontation between the prime minister and the Basque bishops in June 2002. On Aznar's charge that the bishops, who had issued a letter critical of his government's Basque policy, were guilty of 'moral perversion' see *El País*, 4 June 2002, p. 1. For the complete text of the bishops Pastoral Letter see *La Vanguardia*, 7 June 2002, 16.
31 For a small sample of the extensive press coverage in 2004 on this incident – and its political aftermath – see *El País*, 28 January, 1, 14–17; 2 February, 17, 18, 20; 3 February, 14, 15; 5 February, 20; 2 March, 19; and *La Vanguardia*, 3 February 2004, 12–17.
32 For extensive press coverage of these demonstrations, held throughout Spain on 12 March, see *El País* and *La Vanguardia*, 13 March 2004.
33 On the coverage of these events on Spanish state television, see Rafael Duran Munoz, 'La caverna en tiempo de crisis y elecciones: Del 11M al 14M en TVE,' *Revista de Investigaciones Politicas y Sociologicas* 4, no. 2 (Spring 2006): 219–39.
34 Indirect evidence for this assertion is to be found in the election results in small municipalities. Strikingly, relatively similar neighbouring villages – such as Bubión and Capileira in the Alpujarra district on the southern slopes of the Sierra Nevada – moved electorally in opposite directions in 2004. In one of these villages the absolute number of votes for the PP increased from the 2000 baseline, whereas in the other it dropped sharply. In the absence – as of this writing – of systematic national data analysis on this point, this illustrative paired comparison suggests that the micro-

contextual foundation of voter choice was likely informed by highly localized (and varied) interpretations of 11 March and its aftermath.

36 On this phenomenon, see Robert M. Fishman and Suzanne Coshow, 'Setting the Reach of Protest: Institutions, Movements and Social Ties in Spanish Working-class Collective Action,' presented at the Authority in Contention conference, University of Notre Dame, 14–15 August 2002.

37 On the 13 March demonstrations, see Victor Sampedro Blanco, ed., *13M: Multitudes Online* (Madrid: Los Libros de la Catarata, 2005), an important work that clearly establishes the spontaneous character of the 13 March demonstrations.

38 On the ability of some activists and leaders within the PSOE (but most decidedly not others) to forge a poltical style rooted in the combination of social movement and party-institutional experiences, see *Democracy's Voices*, chapter 6.

12 Weber and the Problem of Social Science Prediction

STEPHEN E. HANSON

At first glance, Max Weber's interpretive sociology appears to place little emphasis upon prediction of outcomes in order to test the validity of theoretical hypotheses. After all, Weber clearly dismissed the idea that causation in social science must take the form of invariant, universal 'laws,' insisting that the cultural values that motivate social action in different historical periods, and that also inevitably shape the motivation of social scientists in their choice of subject matter, are constantly subject to change. For these reasons, he argued, 'a systematic science of culture, even only in the sense of a definitive, objectively valid systematic fixation of the problem which it should treat, would be senseless in itself' (Weber 1949, 84).

And yet Weber himself did not shy away from making predictions in his own social-scientific work – most of which, indeed, seem remarkably prescient a century later. At the end of *The Protestant Ethic and the Spirit of Capitalism*, for example, Weber set out three possible futures for the rational capitalistic order as it had emerged in the West by the beginning of the twentieth century: either 'new prophets' would arise to challenge the spiritual meaninglessness of this order, or 'ancient ideals' would be reborn – or 'if neither,' the system would sustain itself indefinitely, leading to a kind of 'mechanized ossification, embellished with a sort of rigidly compelled sense of self-importance' (Weber 2002, 124). In effect, Weber predicted that, despite the unprecedented material power of modern rational-legal capitalism, its decisive subordination of charismatic and traditional forms of legitimacy would likely generate frequent revolutionary challenges by anti-modern charismatic leaders, periodic calls for a return to pre-modern cultural norms, and continuing social alienation in even the most advanced capitalist societies. The history of the twentieth century, it is fair to say, amply bore out Weber's assessment.[1]

A second set of predictions in Weber's work concerns the likely future of state socialism. In *Economy and Society*, for instance, Weber set out his prediction that socialism, far from eliminating the need for formal bureaucracy, would in fact 'require a still higher degree of formal bureaucratization than capitalism' (Weber 1968, 225). However, the attainment of rational bureaucratic control in the absence of market capitalism, Weber argued, would in the longer run likely not be feasible. A socialist planned economy would 'weaken the incentive to labor,' and 'autonomy in the direction of organized productive units would have to be greatly reduced or, in the extreme case, eliminated.' In the end, implementers of a planning system would have to 'accept the inevitable reduction in formal, calculatory rationality which would result from the elimination of money and capital accounting' (Weber 1968, 111), with negative implications for economic efficiency. It is worth emphasizing that Weber was making such predictions a decade before Stalin's Five-Year Plan was introduced, and eighty years before the socialist planned economy succumbed to precisely these problems.

Weber makes yet another set of predictions in connection with his depiction of the dynamics of the charismatic form of legitimate domination. Charisma, he insists, is a relatively unstable form of social order, based as it is on the belief by followers in the 'extraordinary' abilities of the charismatic leader, and his ability to produce 'miracles' regularly. Charisma's hostility to any sort of social routine, Weber continues, forces charismatic movements to rely on irregular forms of economic activity such as plunder or charity; thus 'every charisma is on the road from a turbulently emotional life that knows no economic rationality to a slow death by the weight of suffocation under the weight of material interests' (Weber 1968, 1120). Predictably, charismatic forms of domination will tend to 'routinize' over time; the problem of finding a worthy successor to the charismatic leader, in particular, 'inescapably channels charisma into the direction of legal regulation and tradition' (1123). Weber uses these theoretical propositions to generate a wide range of empirical predictions that still seem highly relevant today: that the most common form of routinization of charismatic leadership would continue to be inheritance of legitimacy through blood ties; that modern democracies would likely see continuing conflicts between charismatic party leaders and bureaucratic party organizations; that despite the tendency for charisma to recede with the development of modern bureaucratic institutions, it would reemerge again whenever an extraordinary event occurs; and so on (1125–48).

One could easily multiply examples of Weberian predictions of this type. Indeed, upon closer examination, the potential for social science theory to generate accurate predictions of future social outcomes is fundamental to Weber's entire conception of the value of the social-scientific enterprise. In the essay '"Objectivity" of Knowledge in Social Science and Social Policy,' the hundredth anniversary of which we celebrate in this volume, Weber insists on this point:

> The question of the appropriateness of the means for achieving a given end is undoubtedly accessible to scientific analysis. Inasmuch as we are able to determine (within the present limits of our knowledge) which means for the achievement of a proposed end are appropriate or inappropriate, we can in this way estimate the chances of attaining a certain end by certain available means. In this way we can indirectly criticize the setting of the end itself as practically meaningful (on the basis of the existing historical situation) or as meaningless with reference to existing conditions. Furthermore, when the possibility of attaining a proposed end appears to exist, we can determine (naturally within the limits of our existing knowledge) the consequences which the application of the means to be used will produce in addition to the eventual attainment of the proposed end, as a result of the interdependence of all events ... Thus, we can answer the question: what will the attainment of a desired end 'cost' in terms of the predictable loss of other values? (Weber 1949, 52–3)

To be sure, Weber is careful to emphasize, twice, the limits of social science knowledge at its current stage of development. But were it altogether impossible to predict the future based on sociological theory, Weber's account here of the utility of a social science free of 'value judgments' for evaluating the value tradeoffs involved in alternative courses of action would become nonsensical.

A glance at the work of the handful of self-identified Weberian scholars within the contemporary political science discipline shows that they, too, embrace prediction as a legitimate goal of social-scientific inquiry. Moreover, I think it is fair to say that the predictive record of the Weberian school – at least in the subfield of communist and post-communist studies, with which I am most familiar – is comparatively quite impressive. Perhaps most famously, Randall Collins was one of the tiny handful of social scientists to predict well in advance the likelihood of the collapse of the Soviet Union, based on its internal problems of legitimation combined with its geopolitical overstretch (Collins 1986; see also Hanson 1991). In the early 1990s, when the vast majority of social scientists studying post-communist societies were enamoured by the optimistic metaphor of successful 'transition' to democracy and the market, Ken Jowitt argued instead that a culture of cynicism about and alienation from politics would likely endure in the region for a long time (Jowitt 1992); recently, careful evaluation by Marc Howard (2003) of survey evidence shows that over a decade since communism's collapse, citizens throughout Eastern Europe remain significantly less willing to participate in civic organizations than their counterparts in post-authoritarian societies elsewhere – let alone in the established democracies of Western Europe. Jowitt's prediction that 'movements of rage' based on hatred of the West would likely emerge to fill the gap left by the collapse of communism and the withdrawal of the Soviet Union from the Third World – a view essentially ignored by mainstream political scientists – also appears, after the events of 9/11, to have been precisely accurate (Jowitt 1992). And at the risk of self-aggrandizement, I'll mention that Jeff Kopstein and I predicted in 1997 that, despite disturbing similarities between Weimar Germany and post-Soviet Russia, fascism would be unlikely to emerge in the medium run in the latter case because of Russia's weak party system and lack of civil society; in a follow-up article written in 2000, I predicted that Russia's party system would disintegrate altogether as a result of the absence of coherent party ideologies in the post-communist cultural milieu (Hanson and Kopstein 1997; Hanson 2003). The sort of pragmatic, 'centrist' authoritarianism now emerging in Putin's Russia thus comes as no surprise to us.

One might think that a theory that has generated so many accurate predictions might quickly take the political science discipline by storm, inspiring generations of young scholars to refine, expand, and promote it. This manifestly has not occurred. Indeed, the neo-Weberian approach, despite having one of the most easily documented records of successful prediction over the past few decades, has only a handful of supporters in the contemporary political science discipline. Meanwhile, other paradigms whose practitioners have ostensibly more embarrassing records of predictive inaccuracy are accorded far more scholarly attention.[2] Obviously, explaining this odd situation is of some personal importance to committed Weberians. But on a more detached level, the professional marginalization of successfully predictive theories, and the professional promotion of predictively inaccurate theories, represents an interesting intellectual puzzle that demands theoretical attention.

In this essay I will argue that at least one important reason no one has noticed the predictive accuracy of neo-Weberian theory is that, surprisingly, there is actually no consensus among contemporary political scientists about the role of empirical prediction in testing theories. Indeed, a substantial number of scholars in the field have given up (explicitly or implicitly) the idea that empirical testing of hypotheses about future outcomes has any role to play in evaluating a social-scientific theory's value. Detached from the anchor of empirical testing, the political science discipline floats in a sea of abstractions, with little relevance to 'science' as it has been understood in the modern world since the Enlightenment. Ironically, at the same time, scholars interested in real-world political phenomena have increasingly tended to reject the ideal of 'political science' altogether – thus ceding the symbolically crucial term 'science' to the disciplinary mainstream.

In what follows, I will first outline several contemporary views on the role of prediction in political science methodology, showing how few scholars now formally accept the idea that repeated incorrect predictions must necessarily falsify a theory. I will then argue for an alternative Weberian approach to understanding the three main ideal-types of 'prediction' – traditional 'wisdom,' charismatic 'prophecy,' and rational-legal 'scientific testing' – each tied to a particular conception of time. I'll then conclude by showing how a neo-Weberian theory of 'regime evolution' succeeds so well in generating specific, testable hypotheses about future developments in global politics.

Political Science and Prediction

The widespread notion that most political scientists accept the accuracy, or inaccuracy, of empirical predictions as the ultimate test of a theory's worth reflects the dominance of this viewpoint in the 1960s, when Carl Hempel's (1952) argument for 'covering law' explanations of social and historical outcomes, and Karl Popper's (1959) related conception of 'falsification' as the engine of scientific progress, became widely popular in the social sciences. Simply put, a 'covering law' is a statement of empirical correlation that takes the form 'if x, then y' – in all times and places. Thus, if one can find evidence of x in some social setting, one should be able accurately and unfailingly to predict the presence of y as well. Social science, from Hempel's perspective, must strive to establish the existence of such 'laws' in order to become more like the successful natural sciences. Popper's argument that science progresses largely through the disconfirmation of attempts to establish such laws helped further to popularize the notion that social scientists (presumably like natural scientists) should develop falsifiable hypotheses about future outcomes, and then seek to disconfirm them. From this 'deductive-nomological' point of view, prediction indeed plays a central role in the social-scientific enterprise.

But the Hempel-Popper perspective came under attack for a variety of reasons. As Thomas Kuhn (1962) famously argued, even within the natural sciences, the methods and standards used to judge what counts as a 'successful' prediction are themselves dependent upon shared 'paradigms' among working communities of scientists concerning the nature of 'good' scientific research. Scientists whose predictions are incorrect will be highly unlikely to toss aside a successful paradigm in the face of a single, or even several, wrong predictions; negative results that might challenge fundamental paradigmatic assumptions can always be explained as a result of faulty procedures or poor research design. If Popper's notion of falsifiability seems unworkable even within the natural sciences, then surely it is even less applicable to the social sciences, which in Kuhn's terms are still 'pre-paradigmatic': that is, agreement among researchers about basic issues of ontology and methodology is still absent.

Kuhn's critique seriously weakened the appeal of the Hempel-Popper approach to falsification. Still, many philosophers of science – and philosophically sophisticated social scientists – objected to Kuhn's insistence on the 'incommensurability' of competing paradigms, which seemed to imply that no rational reason for accepting or rejecting any particular scientific paradigm could exist. If so, 'progress' in the natural sciences was impossible – and the pre-paradigmatic social 'sciences' were doomed to total irrelevance. For these reasons, Lakatos's philosophy of science, which aims to transcend the Popper–Kuhn divide, has become extremely popular among social scientists. Lakatos fully agreed with Kuhn that the simple Popperian perspective on falsification was 'naive': 'Contrary to naive falsificationism, *no experiment, experimental report, observation statement or well-corroborated low-level falsifying hypothesis alone can lead to falsification. There is no falsification before the emergence of a better theory*' (Lakatos and Musgrave 1970, 119, emphasis in original). Scientific 'research programs,' Lakatos argued, could be analysed as containing both a 'hard core' of unchallengeable assumptions and a 'protective belt' of auxiliary hypotheses; only the latter were directly subject to empirical testing, and even here scientists could legitimately 'adjust' the interpretation of such tests in order to preserve a research program's 'core' (Lakatos and Musgrave 1970). The key to preserving the integrity of the scientific enterprise, according to Lakatos, is a commitment among researchers to abandon 'degenerating' research programs – ones in which the adjustments of auxiliary hypotheses take place primarily on an ad hoc basis – for 'progressive' research programs that explain all the empirical content of their predecessors while explaining 'novel facts' as well.

But Lakatos's theory does not satisfactorily establish the criteria by which scientists should decide just when a research program has started to 'degenerate.' He had in mind here groups like Lamarckian biologists after the victory of Darwinism, or defenders of classical Newtonian physics after the development of Einstein's theory of relativity. In cases such as these, the ability of new research programs to explain all old facts while pointing the way toward novel ones seems reasonably clear. Applied to the social sciences, however, Lakatos's views can seemingly justify the defence of just about *any* research program. Since social scientists have established no (or very few) robust causal theories that produce reliable empirical predictions, the Lakatosian demand that competing scholars produce a 'better theory' before current research programs be abandoned makes it impossible in practice to mount an effective challenge to currently dominant research traditions on the basis of disconfirming empirical evidence. Moreover, defenders of dominant paradigms can shrug off their own poor predictive records as irrelevant to the status of the paradigm's 'core,' as long as that core can be presented as possessing some internal logical consistency.

The influence of Lakatos's approach to science can be seen in a wide variety of contemporary political science understandings of the (highly limited) role of prediction in evaluating theories. The authors of *Analytic Narratives*, for example, see their empirical case studies essentially as illustrations of abstract models derived from 'core assumptions' of rational choice theory (Bates et al., 1998). But as Margaret Levi (1997, 33) admits, 'Even when a rational choice analysis offers a logical story consistent with the facts, this hardly constitutes a validation of the explanation.' Gary King, Robert Keohane, and Sidney Verba (1994), who are often described as straightforward defenders of the Hempel-Popper approach (see, for example, McKeown 1999), in fact also describe the role of prediction in political science in essentially Lakatosian terms:

> We have suggested that the process of evaluating theories and hypotheses is a flexible one: particular empirical tests neither confirm nor disconfirm them once and for all. When an empirical test is inconsistent with our theoretically based expectations, we do not immediately throw out the theory. We may do various things: We may conclude that the evidence may have been poor due to chance alone; we may adjust what we consider to be the range of applicability of a theory of hypothesis even if it does not hold in a particular case and, through that adjustment, maintain our acceptance of the theory or hypothesis. Science proceeds by such adjustments; but they can be dangerous. If we take them too far we make our theories and hypotheses invulnerable to disconfirmation. The lesson is that we must be very careful in adapting theories to be consistent with new evidence. We must avoid stretching the theory beyond all plausibility by adding numerous exceptions and special cases (King, Keohane, and Verba 1994, 104).

Here, as in Lakatos, the integrity of science seems to lie in a commitment by scholars to abandon degenerating research programs – but the authors provide no criteria for distinguishing between legitimate 'adjustment' and illegitimate 'stretching' of a theory. This indeterminacy, along with the remarkably poor predictive record of most social science theories over the past few decades, combine in practice to set the bar for empirical testing of political science theories exceedingly low.[3]

Most contemporary critics of Lakatosian approaches to social science, unfortunately, have few workable alternatives to propose. Somers (1998, 773), for example, after persuasively criticizing the non-falsifiability of rational choice approaches to historical sociology, proposes the adoption of what she calls 'relational realism.' But her alternative conception of how to test social science theory against empirical evidence is hopelessly vague: 'Theorizing convincingly about mechanisms, then, is a task requiring neither pure induction nor pure deduction but one that demands devising diverse and creative ways ... to answer the question of whether the theoretical entity being hypothesized can actually be demonstrated to have a relational effect on a specific problem.' Meanwhile, other contemporary critics of mainstream social science often deny the 'scientific' pretensions of the field altogether; for them, the goal of prediction should be discarded altogether in favour of 'interpretation' or 'explanation.' Thus it should not surprise us to see that even political scientists whose empirical predictions have failed utterly and spectacularly – while so many Weberian predictions have come true – can simply shrug off the implications of this result for their favoured theoretical approaches.

A Neo-Weberian Approach to Prediction in Social Science

As this review of the literature implies, it seems to me that any coherent account of the social-scientific enterprise simply has to include success-ful prediction of outcomes as an important criterion for the evaluation of competing theories. Otherwise, there remains literally no scientific check on the ability of empirically incorrect, but deductively consistent, theories to endure indefinitely. By no means does this mean that we should beat a full retreat to Popperian positivism, of course; the cri-tiques of Kuhn and others of 'naive falsificationism' are persuasive. The problem is to find an alternative conception of prediction that takes into account the peculiar subject matter and reflexivity of the social, as opposed to the natural, sciences.

Here Weber's methodological contributions are particularly helpful. In particular, 'social science' prediction itself must be analysed in com-parison with other, more common, social forms of foretelling the future. In this respect, we can follow Weber's theory of the three ideal-types of legitimate domination and distinguish among traditional, charismatic, and rational-legal ideal-types of prediction. Each of these types of le-gitimacy, as I have argued elsewhere, can be seen as reflecting the acceptance of a particular conception of time – and hence, of the 'future' that is supposed to be foretold (Hanson 1997). 'Traditional' forms of prediction are intimately tied to a conception of time as based on the concrete flow of events, usually interpreted as cyclical in nature. In this manner, sages and elders in traditional settings predict that historical outcomes will repeat themselves ineluctably, and insist that acceptance of one's fate constitutes 'wisdom.' Such advice may, in fact, be highly appropriate and accurate in traditional settings. 'Charismatic' forms of prediction are tied to the belief that time (and space) is actually an illusion, and thus those with extraordinary or divine insight can see the 'future' as 'present.' 'Prophecy,' in the true sense, thus involves commu-nication by the charismatic prophet to his followers of what is 'already true' about the future. The experience of successful prophecy – paradigmatically illustrated by the Oedipus myth – has an identity-transforming effect on the recipient of the message.

Finally, 'rational' prediction – the sole form that is 'legitimate' within the institutional context of modern science – is based upon acceptance of the notion that time (and space) is abstract, forming a grid that extends infinitely and linearly from the past, to the present, to the future. As Weber himself puts it, 'The stream of immeasurable events flows unendingly toward eternity' (Weber 1949, 84). To predict concrete outcomes within this framework of rational time requires logical, impersonal procedures designed to ascertain causes at one point in time that can be reliably shown to bring about effects at later points in time. The classic institution of modern science, of course, is the laboratory, where controlled experiments in principle allow the scientific researcher to abstract entirely from particular historical and geographical contexts in order to arrive at 'pure' causal relationships. However, the notion of abstract time that lies behind modern notions of scientific prediction is conceptually separable from the specific institution of the laboratory; hence non-experimental sciences such as cosmology and evolutionary biology can be accepted as fully scientific to the extent that they also strive to verify causal relationships in linear time.[4]

This ideal-typical scheme already helps to pinpoint one reason for the confusion among social scientists about the role of empirical prediction: far more frequently than social scientists realize, the sorts of prediction they are interested in are traditional or charismatic, rather than rational. Weber points to both of these confusions in his methodological essays. To the extent that social scientists enter the profession in order to 'prove' the superiority of particular social arrangements, they unwittingly conflate the task of scientific (linear, causal) prediction with the defence of inherited, traditional values. In contemporary social science scholarship, too, the study of history is often motivated by a search for 'lessons' about the past that can reveal timeless 'wisdom' about the human condition; such scholars 'predict' that abstract schemes to improve the human condition will necessarily fail as a result of their rejection of local knowledge, but they do not embrace the search for testable hypotheses about causal relationships linking antecedent conditions to future outcomes (see, for example, Murrell 1993; Scott 1998). To the extent that scholars attempt to use the lecture hall to dispense 'academic prophecy,' they conflate the tasks of science with those of spiritual leadership. One can see this conflation at work among scholars who explicitly claim that their goal is to engage in 'social engineering' by mastering the laws of social 'physics' (for example, Ordeshook 1995); success in this endeavour would implicitly place social scientists in the role of charismatic leaders, issuing infallible prophecies about the results of particular efforts at institution-building, and 'designing' institutions with perfectly predictable results.

Even in the natural sciences, where laboratory methods allow much more reliable empirical confirmation or disconfirmation of predictive hypotheses, the potential to conflate rational prediction and charismatic prophecy exists as well. Indeed, the conception of the successful natural scientist as 'charismatic prophet' still has a certain amount of purchase among laypeople and scientific practitioners alike; the quest for a unified general theory in physics that would account for all empirical data throughout time and space is one product of this essentially spiritual 'mission.'

Yet natural scientific predictions of the future, however impressively they are confirmed, can for most people be easily compartmentalized and generally have little direct impact on their identities. Adopting an ideal-typically rational approach to prediction in social science, by contrast, would have immense, and, for many, unwelcome implications for the self-understanding of social scientists. To begin with, an abstract and linear view of the unfolding of human history would have to firmly embrace Darwinian evolutionary theory as providing the 'scope conditions' under which social science is even possible. As Weber well understood, a science of interpretive beings – the subject matter that makes social science a distinct field of inquiry – can exist only where, empirically, creatures with the capability of abstract symbolic communication have emerged from the evolutionary process (Weber 1968). Beyond this point, however, a truly 'rational' social science would have to place all religions, ideologies, and scientific paradigms themselves on the abstract time line in order to examine in a procedural and impersonal manner the reasons for their emergence, institutionalization, and disintegration.[5] Thus efforts to establish theoretically the superiority or inferiority of particular 'civilizations' or cultural traditions are, from this point of view, necessarily unscientific. Meanwhile, from the Weberian point of view, the position of would-be 'institutional engineers' becomes not so much immoral or wrongheaded as logically impossible: the first questions one would have to ask about abstract designs for human institutions would be, under what empirical conditions are analysts likely to arrive at these conclusions about which institutional rules are best? And how likely are such designs to be accepted by empirical political actors under the social conditions actually characteristic of the contemporary world? Since scientific (as opposed to ideological or religious) answers to these questions must necessarily indicate the high likelihood of something short of full acceptance and implementation of proposed incentive systems by all human beings, the utopian dream of social-scientific engineering must, from a Weberian point of view, be abandoned.

Yet Weber continues to insist, as we have seen, that prediction is a crucial element of the social science enterprise. Indeed, in nearly every respect, Weber argues, the logical procedures for establishing causal linkages in social science are no different from those used in natural science – since all modern science, as we have seen, must accept a 'rational' conception of time. The only real difference between prediction in the cultural sciences and in the natural sciences is that the social scientist, given the nature of the subject matter, must always consciously place his or her own cultural values into the historical 'timeline.' As Weber puts it, 'The causal analysis of personal actions proceeds logically in exactly the same way as the causal analysis of the historical "significance" of [important events], i.e., by isolation, generalization, and the construction of judgments of possibility.' This procedure must logically be applied to even one's own actions: 'The valid answer to the question: why did I act in that way, constitutes a categorically formed construct which is to be raised to the level of the demonstrable judgment only by the use of abstractions. This is true even though the "demonstration" is in fact here conducted in the mind of the "acting person" himself' (Weber 1949, 177).

Adopting this perspective, however, forces the social scientist to assess the 'causes' of his or her own epistemological, ontological, and methodological stances – including the reasons for his or her very commitment to the modern scientific enterprise. Thus a certain degree of 'subjectivity' is introduced into the social-scientific enterprise that need not be present – or at least, need not be made conscious – among natural scientists. Once one faces the demonstrable fact that modern science is itself a social activity – a collective product of interpretive beings – then there is no way to escape the conclusion that one's choice of profession and of subject matter must reflect on some level the subjective value orientations that one brings to scientific activity as a predictable result of one's upbringing and socialization in a particular historical and geographical context. And yet the logical operations involved in proving or disproving hypotheses about the ideal-typical 'developmental tendencies' of interpretive beings are not thereby changed.

In sum, Weberian interpretive sociology arms the analyst with three crucial conceptual tools for engaging in scientific prediction. First, Weberian analysis, uniquely among major social-scientific paradigms, emphasizes the causal importance of the subjective orientations of social actors in determining the course of institutional development and broader cultural change – a factor often downplayed or ignored by competing theoretical approaches. Second, Weberian social scientists will tend to be especially sensitive to their own subjective biases, and thus be better prepared to guard against the human tendency to let these biases unconsciously colour the conclusions of scientific analysis. Third, forearmed with a clear understanding of the conceptual distinctions among prophecy, wisdom, and scientific prediction, Weberians should, in principle, have an easier time admitting when their favoured hypotheses do fail, since they make no claims to prophetic infallibility or traditional authority that might be damaged by honesty in this sphere. 'In science,' Weber emphasizes, 'each of us knows that what he has accomplished will be antiquated in ten, twenty, fifty years. That is the fate to which science is subjected; it is the very meaning of scientific work ... Every scientific "fulfilment" raises new "questions"; it asks to be "surpassed" and outdated. Whoever wishes to serve science has to resign himself to this fact' (Weber 1946, 138).[6]

Weber's Theory of 'Developmental Tendencies'

We are now brought back to the question with which this essay began: why, exactly, have Weberian and neo-Weberian predictions of social outcomes frequently been so accurate? In fact, Weber's implicit embrace of a non-sociobiological Darwinian perspective on social evolution makes his theory scientifically far more 'rational' – in the sense described in this essay – than is typical of the contemporary political science mainstream. Weber's sociology provides general theoretical predictions about how human belief systems emerge, are consolidated against environmental threats, and then either reproduce themselves over time or become 'extinct.' To restate some of Weber's main propositions in brief: Weberian theory states that only charismatic leaders who convince their followers that their principles are beyond the ordinary constraints of time and space ever manage to create enduring new rituals in turbulent social environments; that such charismatic movements can survive and generate social power only to the extent that they routinize and develop institutions to defend and enforce their principles; that internal conflicting imperatives between formal and substantive rationality can undermine the stability of even the most established and materially powerful regimes; and finally, that informal 'cultural' responses to formal institutional orders may endure long after those orders themselves disappear. These general 'developmental tendencies' in human history generate a wide range of quite testable empirical hypotheses about social development (Kalberg 1994). And the history of the rise, consolidation, and collapse of Leninist regimes presents an ideal empirical context for testing them.

Thus, Collins's correct prediction that the Soviet Union would collapse was built around his simultaneous appreciation of the internal decay of the Communist Party's charismatic legitimation and his evaluation of the increasing geopolitical threat to the Soviet bloc in an era of triumphant Western capitalism, which he argued was producing a rapid decline of the USSR's *Machtprestige* (Collins 1986). Jowitt's correct prediction that 'democratic and capitalist transitions' in post-communist Europe would likely remain incomplete as the result of the cultural legacies of Leninism throughout the region was built upon Weber's proposition that traces longstanding informal cultural values to the earlier imposition of rigidly bounded regime types; thus the continuing evidence of 'neo-traditionalism' in much of the former Soviet Union is unsurprising (Jowitt 1992). That 'movements of rage' advocating radical anti-Western ideologies would emerge after the end of the Cold War, and that in particular, Afghanistan after the Soviet invasion would become a danger to the entire world, could be predicted scientifically from the tendency for new charismatic movements promoting radically novel ways of life (such as the Taliban) to emerge in turbulent, frontier environments (Jowitt 1992). Finally, my own predictions about the fragility of Russia's 'instrumental democracy' were built upon my assessment that no charismatic principle in the post-communist Russian context was likely to inspire 'value rational' commitments to political collective action (Hanson 2001; 2003).

The predictive success of all these risky, falsifiable hypotheses seems to be more than enough reason for scholars to join in the further development of the Weberian social-scientific paradigm. Is this likely to occur? Along the lines suggested in this essay, we can approach this question, too, scientifically. In fact, the embrace of a truly scientific social science seems scientifically unlikely. First, the incentive structures currently entrenched in academic institutions do not tend to reward value-free scholarship: powerful figures in the social science mainstream continue, consciously or unconsciously, to promote younger scholars who share their particular political value commitments, while many students and broader public audiences continue, as in Weber's time, to reward academic social scientists who try to provide prophetic insights rather than simply apply and explain scientific procedures. Instrumentally rational graduate students will thus likely continue to gravitate toward currently dominant social science approaches.

The spread of the Weberian paradigm thus depends upon the very unlikely 'charismatic conversion' of a core group of scholars to a viewpoint that is fundamentally at odds both with the usual charismatic promise of time transcendence *and* with the embrace of traditional conceptions of the good life. Weber's own famous attempt to wrestle with this paradox concluded that science 'as a vocation' – that is, as a charismatic personal mission – meant facing the 'disenchantment of the world' squarely and starkly, since science could never answer the central question of how we should live. Instead, the main value of social science would be its ability to produce 'self-clarification' (Weber 1946). A century later, Weberian social science remains in a distinctly marginal position. The evidence suggests that institutional disincentives, combined with the psychological discomfort necessarily involved in embracing the Weberian theoretical perspective, makes it nearly impossible for Weberians to attract mass professional support. If Weberian theory is right, then, I predict that Weberian social science, despite its predictive accuracy relative to its competitors, will remain a minority viewpoint.

NOTES

The author would like to thank Laurence McFalls and Steve Pfaff for their comments on earlier drafts of this essay. Another version of this essay appeared in Vladimir Tismaneanu, Marc Morjé Howard, and Rudra Sil, eds., *World Order after Leninism*, Seattle: University of Washington Press, 2006, 209–24.

1 Sceptics might say that these predictions about the long-run trends within capitalist society are too vague and general to count as empirically falsifiable hypotheses. Yet when one compares Weber's conclusions at the end of the *Protestant Ethic* to other great social theorists' similarly general predictions about capitalism's future – such as Marx's (1978 [1848]) prophecy of global proletarian revolution, Polanyi's (1944) assertion that only

democratic socialism could forestall the global victory of fascism, and Schumpeter's (1947) forecast that capitalism would be replaced by bureaucratic socialism – the remarkable accuracy of Weber's analysis of future trends within modern capitalism becomes clearer.

2 The work of the eminent political scientist David Laitin – whose work, I should emphasize, is certainly thought provoking and intellectually serious – provides one example. Laitin (1991) predicted – one month after the August coup – that the USSR would not collapse along the lines of its national republics; and Laitin (1998) predicted that Russian-speakers in the non-Russian former Soviet republics would increasingly embrace a new political identity as 'the Russian-speaking population.' Yet no one argues that rational choice theory should be rejected because of Laitin's predictive failures.

3 An admirable exception to this trend is John Gerring (2001, 126): 'A theory that is able to predict election results six months in advance of an election is superior (ceteris paribus) to one that can predict results only a week ahead ... The closer one moves to the outcome of interest, the less useful a prediction is likely to be. Earthquake warnings that arrive seconds before · the earthquake itself are scarcely predictions at all, in the normal sense of the term. Comets, eclipses, and other natural occurrences, on the other hand, have been predicted decades, sometimes even centuries, in advance of their occurrence. These are better.'

4 Goldstone (1998), in his critique of Somers, rightly emphasizes the importance of scientific 'laws' to evolutionary biology – contrary to the assumptions of many historical institutionalists.

5 This, by the way, is the step not taken by sociobiology, which in its assumption that strictly genetic mechanisms are responsible for all forms of social change implicitly leaves relatively short-term changes in political ideologies and regimes (such as the rise and fall of the USSR, which quite obviously cannot be explained by changes in the gene pool) out of the realm of scientific analysis. In this way, sociobiology, despite its scientific pretensions, is actually less threatening to the pride and sense of autonomy typical of contemporary homo sapiens than would be a thoroughgoing rational social science.

6 Some readers may object that Weber's ideal-typical description of scientific modesty merely amounts to an unenforceable call to abandon 'degenerating' research programs that in the end differs little from Lakatos's position. It is true, of course, that no philosophy of science can guarantee the scientific integrity of those who formally embrace it. The emergence of

a corrupt, hegemonic Weberianism whose leading figures fail to admit their predictive errors is admittedly a sociological possibility. It is my contention, however, that the extreme degree of scholarly self-consciousness required by Weber's reflexive sociology acts as a serious check on the tendency of social scientists to justify the endless refining of established 'theoretical' propositions without engaging in sustained empirical testing.

REFERENCES

Bates, Robert, et al. 1998. *Analytic Narratives*. Princeton: Princeton University Press.

Collins, Randall. 1986. *Weberian Sociological Theory*. Cambridge: Cambridge University Press.

Gerring, John. 2001. *Social Science Methodology: A Criterial Framework*. Cambridge: Cambridge University Press.

Goldstone, Jack A. 1998. 'Initial Conditions, General Laws, Path Dependence, and Explanation in Historical Sociology.' *American Journal of Sociology* 104(3): 829–45.

Hanson, Stephen E. 1991. 'Gorbachev: The Last True Leninist Believer?' In *The Crisis of Leninism and the Decline of the Left*, ed. Daniel Chirot, 33–59. Seattle: University of Washington Press.

– 1997. *Time and Revolution: Marxism and the Design of Soviet Institutions*. Chapel Hill: University of North Carolina Press.

– 2001. 'The Dilemmas of Russia's Anti-Revolutionary Revolution.' *Current History* 100(648): 330–6.

– 2003. 'Instrumental Democracy: The End of Ideology and the Decline of Russian Political Parties.' In *The Elections of 1999–2000 in Russia: Their Impact and Legacy*, ed. Vicki L. Hesli and William M. Reisinger, 163–85. Cambridge: Cambridge University Press.

Hanson, Stephen E., and Jeffrey S. Kopstein. 1997. 'The Weimar/Russia Comparison.' *Post-Soviet Affairs* 13(3): 252–83.

Hempel, Carl. 1952. *Fundamentals of Concept Formation in Empirical Science*. Chicago: University of Chicago Press.

Howard, Marc Morje. 2003. *The Weakness of Civil Society in Post-Communist Europe*. Cambridge: Cambridge University Press.

Jowitt, Ken. 1992. *New World Disorder: The Leninist Extinction*. Berkeley: University of California Press.

Kalberg, Stephen. 1994. *Max Weber's Comparative-Historical Sociology*. Chicago: University of Chicago Press.

King, Gary, Robert O. Keohane, and Sidney Verba. 1994. *Designing Social Inquiry: Scientific Inference in Qualitative Research*. Princeton: Princeton University Press.

Kuhn, Thomas. 1962. *The Structure of Scientific Revolutions*. Chicago: University of Chicago Press.

Laitin, David D. 1991. 'The National Uprisings in the Soviet Union.' *World Politics* 44(1): 139–77.

– 1998. *Identity in Formation: The Russian-Speaking Populations in the Near Abroad*. Ithaca: Cornell University Press.

Lakatos, Imre, and Alan Musgrave. 1970. *Criticism and the Growth of Knowledge*. Cambridge: Cambridge University Press.

Levi, Margaret. 1997. *Consent, Dissent, and Patriotism*. Cambridge: Cambridge University Press.

Marx, Karl, and Friedrich Engels. 1978 (1848). *Manifesto of the Communist Party*. In *The Marx-Engels Reader*. Ed. Robert C. Tucker, 469–500. New York: Norton.

McKeown, Timothy. 1999. 'Case Studies and the Statistical Worldview: Review of King, Keohane, and Verba's "Designing Social Inquiry: Scientific Inference in Qualitative Research."' *International Organization*, 53(1): 161–90.

Murrell, Peter. 1993. 'What Is Shock Therapy? What Did It Do in Poland and Russia?' *Post-Soviet Affairs*, 9(2): 111–40.

Ordeshook, Peter C. 1995. 'Engineering or Science: What Is the Study of Politics?' In *The Rational Choice Controversy: Economic Models of Politics Reconsidered*. Ed. Jeffrey Friedman, 175–88. New Haven: Yale University Press.

Polanyi, Karl. 1944. *The Great Transformation*. New York: Farrar and Rinehart.

Popper, Karl. 1959. *The Logic of Scientific Discovery*. London: Hutchinson.

Schumpeter, Joseph A. 1947. *Capitalism, Socialism, and Democracy*. New York: Harper and Brothers.

Scott, James. 1998. *Seeing Like a State: How Certain Schemes to Improve the Human Condition Have Failed*. New Haven: Yale University Press.

Somers, Margaret. 1998. '"We're No Angels": Realism, Rational Choice, and Relationality in the Social Sciences.' *American Journal of Sociology*, 104(3): 722–84.

Weber, Max. 1946. 'Science as a Vocation.' In *From Max Weber: Essays in Sociology*. Ed. H.H. Gerth and C. Wright Mills, 129–56. New York: Oxford University Press.

– 1949. '"Objectivity" of Knowledge in Social Science and Social Policy.' In

Max Weber, *The Methodology of the Social Sciences*. Ed. Edward A. Shils and Henry A. Finch, 49–112. New York: Free Press.
– 1968. *Economy and Society*. 2 vols. Trans. and ed. Guenther Roth and Claus Wittich. Berkeley: University of California Press.
– 2002. *The Protestant Ethic and the Spirit of Capitalism*. Trans. Stephen Kalberg. Los Angeles: Roxbury.

13 Weber, Objectivity, and the Classics of Comparative Politics

JEFFREY KOPSTEIN

During a fellowship year at Princeton I had the pleasure one evening of being seated at a banquet table right next to a famous philosopher. As we ate dinner, the conversation gradually turned to what kinds of readings we assign our graduate students. Eager to show how well educated I was and how much I insisted that my students be educated, too, I informed my conversation partner that I began my graduate core seminars in comparative politics with a three-week tour through the classics of social theory, moving on to the ups and downs of modernization and dependency theory in the post-war United States, and then proceeding to contemporary debates about institutions, rationality, ideas and their impact on modern political life. His response? 'No one should read anything published more than ten years ago.'

After catching my breath, I tried valiantly to defend the proposition that graduate students should be acquainted with the 'classics' in the field so that they know there *is* a field and will be able to teach it. His response? 'Why bother? I promise you that in physics or chemistry nobody is reading anything older than ten years.' But what about in philosophy, what about Plato and Aristotle? I asked. His response: 'If you are interested in the history of philosophy, fine, but if you are interested in *doing* philosophy, then you don't need to read all that old stuff.' I'm afraid that I did not do a very good job defending my position in favour of reading the 'classics' in a given field. He had clearly engaged in this debate many, many times before, and I was ill-equipped both by training and, obviously, by raw intellect to win this battle. What was self-evident, however, is that he was operating with a particular model of knowledge, which postulates that the purpose of inquiry is accumulation and that any pursuit of knowledge over time that is not cumulative may be enjoyable but it is not to be taken seriously.

My intuition tells me that I am right, that we should be reading the classics, and as a Weberian I think that Weber should be able to provide us with some guidance on the matter. Even so, in what follows, I do not attempt a full defence of the proposition that we should be reading the classics. I simply try to make comprehensible the empirical observation that we *do* read them. In doing so, I hope to shed light on some ambiguities in Weber's suggestions to the social scientist and the ambiguous legacy of Weber's writings for North American political science.

My points are simple ones and they are twofold. First, the Princeton philosopher's views were far closer to Weber's own stated views on the subject than I had ever appreciated. Ideal-typical scientific work for Weber is slow and cumulative. We can only thank fate, therefore, that Weber did not follow his own advice.

Second, given that we are still reading Weber one hundred years after he composed both his influential methodological and famous substantive essays (especially *The Protestant Ethic*), it is logical to ask, what makes a classic? Why do some authors and their work get read over and over again, decades, in fact, after their insights have been surpassed or even refuted? What 'causes' a classic? The answer to this question can be approached in a Weberian fashion. On the one hand, Weber's ideal-type of science and the motivations of the ideal-typical practitioner of science would preclude the existence of 'classics.' Nothing old would ever be read. On the other hand, since Weber's ideal-type of science or scientist exists nowhere empirically, the Weberian method suggests that we can look for the causes of real classics in the deviations from the type. With this point in mind, it makes sense to look for the causes of classics in the non-scientific rationalities that co-constitute actual scientific practice. The point here is not simply to use Weber to understand Weber's continued popularity as a phenomenon – though there is nothing wrong with doing so – but rather to inquire about what causes some bodies of work, including Weber's, to be read with fresh eyes by each new generation of scholars. The evidence from political science suggests that the durability of an author's corpus is not only a function of sound scientific method but is also determined by the ethical motivation for the work itself. If methodology constitutes the formal rationality of social science, moral purpose provides the substantive rationality. One without the other renders the enterprise either purely subjective or meaningless.

Weber between Art and Science

Weber's point of departure in 'Science as a Vocation' is much closer to the cumulative model of inquiry than is normally appreciated. After a highly illuminating analysis of the rationalization of German and American academic life that is remarkable for how little has changed since it was written, Weber turns his attention to 'the inward calling' of science. As others have noted, in invoking 'vocation,' Weber's man of science bears remarkable resemblance to the Protestant hero in his study of Western capitalism.[1] The modern scholar works methodically and rationally. Success in science requires above all, Weber tells us, realizing, first, that any significant achievement means specialization. Syntheses across fields are possible but must remain 'highly imperfect.' 'And whoever lacks the capacity to put on blinders, so to speak, and come up to the idea that the fate of his soul depends upon whether or how he makes the correct conjecture at this passage of this manuscript may as well stay away from science.'[2] Weber characterizes the motivation to rational and specialized inquiry as a form of 'intoxication.'[3] Yet even with intoxicated enthusiasm the scholar can never really know whether what he or she has come up with is important or trivial and can never be sure when inspiration will come or what the true sources of inspiration are. For this reason, the scholar can never be certain whether or not he or she will ever distill one important idea in his or her life. In this way, the scholar faces the same sort of uncertainty as the Puritan, though, to be sure, professional obscurity is far more comfortable than eternal damnation.[4]

Weber's emphasis on uncertainty and inspiration leads him to draw the comparison between scientific work and art. Just as with artistic creation, scholarly work requires inspiration. Unlike a work of art, however, which may remain important for hundreds or even thousands of years, modern scientific work 'is chained to the course of progress.' The purpose of art for Weber is 'fulfillment.'[5] The purpose of science, however, is knowledge. Yet knowledge comes only at the price of longevity. 'In science, each of us knows that what he has accomplished will be antiquated in ten, twenty, or fifty years. That is the fate to which science is subjected; it is the very *meaning* of scientific work ... Every scientific "fulfillment" raises new "questions"; it asks to be "surpassed" and outdated. Whoever wishes to serve science has to resign himself to this fact.'[6]

With these words, Weber appears to place himself squarely in the camp that views science as a cumulative project.[7] The implications of this view for Weber, and for the rest of us, are potentially profound. Two at least are worth mentioning. First, cumulative knowledge will be specialized knowledge, and specialized knowledge – even if it requires inspiration – will be a slow, incremental, project – to take a phrase from 'Politics as a Vocation,' akin to the 'slow boring of boards.'[8] The purveyor of the broad synthesis will not approximate the scholarly ideal-type as much as the narrower specialist. Second, because all scholarship will be surpassed, it really does not make much sense to speak of a classic in social science, except in a purely historical sense of work that pushed the field forward in either a small or a large way at a specific point in the development of a discipline. So while historians of science may write book after book about Newton and Darwin, physicists and biologists today do not need to read either, and they do not. The same goes for social science. Why bother with Talcott Parsons or Pitrim Sorokin or Paul Lazarsfeld? Or Max Weber, for that matter?

Two pieces of evidence suggest that Weber's ideal-type of science deviated from actual practice, at least in the case of the social sciences. Even if he was right about how science should be practised (the 'ought'), he was dead wrong about how it actually is practised (the 'is'). In the first place, Weber obviously did not practise what he preached. Instead of working with a model of slow accumulation within a well-defined framework, Weber set out to define the framework itself. Even more importantly, however, Weber was the greatest synthesizer of the twentieth century who became best known for his works drawing on multiple disciplines and languages. Although Weber did not take shortcuts in his scholarship, it would be equally wrong to view him as one slowly boring through scholarly boards. His most enduring work remains his comparative studies on the effects of the great world religions on variations in economic ethics and political authority, a project that spanned two thousand years and several language groups. In short, Weber was anything but an intellectual 'organization man.'

Second, if Weber ignored his own advice, subsequent scholars ignored his advice, too. After all, we are still reading Weber's methodological essays one century after they were written, all in the Faustian hope of great scholarly synthesis and historical insight. Furthermore, political scientists continue to read not only Weber but also important scholars from every decade of the twentieth century, and they read them because they believe that the insights they derive from these books and articles make their scholarship better, deeper, more encompassing, and therefore of more universal and *lasting* value than it otherwise would have been. It is the enduring quality of great scholarship in social science that needs to be examined if the deviations from Weber's ideal-typical model of science are to be explained.

Simply put, there are classics in social science. Some books and articles endure. This empirical observation raises the question, why is this the case? The most obvious hypothesis that comes to mind is that in the social sciences we do not in fact work with a cumulative model of knowledge. A rival hypothesis is that we *do* operate with a cumulative model of knowledge but have made precious little progress in answering any question of social-scientific import. For this reason the questions authors of classics raise are of enduring value and continue to stimulate the scholarly imaginations of subsequent generations. In this view, classics are defined by questions, not by answers or sound scientific procedure. But even these observations, as fundamental as they may sound, still leave open the question of what makes a classic a classic. Why do we read Weber a hundred years after the fact? I have no definitive answer to this question, but several plausible candidates come to mind. In what follows I turn to these questions by way of assessing the role of objectivity in political science.

Objectivity and the Classics of Modern Political Science

If we treat Weber's statement on the rationalization of science from 'Science as a Vocation' as a hypothesis, and if we add onto that the complex treatment of objectivity in his methodological essays, we should expect that in fact there are few enduring classics in the field. Furthermore, following the logic inherent in the Weberian ideal-typical model of science, those few works that do endure should be characterized by exceptionally self-conscious use of concepts and methods, so that scholars may still use them as points of departure in their own work. To what extent is this true? How much attention do the classics of social science devote to questions of method and objectivity in social analysis? In what follows I approach these questions with examples from comparative politics, the subfield of political science whose practitioners have been most influenced by Weber's work.

The consensual classics in comparative politics, such as the work of Reinhard Bendix, Barrington Moore, and Samuel Huntington, all embark upon contextualized comparisons using ideal-typical taxonomies of regime types and carefully selected cases in order to distill carefully bounded generalizations. On the one hand, all of these works reside intellectually within a well-defined framework, primarily as scholarly responses to Parsonian modernization theory. Although these are ambitious, synthetic works, each of these scholars pushed comparative politics forward by chipping away at the edifice of evolutionary social theory. Bendix's *Nation-Building and Citizenship* and *Kings or People* are both designed to highlight the particular experience of the West compared to other parts of the world, in order to illustrate enduring patterns of political authority.[9] Barrington Moore's *Social Origins of Dictatorship and Democracy* illustrates how different class coalitions in the pre-modern world produce systematically different regime types in the modern world.[10] Samuel Huntington's *Political Order in Changing Societies* shows how social change may produce as much political strain as it does democracy.[11]

It is important to note, however, that while each of these books is methodologically very self-conscious in its use of concepts, the authors do not devote an inordinate amount of time to definitional issues. Barrington Moore begins his *Social Origins* without any elaborate discussion of the concepts of class or democracy, even though his book is about the relationship between the two. Furthermore, the first three cases in *Social Origins* – England, France, and the United States – all share similar values on their independent and dependent variables. In sum, Moore illustrates the 'same' case – bourgeois dominance leading to representative government – three times before turning to cases where other classes retain the lions' share of power. No attempt is made to justify the case selection except to say that these were three powerful and independent states.[12] Not only does Moore eschew any conceptual or methodological discussion at the outset of his work, he also refuses to generalize. Instead he dives directly into the histories of England, France, and the United States, and returns to questions of generalization only after all of the evidence has been presented, at the end of the (long) book.

Moving from Harvard to Berkeley, even Reinhard Bendix, a scholar known much more for his commitment to conceptual clarity than causal explanation, is remembered by his graduate students to have issued injunctions against over-conceptualization and needless theorization: they were summed up in his quip about the Weberian conceptual predisposition by quoting the supposed first line of a German train schedule: '*Unter Eisenbahn ist zu verstehen ...*' (By train we mean ...). And on theory, when asked by a graduate student about the absence of a 'theoretical chapter' from Toqueville's *Ancien Regime*, Bendix is reported to have said, 'Aristocrats do not write long methodological introductions,' meaning, among other things, that the theory was embedded in the narrative.[13] Also in Berkeley, Chalmers Johnson, the scholar who invented the notion of the capitalist developmental state in his path-breaking – and by now classic – book on industrial policy in Japan, was heard more than once to warn young job candidates against 'blowing up an outhouse with a howitzer.'[14]

Weber also viewed methodological reflection in purely instrumental terms, as the means to better empirical research, and not an end in itself. As he notes in his criticism of Meyer (in a rare moment of agreement),

> Methodology can only bring us reflective understanding of the means which have demonstrated their value in practice by raising them to the level of explicit consciousness; it is no more the precondition for fruitful intellectual work than the knowledge of anatomy is the precondition for 'correct' walking. Indeed, just as the person who attempted to govern his mode of walking continuously by anatomical knowledge would be in danger of stumbling, so the professional scholar who attempted to determine the aims of his own research extrinsically on the basis of methodological reflections would be in danger of falling into the same difficulties.[15]

For Weber the key point of objectivity is that once a particular 'problem setting' has been discerned, then, and only then, should the analysis of the data be 'an end in itself. It will discontinue assessing the value of individual facts in terms of their relationships to ultimate value-ends. Indeed it will lose its awareness of its ultimate rootedness in the value-ideas in general.'[16] But what kind of practical advice is this? How does one go about ensuring that facts are not assessed in terms of 'ultimate value ideas'? How one accomplishes such a result in comparative historical work is something that Weber does not address specifically in his methodological essays. But he does provide us with important clues. Maintaining objectivity for Weber and the great scholars of postwar comparative politics meant not only conceptual clarity (which obviously mattered to Weber a great deal – otherwise why bother with *Economy and Society* at all?) and maximizing inferential leverage through careful case selection (which Weber also cared deeply about – otherwise why would he have immersed himself in the histories of so many 'exotic' religions and cultures), but it also required cultivating a keen sense of historical irony. The Puritan did not intend to create capitalism, and the capitalist did not intend to create the iron cage of modernity, but that is what happened. The 'irrationality' of religious belief justified and contributed to the creation of modern capitalist rationality, which in turn created a new kind of irrationality – the 'polar night of icy darkness' of bureaucratic politics and economy.[17] A keen sense of irony also informs the classics of postwar comparative politics, because ethically 'good' results (democracy for Moore or stability for Huntington) could often come from ethically 'bad' antecedents (war, repression, violence, Leninism). At the same time, Bendix warned us, movements that cast off the moral restraints of liberalism in the developing world could arise in response to the successful liberalism of the West.

In yet another classic of postwar political science, Ralf Dahrendorf argued in *Society and Democracy in Germany* that Hitler paved the way for postwar German democracy by destroying the pre-modern social order that constituted the foundation of German authoritarianism.[18] The painful irony for Dahrendorf is that if the aristocratic opposition to Hitler (which Dahrendorf labels 'counterrevolutionary') had succeeded in one of their assassination attempts, the future of democracy would have been far less certain than in a defeated Nazi Germany.

This sense of irony is to be found at the very core of Weber's thinking on social science and is summed up in his notion of 'unintended consequences.' Irony is what permits the social scientist to distance him- or herself from the moral valence of root causes being examined or macropolitical outcomes being accounted for and to evaluate both in a dispassionate way. One reason that we continue to read the classics in social science is that they provide us with object lessons in the use of irony for obtaining scholarly objectivity.

So it appears at first glance that Weber's injunctions about objectivity have informed much of modern political science and account to a significant degree for why classics become classics. Each of the books mentioned above deployed concepts self-consciously and carefully; each is meticulous in its selection of cases (Moore, in fact, to the point where he chose the Asian cases of Japan and China for illustrating Fascism and Communism rather than the German and Russian cases, which he knew far better); each is able to achieve scholarly distance from causes or outcomes that may be potentially displeasing.

Yet this is only part of the story, for at the end of the day, each of these books has been subject, more or less, to empirical attack, and yet each of them continues to be widely read. Weber's work on the relationship of

Protestantism to capitalism has withstood over a century of withering empirical attack. The same holds for the decades of criticism endured by Moore's *Social Origins*. After almost forty years, there is hardly anything left in Barrington Moore's book that has not been criticized, repeatedly. His selective use of evidence and historiography in particular stands out. Indeed, when rereading the volume, one is struck by the footnotes and how the same sources are cited over and over again, suggesting to even the non-specialist that there were certain books that 'helped' Moore make his case. In an important essay on the use of historiography in comparative politics, Ian Lustick goes so far as to say that Moore was guilty of selection bias in his use of historiography.[19] Each major issue in the historiography of France or Japan or China contains a great debate, and Moore generally accepts the side in the debate that supports his interpretive needs. This same criticism, as Lustick notes, could be mounted against virtually every major work in comparative politics in the postwar era, and against Weber's own *Protestant Ethic and the Spirit of Capitalism*, for that matter. Note that the point here is not that there are empirical errors in great works but that most authors of the 'classics' in comparative politics do not easily pass a strict version of an 'objectivity' test.

Why then, if not on grounds of scholarly objectivity, do these books continue to be read? I suggest they continue to be read not only because of their methodological rigour but also because of the moral valence of the questions they pose and the answers they provide. It is important to recall that Weber had nothing against the motivation for empirical research deriving from normative concerns. Weber merely held that competing values could not be adjudicated by rational inquiry. Empirical inquiry could inform us about the costs and benefits of pursuing conflicting values in society, but it could not adjudicate which values were the right ones. But once this point was understood, the scholar was free to allow his or her values to motivate the study of a subject.

Let us once again consider Moore in this regard. Moore's volume is actually about many things. In the context of modernization theory it was understood as a book about the multiple paths into the modern world. As a critique of modernization theory, however, it is also an impassioned plea for the importance of violence in each society's pathway from traditional to modern society. It is worth recalling that the book's first chapter, on England, carries the subtitle 'The Contribution of Violence to Gradualism.' The subsequent chapter on France highlights the importance of the terror in ensuring a decisive break with the pre-modern order. And, in the following chapter, Moore's much neglected case study of the United States, the Civil War is portrayed as the 'real' American revolution without which the United States would have been left with a society divided between a highly industrialized North and a slave owning 'Junker'-like South much more akin to the *Kaiserreich* than to England. In short, the road to democracy, or any viable institutional order for Moore, was paved with blood, lots of blood. In the context of when it was published, in 1966, it is easy to see the implication for Moore's American readers: who were they to deny the Vietnamese their own revolution, when it appeared that the precondition of their own modernization was something, if not identical to the carnage of the American Civil War, then at least in the same family of political events? Moore's sense of irony allowed his book to be both 'objective' (in that there was at least some group of historians who would agree with each and every one of his interpretive points, even if none would agree on all) and morally charged at the same time. And it was this combination that helped transform the book from a comparative study of lord and peasant in the modern world to a classic of comparative politics. Similar observations could be made about virtually any book in modern social science that acquires the status of a 'classic.'[20]

Of course, as is so often the case with Weber, rereading Weber's essay on objectivity in the social sciences illustrates that Weber understood this point very well. Indeed, within Weber's own work the evidence is quite convincing that he believed objective analysis could occur only after the substantive end of the inquiry, the value orientation of the scholar, had been clearly identified. As he states in '"Objectivity,"' 'These view points are necessary in order to engage in an empirical science of concrete reality which seeks to understand the cultural significance of individual events in their contemporary manifestations and the causes of their being historically so and not otherwise.'[21]

This much is fairly easy to accept. Ultimate ends motivate objective analysis in a two-stage process where the first (the motivation) does not contaminate the second (the analysis). But even Weber was uncertain whether the two could so easily be quarantined from each other. In '"Objectivity" in Social Science,' after many pages of dense prose, in the deservedly famous final paragraph Weber begins by reiterating the importance of the fact–value distinction for practical research by imploring us to remember that once the purpose of the study has been established, we can 'discontinue assessing the value of individual facts in terms of their relationships to ultimate value-ideas.' He ends the thought with a semi-biblical 'And it is well that it should be so.' At that point, however, Weber provides us with the most important caveat in his thinking on social science methodology.

> But there comes a moment when the atmosphere changes. The significance of the unreflectively utilized viewpoints becomes uncertain and the road is lost in the twilight. The light of the great cultural problems moves on. Then too science prepares to change its standpoint and its analytical apparatus and to view the streams of events from the heights of thought. It follows those stars which alone are able to give meaning and direction to its labors.[22]

These lines have been read any number of ways by students of Weber's thought. In terms of this essay, however, they suggest that Weber was deeply conflicted about a cumulative model of knowledge for the social sciences and about his ideal-type of scientific inquiry. Whereas objectivity required a strict separation of fact from value in the course of inquiry, inquiry itself and external circumstance itself could undermine the very distinction between the two by rendering our concepts meaningless. At that point, we need to review and renew our conceptual apparatus in light of concerns that seem more relevant. That relevance, as determined by the underlying moral motivation and significance of the work, is what makes a classic a classic and accounts, to some extent at any rate, for why we continue to read them.

In this respect, it is useful to recall that the classics of ancient Greece themselves went unread for over one thousand years. Only when circumstances seemed to give them renewed meaning did Renaissance Europeans turn to them. They read Aristotle and Plato because these thinkers spoke to the problems of the age. This suggests that, contrary to the cumulative model of knowledge, with which Weber obviously did not completely agree and was in any case undercut by his understanding that external circumstances may render concepts irrelevant, in the social sciences we return to books written long ago not because they deal with human problems that are eternal – that there are few such problems accounts for the fact that all scholarship appears at some point in time to be obsolete – but because they address problems that eternally recur. For the social scientist, the concerns that Weber raised and addressed in his methodological essays recur time and again, and for that reason his work on the subject is still profitably read.

NOTES

1 Sheldon Wolin, 'Max Weber: Legitimation, Method, and the Politics of Theory,' *Political Theory* 9, no. 3 (1981): 401–24.
2 Max Weber, 'Science as a Vocation,' in *From Max Weber: Essays in Sociology*, ed. H.H. Gerth and C. Wright Mills (Oxford: Oxford University Press, 1946), 135.
3 Ibid.
4 Ibid.
5 Ibid., 13.
6 Ibid.
7 This is admittedly only one way of reading this passage, albeit one that if accurate contains profound implications for Weber's work as a whole. Alternatively, one could argue that the cited passages from *Science as a Vocation* should be read in a Popperian mode as a discussion of the 'logic of discovery' in science, rather than a discussion of the problem of refuting or verifying theories. Without engaging in a lengthy defence of the proposition that Weber supports a 'cumulative growth' model of science, it is enough at this point simply to acknowledge the plausibility of alternative readings of a frequently ambiguous text.
8 Max Weber, 'Politics as a Vocation,' in Gerth and Mills, *From Max Weber*, 128.
9 Reinhard Bendix, *Nation-Building and Citizenship: Studies of Our Changing Social Order* (New York: Doubleday, 1969); Reinhard Bendix, *Kings or People: Power and the Mandate to Rule* (Berkeley: University of California Press, 1978).
10 Barrington Moore, *Social Origins of Dictatorship and Democracy: Lord and Peasant in the Making of the Modern World* (Boston: Beacon, 1967).
11 Samuel P. Huntington, *Political Order in Changing Societies* (New Haven: Yale University Press, 1968).
12 'Does not the exclusion of the smaller Western democratic states produce a certain antipeasant bias throughout the whole book? To this objection there is, I think, an impersonal answer. This study concentrates on certain important stages in a prolonged social process which has worked itself out in several countries. As part of this process new social arrangements have grown up ... which have made certain countries political leaders at different points in time during the first half of the twentieth century ... The fact that the smaller countries depend economically and politically on big and powerful ones means that the decisive causes of their politics lie outside their own boundaries. Therefore a general statement about the historical

preconditions of democracy or authoritarianism covering small countries as well as large would very likely be so broad as to be abstractly platitudinous.' Moore, *Social Origins*, xiii.

13 I am grateful to Laurence McFalls for pointing out an alternative reading of this quip. It is possibly a commentary on the importance of social position in the production of classics. It is true that a disproportionate number of great works have been produced by wealthy outsiders who make their intellectual homes only at the edges of the academy.

14 Chalmers Johnson, *MITI and the Japanese Miracle: The Growth of Industrial Policy, 1925–1975* (Stanford: Stanford University Press, 1982).

15 Max Weber, *The Methodology of the Social Sciences* (Glencoe, IL: Free Press, 1964), 115.

16 Ibid., 112.

17 Weber, 'Politics as a Vocation,' 128.

18 Ralf Dahrendorf, *Society and Democracy in Germany* (New York: Doubleday, 1969).

19 Ian Lustick, 'History, Historiography, and Political Science: Multiple Historical Records and the Problem of Selection Bias,' *American Political Science Review* 90, no. 3 (1996): 605–18.

20 A further attribute of classics is one that does not easily fit into this framework, yet surely counts as one of the non-scientific rationalities that is co-constitutive of actual scientific practice. I refer here to the esthetic quality of a given author's work. It is no accident that many of the classics of social science, such as Moore's *Social Origins* and Huntington's *Political Order*, are beautifully written. Weber himself noted Ranke's artistic genius even as he complained that the historian offered neither original ideas nor new facts. Where the logic of the esthetic appeal in the social science breaks down completely and ironically, is in the case of Weber's own writings. Even his most well-known works, such as *The Protestant Ethic* and *Politics as a Vocation*, are essentially impenetrable.

21 Weber, *Methodology*, 96.

22 Ibid., 112.

14 Also One Hundred Years since Weber Flirted with Ethnography

JAMES A. BOON

Midsummer of 1904 ... This prospect of the New World was so enticing for Weber that he overcame all inhibitions and misgivings and decided to go out into the world with his wife ... They entered New York harbor early one September morning ... Weber could hardly wait for the ... customs inspection. When they went ashore he darted ahead with long, elastic strides ... like a liberated eagle finally allowed to move its wings. They headed for a twenty-story hotel in the ... business district of Manhattan Island where the ... 'capitalist spirit' of that country had created its most impressive symbols. One could virtually smell and taste the dried-up horse manure of these streets, through which heavy traffic roared. Oh God, what a contrast to Italy – Rome, Florence, Naples! Everything struck them as overwhelmingly strange: that loveless barracks for traveling salesmen in which everyone was only a number! An *'elevator'* [English] took them to the height of a church steeple and into a room that was distinguished by its bareness, a telephone, and two enormous spittoons.

Marianne Weber, 1926

The hunch of a dilettante ... may have ... greater significance than a specialist's.

Max Weber, 1919

Today we commemorate Max Weber's ever-slippery theory of objectivity, dating from questions 'customary to ask' *occasioned* 'when a social science journal ... passes into the hands of a new editorial board' (Weber 1949, 50). I heartily join in *our* occasion by co-commemorating Weber's practices of description en route to and from another 1904 occasion: St Louis's centennial and 'universal exposition.' (Contingent celebratory occasions tend to multiply!) Weber's animated travel notes and ethno-graphic sensibilities may seem more *casual* than *causal*, indeed more casual even than 'contextual, multicausal, and conjunctural causal,' in Stephen Kalberg's terms (Weber 2002, lx). Yet whether casually, caus-ally, or perhaps casual-causally ('hunchily'?), Weber's propensity for digressive deviations is patent. As Marianne conscientiously recollected, Max liked to dart hither and yon, often (I'd add) thinking of *there* when one is *here*, of *that* when the subject is *this*, and vice versa.

Might an 'elective affinity' obtain between Weber's flirting with anecdotalism and his vastly contrapuntal 'conjuncturals'? I've a theory that it does; yes, I've a hunch that his *occasional* ethnographic vignettes *underscore* Weber's profound *musicality* in 'thick comparison' (to coin a type). 'Liberated' both spatially and temporally, Marianne's eagle may soar, as in the studies of South Asia, or perch, as in the 'methodology' pieces.[1] Yet signs of such flight – now surging, now receding – never vanish from Weber's many-stranded texts with their 'vanishing media-tors' (Jameson 1988).[2]

My essay provisionally associates 'ethnography' with description that runs wilfully astray, proceeds counter-officially, respects hunches. Of course, ethnography (an ideal-type) can also be routinized and rule governed – as in professional *Notes and Queries*, 'functionalist method,' etc. And these opposed contingencies – openness and system – are not unconnected (judging always from Weber's example). To accentuate discursiveness as part of Weber's 'contrastive spirit,' is neither to ignore nor to belittle his 'objectivity' or the style that conveys it. After dallying with the charismatically casual in Weber, I promise to return to the ostensibly objective.

Via St Louis

No one today can relive Weber's stateside sojourns in 1904 (New York, Chicago, St Louis, Oklahoma, Boston, Mount Airy). We can only trace his travels' textual aftermath (with Rollmann 1993; Peacock and Tyson 1989; Keeter 1981); these include letters home, Marianne's versions, and incidents woven into the 'Protestant Sects' essay and elsewhere. More-over, we can try administering our own ethnographic sensibility when rereading his everyday, chance encounters. Imagine Weber listening, seeing, speaking, smelling, feeling, tasting, and quaffing (beer, at Co-lumbia for sure, in St Louis most likely, and in North Tonawanda perhaps!).[3] Savour Weber rolling across Indian Territory chatting with 'a traveling salesman of "undertaker's hardware" (iron letters for tomb-stones)' about his 'church-mindedness' (1946, 303).

One inviting episode occurs in North Carolina among his backwoods kinfolk whom Weber records and remembers:

> On a beautiful clear Sunday afternoon early in October, I attended a bap-tism ceremony ... to take place in a pool fed by a brook ... It was cold ... About ten persons of both sexes in their Sunday-best stepped into the pond, one after another. They avowed their faith and ... came up shaking and shivering, and everybody 'congratulated' them ... One of my relatives com-mented that 'faith' provides unfailing protection against sneezes. Another relative stood beside me and, being unchurchly in accordance with Ger-man traditions, he looked on, spitting disdainfully over the shoulder. He spoke to one of those baptised, 'Hello, Bill, wasn't the water pretty cool?' and received the very earnest reply, 'Jeff, I thought of some pretty hot place (Hell!) and so I didn't mind the cool water ...' When I asked him after the ceremony, 'Why did you anticipate the baptism of that man?' he answered, 'Because he wants to open a bank in M[ount Airy].' (1946, 304)

Weber's theoretical topic is voluntary sects versus church-by-birth and practices of credit-solidarity; his vehicle of *Verstehen* is 'thick evoca-tion' at least, and thick description incipiently. A single weakness mars (for me) these otherwise stellar 'fieldnotes': Weber names parentheti-cally (with exclamation!) the alluded-to 'hot place.' I suspect that Bill (likely a better humorist) did not: 'native' punch, ethnographers soon learn, lies in the implicit. While Weber's paragraphs may be too precise to be quite accurate, they nevertheless sport overlapping nuance, ricocheting 'points of view,' quoted backchatting, and sarcasm of prac-titioners. His vignette achieves 'play,' you might say – *soit* deep, *soit* superficial. Weber captures ambiguities of consensus *and* fragmentari-ness, action and dissension. He appreciates the interpreted themselves as interpreters and also reports follow-up interviews *after* the ceremony. Weber thereby dabbled in ethnographic excellence by Malinowski's standards as much as Geertz's (or mine).[4]

I love to teach this comparative moment: to fancy Weber regarding, eavesdropping, following through. Lingering here helps anthropology students (and professors) feel a little less 'frightened' by Weber (Geertz 1973), but only a little. He still overwhelms. Indeed, his ethnographette of Mt Airy immersion may be incidental (even 'accidental'), but it is no less intricately plural (rather like Geertz, 'before the fact') than Weber's boldest scale of *Sinn* thundering through time.[5]

Now, anecdotes themselves move around in Weber; they get recycled and conjoined (another habit of ethnographers!). Like Franklin's 'biography' in *The Protestant Ethic*, such 'accidentals' lend a palpable air. For example, Weber's 1904 visit to American-German *Vereine* is retailed in a later footnote's ear for irony-in-translation: 'When asking young German merchants in New York (with the best Hanseatic names) why they all strove to be admitted to an American club instead of the very nicely furnished [*gemütlich*?] German one, they answered that their (German-American) bosses would play billiards with them occasionally, however not without making them realize that they (the bosses) thought themselves to be "very nice" in doing so' (1946, 311).[6]

A 1911 address recalls being invited at Columbia University 'to a proper German drinking bout, with sabres and all that goes with them.' It maps contrasts in American/German voluntarism and credit-praxis: 'The American student like the German student has his societies ... The German societies are more like "insurance institutions"' (Weber 1973, 25).

'Accidence' (and accent) grows exponentially in another 1911 piece that writes of having forgotten 'in the excitement of speaking' notes written previously. Weber punctuates things with a 'brief tale' to illuminate everyday pride in German commercial firms – 'the one about' a travelling salesman who found his prices being challenged: 'The elegantly nasal reply was, almost literally: ... "You should regard the fact that I am a reserve officer as sufficient evidence that I supply only high grade goods at the best prices. I re-gret it ver-ry much." Elegant and dignified withdrawal' (1973, 38–9).

What Weber calls this 'anecdote' conveys in an 'uncomfortable way' subtleties of status snubs among contemporary businessmen. 'The dumfounded manufacturer is still laughing,' Weber quips, tossing in his own 'positionality': 'Since I have been accused ... of taking a contemptuous view of 'clerks,' let me say that my name comes from a Westphalian linen family and that I do not deny my pride in this bourgeois descent' (1973, 39).

Many readers today would want me to credit Weber here (too familiarly, perhaps) with 'reflexivity.' Instead, I'll just observe that Weber *occasionally* enacted *discours* (in the sense Kristeva adapts from Benveniste): contingency-laden and personally voiced writing, as opposed to as-if abstract *énoncé*.[7] Weber was no stranger to first-person narrative or intimate aside; such devices too graced his contrapuntal expanse – extending from 'here and now' ethnography (Mt Airy, 1904) to there-and-everywhere comparatism (over time, lots of it). Moreover, even where anecdote *seems* absent in Weber, a devotion to exception-making lends his oeuvre overall an 'ethnographic' quality. Or such is my hunch that I now diligently exploit.

On 'Objectivity' (with 'India' Perhaps Already Implicit)

I relish both Weber's scarce lapses (or lofting) into anecdote and his 'surplus' style as well: his writing's key of 'objectivity' – illustrated by such sentences as 'These points refer to "class situation," which we may express more briefly as the typical chance for a supply of goods, external living conditions, and personal life experiences, in so far as this chance is determined by the amount and kind of power, or lack of such, to dispose of goods or skills for the sake of income in a given economic order. The term "class" refers to any group of people that is found in the same class situation' (1946, 181).

I pluck such 'precisionings' of 'class' (versus status group and party) from within Gerth and Mills's brackets. They plucked them from elsewhere in *Wirtschaft und Gesellschaft*, presumably to clarify (methodologically) the excerpt, lest readers forget just what the excerpt is 'explaining'! Their volume (one I prize, and still assign) even kicks things off with a displaced definitional *énoncé* (appropriately 'enunciated' *very* precisely): 'Law exists when there is a probability that an order will be upheld by a specific staff of men who will use physical or psychical compulsions with the intention of obtaining conformity with the order, or of inflicting sanctions for infringement of it' (Weber 1946, 180).

Such tinkered-with, pasted-on stipulations appear advisable even where Weber has already subjugated (with caveats) 'causalities' to 'discipline,' 'routinization,' and 'rule-governing' (all Weber's concepts). Yes, in *Wirtschaft und Gesellschaft* too – a 'rationally' outlined and reorganized compilation – readers risk, or enjoy, becoming disoriented (lost even) among endless displacements, complex counter-cases, and constitutive contrast. Readers also experience non-stop negativity: something perhaps not unlike dialectics, only different.

Twenty-some years ago – before I was older (as now) than Weber lived to be – I opined over-boldly,

> The more dialectical dimension of Weber ... detects sociological space where it is least expected. He [foregrounds] the nearly negative (asceticism) and the nearly vacant (mysticism). Even mystics and ascetics are interest groups ... Weber's comparative typology ... commenced with

components ostensibly the most rarified and contextualized them by 'treating the terms asceticism and mysticism as polar concepts' ... He charted the variant ways society and institutions are believed to be circumvented by selflessness in direct touch with divinity ... . Weberian ideal-types are never simply imposed on the flux of time and cultures in some mechanical fashion. Instead, ideal-types emerge from juxtaposing dimensions such as asceticism/mysticism and from allowing the relative form they lend each other to reverberate through substantive creeds (e.g., theodicy). Ultimately, rationality is posed not as a natural reason producing inevitable enlightenment but as a religious value, one that has a history, or rather histories. Weber then reveals its varying tonalities. (Boon 1982a, 74–5).

And here I stand in 2004, nursing a hunch that the same goes for 'objectivity.' But also note this point worth endlessly returning to: Weber's accent on negation extends even to *comparative* negations – as when he speculates (more than once) that Buddhism cancels resentment and thus *disproves* Nietzschean *ressentiment* is the *Grund* (base motive-drive) of, let's say, '*Untermenschen.*' And Weber adds in meticulously contrapuntal critical judgment, 'However fortunate and fruitful the disclosure of the psychological significance of resentment as such has been, great caution is necessary in estimating its bearing for social ethics' (1946, 270).[8]

Max Weber's unstoppably 'different dialectics' and profoundly plural proclivity culminated in supremely sketchy essays – on religions, world-rejections, music(s), etc. – between 1911 and 1915, an inspired, mania-infused period of his writing life (in my 'critical judgment' – Boon 1982a, 269).[9] But Weber's irradiating negativities and backpedalling causalities are already evident in the 1904 essay on 'objectivity,' from which I have digressed, distracted by my affection for his contrastively 'charismatic' style. Back to the subject at hand: Weber's powerfully 'objective' strand.

Whatever 'objectivity' implies in Weber, it is not standardization; indeed, he masterfully befuddles distinctions of average and 'extreme' – as when declaring, 'Finally, we must oppose to the utmost the widespread view that scientific "objectivity" is achieved by weighing the various evaluations against one another and making a "statesman-like" compromise among them. The "middle way" is not only just as undemonstrable scientifically – with the means of the empirical sciences – as the "most extreme" evaluations: in the sphere of evaluations, it is the least unequivocal' (1949, 57).[10]

328 BoonSuch claims reinforce my resolve to *underscore* how *variably* Weber composes in and on the key of 'objectivity' – which, to reiterate, *sounds* like abstract *énoncé* (in our Benveniste-Kristeva sense) as opposed to *discours* (writing 'accented' in interpretive contingencies, as in Weber's travel vignettes). But do recall that for Weber *anything*, including 'objectivity,' can be taken up only with a 'stance' (1978, 192). It was, of course, such 'objective style' (*énoncé*) that Talcott Parsons loved to emulate – to the point of unreadability – although I have a soft spot for Parsons (my teachers' teacher: my 'grandteacher,' so to speak); in 1982, I even defended Parsons's posthumous essays, (quite the unfashionable thing to do in those days).[11]

But the point now (on which I take a precise and insistent stance, as 'objectivity' demands) is that Weber's *énoncés* of 'positive' definition (the very mark of 'objectivity') can occur in counterpoint with dialectic and lack. Here, for instance: 'First we have to ask: with what concepts shall we define a "caste"? Let us ask it in the negative: what is not a caste? Or, what traits of other associations, really or apparently related to caste, are lacking in caste? What, for instance, is the difference between caste and a tribe?' (1946, 397).

Against critics who would deem such (anti)definitional moves 'deconstruction,' I de-deem them that, calling them instead 'disaggregation' (or a 'calling' to disaggregate). This *Beruf* is compatible with Boasian 'disaggregation' in anthropology – another worthy school of contrastively circumstantial cultural comparison (and not just a philosophical shadow-war against metaphysics, per 'deconstruction').[12]

Some critics underestimate Weber's negative-defining (of *casta*, *Varna*, etc.) as merely heuristic; I would remind them that the caste/status group distinction can dissolve empirically – a fact Weber carefully documented: 'The Census Reports plainly show that the Islamic castes lack ... important characteristics of the Hindu caste system, especially ritualistic defilement through commensalism with non-members – even though commensalism and social intercourse among different social strata may be avoided and rather rigidly so, as is often the case, after all, in western society [see below] ... Properly understood, the so-called Islamic castes are essentially status groups and not castes' (1958, 132).

Note too how Weber balances out history's own 'disaggregative' developments with contrapuntal (and wildly comparative) aggregations: 'For some time the Lingayat sect has undergone a ... status differentiation suggestive of the gentility claimed by the descendants of the

Mayflower Pilgrims in New England' (1958, 20). His dynamic South Asian panorama covers diverse registers (Hindu, Jain, Buddhist, Islamic, colonialist, etc.) in various forces (orthodox, heterodox, sectarian), and he methodically criss-crosses such counter-formations as reformist movements and tantric tonalities (the latter resembling ones I address in Hindu-Buddhist institutions of Bali).[13] *Occasionally* Weber even reminds readers that 'one is tempted to think of the Occident' (1958, 26). And there too (the Occident), the same (that is, opposite) is true: as proof, consider three sentences added to the *Protestant Ethic*'s footnote on Lutheran Pietism (versus Calvinism): 'However, the question of the *certitudo salutis* itself was absolutely central for every religion based in non-sacramental salvation, whether Buddhism, Jainism, or any other. This point should not be mistaken. From *this* question arose all psychological motivations of a purely *religious* character' (Weber 2002, 198).

This sudden, inserted comparison (in the 1920 edition) succinctly captures one motive force of Weber's Indian researches – hardly merely a matter of obstacles to 'capitalism' in *othered* religions.

Weber's constant 'temptation' to comparison is both systematic and distracted (compare 'causal' and 'casual'). Indeed, said temptation dimples 1904's 'methodology' piece, whose 'function' (which, however, does not *explain* it!) was partly to *legitimate* a publishing venture. On the distraction side, consider just two of that still-surprising essay's abrupt allusions – to prostitution and to brothels:

> The fact with which we are primarily concerned, namely, the *cultural significance* of the money-economy ... is not derivable from any 'law.' The *generic features* of exchange, purchase, etc., interest the jurist – but we are concerned with the analysis of the cultural significance of the concrete *historical* fact that today exchange exists on a mass scale.
>
> ... An 'objective' analysis of cultural events, which proceeds according to the thesis that the ideal of science is the reduction of empirical reality to 'laws,' is meaningless ... 'Culture' is a finite segment of the meaningless infinity of the world process, a segment on which *human beings* confer meaning and significance. This is true even for the human being who views a *particular* culture as a mortal enemy and who seeks to 'return to nature' ... Thus when we speak here of the conditioning of cultural knowledge through evaluative ideas [*Wertideen*] ... it is done in the hope that we will not be subject to crude misunderstandings ... that cultural signifi-

cance should be attributed only to *valuable* [*valued*?] phenomena. Prostitution is a *cultural* phenomenon just as much as religion or money. (Weber 1949, 77–81)

Weber's arresting suggestions cancel (1) any presumed 'high-mindedness' in his concept of 'culture,' and (2) any aura of ideality (versus spleen!) in his notion of 'Ideal.' His accompanying comparative insight verges on the aphoristic: prostitution is as cultural as religion or money. The same *aperçu* recurs, with variation:

> An 'ideal type' in our sense, to repeat once more, has no connection at all with *value-judgments*, and it has nothing to do with any type of perfection other than a purely *logical* one [hence Parson's recommendation we call ideal-types 'logical-types' – Boon 1982a, 69]. There are ideal types of brothels as well as of religions; there are also ideal types of those kinds of brothels which are technically 'expedient' from the point of view of police ethics as well as those of which the exact opposite is the case. (1949, 98–9)

Indeed. And there are logical-types of 'erotic movements,' to which Weber was eventually privy – in idea(l) and/or in practice. Weber's 1904 allusions to money, prostitutes, and brothels may remind us he had recently read Simmel's *Philosophy of Money* (1978), when emerging from psychic collapse. And those same allusions may foreshadow Weber's later 'casual' involvement (along with Edgar Jaffé, the *Archiv*'s owner) in heterodox circles of the Von Richtofen sisters and Otto Gross's projects 'of and for' sexual liberation. Possibly exaggerated by M. Green (1988), Weber's entanglement in his era's 'erotic movement' nevertheless remains crucial in measured assessments of his *Lebenswerk* by G. Roth, H. Liebersohn, and others.[14]

Apprised of 'methods' that conjoin religion and money with prostitution (read 'sexuality'), students today might well want me to intimate that Weber was 'waiting for Foucault' (virtually). I suggest instead that Weber's last-cited caveat ('the exact opposite is the case') sounds more radically relativist: like Lowie.[15] And a comparative fact deserves trumpeting: Weber's theoretical-anecdotal conjuncture (religion-money-prostitution) anticipates attention he later paid to Indic permutations of pleasure, power, gender, and agency. (Here I capitulate willingly to preferred issues of our era). Weber's eventual notes in this regard deserve daring rereading ('ethnographically'):

The Indian dancers, *Deva-Dasa* (Portuguese *balladeirs*, French *bayaderes*) of medieval times were developed out of the *Hierodulen*, the hieratic – homeopathic, mimitic, or apotropaic – *sakti* and temple prostitutes by the priests (and ... prostitutions of wandering merchants) and are still today primarily bound up with the Shiva cult. They were obligated to temple service through song and dance and had to be literate – until most recent times the ONLY LITERATE WOMEN of India. For the numerous temple festivals ... [they formed] a special caste with its own *dharma* and, especially, inheritance and adoption rights, and were PERMITTED TABLE-COMMUNITY WITH THE MEN OF ALL CASTES GIVEN ACCESS TO WRITING SKILLS IN CONTRAST TO HIGH-BORN WOMEN, for whom writing and literary art were excluded, because they belonged to the *dharma* of temple wench and were held as shameful and likewise not valid ... THE USUAL *dasi* IN CONTRAST to the *Deva-Dasi* WAS A WANDERING PROSTITUTE of the lower castes without relation to temple service. THE TRANSITION FROM THERE TO THE HIGHLY CULTIVATED WOMEN of the type of *Aspasia*, corresponding to the *hetoiral* of classical drama (*vasantasena*) was naturally FLUID THROUGHOUT. The last-named type belonged quite as much as the quite well-educated inner-society of female scholars and female propagandists among the Buddhist philosophers (in the manner of the feminine Pythagoreans), of the old distinguished intellectual culture of the pre-Buddhistic and early Buddhistic times which disappeared with the domination of the *guru*-monk. (1958, 354; majuscules mine)

Thus did the 1904 essay's seed of prostitution flourish cross-culturally in Weber's understanding of South Asian history that qualified 'class/ caste' in extravagantly different-dialectics of Dasi/Deva-Dasi!

Long before such 'charismatic comparisons' (to me) of Indic multiplicities, Weber was hardly unific about anything – even 'objectivity' in 1904. Objectivity for Weber was, in fact, rather relativized – or rather, 'relatively relativized.' (Paradoxically, nothing for him – or for Geertz, Boasians, Marcel Mauss, Montaigne, etc. – is absolute, so-called relativism included.) Weber's 1904 multi-disciplinary foray ended suitably with *Faust*; it was wobbly methodologically, and fluid topically. And long may it remain so! The piece formulated, virtually, what I like to hyphenate the 'economic-*erotique*' – an ideal-type (hybridity?) worth pursuing still, both as Weber did and as he (then) couldn't. Indeed, Weber, having read Simmel, spurred us on to '*cultural significance* of the money-economy.' (Who then needs, or rather desires, Baudrillard?)[16]

In sum, Weber's 1904 composition can be read as less 'methodologi-cal manifesto' than 'blurred genre,' penned to navigate diverse waters: the intellectual, the economic, the erotic, the political. These very 'spheres' (including retro-Decadence!) became key institutional crossroads in Weber's sublimely practice-minded sketch of 'Religious Rejections of the World' (1915), with its uncanny, comparative insight: 'Mysticism is a unique escape from this world in the form of an objectless devotion to anybody, not for man's sake but purely for devotion's sake, or in Baudelaire's words, for the sake of "the soul's sacred prostitution"' (1946, 333).

This astonishing sentence concludes neither the aesthetic sphere nor the erotic sphere (or even the intellectual sphere), but 'the economic sphere.' There's madness (or mania) in Weber's method and a whole lot of (cross-cultural) hunch.

More 'India,' Otherwise Deviated

To further track circumstantial flexibilities reticulating (rather like anec-dotes) through Weber since 1904, I repair again to South Asia – this time its 'commensality.' As always, Weber's topical contrasts are sharp, yet *nothing is absolute*, and contingencies are downright dizzying – even for 'basic' definitions of caste versus guild. Stipulating that neither institu-tion is exclusive to either Europe or India, Weber nevertheless categori-cally contrasts them dynamically: 'The merchant and craft guilds of [Europe's] Middle Ages acknowledged no ritual barriers ... apart from the ... stratum of pariah peoples and pariah workers ... (knacker, hang-man) [who] come close sociologically to the unclean caste of India. There were factual barriers restricting the connubium between differ-ently esteemed occupations, but there were no ritual barriers ... Within the circle of the "honorable" people, ritual barriers to commensalism were completely absent; but such barriers belong to the basis of caste differences' (195, 35).

Weber notes as well an assertive and positive side to this absence of barrier, this lack, in Europe's formations: 'The occupational associations of the medieval Occident ... engaged in violent struggles among them-selves but at the same time they evidenced ... fraternization ... The fraternization of the citizenry was carried through by the fraternization of the guilds' (36).

Common meals, drinking rooms, and processions established 'the cultic community of the citizens' with its most festive form of commensalism, the Lord's Supper (36). Weber adds that commensalism need not be *actually* practised in fraternization, but it must be ritually possible (36); this distinguishes it categorically from caste order, which precludes complete fraternization and full commensality.

Because the contrast, however, is 'not an absolute one' ('nor are transitions lacking'), Weber itemizes a page of exceptions in India; they include commensalism between Rajput and Brahman sub-castes, kings inviting various castes to table, and open soup kitchens during famine (36). (Given ethnographies and histories of South Asia since Weber, his page would today require volumes). The exceptions cited indeed proved the rule: 'It is a long way from this situation to a possible commensalism and fraternization as they are known in the Occident' (37).

The Occident, I hasten to stress, has had its own separations; Weber mentions Paul's letter to the Galatians that reproached Peter for first eating with gentiles and then separating himself as Jew: '[Paul's] shattering of the ritual barriers against commensalism meant a destruction of the voluntary ghetto, which in its effects is far more incisive than any compulsory ghetto. It meant to destroy the situation of Jewry as a pariah people, a situation that was ritually imposed upon this people' (37).

Indeed, Weber brazenly relates Paul's 'universalism' (a manifestly exclusivistic one, by which Paul was indeed 'tempted') to repercussions a millennium later: 'The elimination of all ritual barriers of birth for the community of the eucharists was ... the hour of conception for the occidental "citizenry" ... even though its birth occurred more than a thousand years later in the revolutionary *conjurationes* of the medieval cities. For without commensalism ... no oathbound fraternity would have been possible' (37–8).

Again, the contrast Weber draws with India is dramatic, categorical, doubtless overdrawn, but never (well, hardly ever!) absolute: 'India's caste order formed an obstacle to this, which was unsurmountable, at least by its own forces. [But] the castes are not governed only by this eternal ritual division. A nabob of Bankura, upon the request of a Chandala, wished to compel the Karnakar (metal workers) caste to eat with the Chandala' (38).

In short, commensality is conceivable in India and may be backed by princes, although such possibilities, along with Indian guilds, wound up marginalized. Weber carefully encapsulates this history of contingencies (in credit-solidarity):

By its solidarity, the association of Indian guilds, the *mahajan*, was a force which the princes had to take very much into account ... The guilds acquired privileges from the princes for loans of money, which is reminiscent of our medieval conditions. The *shreshti* (elders) of the guilds ranked with the warrior and priest nobility of their time, ... the power of the castes was undeveloped and ... shaken by the religions of salvation ... hostile to Brahmans. The later turn in favor of the monopoly rule of the caste system not only increased the power of the Brahmans but also that of the princes, and it broke the power of the guilds. For the castes excluded ... politically powerful fraternization of the citizenry and of the trades ... The prince ... could not only play off the castes against one another – which he did – but he had nothing whatever to fear from them, especially if the Brahmans stood by his side. (38–9).

My paramount *énoncé* (plus stance) here concerns Weber's relatively relativist way of 'objectively' typologizing caste/status group/guild. I mentioned above empirical evidence of Muslim transformations of 'caste' into status group. More fundamentally, at key theoretical conjunctures Weber casts 'caste' (or varnas 'grouping' castes) *as* status group. To state the matter precisely: Weber's ideal-typical distinction between caste and status group works like a status–group distinction and *not* a caste distinction. Or, rephrasing yet again Weber's different-dialectic (one I am striving to *verstehen*): even as caste and status groups are opposed, 'caste' tilts to 'status group' (I mean 'methodologically'). This happens patently where Weber asserts:

The Brahmans and Kshatriyas engaged in certain prescribed, exclusive activities which implemented their *styles of life as status groups*: for the Brahmans – sacrifice, study of the Vedas, receipt of gifts (particularly land grants), and asceticism; for the Kshatriyas – political rule, knightly feats of valor. The occupations of a Vaishaya – tillage and trade and, particularly, the *lending of money at interest* – were considered by both upper castes as unbecoming to their rank and station. However, in time of need, when it proved impossible to earn one's living conventionally, it was temporarily permissible, with some reservations, to take up the occupations of a Vaishya.

In contrast to this, the way of life of the Shudra signified 'menial service.' The correct Brahman cannot join the modern army, for he would have to obey superiors from a lower caste or of barbarian descent. (1958, 56; emphasis added)

Manifestly, then, *as a theoretical construct* 'status group' here trumps 'caste' – as elsewhere in Weber it does 'class.' Incidentally, these paragraphs are as far as Weber takes this Indian counterpoint historically. However, there is no reason to assume he would have denied possibilities of subsequent 'exceptions' to restrictions documented. Nothing, I propose, would have surprised Weber less than an emergence of Brahman soldiers in India's modern military or agonistically thriving capitalism and democracy in India today. Similarly, as just shown, Weber's Indian researches revealed that caste-infringing commensality could occur in part precisely because it was prohibited. Such ironies of unintended consequences led Weber to *expect* exceptions – if only as a hunch!

Closing Hunches of a Dilettante (in Pianissimo)

The hunch of a dilettante ... may have ... greater significance than a specialist's. The dilettante is distinguished ... by his inability to exploit the potentialities of his hunch. An imaginative idea is no substitute for work. On the other hand, work is no substitute for imaginative insight; diligent work, no more than passionate devotion is capable of compelling insight. Both – particularly, both together – [can entice the idea]. But ... the best ideas come ... during a walk on a gradually ascending street, or ... when one does not expect them – and not when one is puzzling and pondering at one's desk. At any rate, the scientist ... must reckon with the chance which attends every piece of research – the chance that inspiration might or might not come.

Weber 1973[17]

Weber's 'Science as *Beruf*' affords an alliteration my essay has been half-surreptitiously saluting: the diligent dilettante. To the end of his calling (1920), Weber cultivated interdisciplinary 'hunches' (for example, that Buddhism contradicts Nietzsche's nevertheless worthy theory of *ressentiment*). Alas, hunches about Weber have been bet on by anthropologists with sporadic success at best. More often we have avoided his sweep, given short shrift to his many strands, or bought into easy convictions that he championed Western capitalism's exceptionalism. Some colleagues, however, have invested more in Weber, including South and Southeast Asian specialists: L. Dumont, S. Tambiah, J. Peacock, and C. Geertz.[18] My admittedly parochial list of 'area anthropologists' alert to Weber may harbour affinities with certain interdisciplinary approaches: cross-readings of Weber and Mann by Goldmann (1988);

parallels between Weber and Foucault by Szakolczai (1998); pairings of Weber's 'sects' and Nietzsche's 'monastery' for freer spirits by H. Treiber: 'Comparing Nietzsche means relativizing his uniqueness' (1993, 133). Following such examples, I am also tempted – both openly and furtively – to hitch Weber with select Boasians (for example, Lowie) and post-Parsonians (for example, again, Geertz). And along with Philippe Despoix, I keep pondering Weber's interpretive attraction to music – and not just 'aesthetically.'[19]

Any of these topics could lead back to where this essay began: Weber's 1904 sojourn in St Louis. I'll take just one case in point. To broach Geertz-on-Weber requires revisiting religious rationalization, semiotic webs, kingly charisma, and anti-economistic construals of culture (Geertz 1973, 1983, 2000). His own ethnography-informed histories of infrastructure, labour, and power – on pre-colonialist Bali's statecraft, say, or colonial Java's 'agrarian capitalism' – recall Weber in their evidentiary texture. Geertz's *Negara* (1980) depicts Balinese in ways echoing Weber on peasants: 'politically, personally, and economically subjected to quite different lords' (1946, 377). Geertz's *Agricultural Involution* (1963) analytically resembles Weber's 'Capitalism and Rural Society in Germany' – whose publication, I may have failed to mention, derived from that speech in St Louis – the first public performance Weber managed after his long mental collapse. The assembly was small: 'a handful of people' (Rollmann 1993, 377); teeming audiences would come only near life's end at the *Beruf* lectures. But where was I? Oh yes: Weber's work on rural economies plotted lags in capitalization of productive lands, as did Geertz (1963), who concluded his study of Java with a brazen historical contrast with Japan. Just so, Weber's piece was strikingly contrastive: it criss-crossed East/West of the Elbe in Germany with opposed cases from the U.S. and British configurations, tracking ever-receding 'causalities' relating those differences (1946, 374–6).

Yes, panoramic sweep already pervaded Weber's theoretical calling in 1904, even as ethnographer-Weber engaged in incidental-seeming travels that somehow wound up seasoning the whole. Another claim I earlier staked out bears renewing: Weber was 'ever the semiotic anthropologist' (Boon 1982a, 77). Kalberg's (2002) daunting list of Weber's unfinished projects includes quasi-anthropological ones. And Liebersohn stresses Weber's 'promise to make use of ethnographic material in his sociology of religion' (1993, 126).

It remains nevertheless difficult to craft rapprochements between Weberian interpretation and anthropology today. Yet I am dogged by a hunch that the two enterprises can be 'syncopated.' For example, like Colin Campbell's *Romantic Ethic and the Spirit of Modern Consumerism* (1987), but differently, I want to 'deploy' Weber on world commercial forces (not lacking in 'erotic-ethics'!) and global agencies of consumption. Issues of hyper-commoditization are all the rage in ethnography now; their importance rivals those religions and 'economic-ethics' that Weber incomparably compared.

To entice a Weberian 'gaze' toward commodities he lacked the life thoroughly to inspect, I recommend foregoing any methodological Weber for that poly-sensate Weber who speculatively wandered and read. Recall with me again how discerningly (and reliably) Weber listened: passing through Boston, for example, he paused to deride white Protestant 'community singing': 'Apart from the Negro churches, and except for the professional singers now engaged by the churches as "attractions" ... all that is usually to be heard in America is a kind of caterwauling, unbearable to German ears' (Weber 1978, 156).

Similar discernment marked his vision when encountering 'old and new forms of the social stratification of democratic society.' Indeed, both Max and Marianne scrutinized evidence of racial divides, along with ethnicity, class, gender, and age; neither quite escaped prejudicial formulations of their time (e.g., 'half-breeds'], but each clearly sympathized with the dispossessed. Here, as evidence, are two chance ethnographettes:

Today I [Max] watched whole troops of Indians arrive to get their money; the full-blooded ones have peculiar tired facial features and are surely doomed to destruction, but among the others one sees intelligent faces. Their clothes are almost inevitably European ... I think my host, the Cherokee, will attack the latest Indian policy of the United States in the *Archiv*: his eyes sparkled when he spoke about it. (Cited in Mar. Weber 1988, 294)

They next landed in the little city of Tuskegee in order to see Booker Washington's famous educational institution for Negroes. What they found probably moved them more than anything else on their trip ... They sensed above all the tragedy of the pariahdom of that ever-increasing mixed race of all shades from dark brown to ivory, people who by virtue of their descent and talents belonged to the master race [*Herrenrasse*] but were excluded from its community as though they bore a stigma. According to law there were no longer any slaves, but the white masters of the southern states took revenge by socially boycotting the slaves' children and children's children. (Mar. Weber 1988, 295)

Moreover, Weber – routinely 'hyperactive' – felt 'intoxicated by the dynamics of American work and industry' (Rollmann 1993, 373). Accordingly, he inscribed Chicago's inter-sensory, polyphonic crescendo of cross-cultural experience:

> All hell had broken loose in the 'stockyards': an unsuccessful strike, masses of Italians and Negroes as strikebreakers; daily shooting with dozens of dead on both sides; a streetcar was overturned and a dozen women were squashed ... dynamite threats against the 'Elevated Railway' ... There is a mad pell-mell of nationalities: Up and down the streets the Greeks shine the Yankees' shoes for 5 cents. The Germans are their waiters, the Irish take care of their politics, and the Italians of their dirtiest ditch digging ... The whole tremendous city ... is like a man whose skin has been peeled off and whose intestines are seen at work. For one can see everything – in the evening, for example on a side street in the 'city' the prostitutes are placed in a show window with electric light and the prices are displayed! A characteristic thing here as in New York is the maintenance of a specific Jewish-German culture. Theaters present in Yiddish [Judendeutsch] The Merchant of Venice (with Shylock prevailing, however) and their own Jewish places, which we are planning to see in New York. (Cited in Mar. Weber, 286–7).

Inspired by his manifest ethnographic gifts, my essay-commemoration concludes by imagining a quieter encounter (possibly pianissimo) available to Weber, had he chanced to wander off after speaking in St Louis. (Incidentally, that 'world's fair' *occasion* had ironically been displaced in time – 'syncopated,' you might say – from a Louisiana Purchase centennial intended for 1903, with the *unintended consequence* that St Louis got to host the 1904 Olympic Games as well!). Hurrying by fabulously diverse displays, Weber could have passed an actual Ainu from Japan (a real minority-Asian, face to face!) or Prince Pu Lun from China, 'for the first time in history ... officially participating in a universal exposition. Grandson of the late emperor, the 29 year old Prince stayed in St. Louis for two months, living at the George Washington Hotel in Kings Highway' (Witherspoon 1973, 56–7).

Nudging prophetic signs of his future Asiatic researches, Weber could next have espied the 'most commanding of all the exhibits at the fair': abundant 'specimens' of living Moros, Visayans, and Igorots (Witherspoon 1973, 38). One fetching fellow, in fact (from among '1100 Filipinos') could have helped this Weber I'm imagining (Marianne's

Mrs Wilkins teaching an Igorot the Cakewalk. Courtesy Missouri Historical Society, St Louis.[20]

Max) experience ephemeral intimations of economic-ethical 'exceptions.'
Yes, Weber might have glimpsed omens of eventual caveats in seemingly intractable divides (by race, by class, by gender), not to mention
status-group smugness infecting that national democracy he so busily
'voyeured': *America*!

Gaze then, readers, upon a photograph from St Louis's fair. (Any
curiosity-seeker could be forgiven for wondering just who here is teaching whom!) Needless to stipulate, alas our dazzling conjuncture remained nestled unrebelliously in 1904's patronizing politics of high
colonialism. Still, the conjuncture conceivably (and suggestively) eroded
unjust certainties – manifest norms – of its era. Following a hunch, any
'gradually ascending' Weberian might almost infer affinities with other
dancing duos – such as India's Dasi/Deva-Dasi, who also multiply
contradicted singular categorical distinctions (of caste, class), both institutionally and performatively. (I indicated above Weber's annotating
Dasi/Deva-Dasi this way). In St Louis's midway, Max could have enjoyed nimble prognostications of a radically commoditizing century
(1904–2004) – one destined (or doomed) to *interconnect* U.S. business
(plus military and bureaucracy) to 'popular' consumption worldwide
via dominant ('democratic') practices, including entertainment media
called 'global.'

To interpret these foretokens, I shift my senses from the photo's *look*
to its implicit *sound*, which amplifies still different dialectics. Mrs Wilkins
and an unnamed (yet personable!) Igorot strut their stuff to novel
commercial strains – when two-step is historically transmogrifying into
ragtime, and sheet music into piano rolls, then gramophones, and later
broadcasts (with CDs, iPods, etc. on the transnational technological
horizon). Weber, I note, later lucidly analysed antecedent *techniques* of
art and industry: 'experimental pianos;' this was part of his passionate
work on harmonics and chromatics in musical practice-and-idea over
time, with its composite rhythms and contrapuntal concerns (Weber
1946, 146; 1969; 1978, 378–83). What, then, might Max have made of
ragtime's relentless syncopations (its trademark praxis) and shifting
social contexts: from sleazy saloons and routine prostitution (for which
W.E.B. Dubois defamed it), to marketed respectability in sanitized 'life
styles' that nevertheless still tweaked 'bourgeois' separations of race,
class, generation, gender, and more.

Weber's typological triad of 1904 (religion, money, prostitution) might
well tempt any interpreter toward thicker description of 'pioneer ragtime pianist' Tom Turpin. His style honed in St Louis's raunchiest

district, Turpin authored songs 'later expurgated for polite society' –
such as *Hot Time in the Old Town* 'introduced by the famous New
Orleans octoroon entertainer, Mama Lou, and a chorus line of girls who
wore only skirts and danced on a mirrored floor.' In the 1890s Turpin
owned 'the Rosebud Bar, the mecca for all underground ragtime musi-
cians ... He and his brother Charlie controlled the Booker T. Washington
Theater ... The brothers were the first black politicians in town and ran
gambling houses, dance halls and sporting houses' (Jansen and Tichenor
1989, 28). By 1904 Turpin composed 'The Buffalo Rag': 'The entire
composition has a capricious air: the treble texture is punctuated with
quick chords and abrupt phrasing, contrasted with longer, lyrical single-
note melody lines. The Turpin flair for contrast, surprise, and creativity
was never better displayed ... The title ... may reflect Turpin's hunting
and his Western adventures, but most probably refers to "The Benevo-
lent Order of Buffaloes," a St. Louis lodge in which he was very active'
(Jansen and Tichenor 1989, 33).

Weber would have called Tom Turpin's 'Buffaloes' what they were: a
Verein; he may even have tolerated their singing!

Like some pulsating *pneuma* (see note 17), ragtime 'mesmerized its
turn-of-the-century audience'; its charismatic contradictions were downright multi-conjunctural:

> [Ragtime] combines a syncopated melody accompanied by an even, steady
> duple rhythm ... It was ragtime's relentless syncopation that [was] unset-
> tling to a public accustomed to a sentimental musical diet of dreary
> ballads and buffoonish depictions of 'darkies.' By virtue of the fact that
> ragtime's *melodies* are too abstract and pianistic to be vocalized or even
> hummed, and its *syncopations* too elaborate to lend themselves to dancing,
> ragtime RENOUNCES these two basic components of American pop music
> and black folk music. The customary view of ragtime as a kind of musical
> hybrid created by someone with a Caucasian cortex and African central
> nervous system shortchanges the significance of this RENUNCIATION, which
> Tin Pan Alley sought to obscure by labeling ragtime as dance music.
> (Jansen and Tichenor 1989, 3, 4; majuscules mine)

Could a historical process be more 'Weberian'? Coincidentally, Weber
himself passed through St Louis just before ragtime's centre moved (as
centres do!) to Chicago, with the advent of the Novelty rag: 'The distinctive sound of the Novelty rag is a combination of the influence of
the French Impressionists – Claude Debussy and Maurice Ravel – with

contrasting rhythms as used by the roll arrangers. Chromaticism is at the heart of the Novelty tradition ... in a sequence of ascending chromatic major thirds the top note of every other interval forms the whole-tone scale. Probably the most striking hallmark of Novelty writing is the use of consecutive fourths in the melody voicing' (214–15).

Elective, indeed, were ragtime's diverse and fluid affinities!

Such tokens of 'ragtime-renunciation' possibly cancel polarized, or even hybrid, categories (for example, black/white). With said tokens my essay concludes. I hope to have hinted at popular culture's potential for radically contrapuntal *Verstehen*. Regardless, my fanciful closing anecdote (inspired by Weber's calling for chance inspiration) should suffice to prove that, anthropologically, I have nothing but hunches about Weber – including how, given the *occasion*, he might diligently have 'enticed the idea' of a raggin' Igorot plus *gnädige Frau*. Such were certain syncopated sights and sounds available in 1904, when, as Marianne movingly remembered, Max interpretively meandered with those long, elastic strides.[21]

NOTES

1 Coincidentally, the Kaiser-bestowed bronze eagle displayed at the German Exhibit when Weber visited St Louis later passed to Philadelphia's firm of Wanamaker's, key player in the history of U.S. commercial spirit and 'consumer capitalism' (see Leach 1993). This very eagle (so proximate to Marianne's metaphor-for-Max) became Wanamaker's trademark, installed next to the pipe organ also transported from St Louis. (Wanamaker's even marketed its own house brand of pianos; see Witherspoon 1973, 18). Were Weber alive today and travelling through Philly, he could hear again in that store's successor the very organ's contrapuntal strains, if indeed he heard them in 1904 (as is likely; see Rollmann 1993, 376).

2 Jameson's 1974 essay (in Jameson 1988) places Weber's key topics – Protestantism, prophets, charisma – under the sign of 'vanishing mediator' along with Weber himself. (Bendix [1962] and others also understood Weber as working in a mode of prophecy; see Boon 1982a, 69–70). Here's Jameson: 'Thus the prophet is able to mediate the basic contradiction between ... the magician's concern with immediate gain and ... a bureaucracy that will eclipse his own historical function as well' (1988, 17). Also, charisma that 'cools off' serves as a 'bearer of change and social transfor-

mation only to be forgotten once that change has ratified the reality of the institutions' (1988, 26). Marxist Jameson, however, carries a promising hunch too far ('jumping the gun,' so to speak, on history) when he argues, 'Once Protestantism has accomplished the task of allowing a rationalization of innerworldly life to take place, it has no further reason for being and disappears from the historical scene' (1988, 25). To date, this prophecy (rather dogmatic) is in error! Jameson at moments appreciates subtler dialectics: for example, with Calvinism 'the means now becoming *more* rather than less religious, even while the ends grow even more secularized' (22). But he neglects to doubt radically whether 'secularized' adequately captures such ironies. Invoking 'genuine Marxist' critique, Jameson flirts with assumptions that something like secularism results as history's last cancellation. That 'belief' may avoid endless ironies vital, I suspect, in Weberian 'prophecy.' Jameson also over-synthesizes Weber in claiming that 'the concept of the vanishing mediator characterizes all of Weber's sociological and historical thinking and may be seen as the dominant structure of his imagination' (1988, 25). (For further friendly critique of Jameson for unwarrantedly arguing an 'all,' see Boon 1998a).

Provocatively returning to Jameson's 1974 essay, S. Zizek uses *traumatic* where Weber would likely have used *charismatic* (1993, 227, 284); Zizek (I'd think) would sympathize with shaggy-dog qualities of Weber's receding causalities in 'storytelling,' as Jameson's calls it. Like many of us, Jameson (and, I'd guess, Zizek) insists that 'Weber's *Wertfreiheit* was itself a passionate value judgment that has nothing in common with that positivistic and academic type of objectivity' (Jameson 1988, 3); although here again Jameson lumps critical culprits together too easily and dismissively. Worth savouring (and not unironically) is Jameson's effort (this was 1974, remember) to analyse Weber using Lévi-Strauss!

3 All these 'sites' can be traced in Marianne Weber, including North Tonawanda (1988, 284); see also Rollmann (1993, 376).

4 This paragraph and others herein flirt with issues of 'essentially contested' standards of ethnography articulated throughout Geertz's corpus; for more on Geertz (and Weber), see Boon (1982a, 2000, 2005).

5 'Accidental' meaning – in both 'motivational' and musical senses – occurs in such writers as Lévi-Strauss, William Faulkner, and Thomas Carlyle (Boon [1982b]); musical analogies suffuse certain rhetorics of interpretation, for example, Kenneth Burke (Boon 1999: xx–xxii, 3–16, 90–1).

6 Voluntary associations are crucial in Weber's work on economic-ethics in 'axial religions' and in Robert Lowie's (1920, 1948) work on 'primitive society' and general social theory (Boon 1982: 72, 98–104, 110–11).

7 Kristeva (1989) harnesses Benveniste, Jakobson, Saussure, and other linguists, along with Bakhtin, Lacan, and more (Boon 1998).

8 See also Weber (1946, 190; 1978, chap. 8). Weber gathers his caveats on *ressentiment* into 'Soteriology of the Underprivileged' in *Economy and Society* (1968). Inklings of how Weber may help interpret commodity-life and 'show business' punctuate Boon (1996, 1999, 2000). I note here his keen observation: 'With the exception of Judaism and Protestantism, all religions and religious codes of ethics have been forced to revert to the cult of saints, heroes or functional gods in order to accommodate themselves to the needs of the masses' (1978, 180). Weber's hunch neglects a (then incipient) 'star system' – a component of both Jewish and Protestant consumer culture that has given wiggle room (and even mobility) to 'underprivileged' sectors.

9 I poach 'mania' and 'inspired' from Weber's *'Wissenschaft als Beruf,'* which reminds us to associate mathematics with 'frenzy' (in the sense of Plato's 'mania') and 'inspiration' (1946, 136).

10 Boon (1977, 33; 1982a, 230–37; 1990, title and passim).

11 In a so-called full disclosure (*discours* disguised as *énoncé!*), I'd be obliged to own up to this fact: my early efforts on Weber were prompted by Otto Stammer's (1971) *Max Weber and Sociology Today* – fruit of another centenary *occasion* that convened Parsons, Aron, Marcuse, Horkheimer, Habermas, Bendix, and other giants. That daunting volume was mailed to me as a sample from the Philip Rief and Bryan Wilson series ('Explorations in Interpretive Sociology') in which my first book (Boon 1972) was about to appear. I have never recovered; I never shall.

12 On Boasian anthropology see G. Stocking (1974); elsewhere I relate various Boasian scholars (Ruth Benedict, Margaret Mead, Edward Sapir, Robert Lowie, etc.) to various critical issues, many of them contemporary (Boon 1982a, 1998, 1999).

13 On tantric formulations in Bali and comparatively (as pursued by Dumont, Weber before him, and others) see Boon (1982a, 200–4; 1990, xii–xii, chap. 6–7, 158 ff.; 1999, indexed under 'Tantric codes').

14 Both G. Roth (1993) and H. Liebersohn (1988/9, 1993) artfully blend historiography and biography. Even with their admirable efforts, just how Weber's calling pertained to erotic-ethics (or economic-erotics) – of Otto Gross, the Stephan George circle, etc. – might never be confirmed. Hunches may indeed best suit such interpretation (but see Roth 1993, 9–11). Runciman summarizes some relevant context as 'background' for Weber's letter to Jaffe rejecting Otto Gross's submission to the *Archiv* on Freud: 'Dr. X [in Weber's letter] was in fact Otto Gross (1877–1920) whose

wife Frieda was a friend of Jaffé's wife Else. Gross became the lover both of Else Jaffe (who was later to become, it is now thought, Weber's mistress) and of her sister Frieda (who was later to marry D.H. Lawrence). Weber, as his remarks in this letter show, was responsive both to the claims of a conventional ethic of responsibility and also to the arguments for sexual liberation: but it was characteristic of him to insist that it is impossible to have "the best of both worlds"' (Runciman 1978, 358).

There's renunciation! Drawn directly from Green (1988), Runciman's summary sounds tangled enough, even without mentioning that Weber's presumed mistress (likely known as such to Marianne) had also served in that capacity to his brother, Alfred Weber. (Brothers sharing a sexual *source*, even sequentially, is a whole other leitmotif!). But the (Weberian) irony in this instance is that potential personal involvement in the '"new ethic" of sexual liberation' (Roth 1993, 9) complicates Weber's officially negative assessment of Gross's work (and indirectly of Freud). In a reversal that confirms just how convoluted 'ethical' stances could be for Weber, this very letter (which starts by asserting that it will not exert Weber's editorial 'nay') ends precisely topsy-turvily: 'I must retract my remarks at the beginning. I should be lacking in character if I were to allow myself to be overruled and I make use of my contractual veto' (1978, 388). Presumably, rereading his own letter, Weber persuaded himself to renounce a stance asserted by its author at its outset (1978, 383–8). These 'dialectics' are explicit in 'Freudianism' – one of the 'miscellaneous topics' (along with 'The Stock Exchange,' 'The History of the Piano,' etc.) that conclude Runciman's collection: a tidy way to experience Weber's exceedingly polymathic virtuosity.

Hardly less polymathic was Simmel's 'philosophy,' including its account of the 'typical relation between prostitution and money' that Weber may have been remembering in 1904 and later (Simmel 1978, 376–80). By the way, Marcel Mauss's reception of Simmel would have been influenced by uncle Durkheim's review of *The Philosophy of Money* (see Bottomore 1979, 12). In my book, Simmel (1978) and Mauss (1983, 1990) always warrant further cross-reading.

15 See note 7. My Godot-echoing tease about Foucault is pinched from Sahlins (2002). Any follow-through here would obviously capsize a paper that is too long already; places to start would be Szakolczai (1998) and Goldman (1993). Lowie's radical caveating includes an early mention of Weber's *'Politik als Beruf'* (Boon 2002).

16 About Baudrillard, I'm kidding (Boon 1999, chap. 12, 'Coca-Cola Consumes Baudrillard ... ').

17 This is Shils's delicious translation (Weber 1973, 59–60), with one felicitous phrase (in parentheses) lifted from Gerth and Mills (Weber 1946, 136), from whom I also plucked my concluding subtitle's parenthetical Italian, breathtaking in Weber: 'It is not accidental ... that today only within the smallest and intimate circles, in personal human situations, in *pianissimo*, that something is pulsating that corresponds to the prophetic *pneuma*, which in former times swept through the great communities like a fire-brand' (1946, 155).

18 I cite token works by these worthy scholars in the bibliography. A key corpus is Dumont's, at conjunctures of India and Europe. On Dumont's attention to Weber in hierarchies/stratifications (including Christian) and in comparative individualism/asceticism, see Boon (1999, chap. 9). Geertz and Weber, addressed below, are another long-term concern (Boon 1977, 1982a). Peacock and Tyson give further details of Weber's 'Blue Ridge connection' in North Carolina (1989, 59). They also salute the 'dense allusiveness of Weber's prose' (269). I hope to have shown that Weber's erratic fashioning of a comparative corpus – with 'methodology,' casual anecdotes, and continually caveated comparison – constitutes part of his 'metaphorical complexity' (Peacock and Tyson 1998, 269).On such Weberian 'swoopings,' see also Boon (1982a, 71).

19 Boon (1982a, 1999). Dare I note in the same breath Weber's casual, but conceivably key, mentions of Wagner (for example, Weber 2002, 62) – and '*Meistersänger*, Offenbach' conjuncturals (Marianne Weber 1988, 499)! – and Levi Strauss's systematically ironic returns to Wagner (and Offenbach) throughout his own comparative oeuvre – Boon 1989, 1996)? For more on Tin Pan Alley, mentioned in Jason and Tichneor's incisive analysis of ragtime, see source in Boon (2000).

20 For more photographs from this key occasion in Weber's travels, see Breitbart 1997.

21 Hearty thanks to Laurence McFalls, Philippe Despoix, Mariella Pandolfi, and many more who organized and participated in a memorable conference-experience, for which I originally wrote this essay in March 2004. My essay's motivic use of 'temptations' was first devised to play on Jack Goody's originally announced paper. I underscore, as did Stephen Kalberg at the Montreal conference on the centennial of the 'Objectivity' essay, Weber's ambivalence about rationalizing practice and his non-economistic reading of religion-cum-economy. Some specifics of my personal encounter with Weber's legacy are scattered throughout (including notes 2, 9, 12), in the spirit of hunches about how Weber's won writing was itself composed.

REFERENCES

Bendix, Reinhard. 1962. *Max Weber: An Intellectual Portrait*. New York: Anchor Books.

Boon, James A. 1972. *From Symbolism to Structuralism: Lévi-Strauss in a Literary Tradition*. New York: Harper and Row.

– 1977. *The Anthropological Romance of Bali, 1597–1972*. New York: Cambridge University Press.

– 1982a. *Other Tribes, Other Scribes*. New York: Cambridge University Press.

– 1982b. 'Review of William Morris' *Friday's Footprint*.' *Novel* 15(3): 260–2.

– 1989. 'Lévi-Strauss, Wagner, Romanticism: A Reading-Back.' *History of Anthropology*, Vol. 6. Ed. G. Stocking. Madison: University of Wisconsin Press.

– 1990. *Affinities and Extremes: Crisscrossing the Bittersweet Ethnology of East Indies History, Hindu-Balinese Culture, and Indo-European Allure*. Chicago: University of Chicago Press.

– 1995. 'Panofsky and Lévi-Strauss (and Iconographers and *Mythologiques*) Re-regarded.' In *Meaning in the Visual Arts: Views from the Outside*. Ed. I. Lavin, Princeton: Princeton University Press.

– 1996. 'The Cross-Cultural Kiss: Edwardian and Earlier, Postmodern and Since.' David Skomp Lecture. Department of Anthropology. Indiana University.

– 1998. 'Accenting Hybridity: Postcolonial Theory, a Boasian Anthropologist, and I.' In *Culture and the Problems of the Disciplines*. Ed. J. Rowe. New York: Columbia University Press.

– 1999. *Verging on Extra-Vagance: Anthropology, History, Religion, Literature, Arts, ... Showbiz*. Princeton: Princeton University Press.

– 2000. 'Showbiz as a Cross-Cultural System: Circus and Song, Garland and Geertz, Rushdie, Mordden ... and More.' *Cultural Anthropology* 15(3): 424–56.

– 2001. 'Subtly Showy Lowie, or Anthropology's Ancestors May Be Trickier Than We Think (even Frazer).' Franz Boas Lecture Series. Department of Anthropology, Columbia University.

– 2005. 'Geertz's Style: A Moral Matter.' In *Clifford Geertz by His Colleagues*. Ed. R. Schweder and B. Good. Chicago: University of Chicago Press.

Bottomore, Tom. 1978. 'Introduction to the Translation' of Simmel (1978).

Breitbart, Eric. 1997. *A World on Display: Photographs from the St Louis World's Fair, 1904*. Albuquerque: University of New Mexico Press.

Campbell, Colin. 1987. *The Romantic Ethic and the Spirit of Modern Consumerism*. Oxford: Blackwell.

Dumont, Louis. 1977. *From Mandeville to Marx*. Chicago: University of Chicago Press.

348   James A. Boon

- 1980. *Homo Hierarchicus: The Caste System and Its Implications.* Rev. ed. Chicago: University of Chicago Press.
- 1982. 'A Modified View of Our Origins: The Christian Beginnings of Modern Individualism.' *Religion* 12: 1–27.
- 1986. *Essays on Individualism: Modern Ideology in Anthropological Perspective.* Chicago: University of Chicago Press.
Geertz, Clifford. 1963. *Agricultural Involution.* Berkeley: University of California Press.
- 1968. *Islam Observed.* New Haven: Yale University Press.
- 1973. *The Interpretation of Cultures.* New York: Basic Books.
- 1980. *Negara: The Theater State in Nineteenth-Century Bali.* Princeton: Princeton University Press.
- 1983. *Local Knowledge.* New York: Basic Books.
- 1984. 'Culture and Social Change: The Indonesian Case.' *Man* 19: 511–32.
- 1995. *After the Fact: Two Countries, Four Decades, One Anthropologist.* Cambridge: Harvard University Press.
- 2000. *Available Light: Anthropological Reflections on Philosophical Topics.* Princeton: Princeton University Press.
Goldman, Harvey. 1988. *Max Weber and Thomas Mann: Calling and the Shaping of the Self.* Berkeley: University of California Press.
- 1993. 'Weber's Ascetic Practices of the Self.' In Lehmann and Roth (1993), 161–78.
Green, Martin. 1988. *The Van Richtofen Sisters.* Albuquerque: University of New Mexico Press.
Jameson, Fredric. 1988. *The Ideologies of Theory: Essays, 1971–1986.* Vol. 2. *The Syntax of History.* Minneapolis: University of Minnesota Press.
Jansen, David, and T.J. Tichenor. 1989. *Rags and Ragtime: A Musical History.* Mineola, NY: Dover Publications, 1989.
Kalberg, Stephen. 2002. Introduction. In Weber (2002).
Keeter, Larry G. 1981. 'Max Weber's Visit to North Carolina.' *Journal of the History of Sociology* 3(2): 108–14.
Kristeva, Julia. 1989. *Language: The Unknown.* Trans. A. Menke. New York: Columbia University Press.
Leach, William. 1993. *Land of Desire: Merchants, Power, and the Rise of a New American Culture.* New York: Pantheon Books.
Lehmann, Hartmut, and Guenther Roth, eds. 1993. *Weber's Protestant Ethic: Origins, Evidence, Contexts.* New York: Cambridge University Press.
Liebersohn, Harry. 1988. *Fate and Utopia in German Sociology, 1870–1923.* Cambridge, MA: MIT Press.

- 1988/9. 'Weber and Women: A Review of Marianne Weber, *Max Weber: A Biography.*' *Telos* 78 (Winter): 123–9.
- 1993. 'Weber's Historical Concept of National Identity.' In Lehmann and Roth (1993), 123–32.

Lowie, Robert. 1920. *Primitive Society.* New York: Boni and Liveright.
- 1948. *Social Organization.* New York: Holt, Rinehart, and Winston.

Mauss, Marcel. 1983. *Sociologie et anthropologie.* 8th ed. Paris: Presses Universitaires de France.
- 1990. *The Gift.* Trans. W.D. Halls. New York: Norton.

Peacock, James L. 1978. *Muslim Puritans: The Psychology of Reformism in Southeast Asian Islam.* Berkeley: University of California Press.

Peacock, James L., and Ruel W. Tyson Jr. 1989. *Pilgrims of Paradox: Calvinism and Experience among the Primitive Baptists of the Blue Ridge.* Washington: Smithsonian Institution Press.

Rollmann, Hans. 1993. ''Meet Me in St. Louis': Troeltsch and Weber in America.' In Lehman and Roth (1993), 357–82.

Roth, Günther. 1993. 'Weber the Would-Be Englishman: Anglophile and Family History.' In Lehman and Roth (1993), 83–121.

Runciman, W.G. 1978. Introduction to Weber (1978).

Sahlins, Marshall. 1976. *Culture and Practical Reason.* Chicago: University of Chicago Press.
- 2002. *Waiting for Foucault, Still.* Chicago: Prickly Paradigm.

Simmel, Georg. 1978. *The Philosophy of Money.* Trans. T. Bottomore, D. Frisby, K. Mengelberg. Boston: Routledge & Kegan Paul.

Stammer, Otto, ed. 1971. *Max Weber and Sociology Today.* Oxford: Basil Blackwell.

Stocking, George. 1974. *The Shaping of American Anthropology: A Franz Boas Reader.* New York: Basic Books.

Szakolczai, Arpad. 1998. *Max Weber and Michel Foucault: Parallel Life-Works.* New York: Routledge.

Tambiah, Stanley. 1984. *The Buddhist Saints of the Forest and the Cult of Amulets.* Cambridge: Cambridge University Press.

Treiber, Hubert. 1993. 'Nietzsche's Monastery for Freer Spirits and Weber's Sect.' In Lehman and Roth (1993), 133–59.

Weber, Max. 1946. *From Max Weber: Essays in Sociology.* Ed. and trans. H. Gerth and C. Wright Mills. New York: Oxford University Press.
- 1949. *Methodology of the Social Sciences.* Ed. E. Shils, Glencoe, IL: Free Press.
- 1958. *The Religion of India.* Ed. H. Gerth and D. Martindale. Glencoe, IL: Free Press.

– 1968. *Economy and Society: An Outline of Interpretive Sociology*. Ed. G. Roth and C. Wittich. New York: Bedminster.
– 1969. *The Rational and Social Foundations of Music*. Trans. D. Martindale. Carbondale: Southern Illinois University Press.
– 1973. *Max Weber on Universities*. Ed. and trans. E. Shils. Chicago: University of Chicago Press.
– 1978. *Weber: Selections in Translation*. Ed. W.G. Runciman, trans. E. Matthews. New York: Cambridge University Press.
– 2002. *The Protestant Ethic and the Spirit of Capitalism*. Trans. S. Kalberg. Los Angeles: Roxbury.
Weber, Marianne. 1988. *Max Weber: A Biography*. Ed. and trans. H. Zohn. New Brunswick, NJ: Transaction Books.
Witherspoon, M.J. 1973. *Remembering the St Louis World's Fair*. St Louis: Comfort Printing.
Zizek, Slavoj. 1993. *Tarrying with the Negative: Kant, Hegel, and the Critique of Ideology*. Durham: Duke University Press.

Conclusion: The 'Objectivist' Ethic and the 'Spirit' of Science

LAURENCE MCFALLS WITH AUGUSTIN SIMARD AND
BARBARA THÉRIAULT

Fourteen authors have presented at least as many different manners of reading and using Weber. They have addressed him, in varying combinations, as a revered founding father of modern social science, a co-equal rational interlocutor in the ongoing debates of that science, and the tragic prophet of the disenchantment of the social world through scientific intellectualism. They have treated Weber's oeuvre as an end of knowledge in itself, but also as a means for advancing their own epistemological positions and their practical research objectives. The question for us now remains how to explain these and countless other divergent receptions and uses of Weber's oeuvre.

At first glance, the essays in this volume offer an obvious response. For example, John Drysdale proffers a careful, systematic analysis of the meanings of *objectivity* in Weber's essay on the topic, while Mario Bunge scathingly critiques Weber's apparent epistemological reliance on phantasmagoric idealism in readings that befit the intellectual dispositions respectively of a long-time teacher of sociological methods and theory and of a physicist-turned-philosopher of science in the realist, if not neo-positivist, tradition. Similarly, it is not surprising that the director of a Franco-German research institute, Catherine Colliot-Thélène, should explain the mutually foreign grammars of Durkheim's and Weber's social theories as products of their different politico-academic positions within their national institutional and intellectual climates; that the grandson of a Baptist missionary and nephew of a Catholic archbishop, the Brazilian sociologist of religion Roberta Motta, should be preoccupied with the 'objective' validity of the Protestant-ethic thesis; that students of the late, great Weber biographer and of Berkeley sociologist-cum-political scientist Reinhard Bendix, namely the political scientists Jeffrey Kopstein and Stephen Hanson, should hold Weber up as both exemplary and marginal to their discipline; or that James Boon, a student of the charismatic ethnographer Clifford Geertz,[1] should propose a simultaneously anecdotal and generalizing celebration of Weber's daring cultural comparisons. In other words, their diverse readings of Weber make sense in light of their intellectual biographies.

To be sure, readers and users of Weber cannot, in the German expression, 'jump over their own shadows,' but reception-history cannot stop at the level of intellectual history. To do so would entail a one-sided idealism, in which readers communicate with and interpret authors within the sphere of ideas alone, with readers' biographies merely furnishing the ideational context for interpretation, which then follows a logic divorced from material circumstances. Unfortunately, most reception-histories remain at the level of the dematerialized logical playing out of ideas. For the case of Weber, too, they have suffered from what we can call 'vulgar Weberianism,' that is, the reduction of Weber to the polar, idealist opposite of vulgar Marxism's unilateral materialism.[2] Indeed, in light of this common idealist reading of Weber, Mario Bunge is not unjustified when he takes Weber to task for preaching a misleading methodological subjectivism that he did not, fortunately, practise in his empirical analyses.

In the introduction, we too slipped into a subjectivist reading of Weber when we proposed a typology of reception based on Weber's three modes of legitimate domination. By defining the ideal-typical traditional, legal-rational, and charismatic readings of Weber in terms of readers' beliefs about Weber's scientific authority (personal versus impersonal, ordinary versus extraordinary), we perpetuated the intellectual illusion that reception takes place only in the minds of readers engaged with Weber-as-text (as well as with surrounding secondary literature and scholarly debates). Of course, readers do phenomenologically experience their reading and understanding of an author such as Weber as a personal, socially unmediated experience, as a solipsistic moment. Our ideal-typical, logically exhaustive typology of receptions only *describes* the parameters within which readers subjectively experience their relationship to the author. Yet no later than when readers begin to articulate their interpretations, in teaching or in text in particular, *should* they become aware of their socially mediate position, though scholars prefer to cultivate the self-deceiving, self-legitimating myth of intellectual detachment. From Weber's 'Objectivity' essay, however, we

have learned that all scientific 'truth' is socially and culturally conditioned. So, too, is any reception of Weber. This point does not, of course,
mean that all interpretation is predetermined; individual subjective
representations do have their autonomy and historical effectiveness.
The problem for the elaboration of an adequate theory of reception (as
with any social theory), then, lies in the articulation of the complex
causal interrelations between subjective representations and socio-
structural constraints.

To develop such an account of Weber's reception, we need, once
again, look no farther than Weber's own sociological praxis. In fact, we
need only move beyond the first methodologically individualist level of
Weber's sociology of domination to reveal the reception *regimes* within
which readers experience and interpret Weber. Both rational choice
theorists and cultural interpretivists have latched onto the methodological individualism that Weber espouses, notably in the first
Grundbegriffe chapter of *Economy and Society*, albeit the former in order
to deduce social reality from abstract principles of human nature and
the latter in order to reconstruct it from individual subjective representations. As Catherine Colliot-Thélène demonstrates in this volume, however, Weber's individualism is by no means ontological: social reality
cannot be derived from (or even be heuristically explained by) the more
or less rational motives of individual actors.[3] Weber starts from the
individual in order to avoid the (crypto-) Hegelian reification of collective concepts such as the state, feudalism, or rational bourgeois capitalism, which exist by virtue of the subjective representations and objective
actions of individuals, whose existences are in turn defined by the
complex social relations they (re)produce. This dynamic process of
mutual construction of social structures and of concrete historical individuals is evident in the shifting modes of legitimation that sustain
orders of social domination.[4] Weber introduces his different ideal-
typical modes of legitimation not simply to expose the different belief
bases on which individuals submit to authority, or the subjective glue
that binds society together,[5] but to analyse the different, continual
processes of social organization – ideal-typically communalization
(*Vergemeinschaftung*) and association (*Vergesellschaftung*) – that differentiate societies. This is not the place to attempt to summarize Weber's
social theory; suffice it to say that Weber's interest in the beliefs that
legitimate social orders lies less in their specific contents and consequent motivations for individual action than in the repercussions that
their forms entail for the material organization of society, in particular

the relations between rulers, their administrative staff, and the administered population.[6] For example, a charismatic revolutionary movement has different modes of action and organization from a traditional governing party of local notables (for example, requisition and mass mobilization versus clientelism and demobilization). Since no pure form of legitimate order can statically maintain itself (charisma routinizes, tradition requires renewal, rational-legality begs for meaning), legitimate domination empirically assumes fluid, hybrid forms that rarely approximate one of the ideal-types.

The complex, shifting modes of social mediation characterizing orders of legitimate domination also apply to what we call 'reception regimes.' That is, if we wish to understand how a scientific 'authority' such as Weber has been read and interpreted, we must move beyond the ideal-typical parameters descriptive of possible subjective interpretations of Weber – the traditional, legal-rational, and charismatic readings of his oeuvre – and situate readers in their sociological context. Thus, just as legitimate domination not only describes the simple binary relation between 'master' and 'servant(s)' but applies to the mediated relations between a leader, his or her administrative staff, and the administered population, the scholar who reads and subsequently writes about Weber (or any other 'author-ity') occupies an intermediate position of both submitting to and exercising Weber's authority (over the as yet unschooled 'masses'), especially when using Weber, as in the essays in this volume, in a self-reflexive and hence unavoidably self-justifying manner. A reception regime is, of course, a more fluid and less constraining social structure than most orders of domination, except in the classroom, where an interpreter can exploit the technical means of the examination and grading systems to impose an orthodoxy. In most cases, however, the 'subaltern' secondary reader can simply put aside an interpreter's version of Weber (though not this book, dear reader!), turn to Weber's texts themselves, or turn on the television. Nonetheless, the form, the content, and the effectiveness of an interpretation will vary as a function of not only the subjective creativity of the interpreter but – more importantly from a sociological, if not aesthetic, point of view – of his or her social position. We all know, for example, that the banalities uttered by a Harvard professor will carry more weight than the most brilliant insights of a graduate student from a third-rate university. Can we, however, formalize this sociological commonplace for a meaningful comparative reception-history of Weber's oeuvre?

The answer once more resides in Weber's work, namely in his empirical application of his formal concept of legitimate order in his *Religions-soziologie*.[7] There Weber examines how religious doctrine translates into practical life conduct (more specifically, into economic institutions) according to the social characteristics of the intellectuals who interpret doctrine and thereby participate in the religious 'ad*ministration*' of the faithful masses. Again, we cannot summarize the subtle complexities of Weber's configurational analyses of how particular types of intellectuals – such as the meritocratic literati devoted to the perpetuation of traditional readings of Confucius in not-fully rationalized bureaucratic service of the charismatic emperor of China – act to (re)produce different types of legitimated social and religious orders of domination. From Weber's example, however, we can distill a multi-causal schema for the diffusion of ideas – including his own.

First, Weber certainly does not neglect the causal autonomy, or inherent logic (*Eigengesetzlichkeit*), of ideas themselves. 'Not ideas, but material and ideal interests, directly govern men's conduct,' he writes in a celebrated passage, continuing: 'Yet very frequently the "world images" that have been created by "ideas" have, like switchmen, determined the tracks along which action has been pushed by the dynamic of interest.'[8] Even before ideas meet with interests (their distinction being only ideal-typically possible, of course), though, their inherent logics collide with one another, as Weber shows in his theoretical *Zwischenbetrachtung* (intermediate consideration) within his empirical study of the world religions.[9] That is, at the level of ideas alone, intellectuals, and others, find themselves torn between the competing rationalities of different life spheres, which are as numerous as the possible finalities of life from the religious to the political, scientific, economic, erotic, etc. Indeed, it is the suspension of social actors within the tensions between competing rationalizations of virtually every life value-sphere that defines the 'disenchanted' condition of modern Occidental humanity. Brought back down to the mundane life sphere of the academic reception of Weber's own rationalization of social science, Weber's concept of the logical autonomy of ideas establishes that the rational content of his ideas, his scientific 'doctrine,' switches readers onto certain possible tracks of interpretation. The volume and complexity of Weber's published thought, moreover, means that its receptions must be quantitatively and qualitatively partial, with the selection of Weberian ideas and their interpretation varying according to users' other cultural dispositions and modes of rationalization. In other words, according to this first level of analysis, to which idealist intellectual history generally limits itself, we can explain Weber's varied reception as the product of the diverse cultural and disciplinary milieus within which he has been read.[10]

Second, and more important from a sociological standpoint, Weber, as we have already seen, emphasizes the material (economic) and ideal (status) interests that 'govern men's actions,' including the reception and diffusion of ideas. Thus, in his sociology of religion, doctrinal analysis (conducted moreover with ideal-typical exaggeration in order to tease out social consequences) occupies a less important place than the study of the material conditions and institutional positions of the social carriers (*Träger*) of ideas. To be sure, he by no means seeks to reduce doctrinal interpretation to the expression of class or status group interests.[11] Religious ideas shape the behaviour of a variety of social strata more than the inverse, but received religious ideas are also adjusted to meet religious needs; and while the influence of the interested social stratum that brings about such adjustment may be secondary to the intrinsic logic of the doctrine, that influence is also 'very obvious' and sometimes 'decisive.'[12] Weber's encyclopedic study of the world religions goes on with intricate nuance to describe the practical consequences of doctrinal reinterpretation by intellectuals of social origin ranging from the genteel Brahmans of Hinduism to the plebeian elements of rabbinical Judaism.

As Weber makes abundantly clear at the beginning of 'Science as a Vocation,'[13] status and class conditions shape the development and diffusion of scientific thought probably even more than religious thought. Weber begins his celebrated lecture with the question, 'What are the conditions of science as a vocation in the material sense of the word?' And drawing a comparison between American and German universities, he foresees the further proletarianization and bureaucratization of academic work with the concomitant loss of meaningfulness and values. It is precisely within this material and status context that Weber's oeuvre itself has been received as a traditional and legal-rational justification for scientific specialization as well as a charismatic call for criticism and interdisciplinary regeneration. A differentiated reception-history of Weber would therefore have to distinguish the institutional interests, resources, and prestige of his different interpreters without, of course, reducing their creative (mis)readings to their social positions.

Third, and more subtly, Weber introduces a more specifically historical element to his explanation of the diffusion of ideas, namely the technical means at the disposal of their social bearers.[14] Doctrinal texts do not change in themselves, though new discoveries may appear (in the case of Weber, much of his personal correspondence, in particular from his period of mental illness, remains unpublished to date).[15] What is more, the ideal and material interests of social bearers of ideas (that is, different forms of wealth and honour) vary only in relative importance but, as expressions of always at least theoretically possible ultimate ends, do not change in the sense of historical progress. As Weber argues in his 1917 methodological piece 'The Meaning of "Ethical Neutrality" in Sociology and Economics,'[16] it is possible to measure progress only by the technical means available to realize particular ends. Thus, without judging the justice, truth, beauty, or other ultimate value of contemporary high-tech society, for example, we can say that it offers certain unprecedented efficiencies and possibilities as well as constraints for human action.[17] As for the development and diffusion of ideas, religious and otherwise, the historical progress of technical means can explain part of their effectiveness without judging their validity. For example, the 'objective' difficulty of mastering Chinese ideographic writing probably contributed to the stagnation of Confucian thought and of Chinese socio-economic development, whereas the doctrinal and institutional success of the Protestant Reformation was certainly not unrelated to the invention of the printing press.

Unlike the rationalized technical means that co-determine life possibilities within contemporary society, those that have shaped Weber's scholarly reception may appear trivial, but they have played a decisive role. They concern primarily the accessibility of Weber's oeuvre. For non-German readers in particular, the quantity and quality of translation work, itself a function of initial reception and of the depth of foreign-language skills, has inevitably distorted subsequent reception. The fragmentary reception of Weber in North American social science well into the 1980s certainly owes something to its diffusion in excerpt form in edited volumes such as Hans Gerth and C. Wright Mills's *From Max Weber* (1946).[18] Even in Germany, the accessibility of Weber's texts has been problematic: while the 'social carrier' retired banker Johannes Winckelmann, with his fourth and fifth revised editions of *Wirtschaft und Gesellschaft* and his editing of paperback editions of Weber's works, contributed greatly to the postwar rehabilitation of Weber,[19] the critical edition of Weber's writings was begun only in 1976 and remains an incomplete project. Finally, today, with the availability of Weber's texts in electronic format on CD-ROM[20] and on Internet websites, the technical conditions are ripe for not only universal access and easy citation checks and simple content analyses, but also for rampant plagiarism and for postmodern reception in the worst possible sense: fragmentary, disjointed, arbitrary, and deprived of all context.

In sum, a Weberian historical sociology of the scholarly reception of Weber's oeuvre would have to comparatively situate the various readings and uses of his thought within different reception regimes defined by (1) the pre-existing cultural and scientific normative context of intelligibility and communicability of Weber's thought; (2) the social structures and institutional settings with their concomitant material and ideal interest incentives and resources within which interpreters act; and (3) the technical means at readers' disposal.[21] Such an undertaking would of course be hugely complex – witness the encyclopedic scope of Weber's incomplete comparative study of the economic ethics of the major religions – but no more so than the multi-causal, configurational explanation of any other social phenomenon. Such a study would also require the ideal-typical reduction of reality according to the historically and sociologically conditioned interests of the researchers involved, as Weber explains in the 'Objectivity' essay whose centennial this volume celebrates. As we noted in the Introduction, this volume represents only the first step towards a historical sociology of Weber's reception within, and legacy to, contemporary social science practice, the collected essays offering suggestive source material. Analysing the essays' ideational contents and concrete social contexts of production would require several additional volumes. Nonetheless, drawing on some of the ideal-typical receptions of Weber sketched in the Introduction and on one of the essays from this volume, we can indicate some of the directions that our research on Weber's reception can take.

As we saw in the introduction, certain well-known readings of Weber approximate the traditional, legal-rational, and charismatic ideal-types. Far from being the product of personal idiosyncrasies, these readings arose within particular reception regimes. Thus, for instance, Karl Jaspers's charismatic rendering of Weber, in his eulogy before Heidelberg students a few weeks after his death, as a living philosophy was not simply a personal, grief-stricken heroic immortalization. An anecdote that Jaspers recounts in his *Philosophical Autobiography* points to the institutional context and interests that motivated Jaspers's stance. Five days after Weber's death, Jaspers met to commiserate with the neo-Kantian philosopher Heinrich Rickert, an old friend of Max and Marianne Weber whom Max Weber acknowledges in the 'Objectivity' essay.[22] When in their conversation Rickert referred to Weber as his *Schüler*, however, Jaspers angrily, but presciently, retorted, 'If you think that you and your philosophy will be known at all in the future, you may perhaps be right, but only because your name is mentioned in a footnote in one of Max Weber's works as the man to whom Max Weber expresses his gratitude for certain logical insights.'[23] This incident seems to have played a part in stimulating Jaspers's charismatic characterization of Weber as the greatest philosopher of our time in his *Gedenkrede* a few weeks later. Recently appointed to a chair in philosophy, the medical doctor and psychologist Jaspers, whose qualifications as a philosopher Rickert had called into question, albeit it in a friendly manner,[24] was not simply seeking to justify his own position by claiming that Weber incarnated an active philosophy of life; he was defending his ideal and institutional position within a particular crisis context. Indeed, Jaspers's eulogy of Weber was given at the invitation of students at Heidelberg University, who organized the commemoration after the administration had declined to organize an official ceremony for its former professor. The reasons for the university's decision would require deeper investigation, but whatever they might have been, Jaspers was certainly aware that established, systematic philosophy, of which the neo-Kantian school at Heidelberg was a fortress, was under siege by a new generation of 'existential' philosophers, notably Max Scheler and Martin Heidegger,[25] and their students. Thus, by charismatically appropriating Weber for a new mode of philosophy before this audience of students, Jaspers was participating, as both cause and effect, in an institutional as well as intellectual revolution.

Because, as we saw in the Introduction, ideal-typically charismatic readings of a scientific author signal an extraordinary rupture with existing scientific practice, we can expect to encounter them in a reception regime characterized by at least latent conflict within a particular scientific community. Thus, Sheldon Wolin's well-known charismatic reception of Weber's methodology as 'mind engaged in the legitimation of its own political activity,'[26] echoing and culminating his previous implicit appeals to Weber,[27] expresses to a large degree the longstanding battle for prestige and resources between institutionally marginalized political theorists and the hegemonic purveyors of the '*Herrschaft* of facticity,'[28] that is, behaviouralists, neo-positivists, and their successors in American political science.[29] By contrast, 'traditional' and 'legal-rational' interpretations – which, both being inscribed in scientific practices of paradigmatic continuity, tend to blend into one another – less obviously illustrate the social and historical configurations of their reception regimes. They may, however, better demonstrate the relevance of our historical sociological approach to reception.

The single most important interpretation of Weber for his subsequent reception in Anglo-American social science (and for his re-importation to Germany) was that of Talcott Parsons,[30] which we typed as traditional because of its treatment of Weber as founding father of a cumulative social science. Parsons's reinterpretation of Weber has been widely documented and criticized,[31] though primarily from an idealist perspective on his doctrinal distortions.[32] A brief recounting of Parsons's (mis)use of Weber shows that this reception involved much more than the logic of ideas. Parsons first even heard of Weber in 1925 when, after studies at Amherst College and the London School of Economics, he began doctoral studies in Heidelberg. Reading *Die protestantische Ethik* there was like a revelation to Parsons, its thesis immediately appealing to a New England patrician Congregationalist and prompting him to write his dissertation on Weber's and Werner Sombart's work on the origins of capitalism as well as to undertake the first English translation of *The Protestant Ethic*. Parsons's subsequent enlisting of Weber in his grand project of a universal, progressive, evolutionary yet homeostatic theory of a normatively integrated social order, however, followed from more than an elective affinity between certain Weberian ideas and Parsons's American optimistic liberalism. In the institutional context of American sociology, Parsons could elaborate his theoretical synthesis of European social thinkers, Weber foremost among them, as a counterweight to not only the nativist American empiricism of the Chicago School but also relative to the (albeit socially less significant) Austrian and German emigrant social theorists anchored at the New School, notably the part-time lecturer Alfred Schütz,[33] thanks largely to the institutional prestige and resources available to him at Harvard University. Parsons, moreover, was not unaware of the importance of linguistic technical means in determining as well as justifying his interpretation of Weber. In responding to a polemical call to 'de-Parsonize Weber,'[34] Parsons questioned the linguistic competence of his critics, who, among other alleged shortcomings, sided with native-German-speaker Reinhard Bendix's translation of *Herrschaft* as 'dominancy' as opposed to Parsons's less conflictual 'leadership.'[35] Without specifying further, Parsons accused: 'My reading of the Cohen et al. paper gives me the impression that none of the three authors possesses a thorough command of the German language.'[36] Ironically, Parsons here did not recognize that as a technically competent social carrier (and, literally, translator) of Weber's thought into American social science, he himself had shaped his critics' Americanized reading of Weber.

Having only hinted at the complexities of the reception regime within which Parsons acted, we cannot at this point unpeel these layers of causal interconnection within American social-scientific reception further. Instead, we propose a final example, drawing on one of the essays in this volume. Among our guest authors, we dare lay only our colleague and research collaborator Guy Rocher on the couch of sociological analysis, even the most preliminary.[37] Rocher entitled his contribution to the volume 'Talcott Parsons: A Critical Loyalty to Max Weber,' and we can in turn call our interpretation of his interpretation of Parsons's reception and use of Weber 'Guy Rocher: A Critical Loyalty to Talcott Parsons.' Rocher's essay offers some autobiographical details that go a long way to explaining his sympathy for Parsons and his grand theoretical ambitions: Parsons, by way of the technical means of his English-language translations of Weber, opened Rocher's eyes to Weber's work and to the broad theoretical horizons of European social thought in general. Rocher went on to become Parsons's doctoral student, and following in Parsons's footsteps, he published a major work of general sociological theory early in his career[38] and shortly thereafter a major study of Parsons's work itself.[39] Raised, like Parsons, in a highly religious environment, Rocher had, even before encountering Parsons, a strong interest in the sociology of religion (and later on in the sociologies of law and of medicine).[40] As Rocher's text testifies, the two men had strong intellectual affinities, Parsons's American synthesis of European sociological theory powerfully appealing to a student of Quebec's first social science faculty in search of secular liberal social theory.

What Rocher does *not* write in his essay is that his own position within Quebec society made him the social carrier par excellence of a particular reception of both Parsons and Weber. From a modest, small-town, and Catholic background himself, Rocher over the past half century has personified Quebec society as both interpreter and instigator of its modernization. From his historical doctoral dissertation on the relations between Church and state in colonial New France to his research on Quebec as a multicultural, post-industrial immigrant society, his scholarly work has accompanied – and his career as a secular intellectual materially depended on[41] – the peaceful, progressive evolution of a society that, unlike most, actually corresponded to the optimistic modernization theory that Parsons's systemic social theory had inspired in the 1950s and 1960s. Unlike Parsons, but more successfully than Weber himself, Rocher has engaged in politics and policy-making, and this in a manner that has never called his scientific integrity into question. In the early 1960s he was member of, and author of the five volumes of recommendations of, the royal commission that established Quebec's first Ministry of Education and its universal secular public school system through the junior college level. Somewhat more contro-versially, Rocher, as a deputy minister of culture in the first government of the separatist Parti Québécois in the late 1970s, was one of the principal authors of Bill 101, the language law restricting use of English in defence of French as the language of public discourse in Quebec. Rocher is a modernizing liberal nationalist, as was Weber, but his affin-ity with Weber is more than ideological: as an engaged social actor who has reconciled the vocations of science and of politics, he has intro-duced Weber's thought as not only an idea but as social praxis to three generations of students in Quebec and Canada.[42]

We have been able here only to scratch the surface of what would constitute an adequate sociology of reception of Weber's oeuvre. Such an undertaking in the comparative historical sociology of knowledge will require a much more rigorous and systematic classification of the different receptions of Weber than our simple tripartite ideal-typical schema (just as Weber develops countless hybrid types of legitimate authority in his empirical studies). We shall then have to situate each reading within its intellectual, social, and material-technical contexts in much greater depth before making the configurational comparisons that can allow for some causal inference. As we know from the example of Weber's own empirical work, this kind of research requires encyclo-pedic knowledge, and even then any conclusions remain highly contin-gent and conditional, their 'objective' validity existing only relative to the value orientations of the researchers and their resulting ideal-typi-cal reductions of the infinite complexity of social reality.[43]

In light of the impossibility, from a Weberian epistemological per-spective, of a definitive, exhaustive sociology of Weber's oeuvre's re-ception, it is essential that we recall the normative interest that motivates our study of his reception. Our ambition is certainly *not* to distill the 'essential,' 'authentic,' or 'true' Weber from the plethora of extant inter-pretations, for there can be no such thing, just as there is no ideal essence lurking behind reality. Weber's life work was precisely dedi-cated to debunking such teleological, metaphysical fantasies as epito-mized in Hegel's philosophy and more or less consciously embraced by evolutionary and functional social theories.[44] The social world, for Weber, is flat, his methodological individualism designating the social actor as not only the ceiling but as the floor of sociological intelligibility.[45] That is, social reality neither exists at the level of collectively conceived supra-individual social structures nor does it derive from biological or psychological forces (that is, 'human nature') within the individual; it exists through the relations that are both cause and consequence of action and is hence an entirely open-ended process. For Weber, the refusal to seek a hidden meaning behind or within social reality is a precondition for the scientific, disenchanted or 'demagicalized' (*entzaubert*), understanding of the world. Human reason cannot accede to absolute truth; at best it can aspire to scientific truthfulness, and in doing so assume responsibility for its truth-claims.[46] Weber's sober and modest epistemological position is of course entirely consistent with his admiration for Puritan asceticism deriving from the Calvinist doctrine of predestination, that fully rational solution to the problem of theodicy, which recognizes the human inability to influence or to understand (beyond scriptural revelation) God's will. Whereas the Puritan translated rational theology into a worldly life practice of diligently accumulating capital to no end other than itself, Weber translated his anti-metaphysical epistemological position into a monomaniacal quest for scientific knowledge without possible end.

Regardless of whether or not one agrees with Weber's epistemological position or with his ideal-typical social-scientific method, one must acknowledge his normative devotion to rational, 'objective' scientific knowledge. Whatever the empirical truth-value of Weber's historical sociology – and he was the first to admit the fragility of his scientific claims,[47] what is normatively at stake in the reception of Weber's oeuvre, as we wrote in the Introduction, is whether his readers and followers have seized upon the fragile possibility for scientific truthfulness that his oeuvre instantiates or whether they have missed the opportunity to make social science into something other than glorified ideology. In other words, Weber in his methodological writings defined an ideal-type of rational social-scientific inquiry that he attempted to apply in his empirical research practice. Although it is certainly possible to find fault with his work in both theory and practice, one cannot in principle contest Weber's ideal-typical, analytic distinction between scientific and other rationalities: science is not business, is not art, is not politics, is not kinship, etc. To be sure, actual scientific practice always follows economic, aesthetic, and other incentives as well as the rational criteria of scientific truthfulness ('objectivity'), but to the extent that non-scientific (ir)rationalities enter into scientific practice, it can be called ideological – or to avoid the pejorative connotations of the term, we might say that it is sociological, that is, subject to a configuration of social (and technical) influences. Precisely because Weber's sociology articulates and reflects upon its own conditions of possibility and of validity, an internally consistent and formally valid reception of his oeuvre would have to take into account its own sociological conditioning. Thus, we might say that readings of Weber that fail to acknowledge both his and their own contingency – and here as interpreters we should pause to deconstruct our own positions, at least to ourselves – are not Weberian, with those who read into him a philosophy of history, for example, succumbing to the temptations of his nemesis Hegel.[48]

If indeed Weber's reception to date has not actually been Weberian, as we hypothesize and seek to verify in our projected historical sociology of reception, then Weber's scientific status itself is at stake. In our Introduction, we drew on Foucault's distinction between founders of scientific disciplines and founders of 'discursiveness' to articulate this problem of Weber's eventual status as a scientific authority. As we saw, the reception of a disciplinary founder's oeuvre takes place within a paradigmatic discourse that both arises from and encompasses that oeuvre, whereas the reception of a founder of discursiveness generates competing (proto-)paradigms that appeal differently to the authority of the founder's oeuvre without succeeding in subsuming it. The absence to date of a coherent Weberian paradigm that encompasses both the varying receptions of his oeuvre as well as Weber's thought itself does not, however, mean that Weber was necessarily, by process of elimination, a founder of discursiveness, an uninhibited scientific demiurge who, like Foucault's examples Marx and Freud, proliferates possible meanings that escape 'disciplining' (in Foucault's ultimately pejorative sense). Weber could instead belong to another category of thinker beyond Foucault's distinction. As we saw in the Introduction as well, the reception of what Foucault calls founders of disciplines as well as of derivative authors occurs ideal-typically in what we defined as the traditional and legal-rational modes of reception, that is, personally (traditional) or impersonally (legal-rational) within ordinary regimes of scientific continuity. The reception of founders of discursiveness, by contrast, is charismatic in that interpreters appeal to the exemplary personal authority of the founder in an extraordinary context of scientific rupture or revolution. We noted, however, that a fourth mode of reception, just as a fourth ideal-typical mode of legitimate domination, was logically possible, if empirically improbable: a mode of reception (and authority) that is at once impersonal and extraordinary.

Recent history does offer the unprecedented example of a political revolution with little or no charismatic content in either the form of exceptional personal leadership or of revolutionary doctrine (traditionalized or institutionalized charisma as in religiously inspired movements): the peaceful revolutions that ended Eastern European communism.[49] Still, can such an impersonal but extraordinary form of authority exist in the realm of scientific discourse? According to Thomas Kuhn's model of scientific revolution translated into Weberian terms,[50] ordinary science occurs within the legal-rational parameters of theoretical paradigms, which reinforce their authority with traditional appeals to their longstanding validity when anomalies first call them into question. Although cumulative progress occurs quantitatively within paradigms, a revolutionary shift from one paradigm to another requires a qualitative leap of faith in the promise of an alternative vision of reality that has not yet proven its validity through ordinary paradigmatic research practice. The vision of a new paradigm need not be that of a single thinker, yet its prophetic nature certainly underscores the charismatic quality of scientific revolution; it depends on a personal gift of vision that cannot exist outside of the revolutionary scientists' minds in formal rules or habits. The history of scientific discourse thus depends on the extraordinary charismatic creativity of scientists, but the existence of scientific discourse as a particular form of rational activity per se does not depend on the personal authority of any scientist; for the rational substance of science changes with paradigms and persons, but its formal rationality does not. At the same time, science is an extraordinary activity in that it reveals the inadequacy of existing knowledge and practices for acquiring it.

Extraordinary and impersonal, these are the formal qualities that define a fourth ideal-typical form of legitimate domination, that of science. Weber did not or could not explicitly articulate this possible form, we speculate, because naming is an act of personal, charismatic authority and because logical formalization is an act of legal-rational authority. Indeed, the asymptotic quality of this fourth ideal-type is especially evident since any particular moment of scientific authority immediately tips towards the charismatic or the legal-rational: the scientist who makes a claim to scientific authority automatically appeals to either personal insight or procedural validity. The existence of scientific authority, however, seems implicitly guaranteed in its polar opposite. Whereas traditional authority posits an eternal, sacred order with a surfeit of meaning, science is the only possible authority in a godless, contingent world. This is the kind of world Weber addressed in his methodological and empirical writings, though in doing so, he was attempting the impossible. Facing and embracing an ultimately meaningless world is an act of heroic charisma, and trying to define a method for lending it meaning, however partial and provisional, an act of procedural rationalism. Nonetheless, in this attempt, we can perceive a foundational status beyond those foreseen by Foucault, a status by which Weber would be neither a founder of a particular scientific discourse nor a founder of discursiveness, but the founder of the conditions of possibility of scientific discourse, his own and any other.

What distinguishes Weber from other founding (and hence always at least partly charismatic) authors are his self-reflexive methodological writings exemplified best by his 'Objectivity' essay and practically applied in the *Protestant Ethic*. Indeed, these contemporaneous pieces respond to the same paradoxical question: what might be the ethical origins of a world without normative bearings? Like modern bourgeois rational capitalism's temporally and purposively endless quest to accumulate and to perfect the means of production, the 'spirit' of science – as an ideal-type – resides in its ultimately aimless pursuit of greater knowledge always closer to yet farther from an infinitely elusive reality. Just as he traces the origins of the capitalist 'spirit' to the Protestant ethic of worldly asceticism according to which humans assume responsibility for their productive action in a world from which God has absconded, Weber identifies the key to the scientific 'spirit' in the self-effacing ethic of 'objectivity' that governs the action of the modern scientist. Beyond developing the methodological concept of the ideal-type as an 'objective' means for the social scientist to escape from subjectivism by rationally articulating the hypothetical consequences of particular subjective value orientations,[51] Weber proposes an epistemological self-critique of this method. Indeed, as he signals with his careful use of quotation marks, Weber always simultaneously deconstructs the scientific position he is staking out, that is, he historicizes and relativizes his arguments to underscore their radical nominalism. Thus, the quotation marks around the obviously Hegelian term *Geist* (which he does not but could have applied to science) in the title of *Die protestantische Ethik und der 'Geist' des Kapitalismus*[52] warn the reader that Weber does not pretend to offer the essential 'world-historical' meaning of capitalism but a construct of what capitalism might entail if it were as Weber ideal-typically imagines it. Similarly, 'objectivity' refers not to the certitude of knowledge freed from subjective contingency but to the personal ethical position of the scientist who assumes responsibility for the ultimate meaningless and the contingency that underlie the will for truthfulness. The scientist is a particular type of cultural, historical individual whose normative claims are valid only for those who share a will to be scientifically truthful, just as the capitalist is peculiar to a historical and cultural context that values productivity above all else.

The contingency of 'capitalism' and of 'science' does not mean that these particular ideal-typical rationalities are not historically effective. The whole purpose of Weber's social science is to confront reality with these and other logically possible, empirically improbable conceptual constructs in order to ascribe some causally meaningful coherence to some small part of reality. There is no such thing as capitalism or science, only social actions and relations more or less consistent with the conceptual logics of 'capitalism' or of 'science.' There is also no such thing as Weberian social science, understood as a coherent, systematic practice that allows causal explanation and interpretation of social phenomena including Weber's reception, only as many 'Webers' as there are scholars who seek inspiration in his work. We have seen at least fourteen of these 'Webers' in the essays collected in this volume, and we have constructed yet another 'Weber' in an attempt to impose our own meaningful order onto the reality of social-scientific practice that refers to Weber and invokes 'Weber.' Like the others, our 'Weber' is an ideal-type, but thanks to him we know that our construct is historically, culturally, and socially contingent and that therefore we cannot lock ourselves into an iron cage of Weberianism.

NOTES

1 For many North American social scientists, the first (and often last) exposure to Weber as well as to ethnography is Clifford Geertz's essay 'Thick Description: Towards an Interpretive Theory of Culture,' in his *Interpretation of Cultures* (New York: Basic Books, 1973), 3–30.

2 A notable exception is the work of the late Michaël Pollack, 'Max Weber en France: l'itinéraire d'une oeuvre,' *Cahiers de l'IHTP* 3 (July 1986): 1–70, which employs Bourdieu's genetic structuralist approach for analysing the

dynamic intellectual field of Weber-reception. Although Pollack's approach adapted from Bourdieu builds on Weber, its one-sided structuralism differs from the approach we propose here. Although they do not develop an explicit model, Peter Kivisto and William H. Swatos Jr, 'Weber and Interpretive Sociology in America,' *Sociological Quarterly* 31, no. 1 (1990): 149–63, do offer an institutional and strategic analysis of Weber's American reception, in particular of Parsons's role. See note 22 of the Introduction for the more 'idealist' reception histories of Weber.

3 In this volume, Mario Bunge's critical observation that Weber's empirical sociological practice does not correspond to the subjectivist hermeneutic methodology that he appears to advocate in his methodological essays follows from the disjuncture between Weber's methodological individualism, which is an intellectual strategy for debunking unilateral structuralism, and his ontological constructivism, which expresses Weber's agnosticism about individual versus collective causes of social reality.

4 For a more detailed analysis of legitimation processes, see Laurence McFalls, 'L'État bâtard: légitimité et legitimation chez Max Weber,' in *La légitimité de l'État et du droit: autour de Max Weber*, ed. Michel Coutu and Guy Rocher (Quebec: Presses de l'Université Laval, 2005), 47–60.

5 If that were the case, his sociology would become a static structuralo-functionalist model of the normative integration of the individual into society, as we might caricature Parsons's interpretation of Weber.

6 See Max Weber, *Economy and Society* (Berkeley: University of California Press, 1978), 213: 'But according to the kind of legitimacy which is claimed, the type of obedience, the kind of administrative staff developed to guarantee it, and the mode of exercising authority, will all differ fundamentally. Equally fundamental is the variation in effect.'

7 The bibliography of Weber's sociology of religion is confusing both in the original and in English translation. Weber followed his 1904–5 study of *The Protestant Ethic and the 'Spirit' of Capitalism* with his *Economic Ethics of the World Religions*, published separately under the titles *Confucianism and Taoism, Hinduism and Buddhism*, and *Ancient Judaism*. In German, they all appear in volumes 1–3 of *Gesammelte Aufsätze zur Religionssoziologie* (Tübingen: Mohr-Siebeck, 1988), with the 1920 preface to all four studies of religion appearing before the *Protestant Ethic* and the 1915 introduction preceding the study of Chinese religions. In English, the introduction was published in Hans Gerth and C. Wright Mills, *From Max Weber* (New York: Oxford University Press, 1946), 267–301, as 'The Social Psychology of the World Religions.' Weber also devoted 235 pages of *Economy and Society* to 'Religious Groups,' but this section was published by Talcott Parsons as

Max Weber, *The Sociology of Religion* (Boston: Beacon, 1963). For our purposes here, we base ourselves on Weber's introduction to the *Economic Ethics* and the exemplary illustration of his chapter on the Confucian 'Literatenstand,' translated separately as 'The Chinese Literati,' in Gerth and Mills, *From Max Weber*, 416–44.

8 Weber, 'Social Psychology,' in Gerth and Mills, *From Max Weber*, 280n7.

9 Published as 'Religious Rejections of the World and their Directions,' in ibid., 323–59.

10 Thus, for example, we might paraphrase Agnes Erdelyi, *Max Weber in Amerika: Wirkungsgeschichte und Rezeptionsgeschichte Webers in der anglo-amerikanischen Philsophie* (Vienna: Passagen Verlag, 1992) with the formula: Weber + Anglo-Saxon logical positivism = 'value-free' social science.

11 'It is not our thesis that the specific nature of a religion is a simple "function" of the social situation of the stratum which appears as its characteristic bearer, or that it represents the stratum's "ideology," or that it is a "reflection" of a stratum's material or ideal interest-situation. On the contrary, a more basic misunderstanding of the standpoint of these discussions would hardly be possible.' Weber, 'Social Psychology,' in Gerth and Mills, *From Max Weber*, 269–70n7.

12 Ibid., 270.

13 In ibid., 129–56.

14 We owe this emphasis on technical means to the work of our colleague and collaborator Philippe Despoix, whose work in literary and aesthetic theory has drawn on Weber's sociology of technical progress as articulated notably in his rarely studied *Rational and Social Foundations of Music*, trans. and ed. Don Martindale et al. (Carbondale: Southern Illinois University Press, 1958).

15 See Introduction for the potential significance of previously unknown texts for the paradigmatic status of an author.

16 Max Weber, 'Der Sinn der "Wertfreiheit" der soziologischen und wirtschaftlichen Wissenschaften,' in *Gesammelte Aufsätze zur Wissenschaftslehre* (Tübingen: Mohr-Siebeck, 1988), 489–540. Translation by Edward Shils and Henry Finch in Max Weber, *The Methodology of the Social Sciences* (New York: Free Press, 1949), 1–49.

17 In a more normative, philosophical reading, we would note that in the modern age the rationalization of means, such as capitalism, has become an end in itself producing the alienation, or disenchantment, of life within various iron cages of contemporary forms of technical rationality.

18 A fascinating contribution to the reception history of Weber in the United States is Guy Oakes and Arthur Vidich, 'Friendship, Ethics, and

Careerism: Gerth, Mills, and Shils: The Origins of *From Max Weber*,'
International Journal of Politics, Culture, and Society 12, no. 3 (Spring 1999):
399–434, where they detail the partnership of convenience between the
theoretically and linguistically qualified Gerth and the politico-academi-
cally astute Mills.

19 Walter M. Sprondel, Constans Seyfarth, et al., '"Soziologie soll heissen ... "'
Kölner Zeitschrift für Soziologie und Sozialpsychologie 32, no. 1 (1980): 4.

20 Karsten Worm, *Max Weber im Kontext* (Berlin: InfoSoftWare, 1999).

21 Our schema bears a certain resemblance to Pierre Bourdieu's theory of
social 'fields,' in this case the academic field, with the first level of our
model corresponding to the cultural 'capital' that scholars bring into the
social game of their field, the second corresponding to their diverse forms
of social capital, and the third to the material capital at their disposal. This
resemblance is not due to our reliance on Bourdieu but rather to his on
Weber. In the one article that he explicitly devotes to Weber, written well
before his ascent to hegemony within the field of French sociology, 'Une
interpretation de la théorie de la religion selon Max Weber,' *Archives
européennes de sociologie* 12, no. 1 (1971): 3–21, Bourdieu, in an operation
of appropriation of Weber's authority within his own field, literally and
figuratively translates Weber's *Religionsssoziologie* (in the form in which he
summarized it in *Economy and Society*) into the language of his social field
theory. Although Bourdieu is not known for his command of German, his
article presents what appear to be his own translations of Weber's texts,
which had not yet been translated into French, thereby appropriating and
exploiting technical means of linguistic capital.

22 Weber, *The Methodology of the Social Sciences*, 50.

23 Karl Jaspers, *The Philosophy of Karl Jaspers*, ed. Paul A. Schilpp (New York:
Tudor, 1957), 32–3; cited in Christopher Adair-Toteff, 'Max Weber as
Philosopher: The Jaspers-Rickert Confrontation,' *Max Weber Studies* 3, no.
1 (2002): 18.

24 See Adair-Toteff, 'Max Weber as Philosopher,' for a summary of Rickert's
published reviews of Jaspers's works.

25 See Martin Heidegger, *Sein und Zeit*, 10th ed. (Tübingen: Niemeyer, 1963),
9–10, where he describes this, his first published work, as a response to
the 'foundational crisis' shaking all sciences.

26 Sheldon Wolin, 'Max Weber: Legitimation, Method, and the Politics of
Theory,' *Political Theory* 9, no. 3 (1981): 406.

27 Sheldon Wolin, *Politics and Vision* (Boston: Little, Brown, 1960); 'Political
Theory as a Vocation,' *American Political Science Review* 63 (1969): 1062–82.

28 Wolin, 'Max Weber,' 420.

29 For an outstanding analysis of the material and ideal interests at stake in this battle, see John G. Gunnell, *The Descent of Political Theory: The Genealogy of an American Vocation* (Chicago: University of Chicago Press, 1993); on Wolin's part in this battle in particular, see John G. Gunnell, *Between Philosophy and Politics: The Alienation of Political Theory* (Boston: University of Massachusetts Press, 1986), 117–33.

30 In the French-speaking world, Raymond Aron played a comparable role, notably through his *La sociologie allemande contemporaine*, 4th ed. (Paris: Presses Universitaires de France, 1981), and his interpretations – initially charismatic à la Jaspers in the 1930s and subsequently more traditional, with Weber portrayed as the culmination of the sociological tradition starting from Montesquieu – quite clearly express the French reception regime in which Weber offered a political, institutional, and intellectual alternative to Durkheimian ahistoricism and Marxist materialism.

31 See Guy Rocher's contribution to this volume; Erdelyi, *Max Weber in Amerika*; Richard Swedberg, 'The Changing Picture of Max Weber's Sociology,' *Annual Review of Sociology* 29 (2003): 283–306; Peter Kivisto and William Swatos Jr, *Max Weber: A Bio-Bibliography* (New York: Greenwood, 1988); Arthur J. Vidich and Stanford Lyman, *American Sociology: Worldly Rejections of Religion and their Directions* (New Haven: Yale University Press, 1985).

32 Most polemically in Jere Cohen, Lawrence Hazelrigg, and Whitney Pope, 'De-Parsonizing Weber: A Critique of Parson's Interpretation of Weber's Sociology,' *American Sociological Review* 40 (April 1975): 229–41, and by the same authors, 'On the Divergence of Weber and Durkheim: A Critique of Parsons' Convergence Theory,' *American Sociological Review* 40 (August 1975): 417–27. By contrast, Peter Kivisto and William Swatos Jr, 'Weber and Interpretive Sociology in America,' *Sociological Quarterly* 31, no. 1 (1990): 149–63, situate Parsons's reading within the contexts of the historical, institutional development of American sociology and of Parsons's institutionally privileged position at Harvard University.

33 On Parsons's patrician snub of the founder of phenomenological sociology, see Kivisto and Swatos, 'Weber and Interpretive Sociology,' 159.

34 Cohen et al., 'De-Parsonizing Weber.'

35 Ibid., 236–9.

36 Talcott Parsons, 'On '"De-Parsonizing" Weber,' *American Sociological Review* 40, no. 5 (October 1975): 668.

37 Indeed, the preliminary character of our analysis requires that we make stereotypical generalizations (for example, about Parsons's 'privilege' as a Harvard professor), which courtesy prevents us from applying to our

invited authors. For our analysis of Rocher, the facts that our average age is less than half of Rocher's, that our scholarly experience and expertise is only one hundredth of his, and that our reputations within the Québec and Canadian scholarly communities are only a millionth of his means that our reading of Rocher takes on both traditional (patriarchal) and charismatic (hero-worshipping) tones

38 Guy Rocher, *Introduction à la sociologie générale*, 3 vols. (Montreal: H.M.H., 1968–9). An edition adapted to the French and international francophone market was published by Seuil and subsequently translated into English, Spanish, Portuguese, Italian, and Persian.

39 Guy Rocher, *Talcott Parsons et la sociologie américaine* (Paris: Presses Universitaires de France, 1972), subsequently translated into Italian, English, Dutch, Portuguese, and Japanese.

40 Parsons's less well-known empirical work concerned medicine. On the centrality of law to Parsons's appreciation of Weber, see our Introduction.

41 Rocher belongs to a generation of new francophone elites whose ascendancy depended on the expansion of the economic and social roles of the secularized, technocratic Quebec state that emerged from the Quiet Revolution ushered in by the Liberal government of Jean Lesage elected in 1960. Along with the expansion of the role of the state, notably with the creation through nationalization of the industrial giant Hydro-Québec, the Quiet Revolution was a cultural transformation, within a few years, from a religious, natalist society to one of the world's most secular societies with the lowest birth and marriage rates in the industrialized world.

42 Rocher has not widely published directly on Weber – exceptions being 'La réception de l'oeuvre de Max Weber dans la sociologie et la sociologie du droit aux États-Unis,' *Droit et société* 9 (1988): 255–80, and his participation in the translation and editorial introduction of Weber's critique of Stammler – Michel Coutu, Dominique Leydet, with Guy Rocher and Elke Winter, *Max Weber, Rudolf Stammler et le matérialisme historique* (Quebec: Presses de l'Université Laval, 2001) – but his work is always Weberian in its comparative, historical, configurational, multi-causal perspective and its interest in the social carriers of ideas.

43 In Weber's own work the possibility of an infinite causal regress takes on almost comic proportions in his *General Economic History* (London: Allen and Unwin, 1927), incidentally his first work (actually a series of lectures) translated into English, where every few pages, in his fourth chapter summarizing his entire work on the origins of modern capitalism, he identifies another absolutely essential or decisive cause ranging from double-entry bookkeeping to speculation on loss and worldly asceticism.

44 In a letter to Franz Eulenburg dated 11 May 1909, Weber wrote, 'Two paths are open before us: Hegel or my manner of handling things.' Cited epigraphically at the beginning of Catherine Colliot-Thélène, *Le déesenchantement de l'État de Hegel à Max Weber* (Paris: Éditions de Minuit, 1992).

45 See Catherine Colliot-Thélène's contribution to this volume.

46 This what Karl Löwith, as we cited in the Introduction, calls Weber's 'will to unconditioned truthfulness [*Willen zur unbedingten Wahrhaftigkeit*]' in his essay 'Die Entzauberung der Welt durch Wissenschaft, *Merkur* 6 (1964): 515. Löwith goes on to explain that this 'demoniac will' rests on the 'precondition that we are not in the truth [*Voraussetzung, dass wir nicht in der Wahrheit sind*].'

47 See what Wolin, 'Max Weber,' 420, calls Weber's 'secular [self-]crucifixion' in his preface to his studies of religion, Max Weber, *The Protestant Ethic* (New York: Scribner's, 1958), 28. There Weber admits, '[These studies] are destined to be superseded in a much more important sense than this can be said, as it can be, of all scientific work.'

48 See Roberto Motta's contribution to this volume.

49 The absence of clear and effective leadership, of a revolutionary project or ideology, and of violence has led some observers to contest the revolutionary character of this world-historic event. This terminological debate stems of course from the empirical expectation of an association between charisma and the extraordinary, a form of magical thinking that attributes upheaval to (quasi) divine intervention.

50 Thomas Kuhn, *The Structure of Scientific Revolutions* (Chicago: University of Chicago Press, 1962).

51 See our Introduction, as well as John Drysdale's and John Gunnell's analytical summaries of the 'Objectivity' essay in this volume.

52 Significantly the quotation marks disappear in Parsons's translation, inviting interpretation in the sense of a Weberian crypto-Hegelian philosophy of history.

Contributors

James Boon is professor of anthropology and department chair at Princeton University. He works in the interdisciplinary history of anthropology and critical theory. He has done fieldwork in Java and Bali, research on colonialist Indonesian studies, and cross-cultural writings on hybrid arts. He blends social-scientific and literary readings of comparative discourse (including Weber's) in diverse books: *Verging on Extra-Vagance: Anthropology, History, Religion, Literature, Arts ... Showbiz*; *Affinities and Extremes: Crisscrossing the Bittersweet Ethnology of East Indies History, Hindu-Balinese Culture, and Indo-European Allure*; *Other Tribes, Other Scribes: Symbolic Anthropology in the Comparative Study of Cultures, Histories, Religions, and Texts*; *The Anthropological Romance of Bali, 1597–1972: Dynamic Perspectives in Marriage and Caste, Politics and Religion*; and *From Symbolism to Structuralism: Lévi-Strauss in a Literary Tradition*. Boon's first exposure to Weber came from his teachers (Jim Peacock, David Schneider, Cliff Geertz) who had studied (not uncritically) with Talcott Parsons – whom Boon thus calls (with a wink) his 'grand-teacher.'

Peter Breiner is associate professor of political science at the State University of New York at Albany. His research interests include Max Weber as a political theorist, the influence of Weimar émigrés on American political science, and the role of judgment and examples in political theory. Among recent publications are: *Max Weber and Democratic Politics*; 'Weber's *Protestant Ethic*: Hypothetical Account or Historical Explanation of Capitalism,' *Journal of Classical Sociology*; 'Unnatural Selection': Max Weber's Concept of 'Auslese' and His Criticism of the Reduction of Political Conflict to Economics,' *International Relations*; and 'Translating Max Weber: Exile Attempts To Forge a New Political

Science,' *European Journal of Political Theory*. Breiner became interested in Weber during graduate school when he had a DAAD grant to do research on Weber's political writings in Germany and read Weber in the original. He wrote his dissertation and subsequently a book on Weber. He is interested in Weber's implications for a political theory that places political ideas in the sociological context in which they are contested.

Mario Bunge is the Frothingham Professor of Logic and Metaphysics at McGill University with expertise ranging from theoretical physics to social theory. He holds fifteen honorary doctorates and four honorary professorships. Author of the monumental *Treatise on Basic Philosophy*, Bunge has recently devoted several books to the social sciences: *Finding Philosophy in Social Science*; *Social Science under Debate*; *The Sociology–Philosophy Connection*; and *Emergence and Convergence: Qualitative Novelty and the Unity of Knowledge*. A distant relative of Weber's himself, Bunge approached him through his critical reading of neo-Kantian philosophy.

Catherine Colliot-Thélène is professor of philosophy at the Université de Rennes I and was through 2004 director of the Centre Marc Bloch in Berlin. She recently published a new translation of Weber's lectures on politics and science as vocations, and she collaborated on the first French translations of Weber's *Confucianism and Taoism* and of *Agrarian Conditions in Antiquity*. Her interpretive work on Weber includes: *Études wébériennes. Rationalités, histoires, droits*; *Le désenchantement de l'État. De Hegel à Max Weber*; and *Max Weber et l'histoire*. Colliot-Thélène first read Weber, in the original German, while she was teaching French to American students at Harvard University.

John Drysdale is emeritus professor of sociology at Concordia University and was visiting professor of sociology at the University of Iowa, 2002–4. He is currently working on a book on concept formation in the sociology of Max Weber. His publications related to Weber include: 'How Are Social-Scientific Concepts Formed? A Reconstruction of Max Weber's Theory of Concept Formation,' *Sociological Theory* and 'The Paradoxical Relation of Knowledge and Values: On Schluchter's Analysis of the Value Theme in the Work of Max Weber,' *International Journal of Culture, Politics, and Society*. He first seriously read Weber's methodological essays in the 1960s as continuing the legacy of Wilhelm Dilthey and the German historical tradition. This experience was extended by studying Weber's substantive works in the seventies, especially during a year as *Gastprofessor* at the Max-Weber-Institut of the University of Munich. His further studies of Weber's work in relation to the contemporary German context were advanced by sabbatical research appointments at Harvard University's Center for European Studies twice in the 1990s.

Robert M. Fishman is professor of sociology and Kellogg Institute Fellow at University of Notre Dame where he works in political sociology and in the sociology of culture, economic sociology, and the sociology of religion. His current research projects include a comparative analysis of enduring legacies of reform and revolution in transitions to democracy and a cross-national study of the evolution in priestly vocations. His books include: *Democracy's Voices: Social Ties and the Quality of Public Life in Spain*; *Working Class Organization and the Return to Democracy in Spain*; and *The Year of the Euro: The Cultural, Social, and Political Import of Europe's Common Currency* (co-edited with Anthony M. Messina). Fishman learned his Weber from the great comparative sociologist and political scientist Juan Linz during his studies at Yale University, though political theorist Seyla Ben Habib first introduced him to the 'Objectivity' essay.

Jack R. Goody is Emeritus William Wyse Professor of Social Anthropology at St John's College, Cambridge University, where after undergraduate work in literature he studied anthropology with Evans-Pritchard. While drawing insights from Weber's analysis of technical means, Goody's enormous corpus of works has attacked the Eurocentrism of Weber's and others' social theory. Among his better known books are: *The East in the West*; *The Interfaces between the Written and the Oral*; *The European Family*; *Cooking, Cuisine and Class*; and *The Domestication of the Savage Mind*. Goody first learned about Weber from Talcott Parsons when he taught a seminar at Cambridge in the late 1950s.

John G. Gunnell is Distinguished University Professor of Political Science at the State University of New York, Albany, and the leading intellectual historian of American political science and political theory, with a particular interest and insight into the influence of the Weimar émigré intellectuals on the genealogy of political science. His books include: *The Descent of Political Theory: The Genealogy of an American*

Vocation; The Orders of Discourse: Philosophy, Social Science, and Politics; Imagining the American Polity: American Political Science and the Discourse of Democracy; and *Between Philosophy and Politics: The Alienation of Political Theory.* He first seriously read Weber's work in the late 1960s when he was looking for alternatives to the positivist conception of social-scientific explanation. Over the decades he has revisited Weber, coming to recognize the centrality of his thought to what Gunnell calls the 'Weimar conversation.'

Stephen Hanson is Boeing International Professor in the Department of Political Science and the director of the Ellison Center for Russian, East European, and Central Asian Studies of the Jackson School of International Studies at the University of Washington. He has published numerous articles on post-communist Russia and co-edited and co-authored four books in the field of comparative post-communist studies. His monographs include: *Time and Revolution: Marxism and the Design of Soviet Institutions* and *Uncertain Democracies: Ideology and Party Formation in Third Republic France, Weimar Germany, and Post-Soviet Russia.* Hanson was introduced to Weber during his doctoral studies at the University of California, Berkeley, where a 'Weberian school' of Soviet and communist studies has formed, notably around Ken Jowitt.

Jeffrey Kopstein is professor of political science and director of the Joint Initiative for German and European Studies at the University of Toronto. Co-editor of the leading textbook in comparative politics, he has published numerous articles on interwar, communist, and post-communist Eastern and Central Europe and on the political economy of the enlarged European Union. Recent publications include: *The Politics of Economic Decline in East Germany, 1945–1989;* 'Post-Communist Democracies: Legacies and Outcomes,' *Comparative Politics;* and 'Bad Civil Society,' *Political Theory* (with Simone Chambers). Like Hanson, Kopstein was a student in Berkeley's 'Weberian school' of communist studies. He also studied with the late, great Weber-biographer Reinhard Bendix.

Laurence McFalls is professor of political science at Université de Montréal and a former director of the Centre canadien d'études allemandes et européennes, where he leads a research group on the contemporary legacy and relevance of Max Weber's thought. He has recently co-edited volumes on eastern Germany and on the post-communist Balkans. His other publications include: *Communism's Collapse,*

Democracy's Demise? The Cultural Context and Consequences of the East German Revolution; 'L'État bâtard: légitimité et legitimation chez Max Weber', in *La legitimité de l'État et du droit*, ed. Michel Coutu and Guy Rocher; and 'Illegitimate Unions? German and European Unifications Viewed in Comparative Perspective,' in *Germany's Two Unifications*, ed. Ronald Speirs and John Bruilly. He first seriously encountered Weber when one of his doctoral supervisors at Harvard University, Robert Fishman, suggested he read the 'Objectivity' essay as an alternative to the epistemologically impoverished methodology of contemporary political science.

Roberto Motta is professor of social sciences, Universidade Federal de Pernambuco, Recife, Brazil, and holds a doctorate in anthropology from Columbia University. He has written extensively on religion (including the Afro-Brazilian sects), on race relations, and on social thought. His recent publications include: 'L'expansion et la réinvention des religions afro-brésiliennes : réenchantement et décomposition,' *Archives de Sciences Sociales des Religions*; 'Paradigms in the Study of Race Relations in Brazil,' *International Sociology*; and 'Ethnicity, Purity, the Market and Syncretism in Afro-Brazilian Cults,' in *Reinventing Religion*, ed. Sidney Greenfield and André Droogers. About his interest in Weber, he writes, 'Being, at the same time, the grandson of a Presbyterian minister and the nephew of a Catholic archbishop, it is not necessary to be an orthodox Freudian to imagine that my keen interest for Weber arises from a problem of identity.'

Anthony R. Oberschall is emeritus professor of sociology at the University of North Carolina at Chapel Hill. After studying physics, Oberschall undertook a doctorate in sociology at Columbia University, where in collaboration with Paul Lazarsfeld he published 'Max Weber and Empirical Social Research' (1965). His research interests in comparative sociology have ranged from social movements to entrepreneurship and ethnic conflict and have taken him around the world for fieldwork and teaching. His best-known books include: *Empirical Social Research in Germany*; *Social Conflict and Social Movements*; and *Social Movements: Ideologies, Interests, and Identities*. He first read Weber at the beginning of his graduate studies when his mother, a historian, gave him a copy of *Wirtschaft und Gesellschaft*. He still turns to that copy and his original marginal notes for inspiration on the highly diverse subjects of his empirical research.

Guy Rocher is professor of sociology at Université de Montréal, where he is also affiliated with the Centre de recherche en droit public in the Faculty of Law. As the more detailed biographical sketch in the Conclusion to this volumes shows, Rocher has been the social carrier par excellence of Weber's thought in Quebec and Canada over the past fifty years, embodying the Weberian ideals and ideal-types of the scholar and the partisan. His work on Weber bears the marks of his *Doktorvater* Talcott Parsons. In recent years he has developed particular interest in Weber's sociology of law, participating in the translation and editing of Weber's critiques of Stammler. Among Rocher's internationally renowned and translated works are: *Introduction à la sociologie générale* (3 vols.) and *Talcott Parsons et la sociologie américaine*. As he writes in his contribution to this volume, Rocher first encountered Weber in Talcott Parsons's translations and interpretations.

Augustin Simard is assistant professor of political science at the Université de Montréal. He completed a doctoral dissertation on constitutional legal theory in the Weimar Republic at the École des hautes études en sciences sociales in Paris. His work addresses the legacy of Weber's concept of legitimacy of law in constitutional debates that notably opposed Carl Schmitt and Otto Kirchheimer. As a research fellow at the Centre canadien d'études allemandes et européennes, he has coordinated the activities of the research group on Max Weber's contemporary legacy. The publication of his master's thesis on political theorist Claude Lefort is forthcoming, as are several articles on Weber's sociology of law.

Barbara Thériault is assistant professor of sociology at Université de Montréal and was formerly a doctoral fellow at the Max-Weber-Kolleg at the Universität Erfurt. A sociologist of religion and of politics, she has studied the institutional transformation of Churches in eastern Germany and is currently leading a comparative study of Islam in the public spheres of Canada and Europe. She is one of the initiators of the Weber research group at the Centre canadien d'études allemandes et européennes, of which she is currently assistant director. Her recent books and articles include: *'Conservative Revolutionaries': Protestant and Catholic Churches in Germany after Radical Political Change in the 1990s*; 'The Carriers of Diversity within the Police Forces: A 'Weberian' Approach to Diversity in Germany,' *German Politics and Society*; and 'Ordres légitimes et légitimité des ordres : une approche 'wébérienne' des institutions,' in *La légitimité de l'État et du droit*, ed. Michel Coutu and Guy Rocher.

Naoshi Yamawaki is professor of social thought and public philosophy in the Department of Advanced Social and International Studies at the University of Tokyo, where he is a strong advocate of the interdisciplinary mission of its Komaba Campus. He completed his doctoral dissertation on the epistemological controversy between Popper's critical rationalism and Apel's transcendental pragmatics at the Universität München. He subsequently turned his attention to the antecedent *Methodenstreit*, elaborating his critical stance towards Weber in three major publications in Japanese during the 1990s: *The History of European Social Thought*; *Toward a New Philosophical Foundation of Social Science*; and *Manifesto for a New Transdisciplinary Social Philosophy*. Yamawaki first encountered Weber's thought while studying economic theory as an undergraduate at Hitotsubashi University under the guidance of Professor Yuichi Shionoya, who is now internationally eminent as an economic philosopher. This early exposure testifies to the significant Weber reception in Japan, which boasts more than half of all subscriptions to the ongoing complete critical edition of Weber's works.

Index

action: collective, 245, 256n2, 303; communicative, 18, 180; empirical science of, 138–42; human, 100, 102, 156, 226, 242, 244, 357; individual, 75, 122, 149, 164n73, 192, 242, 257n6, 301, 353; meaningful, 63, 67, 69, 81, 123; political, 72, 106, 108; purposive (logic of), 100, 146, 157, 212, 215; rational, 46, 100, 212; social, 31, 81, 93, 100, 101, 125, 157, 290, 367; subjective meaning of (understandable), 75, 120, 143, 145, 156–8; theory of, 13, 248; traditional, 100; unintended consequences of, 285n1; value-rational, 100
alienation, 290, 293, 369n17
America, North, 165; Latin, 185, 190; Weber's visit to United States, 5, 323, 337–8, 342–3, 345n14
Archiv für Sozialwissenschaft und Sozialpolitik, 3, 32, 60, 161n37, 225, 330, 337
Aron, Raymond, 138–9, 167, 344n11, 371n30
art and artists, 81, 311–13; artistic development, 238; techniques of, 340

asceticism, 327, 334, 348, 363; (inner-) worldly, 4, 15, 52, 189, 195–7, 203–4, 372n43; otherworldly, 194; Puritan, 126, 363
Austin, J.L., 61

Bacon, Francis, 46
Baudelaire, Charles, 332
Benda, Julien, 118
Bendix, Reinhard, 313–16, 344n11, 351, 360
Beruf (calling, vocation), 4, 6, 14, 45, 52, 192–6, 311, 328, 335, 336
Bismarck, Otto von, 48
Bourdieu, Pierre, 367n2, 370n21
Braudel, Fernand, 131, 225–37
Brentano, Lujo, 193
Buddhism, 213, 238, 327, 329, 335
bureaucracy, 100, 127, 174, 212, 291, 340; bureaucratic conservatism, 108; bureaucratic party organization, 99, 291–2; bureaucratic service, 355; bureaucratization, 227, 291, 356
Burger, Thomas, 24n38, 101, 114n16

calling. *See Beruf*

GERMAN AND EUROPEAN STUDIES

General Editor: James Retallack